The Digital Dystopias
of *Black Mirror* and
Electric Dreams

The Digital Dystopias of *Black Mirror* and *Electric Dreams*

STEVEN KESLOWITZ
Foreword by Marshall Julius

McFarland & Company, Inc., Publishers
Jefferson, North Carolina

ISBN (print) 978-1-4766-7868-9
ISBN (ebook) 978-1-4766-3759-4

LIBRARY OF CONGRESS ANDBRITISH LIBRARY
CATALOGUING DATA ARE AVAILABLE

Library of Congress Control Number 2019056115

© 2020 Steven Keslowitz. All rights reserved

No part of this book may be reproduced or transmitted in any form or by any means, electronic or mechanical, including photocopying or recording, or by any information storage and retrieval system, without permission in writing from the publisher.

Front cover image by Lia Koltyrina (Shutterstock)

Printed in the United States of America

*McFarland & Company, Inc., Publishers
Box 611, Jefferson, North Carolina 28640
www.mcfarlandpub.com*

For my wonderful wife, Lital, and
our two incredible girls, Layla and Eliana.
You are the bright lights in my world.

Too often man becomes clever instead of becoming wise. He becomes inventive, but not thoughtful. And sometimes … he can create himself out of existence.
—Rod Serling's narrative conclusion to *The Twilight Zone* episode "The Brain Center at Whipple's," which aired on CBS, May 15, 1964.

Table of Contents

Acknowledgments — ix

Foreword by Marshall Julius — 1

Introduction: Using Pop Culture as a Lens to Understand Our Technology-Obsessed World — 5

1. Reflections Through a Black Mirror — 11
2. Technology and Political Manipulation: An Examination of "The Waldo Moment" and "Safe and Sound" — 41
3. Rate Me, Like Me, Follow Me, Control Me, Love Me, Kill Me: A Dystopian Guide to Social Media and Online Dating — 73
4. Privacy and Security-Related Considerations in a Hyper-Techno World — 97
5. Alternate Realities, Digital Clones and the Meaning and Value of Life — 139
6. Dreading a Post-Apocalyptic Future: From "Metalhead" to "Autofac" and Beyond — 190

Conclusion: Waking Up from an Electric Dream — 216

Appendix A: Black Mirror and Electric Dreams Episode Lists — 223

Appendix B: Television and Film Sources — 225

Chapter Notes — 235

Bibliography — 275

Index — 291

Acknowledgments

I have many people to thank in connection with this book. Over the years, I have received so much encouragement from professionals within the media, publishing, public relations and television fields. I am grateful for your friendship and support.

I am blessed to have such a wonderful family—

To my wife, Lital, thank you for being an incredible wife and for reviewing and commenting on drafts of the manuscript. You are the best mom to our girls and we all love you so much. I could not ask for a better partner to share my life with.

To our daughters, Layla and Eliana. Mom and I love you more than you will ever know. You bring such light and joy into our lives. We are very proud of you in every way. I feel extremely lucky to share so many wonderful experiences with you, from our dance parties to the "daddy train" to "days at the beach" to eating oranges in the park and so much more. No words can describe how wonderful it feels to be your dad and to help raise such amazing children. One of the greatest blessings of my life is to have a job that allows me to spend so much time with you, watching you grow and become such wonderful people. Always remember that each of you has something very special in your heart.

To my parents, Alan and Helene, thank you for always encouraging my writing and for supporting me in so many ways. You are exemplary parents and I can only hope to apply what I have learned from you as I raise my own children. Your sound advice and our thoughtful, engaging discussions always have a profoundly positive effect on me.

To my brother, Justin, thank you for being an awesome brother. You are also a superb lawyer and basketball player. (That basketball part might have a been a typo....) Thanks for your enthusiasm and encouragement, always, and for allowing me to borrow some of your expertise in the form of a quote for the privacy chapter of this book.

Thank you to my grandparents; my childhood is filled with so many memories of such happy times spent together. Thank you, also, for your unconditional support. I continue to be inspired by my grandfathers, who have passed away.

* * *

I have enjoyed every moment of my writing and publishing journey. I have been very fortunate to meet, work with and become friends with many kind and talented folks along the way. My experiences—ranging from watching a table read of *The Simpsons* to greeting Kiefer Sutherland with a copy of my *24* book to attending the red carpet premiere of *Better Call Saul*—have been incredible. Our lunches, conversations and studio tours have always been quite enlightening and memorable. Thank you for welcoming me with open arms into the world of television.

I would like to think my agent, Stacey Glick, of Dystel, Goderich & Bourret Literary Management for your encouragement over the years. Thank you to: all the publishers, editors, publicists and everyone else who I have worked with in the publishing field—especially Charlie Perdue and the McFarland team; Sam Henrie, Mindy Burnett, Peter Lynch, Lori Conser and the Sourcebooks and Presigio Editorial teams; Joe Fodor, Duncan Dobbelmann, Dr. Laura Schor, *The Excelsior*, Brooklyn College and the Macaulay Honors College for your support for my publications about *The Simpsons*; the Benjamin N. Cardozo School of Law, the *Cardozo Law Review* and professors Richard Bierschbach, Max Minzner and Peter Goodrich; my enormously talented friends at *The Simpsons*, especially Mike Reiss, Mark Kirkland, Matt Groening, Mike B. Anderson, Charles Ragins and the rest of the brilliant and welcoming writing, animation and voice-over teams; the incredibly gifted creative team behind *24*, especially Howard Gordon, Manny Coto and Evan Katz; the brilliant creative teams behind, and casts of, *Breaking Bad* and *Better Call Saul*, especially Vince Gilligan, Peter Gould, Bob Odenkirk, Rhea Seehorn, Patrick Fabian, Michael McKean and Brandon K. Hampton; Rick Miller, the talented star of *MacHomer*; all the folks who have interviewed me for print articles as well as television, radio and podcast interviews; and to my professional colleagues past and present at the international law firm Debevoise and Plimpton and the AXA Equitable Life Insurance Company, especially the fearless leader of the Commercial Transactions team, Darryl Gibbs.

Foreword
by Marshall Julius

Advancements throughout human history have invariably been met with suspicion or optimism. With anger or excitement. Though it's in our nature to constantly strive for more, better, faster and sexier, it's equally human to doubt, worry, fear and protest.

Fire was likely largely well-received by Homo erectus millions of years ago. Likewise the wheel by the late Neolithics. Even then, though, I suspect there were naysayers. Like, someone might have overcooked their Bronto Burgers, forever after eschewing flamed meats. Or had a toe or two squished by a passing cart, subsequently declaring the good old days of schlepping heavy things on their back to be a long-lost golden age.

Whether or not you view it as progress, however, technological advancement is inarguably an unstoppable force. Passionate though they were, the Luddites could no more halt the development of textile machinery in the 19th-century than one could stop a tsunami by standing defiantly on a beach, shouting, "STOP!"

Born just months before Armstrong's giant leap for mankind, I've seen the world transformed by tech, from VCRs and game consoles to home computers and, of course, the Internet.

I remember, way back in the late Seventies, spending weeks compiling a mix of my favorite theme tunes, waiting impatiently for each show to air, then demanding absolute silence of the household as I held a cassette tape recorder to the TV's mono speaker and, holding my breath, simultaneously pressing play and record as the music began. Later, playing back the clicking, hissing, tinny tune…. Honestly, I was thrilled.

Today, of course, you need only utter a few magic words to achieve a much higher quality result. "Alexa, play Spider-Man theme tune." I'm glad I got to do it the analogue way first, though, if only to appreciate how incredibly spoiled we are today.

I remember reading a short story at school, "The Machine Stops." A disquietingly prescient tale written by British author E.M. Forster, it was first published in 1909, and told a tale of humanity pampered to the point of utter uselessness, subservient to the machine that caters to their every need and whim. It's a cautionary tale we'd best pay closer attention to in the coming years. An exaggeration certainly, but maybe not so much, a century from now.

Like the people in Forster's story, who communicate entirely via electronic means, I've never met the author of this fascinating book in person. We first became aware of one another via Twitter, my virtual kingdom, bonding over a shared love of geeky things, principally sci-fi and *The Simpsons*.

I've made a lot of friends this way, and yes, I do consider them friends, though we've never gone out for a beer or sat eating popcorn, watching a movie together. Much as I'd like to share those experiences with Steven, I'm a Londoner, he's a New Yorker, and there's something of an ocean between us. Ours, then, is a rather more modern—but no less valid—mode of friendship.

Though it appears to the outside world—at least to those who don't also have their faces buried in their phones—that I'm the opposite of social, I'm continually interacting with others, and on a much larger platform than if I restricted my exchanges to those within spitting distance. Though I appreciate the value of personal interaction, of looking into someone's eyes as we speak, the opportunity to connect with like-minded people around the world, often thousands at a time and instantaneously, is, I feel, nothing to sniff at.

Technology changes everything. The way we live. The way we work. The way we interact as a species. It's a relationship that ceaselessly, and ever more speedily evolves, and we don't always have the upper hand. Truth be told, sometimes I'm not sure whether the device in my hand is my phone, or if I'm *its* human.

Reading this book made me consider how profoundly my life has been affected by tech. For worse, but also for better, in perhaps equal measure. Ultimately, I believe, it's a balancing act. For every loss we incur as a species, we're dealt a gain. For every industry that grinds to a redundant halt, fresh industries grow in their place. Video killed the radio star. The Internet murdered professional journalism. And maybe one day robots will replace people. But then something will come along to replace robots, something non-corporeal and Star Trekky. So don't get too comfortable, AI.

The trick to survival, at least until Skynet becomes aware, is to adapt. Yes, the Internet's a monster, and maybe once you've even felt its claws tear deep into your chest until your heart plopped out onto your shoes. But monsters can be tamed. Study them till you understand them, catch one, stick a saddle on it, then ride it to glory!

Foreword by Marshall Julius

While I was previously a print hack, a film critic and feature writer for those papery things you could buy in those bricky things, these days I'm a social media wiz. Commissions are now multiples of 280 characters, rather than thousands of words. But I've embraced communicating in the short form. And while writing was once a lonely pursuit akin to stuffing messages into bottles and hurling them out into the sea, today it's a lively two-way conversation rich in feedback and surprise.

My greatest success so far has been to build a personal Twitter following of more than 100,000 nerds much like myself, a lively community where politics and trolling have no place, and films, TV, comic books, videogames, toys, beer and bacon are everything. I'm easy to find—@MarshallJulius—so come say hi.

Ironically, my online success made it possible for me to score my first substantial print commission in years, a quiz book called "Vintage Geek" that celebrates a varied selection of 20th-century fandoms. By the time you read these words—unless you wisely skipped them and went straight to the main text—my book will likewise have been unleashed. It's an analogue anomaly I couldn't be prouder of. I hope Steven's equally thrilled with what he's accomplished here, because I'll tell you what, you're in for a ride.

When creating fiction, it's a writer's job to explore possibilities. And since there's very little entertainment value in stories where everything's fine and nothing goes wrong, cautionary tales of unsettling dystopian futures, of tech-gone-awry and scientists more concerned with whether they *could*, than if they *should*, are obviously much more popular, and indeed necessary.

Shows like *Black Mirror* and *Electric Dreams* ask essential questions. They explore the moral implications of developing tech. They force us to confront often troubling truths about where humanity is now, and, looking forward, how easily it could be tipped into murkier waters.

An intriguing exploration of provocative themes, Steven's book sent my mind, at times, to far scarier places than I usually dare visit. But I survived those trips and am all the better for them. It's the print equivalent of slipping on the sunglasses from Carpenter's *They Live*. Finally, I see the world for what it is. More worryingly, I see it now for what it could become, if we don't pay attention.

So pay attention.

Marshall Julius is a veteran nerd with unbounded enthusiasm for everything you love. He is a film critic, blogger, broadcaster, collector and author of a quiz book, Vintage Geek, *from September Publishing. Though his lifestyle appears sedentary, he's actually wildly active on Twitter (@marshalljulius).*

Introduction
Using Pop Culture as a Lens to Understand Our Technology-Obsessed World

This book examines the ways in which popular culture—especially the science fiction anthologies *Black Mirror* and *Electric Dreams*—explores the infiltration of modern technology in contemporary society. I discuss technology's role in disrupting existing norms and the ways in which *Black Mirror* and *Electric Dreams* and other television shows and films highlight these potentialities. I analyze the techno-dystopian worlds of *Black Mirror and Electric Dreams* (including the aesthetics thereof), while taking a deep and critical look at the issues and concerns presented by unchecked advances in technology. I examine the potential breakdown of certain socio-economic constructs due to the introduction of powerful technologies, showcasing the ways in which popular culture presents these scenarios. This disruption may create certain opportunities at both macro and micro levels, but it also poses significant threats to the ways in which we define and experience life—not to mention to the existence of life itself.

I also explore the new paradigms produced by technology's pervasive intrusion into various facets of our lives. The fact that some of the political, social, economic and emotional effects of the infusion of technology have been examined for many years (on shows such as the cutting-edge *The Twilight Zone*) demonstrates some level of consciousness and concern regarding the general impact of technology over time. As technology becomes more advanced, so, too, has our focus increased as we zero in on many potentialities that would have been difficult, if not impossible, to have imagined even a relatively short while ago.

As a practicing intellectual property and technology attorney, I see many of the benefits of technology firsthand. For example, the rapid collection and utilization of "Big Data" has transformed the ways in which financial services companies conduct business, including the way they manage and assess risk. The introduction of blockchain processes has streamlined the way business is conducted. The use of artificial intelligence in the context of contract review, negotiation and management is a critical component of managing legal costs and allocating resources effectively in a growing number of companies. The implementation of advanced software tools has disrupted and supplanted standard industry practices. The result has been the creation of economic efficiencies across a broad swath of industries. Companies can reduce operating costs and thereby increase profits by reducing labor costs. The transformative nature of technology has empowered companies to solve problems more quickly and has disrupted many traditional business practices.

Armed with a host of powerful new tools at their disposal, employees can work smarter and spend less time on tasks that were previously handled manually—or, in some cases not at all. Technology has allowed folks to conduct business in ways previously considered impossible. For example, in the mergers and acquisitions space, lawyers can use redline programs to exchange working drafts of complex agreements. Use of typewriters would not have allowed the type of back-and-forth negotiations and resultant detailed nature of the contractual documents to be executed. Those companies that employ advanced technology and modern techniques for conducting business—irrespective of the industry—possess a distinct competitive advantage over those companies that arrive late to the technology game.[1]

I chose to write this book because of the centrality of technology in everyday life. While other works address many of the issues presented by the current and forthcoming technological revolutions, this book is the first to examine the ways in which the popular television shows *Black Mirror* and *Electric Dreams* tackle such concerns. The power of satire and sharp social commentary to raise awareness of issues and induce change can be significant. In my view, the issues presented on both *Black Mirror* and *Electric Dreams* merit serious attention and examination by scholars, policymakers and the general public. *Black Mirror* is considered such a fundamental component of the public discourse on these issues that television critic James Poniewozik of *The New York Times* declared it to be "hands down the most relevant program of our time, if for no other reason than how often it can make you wonder if we're all living in an episode of it."[2]

My other books have focused on other well-developed television shows (i.e., *The Simpsons*, *24*, *Breaking Bad* and *Better Call Saul*) from which important issues can be examined and discussed.[3] I believe that both *Black Mirror* and *Electric Dreams* satisfy this criterion as well. The episodes are ripe for scholarly review and critique.

Introduction 7

Because of the ubiquity and pervasiveness of technology in our everyday lives, a writer examining the introduction of novel technologies as presented throughout popular culture needs to be selective in terms of topics and issues to cover. One of the challenges of writing this book was determining what aspects of technology should comprise the core focus of this book. Popular culture provides a window into the types of technological innovations that may present the most significant opportunities as well as the gravest concerns. By analyzing the 30 techno-dystopian worlds presented on *Black Mirror* and *Electric Dreams*, I cultivated a picture of those technologies that tend to engender a sense of urgency in contemporary society. Examining those episodes—along with other references to technological innovation throughout popular culture—allowed me to formulate a substantive critique of the technologies presented therein as well as an analysis of the television shows themselves. I also used a host of other television shows and movies as a springboard for a deep discussion of the socio-economic, political, legal and ethical issues resulting from the introduction (in some cases potential introduction) of such technology into society. My analysis of the foregoing was supplemented by a review of academic literature and popular books and articles covering media theory, legal issues, and, of course, technology.

The popular television shows *Black Mirror* and *Electric Dreams* present futuristic worlds where many of the advantages and threats of artificial intelligence, robotics, social media and virtual reality are on full display. Both shows reflect many contemporary anxieties and fears about the future, and this book examines the ways in which specific episodes of these anthologies explore these issues. In addition to *Black Mirror* and *Electric Dreams*—the two shows that comprise primary focus of this book—it also addresses the ways that a host of other television shows (such as *The Twilight Zone, Humans, The Office, The Simpsons* and *Parks and Recreation*) and films (such as *The Truman Show, Eternal Sunshine of the Spotless Mind, The Matrix* and *The Wizard of Oz*) tackle issues related to technological development, defining humanity and escapism from traditional environments. While technology is not the primary focus of some of these other television shows and films, technological concepts, themes and ideas frequently serve as critical background elements in the fictional worlds presented onscreen. It is nearly impossible to produce a television series or film in which the society depicted therein is not heavily dependent on technology in a myriad of ways.

Notwithstanding the benefits of technology (many of which are enumerated herein), this book argues that humanity may be vulnerable to succumbing to certain dangers depicted on the futuristic worlds of *Black Mirror* and *Electric Dreams*. In my view, the issues covered in these anthologies fall into five broadly-defined categories. The episodes examine: (1) the influence of technology on the dissemination of information and political discourse and the power to manipulate; (2) technology's impact on the ways in which folks interact and form relationships with each other; (3) privacy and security-related considerations in hyper-techno, dystopian worlds; (4) the ways in which technology influences the ways we value, define and experience human life; and (5) the feasibility of cohabitating with our technological creations, especially those possessing advanced intelligence capabilities. This book tackles each of these issues, which tend to overlap with one another in some respects, in turn:

Chapter 1 provides an overview of humanity's overreliance on technology and its profound influence throughout society. I discuss the ways in which technological innovations have significant social, political, economic and emotional consequences. I also provide an overview of how technology has been examined throughout popular culture, from *The Twilight Zone* to *Black Mirror* and *Electric Dreams*. I argue that a close examination of these shows, along with other references to technological advancements in films and other shows, provides scholars with keen insights into the potential benefits and harms resulting from their introduction into contemporary society. We can learn much about our potential reactions to the infusion of new technologies by examining characters' reactions to such technologies in our popular culture.

Chapter 2 examines the influence of technology on modern political discourse and the dissemination of ideas. The chapter uses applications of Marshall McLuhan's media theories and the *Black Mirror* episode "The Waldo Moment" as a springboard for discussion of populist politics, including the meteoric ascent of United States President Donald Trump. The chapter also discusses the dangers of misinformation, disinformation and "The Big Lie" in contemporary society, and the role that technology has in the rapid communication of ideas that have not been adequately vetted for veracity. Here, I argue that the fast-paced, largely unchecked exchange of ideas can have deleterious effects on the democratic state. I describe some of the ways in which strategically disseminated disinformation can adversely affect society. In the context of the Internet, I discuss the "Google effect" and the failure to advance the ideal of "net empowerment." While political actors attempting to use the media to manipulate the truth and advance a political agenda in a disingenuous fashion is not a new phenomenon, the power of such actors to achieve desired results has increased exponentially because of the availability of advanced technology. A close examination of the *Electric Dreams* episode "Safe and Sound" highlights this issue.

Chapter 3 analyzes the effects of social media and online dating websites on contemporary human interaction, using the *Black Mirror* episodes "Nosedive," "Hated in the Nation" and "Hang the DJ" as case studies. This chapter discusses studies indicating that individuals addicted to social media outlets may be more inclined to exhibit symptoms of depression, loneliness, and anxiety. Social media platforms have engendered new social dynamics and constructs. While connecting billions of people globally, social media has also, quite paradoxically, limited the way in which humans interact with one another. It has also fostered a rating system culture—one in in which individuals rank each other against specified criteria. Such platforms have enabled governments, quite jarringly, to rank and manage their citizens.

Chapter 4 discusses the constant struggle to strike an acceptable balance between preserving individual liberties while ensuring security. I argue that, in the privacy space, contemporary legal systems and regulatory regimes have been outpaced by advances in modern technology. It also discusses the viability of regulation by and of the government in the privacy and security arenas. This chapter examines the use of technology as a potential mechanism for both creating safety—a questionable premise examined therein—and taking away the privacy of individuals. I explore the question of whether we have a deep appreciation for the ideal of privacy or, conversely, whether technology has diminished the value that we place on such an ideal. I discuss the concept of informed consent in the context of implementation of invasive devices, as explored in the *Black Mirror* episode "Men Against Fire." The chapter discusses the dangers arising from the collection of information by examining the consequences of security breaches. The chapter uses episodes from both *Black Mirror* ("Arkangel") and *Electric Dreams* ("Safe and Sound" and "Kill All Others") to illustrate potential concerns with implementing electronic tracking and monitoring devices. I also discuss the ways in which these anthologies examine technology's impact on privacy norms in the context of memories ("The Entire History of You," "Crocodile"), thoughts ("The Hood Maker") and dreams ("Men Against Fire").

Chapter 5 examines the ways in which both *Black Mirror* and *Electric Dreams* provide sharp commentary on human dignity and the meaning and purpose of human existence, particularly in altered and alternate states of reality. This chapter discusses the emergence of powerful virtual reality and augmented realities technologies, with a focus on how *Black Mirror* and *Electric Dreams* explore the use of such technologies as a mechanism for escapism. I discuss the ways in which popular culture has explored the theme of escapism in a variety of contexts. I also discuss the ways in which technology can simultaneously enhance the quality of life while redefining its characteristics. Here, I question whether a virtual existence (such as in the futuristic world presented on the *Black Mirror* episode "San Junipero") enables humans to experience life in a meaningful way. I explore whether digital copies of individuals and other artificially-created beings on the "spectrum of humanity" possess characteristics that demand that they be treated fairly and perhaps be afforded certain legal protections.

Chapter 6 discusses the impact of artificial intelligence and robotics on humankind, including with respect to workforce displacement and the creation of economic efficiencies. Here, I analyze scientific theories and predictions in this arena set forth in books and peer-reviewed academic articles. I discuss the concept of a "replacement culture," as identified on the *Electric Dreams* episode "Autofac" and analyze this idea in connection with Walt Disney's "Carousel of Progress." I also apply cultivation theory to an examination of a host of *Black Mirror* and *Electric Dreams* episodes in support of my argument that the television shows that we watch are not only informative but also influential in terms of the way in which an audience considers novel issues. Finally, citing the *Black Mirror* episode "Metalhead," I argue that the unchecked introduction of artificial intelligence could potentially lead to a tragic loss of innocence and a competition for scarce resources.

1

Reflections Through a Black Mirror

"It is not a technological problem we have; it's a human one."
—Charlie Brooker[1]

In *The Simpsons* episode "Itchy & Scratchy Land" (1994), the Simpsons family visits the Disneyland-like theme park Itchy & Scratchy Land. The park has many Itchy robots, each designed to attack their counterparts (Scratchy robots)—mimicking the violent cartoon series featuring those characters. The family members find themselves in a fight for their lives after the robots go rogue and start attacking human visitors.[2]

The fear of robots taking over the world and destroying humanity has been a staple of both science fiction and mainstream popular culture for decades.[3] But what if our creations do not seek our physical destruction but instead cause us to lose something else? In *The Twilight Zone*'s "The Lateness of the Hour," a family isolates itself from society and relies on robots to perform daily tasks.[4] The family members become so dependent on their robot servants that they run the risk of losing the ability to care for themselves. Is it unreasonable to suggest that, due to this dependency, the robots exert implicit control over the lives of the family members? Given our own pervasive use of and reliance on technology, have human beings lost the battle with our creations before we (or they) even realized that it has begun?

As modern technology has become more advanced, so, too, has the perceived threat of artificial intelligence and its potentially destructive consequences. We are faced with many important questions: How do we reap the benefits of technology powered by artificial intelligence while avoiding harms caused by its introduction into society? Do we have effective legal and regulatory controls in our arsenal to sufficiently address potential threats? If humanity is unable to tame and control its own technological creations, is it possible that our future as a species is in jeopardy? How do we manage technology so that it does not manage *us*?

Overreliance on Technology

In the *Black Mirror* episode "Fifteen Million Merits" (2011), individuals must pedal on stationary bicycles to earn "merits" that in turn can be used to power the technological innovations surrounding them. The merits are necessary for all aspects of life in this futuristic, techno-dystopian world—from brushing your teeth in the morning to having the ability to switch channels on digital screens. Instead of using technology as an option to save time and energy, the folks living in this society work hard so that they can access technology.[5] This perversion of the intended purpose of technology leads us to question whether gaining the right to use technology is worth the physical effort required in connection therewith. The use of technology is a costly privilege in this society—but it seems necessary to achieve happiness. The failure to earn enough merits could lead an individual to lead a largely isolated and sad existence. While our contemporary usage of technology is not tied to formal prerequisites (such as frequent exercise), the reliance on technology in this episode for daily tasks is not so far removed from our own experiences and interactions with technology. The episode forces us to ask whether exchanging our hard-earned money for Internet access is qualitatively different from the merit-based technology access system presented in the episode. It also leads us to question whether we are in control of our technological creations or whether we rely on technology so heavily that our thoughts, emotions and behaviors are effectively dictated by our desire (and perceived necessity) to make use of it in our lives.

Our ubiquitous use of, and reliance on, technology is undeniable. For many of us, the first and last moments of our day consist of checking our phones. But are we cognizant of the voluminous ways in which technology is affecting our thoughts and behaviors? Even if we were so aware, would we be able to resist the temptation to use technologies to which we have become addicted? *The Twilight Zone*'s "A Thing About Machines" explores our reluctance to make a clean break from technology despite its potential to cause harm.[6] In the episode, a man is in possession of machines that appear to be haunted. After they attempt to kill him, he breaks them in self-defense. Incredulously, he then engages a repair man to fix the machines. The broader message here is that we are largely incapable of eliminating technology from our lives—even if it causes us harm—because we rely on it so heavily.

We frequently adjust our daily behaviors—the ways in which we interact with each other, develop relationships and perform our jobs—based on the introduction of ever-evolving technologies. And some experts argue that we have not yet adapted to an environment that is, and will continue to be, a moving target. *New York Times* journalist and author of "A Deadly Wandering: A Tale of Tragedy and Redemption in the Age of Attention" Matt Richtel documents the disparity between the "pace of innovation" and the "pace of evolution," arguing that human beings need to "learn to adapt to technology in a world that is changing way, way faster than we can evolve."[7] Richtel analogies our experience with technology with the way we confront junk food, pointing out that "just as we have not changed at the pace that food has industrialized, so [too] we don't metabolize junk food any better than we did 50 years ago."[8] The difference, according to Richtel, is that we have learned that we must be careful with junk food and limit its consumption.[9] We have not yet learned to effectively modulate our intake of technology, exposing ourselves to the potential consequences emanating from overuse thereof.

As Richtel persuasively argues, our pervasive use of such technologies may go a bit too far. Even business executives within the technology space—folks who have a clear vested interest in continued use of technology by as many people as possible throughout society—have hinted that our immersion in technology may be a bit extreme. Apple CEO Tim Cook, for example, stated that "Honestly, we've never wanted people to overuse our products. We want people to be empowered from them and do things they couldn't do otherwise, but if you spend all your time on your phone, then you are spending too much time."[10] Cook's comments suggest a growing awareness and concern over our ever-increasing level of digital connectedness. This enhanced connectivity has created a new paradigm, one in which many folks are, effectively, slaves to their devices because of their refusal to temporarily disentangle therefrom. We should actively seek to temporarily disconnect from such devices and avoid becoming so tethered to our devices that we cannot escape. This idea was satirized on *The Office* episode "WUPHF.com," when Ryan Howard develops the "WUPHF" application, which simultaneously sends uber-connected users the same communication via text, social media, fax and telephone.[11]

Taking periodic breaks from technology could serve as a means of cleansing ourselves—a detox of sorts—in which we become reacquainted with our value systems. When Tom Haverford, for example (in the *Parks and Recreation* episode "Sex Education"), becomes addicted to social media and has a car accident while tweeting, a judge orders him to avoid accessing any screens for a week.[12] Haverford acknowledges that he uses technology to distract from problems in his personal life—he relies on modern technological devices to temporarily exit the natural world. While Tom uses technology to escape, a strong case can be made that we often need a reprieve *from* technology—especially when it results in tangible, identifiable harms. Observers of Judaism enjoy the benefits of this reprieve every Sabbath for 25 hours, a time during which folks put down their electronic devices in respect and observance of the holy day. Setting aside time for such a break helps folks to reengage and create meaningful connections with each other—and not rely on shiny screens to communicate messages with the outside world or count the number of likes they receive on a post.

By and large, the appropriate response to technology is not to ban or prohibit its usage over prolonged periods of time—as *The Simpsons*' Sideshow Bob proposes in response to Springfield's overuse of television—but rather to use it in moderation; make use of it in positive, constructive ways; and exercise proper discretion.[13] We rightfully condemn the actions of the Luddites, who, during the 19th century, broke into factories and destroyed the machines that had replaced them.[14] But a careful consideration of the Luddites' concerns about technology in a society frequently defined by its willingness to make substitutions and replacements is warranted.[15] It is critical to acknowledge some of the risks that the abuse and misuse of technology can have not only on individuals but on society generally.

Some folks have already begun to reduce their usage of modern technologies, particularly in the context of raising children. Bill Gates and Steve Jobs both reportedly placed strict limits on the amount of time their kids spent using smartphones and other devices, for example—with Gates prohibiting his children from having cell phones until they reached age 14.[16] Nellie Bowles of *The New York Times* reports that other wealthy parents who work for technology companies have also sought to significantly limit (if not entirely ban) the amount of time that their children spend using screens.[17] While introducing technology in the classroom has historically been a laudable goal, this dynamic is gradually changing, according to educators Joe Clement and Matt Miles—coauthors of the book "Screen Schooled: Two Veteran Teachers Expose How Technology Use is Making Our Kids Dumber."[18] Chris Anderson, the former editor of *Wired* magazine, observes that "The digital divide was about access to technology, and now that everyone has access, the new digital divide is limiting access to technology."[19] This shift is most pronounced in wealthy neighborhoods and parents with professional backgrounds in technology. As Bowles notes, "a dark consensus about screens and kids begins to emerge in Silicon Valley," with one Silicon valley parent opining that "I am convinced the devil lives in our phones."[20] Such sentiments (minus the hyperbole) are supported by studies indicating that use and reliance on smartphones may stunt cognitive development and have an adverse impact on the ways in which our brains function.[21]

The slowly emerging trend known as the "new digital divide," however, should not be overstated. Notwithstanding this very gradual shift away from the usage of technology by children in high income circles, virtually every facet of our contemporary world relies on technology in some way—from business to security to healthcare, and so much more. Technology is a powerful resource and mechanism for rapid communication, education, accomplishing tasks, creating efficiencies and entertainment. It has changed our behavior in countless ways. Take online interactions for example. While the intended purpose of social media platforms was (and perhaps still is) to connect individuals in new ways, such platforms have also disrupted existing privacy norms and preferences. As Hannah Baker acutely observes on the *Netflix* series *13 Reasons Why* (2017–present), "Facebook, Twitter, Instagram— they've made us a society of stalkers. And we love it."[22] And in other contexts, social media is, ironically, used as an outlet by folks to vent their frustrations about the impact of technological advances on their lives.[23] Technology can also be used to engender and disseminate disinformation and manipulation.

Humanity continues to embrace technology, and, in many ways, technology has become an extension of our species. Humanity's over-reliance on technologies—largely to obtain the benefits and advantages of the efficiencies created thereby—can leave our species, and the world at large, vulnerable to the effects of significant disruptions and failures of such technologies. For example, the global community feared catastrophic consequences from potential computer malfunctions or failures on January 1, 2000, because of computer bugs related to the storage and formatting of data for calendar dates. While the Year 2000 (or "Y2K") disaster was largely averted, the fear jolted many governments, businesses and individuals and served as a reminder about some of the adverse effects that could result from humanity's over-reliance on technology.[24]

Another example is the potential impact of data security breaches, which leave individuals' sensitive personal information exposed, potentially opening the door to identity theft and other serious financial and emotional consequences. This concern is highlighted on the *Black Mirror* episode "Shut Up and Dance" (2016), when a hacker gains access to individuals' embarrassing videos and other sensitive information and uses such materials and information to blackmail them. The television series *You* (2018–present) explores the ways in which a stalker who gains access to a target's phone and social media accounts has the power to not only disrupt but effectively control her life, uprooting her existing relationships by sending falsely attributed communications to friends.[25] And in the Netflix film *Cam* (2018), a webcam performer's account and identity are stolen by a malicious actor.[26] The paradox here is that we rely on advanced technological systems to keep us safe and protect our data. But as those devices become more complex—built with more parts from various sources—the risk of a malicious actor successfully breaching the device increases. More penetration testing must be performed to test our devices. As Dr. Jacob Mendel, head of research cooperation at Tel Aviv University's Interdisciplinary Cyber Research Center advises, security experts must "attack it, to use the maximum knowledge we have today to protect it."[27] While technology has provided enormous benefits in terms of maintaining security, it has also created intractable and sometimes insuperable challenges.

And the adverse consequences that could result if an individual is affected by a breach could be significant and life-altering. Viewed holistically (and without regard to the effect on a specific individual), the benefits of the utilization of technology for creating efficiency in terms of maintaining security may outweigh potential harms. And a reasonable observer could argue that despite acknowledged ills, harms and missteps, technology will ultimately serve a greater good and therefore justifiable from a Bentham utilitarianism perspective: you cannot make an omelet without cracking a few eggs, as the saying goes.[28] Alternatively, it may be the case that, at some point during our quest for technological achievement, we come to realize that our inventions are hurting us on a grand scale. As culture editor Jason Parham asks: "What if we're stuck in a loop, slave to new innovations that only amplify hate, human flaw, and social fragility?"[29] Either way, this dichotomy merits both consideration and further examination and is the bedrock of many *Black Mirror* and *Electric Dreams* episodes.

Failures of technology can also be disruptive, given humanity's reliance on its functionality and performance. Society has adjusted certain existing norms to reflect this reality. For example, take the Latin phrase *"force majeure"* (meaning "acts of God"). This term is often included in service-related contracts and is intended to provide a performing party an excuse to suspend performance (and not be held to have breached the contract) during the duration of certain exigencies. In recent years, this term has been expanded to typically include technological failures, malfunctions, and disruptions. This shift makes practical sense, given the deleterious impact that failures of technology could have on areas not only in our daily lives but also in the context of, say, the economy and national security. Companies have already been adversely affected by technological malfunctions. In 2012, for example, an electronic trading company, Knight Capital Group, reportedly lost more than $450 million in thirty minutes due to a faulty algorithm's decision to buy stocks in a range of companies, paying more for the shares as the stock prices continued to rise.[30] And in the context of national security, military leaders frequently devise strategies that rely heavily, if not exclusively, on the proper functioning of technology, such as smart bombs and drone systems. And when such technology fails, lives and missions are at risk. Television shows such as *24* (2001–2010) and *Jack Ryan* (2018–) provide a window into how critical missions of field operatives could be compromised due to cell phone failures and other technical issues.[31] Modifying our language, expectations and behavior to reflect these realities are but some of the many ways in which we have adjusted and adapted our focus due to the incursion of technology in contemporary society.

Ambition and Responsibility

In his final breath, Dr. Victor Frankenstein advises us to "seek happiness in tranquility and avoid ambition, even if it be only the apparently innocent one of distinguishing yourself in science and technology."[32] Dr. Frankenstein's perspective on the perils of an ill-defined and open-ended notion of progress is understandable, having created a monster and suffering from a host of painful consequences resulting from unleashing him unto the world. But does our contemporary technology-driven society seek to achieve an appropriate balance between unbridled, unimpeded innovation and a more cautious approach to the development and introduction of powerful technologies?

The scientific model of technological innovation as a means of achieving ever-increasing efficiencies demands that its prowess be continuously expanded and exploited in ways that may not be predictable or even comprehensible at a given moment in time. Scientists typically do not seek to find a happy medium with respect to developing a technology that reasonably satisfies our species and achieves specific goals.[33] Rather, technological innovation entails constant expansion and development, thereby potentially leading to consequences (both positive and negative) that deviate from the initial focus and objectives of introducing the technological development. As Tesla and SpaceX founder Elon Musk observes, "sometimes what will happen is a scientist will get so engrossed in their work that they don't really realize the ramifications of what they've done."[34] Consistent with this notion, Michigan State University Assistant Professor and scientist Arend Hintze admits that "My focus is not on determining whether I like or approve of something; it matters only that I can unveil it."[35] This sentiment (along with a warning attached thereto) is also echoed on an episode of *Humans*, as a protester at a "We Are People" rally cries, "We're so in love with progress, in such a rush to move forward [that] we're leaving our values behind."[36] It is often the unintended consequences of innovation that generate the most significant concern.[37] While there is nothing inherently harmful with allowing employees at a Swedish company to voluntarily have microchips implanted in them to create workplace efficiency, for example, it is the unknown next step that causes societal angst.[38] Patrick Mesterton, the co-founder and CEO of the company (Epicenter) acknowledged the uncertain direction and presented a relatively nonchalant attitude towards the introduction of such technology, stating "We're just doing this because it's interesting. We want to play around with technology."[39]

A perfect example of the potentiality described above is examined in the first part of the *Black Mirror* episode "Black Museum" (2017). The segment features a doctor who uses a device to transfer his patients' pain to himself so that he could diagnose them with more ease and accuracy. While the purpose is noble, it is not difficult to envision catastrophic results. The episode invites us to imagine a scenario in which the subject doctor could become addicted to the feeling of pain after exposure to the intense new experience, causing the subject to harm himself or others to experience the sensation.[40] It is conceivable that "playing around" with technology in this instance may ultimately prove extremely harmful. For this reason, producers, distributors and purveyors of powerful technologies have a special obligation to be cognizant and cautious about what they introduce into society. As *Spiderman*'s Uncle Ben acutely observes, "With great power comes great responsibility."[41] It is not enough to simply create as much as possible without considering the potential ramifications related to the implementation thereof. And we must be thoughtful and empathetic as we develop and implement new technologies—a lesson expressed in the final intertitle of the science fiction film *Metropolis* (1927): "The mediator between the head and the hands must be the heart."[42] The true innovators are those who can convert novel innovations into practical applications to be used in a responsible way.

One counter-argument to this cautious approach is that the world will be deprived of greatness if we demand that innovators implement a rigid model for balancing stated objectives and potential harms. Because an innovation is, by definition, something new that has not been widely tested, it is often impossible to predict the potential dangers that could result from its introduction. Aside from the lack of practicality of implementing such an approach, we will never know what we might lose, what innovations will never see the light of day because of these restrictions. This is the observation of an inventor in the film *Ex Machina* (2014), who notes that great artwork would never have been produced if the artist was required to map out a specific blueprint for the work before painting it.[43] The freedom and flexibility to create, to produce, in a free-flowing, uninhibited way has led to ineffable developments. The marvels of the world have been produced not by strict adherence to prescribed frameworks; rather, greatness is often born as a result of trial-and-error, a lack of fear of failure and a wide-eyed belief in the beauty that could be created by an unrestricted ability for humans to produce magic.

If society is willing to breach the ideal of unbridled, unfettered creative license (angering not only many inventors but also folks with a libertarian political perspective) and demands a more measured approach to the development and introduction of technology to avoid dramatic surprises and unintended harms, one potential solution is the creation of an independent commission providing for the regulatory oversight of new technological innovations. Such a commission would function like the Food and Drug Administration in the United States, requiring that certain criteria be met prior to the introduction of technology into society. There are, of course, inherent risks and disadvantages in moving forward with such an approach. Innovators may feel less incentivized to develop inventions, given a predictably long and expensive review process with no guaranteed promise of a mainstream rollout. Despite the dual aspirational goals of independence and transparency, the process may well become politicized—with receipt of approval requiring connections on Capitol Hill to move the process forward. Prior to implementing such an approach, we would need to carefully consider whether we would be comfortable permitting lobbyists to effectively help determine which innovations meet the gatekeeper's standards for acceptance and release.

Commentators have observed that our contemporary legal system lacks the sophistication to deal with the introduction and implementation of novel technologies within society. Many argue that our laws are too antiquated to effectively contend with modern technology—a theme to which we will return throughout this book. In the context of privacy laws, for example, the American Civil Liberties Union (ACLU) argues that "Technological innovation has outpaced our privacy protections."[44] In describing the "land rush phenomenon," the ACLU observes that "All too often, the deployment of new technologies happens faster than our social, political, educational or legal systems can react, producing a 'land rush' in which companies and government agencies deploy new privacy-invasive technologies before subjects are aware that they exist—and certainly before we have consented to their use through our democratic political system."[45] Some might argue, however, that the backlash sometimes goes too far. If a cyber-related crime is committed, for example, is it overly burdensome to demand that law enforcement determine, beyond a reasonable doubt, that a named individual used the device in question? Or would it be sufficient to determine that such individual owned the device, tie the device to the alleged crime and require the defendant to prove that the device was stolen by another individual?[46] Would such a standard uproot centuries' worth of jurisprudence in the context of criminal law? If so, is it justifiable given the challenges created by the introduction of technologies? Have those in a position to shape public policy given sufficient consideration to these thorny questions?

This theme of premature introduction of potentially dangerous technologies is explored in *Black Mirror* episodes such as "Black Museum" (where digital transference technology was introduced but then subsequently banned) and "Arkangel" (where the invasive tracking and monitoring device is similarly implemented but then prohibited by law). The failure of the legal system to "catch" these technologies in time is partially due to structural and procedural limitations of our judicial system, but also partially due to the nature of the innovations. Given their novel attributes, it is difficult to anticipate all the potentially adverse consequences that might result from misuses and abuses of the technologies at issue.

This issue is perhaps nowhere more pronounced than in the context of artificial intelligence applications. Artificial intelligence presents a wide array of unique challenges to our legal system. The introduction of commercial applications of artificial intelligence, for example, may affect the way in which we ascribe liability and seek to prohibit discriminatory practices. Existing business norms and applicable legal standards are called into question by the introduction of artificial intelligence. In the context of product liability, for example, is it reasonable to hold a manufacturer liable for the potential failure of artificial intelligence to produce a product that caused a consumer harm? *Black Mirror*'s "Crocodile" (2017) briefly touches on this question, as an insurance adjuster describes the tensions involved in promulgating and enforcing standards of liability for self-driving cars.

These issues arise in the employment context as well. For example, how can employers police their algorithms to avoid discrimination in hiring practices against folks based on factors such as zip codes? What if the algorithm discriminates against such folks from a given zip code because it deems folks from that area to be less qualified? These issues, among others, arise due to the very nature of artificial intelligence. As artificial intelligence expands and makes decisions on its own, we are no longer truly in control and it may not be reasonable to expect existing standards for assigning fault and liability to subsist.[47]

Amazon's focus on artificial intelligence provides an opportunity for a case study. For example, Amazon reportedly scrapped a recruiting tool that used artificial intelligence because the tool demonstrated bias against women.[48] Had Amazon moved forward with the tool, legal experts could debate whether—and, perhaps more interestingly—to what degree Amazon should be held legally responsible for violations of anti-discrimination laws. As in other contexts, our legal system does not seem to be sufficiently advanced to appropriately handle novel questions arising from the introduction of such technology.

Because Amazon has the power to shut down the tool, it seems that it should be held liable—at least to some extent—for the output of the tool. But should the degree of liability be considered and determined on a defined spectrum—where a company's financial responsibility is in proportion to the control exerted in, and influence over, the creation of both the algorithm and its output? If the artificial intelligence is so powerful that it makes decisions without any human involvement or guidance from a corporate actor, is it fair to hold the company fully responsible for the consequences of such decisions? Is it reasonable to advance a strict liability standard in this context, wherein an actor is liable for a result even though it may not have done anything wrongful, negligent or otherwise unlawful? Or must it be demonstrated that companies such as Amazon acted outside of legal and regulatory guidelines and / or its own best practices and protocols to hold such corporate actors legally responsible? Is the argument against such a strict liability standard akin to that of YouTube, which argues that it should not be held liable for third-party claims related to content posted by users—even though YouTube ultimately controls the platform?[49] (YouTube is in fact protected under Section 230 of the Communications Decency Act of 1996, which provides, in relevant part: "No provider or user of an interactive computer service shall be treated as the publisher or speaker of any information provided by another information content provider.")[50] Are both situations examples of companies releasing technology without adequately policing its use or exerting power over it?

Perhaps a strict liability regime would help to advance the objective of incentivizing corporate actors to become more reflective corporate citizens, effectively using economics to force companies to consider the potentially adverse consequences that could result from newly introduced technologies. Might companies then devise and adhere to a more careful, end-user friendly set of business practices? Or would enacting such a standard disincentivize corporations to explore and produce new technologies, depriving end users (and society at large) access to incredible and potentially beneficial innovations? If a strict liability standard is used, would developers and licensors of artificial intelligence tools be willing to indemnify companies for actions of and omissions by the tool? As artificial intelligence becomes more advanced, it is important to carefully study and consider these issues and enact rules intended to create a fair and just system for both companies and the folks who may have been wronged due to the decisions and actions of artificial intelligence produced by such companies.

As Seen on TV: An Introduction to the Award-Winning and Aesthetically Powerful Black Mirror *and* Electric Dreams

Popular culture has both reflected and examined our collective fascination with the development and introduction of technology, documenting the drama and frequent tensions involved in its creation on television shows such as *Halt and Catch Fire* (2014–2017) and *Silicon Valley* (2014–present) and in films such as *Steve Jobs* (2015) and *The Social Network* (2010).[51] The consequences that may emanate from humanity's over-reliance on technological innovation is expertly examined on both *Black Mirror* and *Electric Dreams*. As columnist Chris Li observes, these shows use technology as a "thematic backdrop" and "mirror back the realities of today's society in a larger sense."[52] The science fiction series *Black Mirror* debuted on December 4, 2011, on British television and has completed four seasons, with a current total of 19 episodes.[53] The series was recently renewed for a fifth season. The show was purchased by Netflix in September 2015, enabling the critically-acclaimed series to reach a significantly larger audience.[54] The show was created by Charlie Brooker, who describes it as a collection of hypothetical futuristic worlds that examine "the way we live now—and the way we might be living in 10 minutes' time if we're clumsy."[55] The series has been nominated for 79 awards, winning 21 of them. Those awards include Best TV / Miniseries at the International Emmy Awards (November 2012), Outstanding Television Movie and Outstanding Writing for a Limited Series, Movie or Dramatic Special (the latter two received at the Primetime Emmy Awards for the episodes "San Junipero" and "U.S.S. Callister").[56] The series *Electric Dreams* is a ten episode anthology series that premiered in the United Kingdom on September 17, 2017, and on Amazon Video in the United States on January 12, 2018.[57] Like *Black Mirror*, it is a science fiction series, with a special focus and emphasis on technology. The *Electric Dreams* episodes are all based on short stories penned by author Philip K. Dick.[58] The show was developed by Ronald D. Moore and Michael Dinner, and can be viewed as Amazon's competitive response to Netflix's purchase of *Black Mirror*. *Electric Dreams* was nominated for two Saturn awards.[59]

Both shows are aesthetically powerful and include special effects, music, backgrounds and imagery typically intended to convey a sense of hypermodernity and futurism. Some of these elements set the stage for events that occur and major plot reveals later in an episode—such as the secret nature of the environment in which Frank and Amy reside in the episode "Hang the DJ."[60] Some episodes, such as *Black Mirror*'s "Metalhead" (2017)—which was filmed entirely in black and white—incorporate design elements that seek to portray a dark and dreary setting. The moods and dispositions of the characters in these anthologies are often reflective of their surroundings, some of which are more defined than others. "Crocodile" director John Hillcoat describes his approach to mapping out the scenery for the episode and the ways in which the choice of physical settings is influenced by the plot: "The story's coldblooded aspect fitted like a glove with Iceland during its winter. I always feel like the environment should be equal to the main characters, because people are profoundly affected by their environment. The strange, vast and primeval landscapes with blackened soil felt like they could enhance the cruel inescapable logic of Mia's fatal choices."[61] Some episodes are set in dynamic and colorful settings, such as "Nosedive," where flashiness and the pastel-colored clothing worn by folks influences social rankings. Other societies are defined by darker colors, displaying a sense of hopelessness and sadness (such as the sober, process-oriented world depicted in *Electric Dream*'s "Autofac" [2018]). Sometimes, monotonous design elements are incorporated to reflect the repetitiveness in a society—such as the sameness of the rooms depicted on *Black Mirror*'s "Hang the DJ" (2017).

The music selections played during certain episodes—including 1980s hits, such as *Heaven Is a Place on Earth* (1987) during the period piece "San Junipero"—create powerful settings intended to portray a particular place, time and theme.[62] Some of these unique characteristics help to differentiate our contemporary society from the ones that we see on our television screens. Many episodes feature songs that foreshadow or otherwise highlight the themes presented on the series. *Black Mirror*'s "Black Museum"—an episode focused, in part, on the transference of digital consciousness between hosts—for example, features the single *(There's) Always Something There to Remind Me* (1964) as the protagonist travels to and from the museum.[63] The use of technological devices within various episodes also conveys a powerful, frequently unsettling message. In "White Bear" (2013), for example, the image of (apparent) bystanders calmly pointing their phones at a frantic woman in desperate need of assistance produces a portrait that is seared in our psyches.

Folks are tethered to their fancy gadgets and some unknown force seemingly causes folks to reinvent themselves as zombie-like and emotionless beings—lacking the empathy that we so often argue differentiates humans from our artificially-intelligent creations.

The anthologies employ a relatively unique narrative structure that allows the audience to enter a new world and continue to learn about that world throughout the episode. The episodes range in duration, allowing the writers and directors flexibility in their storytelling and ability to explore issues without adhering to strictly confined and uniform minutes requirements. Certain elements of the world that are not directly relevant to the main plot may be presented as part of a backdrop to add a bit of contextual depth to the fictional society. Additional creative freedom is a byproduct of the anthological structure. For example, the writers and directors are free to cherry pick which elements of a society they wish to explore—and how deep they wish to dive into such elements. They can touch on strange elements (such as some of the odd features of the society depicted on "Crazy Diamond" [2018]) without going into significant depth. This enables the team to show a lot of eyebrow-raising aspects of a world as part of the setup, irrespective of whether the societal formation is realistic. Character development is not a fundamental staple of these shows, as their anthological composition does not provide sufficient time for the writers to craft complex backstories or explore nuanced personality traits.[64] The focus, instead, is on the nature—and, especially, the current state—of the society presented to the viewer.

While *Black Mirror* and *Electric Dreams* can both be helpful in terms of serving as warning signals of what our own society may look like if we are not sufficiently careful, certain episodes are less useful in that regard to the extent the background elements are not fully explained. How can we guard against an exercise-based earned merit system ("Fifteen Million Merits,") for example, if we do not know what led to the development of the system? While the audience may be dismayed by certain aspects of the society at the outset (or the set-up phase), continued immersion in the society as the story builds and conflict results sometimes helps to justify certain elements that were initially deemed abhorrent or seemingly unsustainable. Some episodes—such as *Black Mirror*'s "White Christmas" (2014), "Playtest" (2016), "San Junipero" (2016) and "Black Museum" (2017)—employ plot twists near the end of episodes that disrupt the audience's previous understanding of the nature of the situation presented up to the point of the twist. Some of these surprises are so significant that our view of the fictional world presented on the episodes makes a 180-degree turn. As television columnist David Sims writes about the *Black Mirror* "White Bear," for example: the episode "throws us into a weird, disorienting world, establishes the rules for us as we go along, then pulls the plug out with 15 minutes to go with one of the most devastating and mind-boggling twists imaginable."[65] Other episodes—such as *Black Mirror*'s "White Christmas" and "Black Museum"—require viewers to connect the dots between episode segments that are interwoven in both overt and nuanced ways. Although the series is anthological by design, the individual episodes contained within the series frequently make self-referential, intertextual connections between and among the techno-dystopian societies presented therein—often by means of hidden Easter eggs.[66]

The *Electric Dreams* episode "Safe and Sound" (2018) serves as a case study of a portion of the narrative structure described above. While the enhanced security systems presented near the beginning of the episode seem overly restrictive, we come to understand their purpose and utility as we learn of the apparent epidemic of terrorist attacks. The veracity of the occurrence of the terrorist attacks is appropriately called into question at various points throughout the episode, leading us to view the measures with disdain and contempt.

Black Mirror and *Electric Dreams* each provide sharp satirical social commentary on the potential consequences of unregulated technological advances, including with respect to artificial intelligence and robotics. Both shows serve as frightening portraits of dystopian societies built on the anticipated results of the failure to manage technology. They serve as a unique and purposeful form of art. As Clay Jensen states in *13 Reasons Why*, "A work of art is only good if it arises out of necessity, from need.... Art should be confrontation. It should shock and scare you."[67] The episodes peek into worlds that are powered by technology and are often in complete disarray. As Parham observes with respect to *Black Mirror*, Brooker's "stories are of a world in the throes of madness—be it dread brought on by devices that govern human emotion ('Nosedive'; 'The Entire History of You') or the mayhem that arises out of one's inability to access, or sustain a particular social standing ('The National Anthem'; 'Shut Up and Dance')."[68] These confrontational shows—defined by disorderly universes where technology dominates and morality often takes a backseat to competing agendas—were preceded by one of the most powerful and influential science fiction shows in television history, namely *The Twilight Zone*.

The Twilight Zone

The *New Yorker* calls *Black Mirror* a "*Twilight Zone* for the Digital Age."[69] *The Twilight Zone*'s impact on the genesis and birth of *Black Mirror* is evident from early pitch documents for the latter, one of which, according to Charlie Brooker, read "Just as *The Twilight Zone* would talk about McCarthyism, we're going to talk about Apple."[70] Both shows provide unique stories intended to caution viewers about contemporary trends and tendencies. Each starts with the premise that a knowledgeable audience—one that is keenly aware of potential risks and dangers afoot—is, perhaps, humanity's best hope for salvation.

One theme common to both shows (as well as *Electric Dreams*) is the presupposition of the "products" produced by artificial intelligence and robotics as indifferent at best, and cold, steely, and devoid of empathy—and, perhaps, even possessing an innate or acquired *desire* to harm humanity at worst. In the distinct worlds presented on these anthologies, technology is a highly dominant and overbearing feature of life. Humans are often subject to the agendas of technology—or at least to the agendas of those who (at least in certain of these worlds) have managed to maintain and exert some degree of control and influence over these technologies. By and large, the worlds presented on these shows are *run* by technology, with humans presented as technology's restricted subjects, if not slaves.

The most frightening episodes of the three anthologies are those in which the worlds are only slight reimaginations of our existing world. The universes presented in such episodes are akin to carnival funhouse mirrors. We remain recognizable in such mirrors but the images reflecting back at us are distorted—and frequently grotesque—versions of reality. Those that are closest to our own collective experience are the greatest cause for concern. As Parham observes with respect to *Black Mirror*, "What at first feels like a twisted fairytale slowly unravels into a vision of the quotidian, as if Brooker is saying: our emerging reality is much more unnerving than pure fiction."[71] So many of our fears relate, in some fashion, to the potential that future circumstances might leave us vulnerable to loneliness, isolation and an inability to communicate effectively with others—all of which are issues examined both directly and indirectly on *Black Mirror*, *Electric Dreams* and *The Twilight Zone*.

Like *Black Mirror* and *Electric Dreams*, *The Twilight Zone* (1959-1964) explored humanity's fears of the unknown, often employing a narrative structure that relied heavily on plot twists and misdirection, climaxing with a creepy ending. During its time, contemporary fears included alien invasion, robotics, artificial intelligence, nuclear war, automation, government censorship and authoritarian rule, among others.[72] By providing an avenue through which humanity's gravest concerns could be examined, *The Twilight Zone* provided a window through which to watch how individuals may react in such scenarios. The success of *The Twilight Zone* can largely be attributed not to the often-predictable episode conclusions, but rather to the show's ability to address contemporary fears in a widely accessible manner. By providing a visual conduit through which issues such as the unchecked introduction of artificial intelligence could be explored, for example, it presented viewers with a clear perspective as to some of the potential benefits and harms arising from such implementation. No longer were those fears confined to pedantic explorations in academic articles and treatises. By reaching a mainstream audience—many of whose members had little to no conception of what problems would look like in a futuristic, sometimes dystopian world—individuals were cultivated into a specific way of viewing a world affected by such issues. For example, while general fears and concerns persisted as to potential alien life forms, *The Twilight Zone* (and similar movies and television shows of the era) gave the audience a perspective as to what could be expected were we to encounter alien beings (see "To Serve Man" and "Will the Real Martian Please Stand Up?," for example).[73] When we visualize aliens, we often picture those presented in our popular culture. This observation provides support for *cultivation theory*, which dictates that television is a powerful sphere of influence in those arenas where the mainstream audience lacks other perspectives or acute knowledge or beliefs about a given subject area.[74] Like *Black Mirror* and *Electric Dreams*, *The Twilight Zone*—though fictional—provides an important frame of reference for the audience's general fears about a specific issue of which such audience lacks the necessary knowledge to produce competing perspectives.

The Twilight Zone's focus on mankind's complicated relationship with technology is particularly instructive and relevant to our contemporary experiences. The series is reflective of societal fears—both then and now—of the possibility that machines may conspire to harm human beings (see "A Thing About Machines," for example).[75] The popularity of the show also stems from our overt fascination with exploring the theoretical (though sometimes wholly fantasy-driven) capabilities of machines and other objects, be it self-driving automobiles ("You Drive"); haunted fortune-telling machines, casino slot machines, toy phones, cars, cameras, radios and pianos ("Nick of Time," "The Fever," "Long Distance Call," "The Whole Truth," "A Most Unusual Camera," "Static" and "A Piano in the House," respectively); time-travel helmets ("Once Upon a Time"); or clocks whose proper functioning we may rely on for our very existence ("Ninety Years Without Slumbering").[76] Other episodes focus on our emotional attachments to robots, blurring the lines between humans and the machines with whom they interact. Such connections include falling in love ("The Lonely") and developing familial relationships ("I Sing the Body Electric" and "The Lateness of the Hour").[77] Still other episodes lead us to consider broad societal negative implications as a result of the introduction of technology, not only in terms of automation ("The Brain Center at Whipple's") but also the potentially harmful emotional effects of the development of flawless beings that could supplant humanity ("The Lateness of the Hour"). This concept is also explored on *The Jetsons* (1962–1963), a contemporary of *The Twilight Zone*, which portrays a family who forms a close bond with Rosie, a robotic maid.[78] An occasional episode (such as "The Old Man in the Cave") provides an overwhelmingly positive snapshot of technology, showcasing its potential to assist humans as they navigate difficult circumstances.[79] As part of its exploration of the potential benefits and consequences of technological innovation, *The Twilight Zone* provides a critical lens through which we could analyze who we are as a species and how we may react to new technology. As Adrienne LaFrance notes: "The modern-day response to such technology is often a combination of awe and unease, and it mirrors the sense of uncanniness *The Twilight Zone* captured so well 50-plus years ago."[80]

By exploring a range of human emotional responses to technology (as well as reactions to other out-of-this-world phenomena)—such as fear, hope, greed, elation, anxiety and depression—creator Rod Serling was able to develop an effective and emotionally realistic drama based on alternate realities. LaFrance correctly observes that "*The Twilight Zone* is at its core an exploration of the human condition and commentary on how people cope with fear of the unknown."[81] As previously noted with respect to both *Black Mirror* and *Electric Dreams*, the scariest episodes of *The Twilight Zone* (and the ones that we internalize the most) are those that deviate only slightly from our own world. The implementation of unchecked automation, for example, when taken to its logical conclusion, leads to *complete* workplace displacement and social and economic chaos—not unlike the gloomy scenarios explored on "The Brain Center at Whipple's" episode.[82] Rod Serling explained that his approach to writing was to produce episodes that present potentially foreseeable futures, as opposed to more creative, outlandish scenarios: "I would probably shy away from the year 2500. I would much rather deal in 1998. The hardware that I use, I think, should be identifiable. I like to know what happens Thursday, not in the next century."[83] Serling's conscious desire to have his work deal with the not-too-distant future is comparable to Brooker's preference to examine very near-term potentialities. The closer connection the audience feels with a given situation, the more relatable and powerful the message. As *Black Mirror* production designer Joel Collins pointedly notes, "The art of *Black Mirror* is to stay within a box that isn't too far from people's perspectives. So then they fall into the box with you, and you can shake the box around, bang their heads and upset them a lot."[84]

In the course of presenting futuristic worlds where modern technological advances disrupt society, Serling's *The Twilight Zone* led the audience to question the definition of dignity, self-worth and life itself. Do the apathetic robots that either live side by side with humans or displace humans altogether possess any inherent value beyond their usefulness as tools? If not, then what differentiates human beings from such robots? As La France notes, "*The Twilight Zone* obsessed over questions of authenticity and identity, prompting questions about what human interaction with robots would ultimately mean for society."[85] A close examination of the series allows scholars to extract deep meaning from many episodes that, on first glance, may seem to just show robots and aliens having a good time roaming around and exploring our planet. But those aliens are invaders, and a contemporary screening of the series leads us to ask whether modern innovations, including the advancement of powerful artificial intelligence, can similarly be viewed as outside forces that impact (and may potentially destroy) our conception of life—if not life itself. We can learn a great deal about potential human reactions to the introduction and, yes, *invasion*, of new and complex technologies by watching *The Twilight Zone*.

The Dangers of Technology

Our contemporary experience with technology underpins the dichotomy between usage for positive purposes and disastrous consequences emanating from technology's existence.[86] Director of Engineering at Google and noted futurist Ray Kurzweil correctly states that "technology is a double-edged sword. Fire kept us warm and cooked our food but also burnt down our houses. Every technology has had its promise and peril."[87] Richtel argues that "Things that have enormous power to serve us can also have enormous power to take advantage of us."[88] The late Israeli Prime Minister and President Shimon Peres warned of the dual dangers of ignoring technology and using it without appropriate caution and safeguards: "Technology without values will endanger humanity, while values without technology will bring about hunger and stagnation."[89] Other folks—such as Douglas Hodge, the actor who portrayed Rolo Haynes in *Black Mirror*'s "Black Museum" (2017)—take a more one-sided, pessimistic view, focusing entirely on the negative consequences emanating from the introduction of technology. When I interviewed Hodge via email, he told me that, in his opinion, *Black Mirror* "does tend to expect that technological and scientific advances will be dystopian mainly because history tends to warn us that nearly all extraordinary breakthroughs tend to get commandeered in the name of war and violence."[90]

As we speed ahead towards a *Black Mirror*-style technological revolution, how will we adapt to a world in which the balance of power between humanity and its creations shifts toward the latter? As we continue to rely on technology for so many purposes, we need to be aware that technology could have a significant impact on how much control we have over our own lives. One potential danger examined on both *Black Mirror* and *Electric Dreams* is that technology could shape and mold us.[91] We could become more isolated and detached, and, in some sense, less human if we allow technology to decide how we live our lives. This social fear is explored on the *Black Mirror* episode "Hang the DJ" (2017), where individuals permit "The System," an advanced technological device, to dictate who they date and for how long—irrespective of the individuals' feelings towards each other. The folks in this techno-dystopian world appear to relinquish free will when they sign up to the dating service and are willing to forfeit the expression of emotion and instead subject their love lives to the output of technological algorithms. It seems that these individuals knowingly, and in some cases eagerly, give up the most personal aspects of human free will—such as who to date, love, marry and have sex with—and place full faith and confidence in the results of algorithms and calculations produced by a technological device. This scenario seems less unrealistic when we consider the expanded presence and influence of artificial intelligence in our daily lives. As Roey Tzezana, a researcher in futures studies explains, algorithms shape the behavior of the stock market, determine the prices on Amazon, decide whether a bank will issue a loan, and recommend friends and products for you.[92]

Technology can also be used and manipulated by bad actors to promote agendas that are harmful to civilization. Terrorist groups, for example, use technology to spread propaganda and build support on the Internet—in particular, through social media outlets. While such terrorist groups typically cling to a tribal, jihadist worldview in which they reject Western civilization and the cultural norms appended thereto, the means that they use to resist such perspectives are, ironically, created by the West. As part of their resistance to McWorld—or contemporary globalization—many terrorists utilize McWorld's interconnected networks for the purpose of disrupting and decrying the same interconnectedness that defines Western civilization.[93] This phenomenon is reminiscent of Sideshow Bob's threatening appearance on a television screen to denounce Springfield's obsession with television. In *The Simpsons* episode "Sideshow Bob's Last Gleaming" (1995), Sideshow Bob

1. Reflections Through a Black Mirror   31

threatens to blow up the city with a nuclear bomb unless Springfield ceases broadcasting all television shows. Bob acknowledges the hypocrisy of his choice of medium: "By the way, I'm aware of the irony of appearing on TV in order to decry it, so don't bother pointing that out!"[94] Technology is so pervasive and useful a resource that its opponents would be foolish were they to disregard the significant advantages of communicating through newly developed mediums facilitated by technological advances to quickly disseminate ideas.

Both *Black Mirror* and *Electric Dreams* make important statements about the feasibility of humanity's co-existence with powerfully enhanced technologies. Living in a world devoid of technology is not a realistic notion for most folks.[95] We therefore need to continuously adapt to new technologies as they are introduced and change the landscape of life. To paraphrase Woody Harrelson's character Rex in the film *The Glass Castle* (2017), it is not fruitful for folks to cling to the side their whole lives out of fear.[96] If they do not want to sink, he advises his daughter, they must learn to swim. So, too, in terms of our co-habitation with technology; we generally cannot effectively hide from it, but rather must learn to deal with it in a healthy and beneficial way. Kurzweil believes that humanity will be able to successfully meet these challenges and not only adapt to change but thrive because of it. He predicts, "We're going to get more neocortex, we're going to be funnier. We're going to be better at music. We're going to be sexier. We're really going to exemplify all the things that we value in humans to a greater degree."[97]

But not all experts share Kurzweil's flowery and optimistic vision for the future. As discussed in detail in Chapter 6, some technology leaders believe that the uninhibited introduction of powerful technology will cause humanity's downfall. In any event, both optimists and pessimists share the belief that technology will change our lives in ways that would have been inconceivable until recently.

Some industry insiders, for example, have made predictions about our future not dissimilar to the situations in which humanity finds itself in these anthologies. Elon Musk hypothesizes that humanity ultimately may need to undergo "some sort of merger of biological intelligence and machine intelligence" to survive.[98] On another occasion, Musk noted that "we're already cyborgs. Your phone and your computer are extensions of you, but the interface is through finger movements or speech, which are very slow."[99] A similar sentiment is expressed by Kurzweil, who observes that today "What is actually happening is [machines] are powering all of us. They're making us smarter."[100] Such hybrid amalgamations of natural and digital lead to ethical and legal questions about whether we treat our creations fairly, demonstrating that inventions not only come tagged with a responsibility but also burdensome questions begging to be fiercely debated and ultimately answered in a satisfactory way.

While these shows often offer a bleak assessment of our potential ability to cohabitate Earth with technology as humanity's master, it is undeniable in both our world and the worlds presented on these shows that technology richly enhances our lives. Advances in medical technology, for example, prolong and save countless lives. The Internet connects billions of people, leads to the creation of relationships, and allows for the development and implementation of efficiencies across a broad range of sectors. The benefits of technology are significant, both in scope and impact.

The Advantages of Technology

We are, rightfully, impressed by technology. We are frequently left in awe of devices that could perform actions and functions that we cannot perform on our own. Our innovations are superior to humans in various ways: a bullet from a rifle can pierce the body and organs of the strongest human; an advanced computer can beat us at puzzles and games. In sum, technology can do many things that we cannot do and also often outperform us in head-to head competition.[101]

And if we are wise, we can exploit technology in ways that benefit us. Technology enables us to advance ideas at a rapid pace and gives us the opportunity to access an infinite amount of information at our fingertips within seconds. It also connects us in a variety of ways—through the Internet or via virtual environments. The possibility of forging and maintaining meaningful relationships through the successful exploitation of innovative technologies exists, even as detractors and critics warn of the dangers lurking in the misuse, abuse and overreliance on the power of such connectivity. The benefits of technological advances throughout our history—and, particularly within the past twenty years—are impossible to adequately enumerate in just a few words. Suffice it to say that humanity's existence would be significantly different, and perhaps unrecognizable, were it not for the technology developed over a relatively short period of time. The anticipated expansion and further development within the technology sphere are not only exciting but provide us hope for the future. A few quick examples: advances in Israeli water technology have saved countless lives. Drones have the potential to reduce costs for consumers if employed by retailers as a means of shipping (per the *Electric Dreams* "Autofac" episode). Self-driving cars have the potential to decrease the number of automobile accidents due to the elimination of human driver error. Virtual reality and augmented reality technologies enable us to explore the world in new and exciting ways with great efficiency. Both *Black Mirror* and *Electric Dreams* highlight some of the advantages of technology. Many of the futuristic worlds presented on these anthologies appear to function in a highly efficient and disciplined manner, are well-organized, and, for the most part, seem to allow for quite a productive existence—all of which are positive consequences attributable to the technology-obsessed cultures represented in these societies.

Because of the voluminous benefits of technology, restricting and regulating its introduction is not necessarily on the radar of lawmakers in the same way as other dangers, like, say, climate change. Technology is often not found in the strictly negative list of issues that could plague humanity. Will this blind spot ultimately cause us harm? Perhaps technology's most dangerous attribute is the fact that it provides us with a great deal of advantages, distracting us from its destructive power and negative consequences.

Workplace Displacement

The relationship between man and machine in the workplace is complex. On the one hand, the introduction of automation in the workforce has enabled the corporate world to implement solutions at a quicker pace and grow more expeditiously. Robots have been creatively used to produce jobs for some severely disabled individuals: a Japanese café reportedly uses robot waiters who are remotely controlled by such individuals, thereby helping them find gainful employment within society.[102] On the other hand—and in a far more common scenario—machines have displaced what many deem to be the heart and soul of a business: the worker. Query whether there is any industry where workers can legitimately feel a sense of job security, given expected advances in robotics and artificial intelligence. As we create machines that are able to think, move, develop and create, the conception and structure of the traditional workplace is necessarily placed under stress in a fundamental way.

The dynamics within the corporate technology industry highlight the dichotomy described above. As journalist Alana Semuels observes, some folks employed by large, multinational technology companies (such as Amazon) benefit financially from the massive growth within the industry, while individuals hired to perform the company's lower-level jobs (such as delivery positions) struggle supporting themselves in frustrating work environments with low salaries.[103] Even the new types of positions created within the technology space serve as an example of the complicated relationship between technology, people and society. Recounting her experience working as an Amazon Flex independent contractor for a day, Semuels observes that "Technology was allowing [the higher-level employees] a good life, but it was just making me stressed and cranky."[104]

Popular culture has, in the past, warned us about the consequences of the unchecked introduction of automation in society. For example, in *The Twilight Zone* episode "The Brain Center at Whipple's" (1964), we watch the "historical battle between flesh and steel, between the brain of man and the product of man's brain" unfold.[105] In the episode, a steely, apathetic corporate executive lays off thousands of employees and replaces them with machines. His senior engineer decries this exchange of "pride" and "craftmanship" for "efficiency."[106] Mr. Whipple acknowledges that his "only concern" is efficiency, not the well-being of employees or the intangible aspects of human-produced work product. The underlying message—and warning for those executives and managers like Mr. Whipple who are more than willing to dispense with others' careers and livelihoods—is that those in power need only look in the mirror when searching for folks to expel to save a few bucks. Humans may not be needed at all anymore, as their only useful purpose was to create technology that now manages itself. Their dismissal from the workforce is a direct byproduct of the ideal of efficiency for which many empowered individuals had so strongly advocated.

Other television shows have focused on the emotional consequences resulting from the introduction and implementation of artificial intelligence in society. In the television series *Humans*, for example, humans compete with artificially-created beings called "synths."[107] At a "We Are People" rally, a speaker expresses humanity's collective frustrations with, and fears of, the synths, proclaiming that folks are relinquishing not only their jobs but also other elements that made them human in all facets of life—their responsibilities, purpose and dignity. And the *Electric Dreams* episode "Autofac" serves up biting satirical commentary on the threat of automation running amok, showcasing what appears to be a frustrated and restless community nearing extinction. The factory, not the worker, is the dominant structure in this dystopian techno-future.

In the *Electric Dreams* episode "Kill All Others," we see similar emotional effects of technology on a depleted workforce. Three laborers are tasked with running an entire factory after hundreds (if not thousands) of employees are laid off. Automation has eliminated the need for those jobs, and the remaining three workers even question the need for their positions to be retained in this futuristic world where so many former employees have been displaced. While technological advances have led to worker alienation and changing roles for employees, the widespread implementation of automation is expected to occur at an unexpected scale and magnitude in the future. Some experts project that by the year 2030, up to 800 million jobs worldwide may be lost due to automation, including up to 73 million in the United States.[108] This shifting paradigm requires employees to re-market themselves (which likely requires new training and education) to remain attractive workplace candidates.[109] While the changing dynamics in the economy due to innovation is expected to result in the creation of new types of positions (some of which should be able to offset some of the positions lost due to automation), many observers wonder whether the quality of those jobs will serve as adequate substitutes for the displaced jobs. For example, Steve Viscelli, a sociologist at the University of Pennsylvania predicts that as the e-commerce industry expands, "we're going to take the billion hours Americans spend driving to stores and taking things off shelves, and we're going to turn it into jobs."[110]

Automation certainly has some advantages, particularly at a macro level. As legendary stock market investor Warren Buffet states, "The idea of more output per capita—which is what the progress is made on productivity [would mean]—that that should be harmful to society is crazy."[111] But the widespread implementation of machines in the workplace may have severe economic and emotional effects on individuals. Mr. Whipple (much like the aforementioned "We Are People" protesters in *Humans*), finds himself in a psychological struggle to determine his own worth as an individual. For many employees, work is more than a means to achieving an economic end. It also imbues in them a sense of value, pride and self-identification. If a machine is deemed superior to the individual because of the economic efficiencies created by the machine, he or she may come to question his or her role and purpose in the world. These questions can lead to depression and other severe psychological issues.[112]

The dichotomy of technology's positive and negative aspects is both pervasive and multifaceted. While advances in technology have expanded and grown the global economy exponentially, automation has also led to a loss of jobs, a trend that will almost continue and expand in both scope and degree in years to come. The many individuals that will be affected by a vast robotic workforce will likely not be able to fully participate in the significant benefits of a global economy that has expanded because of advances in technology.

A Board So Big That It Will Destroy Us All

Even with respect to advances in medical technology—rightly seen as an objectively moral and significant benefit to humankind—population experts correctly fear that the increased longevity of life (or in a *Black Mirror*–type world, the creation of immortal super-beings) could, quite morbidly, lead to catastrophe if the planet runs out of space. Other technological advances could perhaps salvage humanity in such a scenario, such as interplanetary colonization and the widespread use of genetically-produced food to defeat famine. Still, technology's benefit to the individual is a potential harm to humanity at large—arguably the converse of the global workforce versus the displaced individual example described above. This dichotomy is expressed during a soliloquy by the alien Kang on *The Simpsons*, who, after having been repelled by humans (by use of a technologically "advanced" weapon, namely a large wooden board with a nail) predicts that eventually human innovation will go too far and destroy humanity with even more advanced weaponry (i.e., a much bigger wooden board with a bigger nail).[113] The sentiment expressed by Kang serves as an acute warning to humanity. Are our technological innovations causing us to stumble, in an oblivious, semi-conscious state toward undesirable realities? Do we possess a blind spot for the risks and dangers posed by technology, grossly underestimating its potential to cause us harm? Do we fail to devote proper time and attention to investigating these potential harms, as well as formulating strategies to combat those risks and dangers? Perhaps, as Rod Serling suggests, we need to be more *thoughtful* in addition to being merely *inventive* as we seek to develop and introduce new technologies.

Sadly, many of us feel lost when we lose temporary access to our screens. As addicts, are we in control when it comes to the ways in which we use our devices? And we must remember that even though we push the buttons on our devices—seemingly in control of the applications and various functionalities contained therein—it does not mean that we are in charge of how they function, what data they collect about us, how they affect our behavior and the ways in which we think about the world.

* * *

Socrates famously stated that "the unexamined life is not worth living."[114] The inherent premise in this remark assumes that the world is a place replete with potential, yet one that requires close study and possible adjustments and improvements. When assessing the hypothetical futuristic worlds presented on *Black Mirror* and *Electric Dreams*, it is fair to ask whether the life that we are examining would be livable, or worth living. It is important to view these worlds with a critical lens to gain an understanding of a variety of potentially dark future states, enabling us to hopefully devise successful strategies to avert disaster. The most helpful episodes in this regard are those that enable us to understand how the conditions and unseemly elements of the fictional society therein came to fruition.

While both shows examine the potential impact of technological advances, they are not solely focused on technology. Parham acutely observes that "For all its technological sprawl, *Black Mirror* is a show about the flesh and bone of human suffering: the different ways individuals hurt and grieve, the way human innovation expands the distance between people, communities, and ideologies."[115] When we turn off our televisions, we are faced with the question of how we view ourselves in the reflections of those dark mirrors. The diverse ways in which we utilize technology reveals much about who we are as a species. As Li observes, "as powerful as technology becomes, its greatest power is in how it reflects who we are and what we choose to do."[116] Questions about human psychology, empathy, stubbornness, persistence, political disposition, risk awareness, hope, fear and motivation arise from a close examination of these shows.

Black Mirror creator Charlie Brooker acutely states that "It is not a technological problem we have; it's a human one"—a theme to which we will return throughout this book.[117] Brooker has even expressed frustration at the notion that when the series is characterized by many folks as a red alarm about the dangers of technology.[118] He likens such a description to folks portraying Alfred Hitchcock's *Psycho* (1960) as a "warning about the dangers of silverware."[119] Brooker asserts that "*Black Mirror* is not really about [technology] … except when it is, just to fuck with people!"[120]

Humans are the creators and users of technology; therefore, a fundamental understanding of human nature is a prerequisite to taking a deep and critical look into how and why technology functions the way it does. Technology is a disruptive force, but it is human desire that demands such disruption to reduce or eliminate inefficiencies in various aspects of life. For example, contemporary trends that demonstrate the ways in which our economy is shifting to overreliance on online platforms can be explained as a function of a human desire to press a button to receive a service as opposed to participating in more traditional modes of commerce. The displacement of many brick-and-mortar stores, as one example, is not the fault of technology. It is the result of a human inclination to save time and energy—a virtue provided by technology powerhouse platforms such as Amazon. From a communication perspective, it is unfair to blame technology for our apparent desire to express messages in 140 characters. Social media provides a mechanism for folks to communicate in new ways, but Congressman Mike Gallagher's unequivocal assessment that "Social media is making us all stupid" is, ironically, over-simplistic and insufficiently nuanced.[121] And when we use technology for destructive purposes, it is not the fault of our innovations—mere avenues exploited by humans to achieve ignoble ends.

When analyzing the impact of technology at a macro level, it is important not to cede too much credit or place too much blame on our innovations. Our natural predispositions inform what we create and how we make use of such creations. An examination of technology without exploring the roots of human action and inaction, infused by our innate desires, would be incomplete. A close study of the messages underlying *The Twilight Zone* suggests that Rod Serling tended to agree with this principle as well. It may not be the aliens from outer space or the robots from Mr. Whipple's company that destroy us; rather, history—as explored through episodes such as "The Obsolete Man" and "Deaths-Head Revisited"—provides support for the unfortunate reality that human beings lack neither the capacity nor will to eliminate one another.[122]

And our technologies, in many respects, reflect who we are. As technology advances and fine tunes its ability to function as a mirror, we may be more likely to recognize ourselves in the reflections of our black screens. Professor Jordan B. Peterson identifies this mimicking as a "fundamental" concern, arguing that if machines reflect us ethically, we should be frightened because our "ethical house" is not "particularly in order."[123] But it is critical to understand the difference between reflection and cause. Folks frequently blame technology for our vices—be it addiction to screens or texting while driving. But technology did not invent addiction or a desire to connect with one another, even when doing so is dangerous. This phenomenon is exemplified by the reaction of *The Office*'s Oscar Nunez (on the episode "The List") to his colleagues' decision to act out a viral sensation: "Welcome to the Internet!," Nunez exclaims.[124] While the Internet makes it easier for folks to connect, it did not create the human predisposition for conformity, to mimic each other's actions or to jump on a bandwagon. The Internet is frequently and unfairly marked as the scapegoat for humanity's impulses and flawed decisions. And those poor decisions will continue to subsist for so long as human nature remains relatively constant.

The infamous fable of "The Scorpion and the Frog" is relatable in this context.[125] A frog is asked by a scorpion to ride on his back so that the scorpion may cross the river safely. The frog hesitates, keenly aware of the scorpion's penchant for causing other animals harm. The scorpion assures the frog that stinging the frog while crossing the river would kill not only the frog but the scorpion as well. When the scorpion stings the frog, dooming them both, the frog asks why. The scorpion responds that it is in his nature to do so. The scorpion is unable to limit his impulses—even temporarily—despite his awareness that his actions will inevitably lead to his downfall. Is our ambition to innovate and achieve "progress" by almost any means necessary an immutable component of our make-up? Will we be able to effectively defy or re-define human nature if the risks of introducing powerful technologies are staring us in the face?

Attempts to circumvent human nature by use of technology will likely fall short. Oedipus famously stated that "Nothing can make me other than I am."[126] While we can always aspire to self-improvement, we should also acknowledge the inherent limitations that define who we are, collectively, as a species. A more grounded position is that technology (unlike beer, in Homer Simpson's view) is not the cause of or solution to all of life's problems.[127] Problems that derive from human nature—those that are hard-wired into our internal make-up—may not be easily resolvable. As law professor Abe Petrovsky observes with respect to the human decision-making process in the film *Rounders* (1998), "We can't run from who we are. Our destiny chooses us."[128] Parham posits that "Humans get into trouble not when we make progress, but when we try to overcome humanity by treating emotion and spirit like science—the quest to articulate and optimize the ineffable."[129]

We seek to gain advantages by using technology not only with the objective of creating efficiencies, but also, regrettably, to outdo and even harm each other. As our technological developments provide us with the opportunity to imagine infinite possibilities, we must acknowledge the flaws inherent in human nature as we seek to effectively control our usage of such innovations. As Swiss psychiatrist Carl Jung poignantly observed, "Who looks outside dreams; who looks inside awakes."[130] *Black Mirror* chillingly and quite cynically enumerates the ways in which we might use technology for deleterious purposes—whether it be ranking and shaming each other online; hacking each other's accounts; locking each other up in digital environments that effectively serve as prisons; transferring folks' consciousness to other hosts without their informed consent; torturing artificially-created beings; or destroying livelihoods by replacing man with machine. If we wish to avoid these scenarios, we must not only manage technology but also ourselves.[131]

Ultimately, *Black Mirror* and *Electric Dreams* are important television shows because they serve as a possible lens for what scientists and developers may have in mind for technology, and, in turn, what technology may have in mind for humanity. Each series examines technology in a serious fashion, taking stock of practical threats and dangers—as opposed to using distrust of technological innovations as a comical punchline. In this regard, both shows can be distinguished from the lighthearted or sarcastic ways in which technology is sometimes referenced on other shows. A prime example occurs on *The Office* episode "Search Committee," when we learn that receptionist Erin Hannon is (ludicrously) prohibited from using voicemail because acting manager Dwight Schrute does not trust robots to give messages to humans.[132] Perhaps the most important lesson that we can learn from a careful consideration of *Black Mirror* and *Electric Dreams* is not to quickly dismiss or brush aside potential concerns that we might have about technology. It is prudent to take the immense power of technology into account when crafting strategies about how to develop it, regulate it, and, ultimately, engage with it.

Some episodes of these anthology shows are frightening if we consider the cold, emotionless worlds that technology has come to conquer and control. Viewed more optimistically, however, the human species can use these shows to demonstrate—at least to itself—that we may be one step ahead of technology. It is best to be proactive, as opposed to merely reactive in the face of potential threats. The fact that we can imagine such worlds and anticipate possible struggles may help us triumph if faced with such seemingly dire situations. Perhaps we can even avoid such scenarios if we view these episodes as a wake-up call, sounding the alarm for a potentially dark future. Humans have managed to survive and thrive in other precarious situations in the past. We have survived many wars, famines, diseases and other calamities, albeit suffering very painful losses along the way. Humans have demonstrated a capacity to overcome adversity, and, at times, grow stronger. Despite the sometimes-dreadful worlds presented on *Black Mirror* and *Electric Dreams*, technology has not yet proven that it can overtake humans or win any potential future wars with its inventors. Even if we lose some battles, failing to win head-to-head fights with our machines—a scenario examined quite literally on *The Twilight Zone*'s "Steel" episode—we refuse to throw in the towel.[133] If we are to endure, rising high above our competitors, it may not be our wisdom or brute strength that sustain us; rather, our bravery, temerity and tenacity may enable us to continue to thrive.

Now let's turn to a critical examination of the 30 techno-dystopian worlds presented on *Black Mirror* and *Electric Dreams*.

2

Technology and Political Manipulation
An Examination of "The Waldo Moment" and "Safe and Sound"

> "The conscious and intelligent manipulation of the organized habits and opinions of the masses is an important element in democratic society. Those who manipulate this unseen mechanism of society constitute an invisible government which is the true ruling power of our country. *We are governed, our minds are molded, our tastes formed, our ideas suggested, largely by men we have never heard of.*"
> —Edward Bernays (the "father of public relations")[1]

Marshall McLuhan and the One Candidate

On October 30, 1938, a live broadcast of the radio program *The War of the Worlds* caused panic among some listeners.[2] The broadcast was introduced as an adaptation of H.G. Wells' 1898 novel *The War of the Worlds*, but folks who tuned in late missed that opening communication.

The one-hour program was interrupted several times by a series of faux "news bulletins" detailing explosions observed on Mars and climaxing in a description of an alien invasion and the aftermath of its occupation of Earth. A "survivor" is interviewed and provides her account of the frightening events. The news-bulletin format of the program caused unrest and was widely condemned by folks in the coming days. The structure of the program—a continuous broadcast without commercial interruption for the first 30 minutes—also contributed to the confusion.

The folks who had been duped had relied on the legitimacy of a radio broadcast—a trusted medium through which information about events taking place in the world is frequently communicated—to deliver the news. The understandable angst experienced by uninformed listeners demonstrates that a message disseminated through a respected channel could have a significant effect on how such a message is received.

Media scholar Marshall McLuhan famously posited that "the medium is the message."[3] In coining this phrase, McLuhan was attempting to describe the symbiotic relationship between the medium through which an idea is presented and the way in which the message is received by an audience. Academics have explored the ways in which various means of communication influence an audience's interpretations of, and direct and indirect responses to, ideas. This relationship helps to explain the infamous *The War of the Worlds* fiasco described above.

The relationship between the medium through which an idea is expressed and its reception by the audience is examined in *The Simpsons* episode "They Saved Lisa's Brain."[4] In the episode, physicist Stephen Hawking visits Homer Simpson's town of Springfield. Hawking expresses genuine interest when Homer presents his model of a donut-shaped universe. Hawking's receptiveness to Homer's idea requires him to dismiss any *ad hominin* attacks on the intelligence (or lack thereof) of the imperfect medium for the theory, namely Homer. From a normative perspective, a critical examination of the substantive ideas should be more important than reaching a conclusion about the medium through which such ideas are expressed or the forum through which they are communicated.[5] Truth seekers should attempt to look beyond the superficial surface of a medium and conduct diligence on the substantive information to determine its value. However, it may be difficult, as a practical matter, to effectively disentangle our biases and preconceptions about a medium from the ideas passed through it.

Hawking's approach is in sharp contrast to Marshall McLuhan's theory regarding the symbiotic relationship of the medium and the message. McLuhan would likely suggest that the fact that the idea came from Homer is likely to affect Hawking's assessment of it, and might even lead the physicist to reject the idea without any examination of its merits. While Hawking is willing to listen to Homer's vision, however, the same idea presented by an authoritative expert in theoretical physics would undoubtedly carry more weight. So, too, with political ideas presented by media outlets believed (perhaps incorrectly) to present stories in a neutral, unbiased manner. And it is often extremely difficult for an audience to respect or latch onto a message presented by a medium viewed with disdain.[6] The Netflix documentary *The Rachel Divide* (2018) explores the account of Rachel Dolezal, a former leader of the NAACP branch in Spokane, after she is exposed for faking her black heritage.[7] While she exhibited strong advocacy and leadership on behalf of the African American community prior to being exposed, the community largely exiled her and refused to allow her to continue in her role—even in a less formal manner—after her identity is discovered. All attempts by Ms. Dolezal to continue her advocacy work were met with resistance. Her message was on point and would have been met with approval had the messenger herself not been so deceptive and had she had an actual ancestral connection with the community.[8] She was the worst possible medium through which to convey the message, and that fact significantly affected the way in which her message could be heard.

Electric Dreams' "Kill All Others" also examines the phenomenon of the rejection of statements and appeals not due to the message itself, but because the messenger is viewed in a specific way. When the "One Candidate" spews fascist hate speech—threatening to kill those perceived as outsiders—her words are largely disregarded by many in society. Members of her base heed her words and a few dissenters object, but most folks appear to dismiss her rhetoric by referring to their own distrust of anything that a politician might say. Such folks believe that there is no real cause for concern over the inflammatory words and threats, given the conventional wisdom that politicians will say anything to rally their supporters and secure power. Many decent folks in the episode express only mild condemnation of her statements—not necessarily because they agree with the One Candidate's proposals, but because they doubt her sincerity. When the protagonist raises concerns about the One Candidate's threatening language, for example, his coworkers advise him not to worry. They casually dismiss politics as entertainment, arguing that words spoken by politicians on stage should not be taken literally or seriously. A McLuhan-like analysis tends to justify this perspective: if politicians are generally not trusted, it is easy to understand why their messages may not be taken seriously. Folks employing this calculus take an enormous risk, however, by potentially misjudging the sincerity of leaders.

A miscalculation in this regard likely leads to some degree of complacency. It is on this level, among others, that the episode sparks comparisons with Donald Trump's rise to power and use of rhetoric that many observers deem irresponsible.[9] A meme circulated on the Internet shows a throng of Trump supporters with the following comic quote bubble pictured above the group: "He didn't say that. And if he did, he didn't mean that. And if he did, you didn't understand it. And if you did, it's not a big deal. And if it is, others have said worse."[10] If we object to speech on its merits, it behooves us to denounce such speech—and not make excuses for it. Our lives will be significantly less rich and more robotic if we fail to react to speech that bothers us but not enough to act. As Holocaust survivor and Nobel Peace Prize winner Elie Weisel stated, "The opposite of life is not death, it's indifference."[11] And Dr. Martin Luther King, Jr., opined that, in the context of civil rights struggles, "History will have to record that the greatest tragedy of this period of social transition was not the strident clamor of the bad people, but the appalling silence of the good people."[12]

Empirical analyses of history teach us that the implicit acceptance or failure to forcefully reject arguably dangerous and reckless speech often leads to serious consequences. To quote Dr. Martin Luther King, Jr., again: "He who passively accepts evil is as much involved in it as he who helps to perpetrate it. He who accepts evil without protesting against it is really cooperating with it."[13] Dictatorships often begin not with guns, but with words: messages to which a minority of a population may latch on, and a majority that fails to act due to apathy, or, as in "Kill All Others," a misguided belief that the dictator does not mean his words literally—inevitably leading to the conclusion that the communication therefore should be of little consequence or concern. "Kill All Others" warns us that extreme and dangerous ideas that are repeated with sufficient frequency could result in implicit acceptance of such ideas as mainstream—even if decent folks might still object to the ideas on their merits. The failure to denounce and express a requisite level of outrage at destructive rhetoric can ultimately have the same or similar impact as if such language had gained enthusiastic support from a wide audience.

A misguided reliance on a false belief about the lack of seriousness of a source due to the perceived symbiotic relationship between the messenger and the message could present significant dangers. The decision not to take rhetoric seriously could result in a population that is vulnerable to heavy-handed, oppressive actions by an aggressive power. The failure to push back against contemptible speech could lead the empowered force to view the public as indifferent and apathetic—one that is easily manipulatable and subject to abuse. The refusal to take the One Candidate—or, some would argue, Donald Trump—seriously may come at a population's peril.

These risks are further explored on *Black Mirror*'s "The Waldo Moment" (2013).

The Trump Moment

Critics have observed (and often lamented) that political discourse in the age of President Donald Trump has shifted to frequent reliance on rapid means of communication of complicated ideas via Twitter.[14] Twitter lacks sufficient versatility for the messenger to properly disseminate complex thoughts, strategies or ideas. As a means of communication, its distinguishing characters are speed and brevity. The strict character limit requires the author to consolidate a message. Nuance is a frequent casualty of such consolidation, and the medium in such instances effectively defines the way that a message is understood. Even when serious ideas are expressed in a comprehensible manner on Twitter, the very use of the tool as a means of transmission—according to a McLuhan-type analysis—hinders the audience's ability to fully appreciate, engage with and embrace the message that the author was attempting to communicate. That is not to argue, however, that tweets cannot have significant influence. Quite the contrary: A 140-character tweet by the President of the United States has the potential to rock global markets, upend the political order, and disrupt the lives of billions of people in numerous ways. If Twitter is a preferred means of conveying consequential ideas by the leader of the free world—irrespective of whether it is responsible to use social media for this purpose—query what other mechanisms could be employed for such purposes, particularly given advances in modern technology.

Enter Waldo, a crude, obnoxious computer-generated cartoon bear, to whom we are introduced on the *Black Mirror* episode "The Waldo Moment."[15] Waldo is the offspring of the ubiquitous (and, arguably dangerous) intersection of politics and entertainment, routinely appearing on a late-night television comedy program to poke fun at contemporary events and politicians. He spews foul and hateful rhetoric (including what the voice-over actor / comedian Jamie describes as "dick jokes") directed at a candidate (Liam Monroe) in a parliamentary election in the United Kingdom. Initially, the program's agenda is simply to get a few cheap laughs and increase ratings. Soon, however, Waldo takes on the role of attempting to disrupt the election.

We first watch Waldo engage the candidate in a *Colbert Report–style* sit down interview, asking an unsuspecting and oblivious Mr. Monroe trick questions to elicit uncomfortable, awkward and cringe-worthy responses from the candidate, followed by laughter from the audience. Waldo then interferes with the candidate's campaign events by rolling up on a truck and appearing onscreen. Waldo possesses no substantive ideas; he simply insults politicians so much that their campaigns become largely untenable. The episode invites the audience to envision a society in which a character such as Waldo takes power, perhaps in a re-imagined, dystopian fascist society.

In a system dominated by political elites, perhaps an agitator such as Waldo could hold some value. He demands that folks question the status quo and rebel against authority figures. Such actions may be warranted if the ruling class abuses its power. In this way, he can be viewed as a necessary check on authoritarian control. Waldo might have served a useful purpose, for example, had he existed in the dystopian world portrayed on "Kill All Others." Perhaps dissenters (such as Philbert) would have been less isolated had they been able to coalesce around a disrupter such as Waldo. Without a sound strategy to defeat the "One Candidate" and prevent her totalitarian regime from taking power, the voices of dissidents might fall on deaf ears. Channeling a loud, obnoxious cartoon bear to express collective frustrations with those seeking power would have made the drowning out of voices such as Philbert's less likely.

Waldo is the conduit through which controversial ideas and political agendas could potentially be expressed and furthered, giving the voice actor behind this cartoon the ability to hide behind the mask—perhaps without fear of attribution. While a McLuhan-type analysis suggests that the audience may not take Waldo seriously given his cartoon nature, he apparently gains sufficient support to rise to power. The introduction of Waldo and Twitter as channels through which ideas can be communicated arguably democratizes the dissemination of ideas in such a manner so as to make us question the applicability and perhaps validity of McLuhan's theory.

Waldo's presentation as a cartoonish mask behind which political actors may hide is reminiscent of the Wizard in the film adaption of L. Frank Baum's *The Wizard of Oz* (1939).[16] In the movie, Dorothy and her friends encounter a powerful and intimidating image of a man on a screen, with fire brimming at the edges of the screen. The characters are frightened by his boisterous voice and threatening persona. The man hiding behind this smokescreen is a charlatan, a feeble and unimposing man. He is weak and inept—unable to produce the grandiose results desired by Dorothy and her friends. The "Wizard" imagery on the screen influences and informs the characters' misperception of him as "great and powerful." This perception is critical to the characters' conscious decision to believe his false promises and follow his instructions to kill the Wicked Witch of the West and deliver her broomstick to the Wizard. The medium through which the Wizard's words are presented have a potent and symbiotic relationship with the characters' belief in, and reception of, the charlatan's words. Like the man hiding behind the wizard screen, the voice actors behind Waldo are not nearly as uninhibited or brave when viewed without the Waldo cartoonish mask. The masks in both situations influence those wearing the masks to act boldly, and the audience's reception to the messages presented.

Waldo is arguably a populist figure, seeking to disrupt the existing political discourse and establishment.[17] In an interview, he declares that he is "less fake" than Monroe, pointedly noting that nobody takes Monroe too seriously.

Waldo's argument is that no ideas and a lack of substance is the preferred option over a political establishment that, in his words, "keeps things shitty." Even though Jamie is disturbed by the fact that Waldo is not real, he is quieted by his producer who declares that Waldo is more real than his political opponents. The producer extols the virtue in not pretending to stand for a particular set of principles of ideals as politicians often do.

Observers can draw many parallels between Waldo's ascent and then-presidential candidate Donald Trump's meteoric rise to power—as well as the fundamental role of technology in each case.[18] *Black Mirror* co-creator Charlie Brooker acknowledged these similarities, noting that he could not have "foreseen the specificity of how close [the episode was to Trump's meteoric rise]."[19] Brooker also stated that "The Waldo Moment" was inspired by politics—and politicians—in the United Kingdom: "There was a great deal of anger in the U.K. at the time at established politicians. They seemed like an alien species that no one could relate to anymore. So the politicians that started to gain traction were these cartoonish buffoons.... It felt like people just wanted authenticity, even if it was ugly authenticity."[20]

Both Trump and Waldo eschewed the political correctness of other candidates, replacing smooth, polished rhetoric with a loud and brash means of communication. Many folks underestimated the force of the political movements giving birth to Trump and Waldo. The political establishment in both situations did not take the anti-establishment sentiments and uprisings seriously, as the establishment politicians were even hesitant to engage in direct debate. The political elites believed that each candidate would ultimately end up in the dustbin of history. The fact that each successfully overcame not only widespread opposition from the media and political opponents but also the traditional definition of a politician demonstrates an ability to disrupt the existing world order that many seasoned political commentators and strategists deemed unimaginable. This ability to disrupt has led some observers—such as legendary filmmaker David Lynch—to predict that Trump "could go down as one of the greatest presidents in history."[21]

Voting for each candidate was reactionary, a statement made by a public that was thoroughly disappointed by the status quo. Both candidates offered hope for a new approach to politics: an in-your-face, no holds barred, bold way of mocking career politicians for their dishonesty, corruption and ineffectiveness. That is not to say that Trump was necessarily trusted by voters: as discussed earlier, it may be the case that his rhetoric was not taken too seriously by a sizable portion of the populace. Still, both Trump and Waldo represented, to many voters, a welcome departure from the status quo. Waldo is referred to by an interviewer as "an official mascot for protest voters," a tagline that can appropriately be used to describe Trump. Waldo's rude and obnoxious demeanor is a characteristic that many voters find in Trump as well: a Suffolk University poll of 1,000 adults conducted in September 2015 found that the most popular terms used to describe Trump were "idiot / jerk / stupid / dumb," followed by "arrogant," "crazy / nuts," and "buffoon / clown / comical / joke."[22]

It is more than mildly ironic that Trump and Waldo came to power during the "information age"—an era where folks have access to more information than at any other time throughout history. Several important questions are raised by their political ascent. With so much data at our fingertips—and with so much capital and energy invested in populating an expansive and ever-growing Internet—how can we explain the rise of a populist who frequently expresses *disdain* for facts, truth and information? Does Trump's victory reflect a backlash against the 24-hour, frequently politically-slanted cable news cycle—a compendium of incessantly noisy chatter that may not reflect the interests of the populace? Did the data that we accessed about the election inform us that Trump was, in fact, the "best" choice? Perhaps. Or are there background forces at work, attempting to manipulate the information that we access and disrupting the ideal of a free and open marketplace of ideas? As discussed later in this chapter, it is likely that such forces are indeed lurking in the background. Coming to definitive conclusions about their impact on the outcome of the 2016 election is, however, a daunting challenge.

The impact of technology in "The Waldo Moment" cannot be overstated. Waldo's producer posits that politicians are wholly unnecessary because individuals all have access to technology (such as iPhones and computers) that enable them to vote online, with the majority determining society's direction on an issue. In this vein, technology can be viewed as a democratizing force—a great equalizer, given its widespread and pervasive accessibility by the masses. Jamie counters that YouTube is similarly democratizing, and yet the most popular video on the site is crude and embarrassing. Perhaps unabridged, unbridled democracy is not a laudable goal—especially if the public cannot be trusted to act in a responsible manner.

Technology gave birth to a political candidate (and movement), even without such birth being the initial objective of the creators of the cartoon. Because of the pervasive nature of technology, Waldo's producers seized a moment in time and created a grassroots political campaign. Waldo became a viral Internet sensation, and the fact that he was a fictional character was not sufficient to discourage many individuals for voting for him—and *against* actual polished politicians. The Internet turned a boorish, fictional cartoon into a dominant political force that had the potential to disrupt and upend the global political order. Similarly, Trump's rise from businessman and reality television host to politician is due in large measure to his pervasive use of technology—particularly his active Twitter account—to mock the establishment, bully his enemies, and, ultimately, endear himself to a large segment of the voting public. Many still question whether Trump's initial motivation was to emerge victorious, or whether, like Waldo's producers, build his brand by attacking others and offering a few cheap shots at the world. Trump's complicated relationship with the mainstream media notwithstanding, his astute use of social media enabled him to tap into a dissatisfied (and angry) portion of the American public that had felt disenfranchised. Many voters of both Waldo and Trump arguably voted against the establishment, rather than "for" what their candidates offered by way of concrete ideas or political solutions to complicated issues.

Trump repeatedly decried the U.S. political system as "rigged" and controlled by powers whose interests were averse to those of the average American. By doing so, Trump fomented a deep distrust in the U.S. justice system and democratic republic. Political enemies of both Trump and Waldo argue that these candidates attempt to sow discontent as a means of distracting voters from their own lack of substantive solutions of well-reasoned political agendas. Like Trump, Waldo offers his lack of political experience as a strength, not a weakness. Neither figure is encumbered by the baggage accompanying the political elites. On the surface, it would seem as though both candidates would have problems connecting with voters. Trump can arguably be viewed as an out of touch billionaire; Waldo is a fictional, crude cartoon bear. But each candidate managed to attract voters to their united cause of distrust of mainstream political figures and the unsatisfactory status quo. The ability to maintain—and manipulate—media coverage was essential to their respective success stories.

Media Manipulation

Jay Stanley, a Senior Policy Analyst at the ACLU, argues that "In the first half of the 20th century, Americans gained a new awareness of the malleability and manipulability of the human mind, and the result was a wave of concern over 'propaganda' and other techniques of influence. Today we may be seeing a new wave of similar fears as we begin to wonder whether the ways we use and rely upon technology today are making us susceptible to new, dangerous forms of manipulation."[23] It behooves us to understand this new paradigm so that we can resist it.

Mediums such as television and the Internet, at least partially due to their pervasive nature, have the potential to influence the way in which a message or idea is both communicated and understood on a wide scale. Popular culture has examined some of the ways in which folks seek to use such mediums to exert influence and achieve a specified agenda. Some of these strategies involve use of television to disseminate messages in a subliminal way. On *The Simpsons* episode "New Kids on the Blecch," for example, the United States Navy recruitment—in a covert attempt to enhance recruitment—produces a music video widely aired on television displaying the words "Yvan eht Nioj!" (or, if read backwards, "Join the Navy").[24] A similar tactic is employed on a smaller scale on the *Saved by the Bell* episode "The Zack Tapes," where Zack Morris tries to use subliminal messages recorded on a video cassette to influence Kelly Kapowski to go to the dance with him.[25] And on "Kill All Others," the words "Kill All Others" flash across a screen intermittently, presumably with the intent of gaining semiconscious but widespread support for the One Candidate's insidious policy proposal.

Brand name media outlets and independent sources also use mediums such as television and the Internet to disseminate messages quickly. The media is often far from objective, a fact that presents challenges for those who fail to see behind the curtain and question sources. The failure (intentional or otherwise) of a source to confirm the veracity of a report prior to disseminating its content broadly may have the same or similar effect as intentionally deceiving the public through means such as subliminal messaging. Folks are heavily reliant on their screens, and the media has an obligation—which it frequently fails to satisfy—to present ideas openly and honestly without any subterfuge.

Former United States Federal Bureau of Investigation Director James Comey once stated that "In the age of the mobile device, a lie goes 100 laps around the world before the truth gets out of bed."[26] Contemporary media outlets have the potential to influence the political viewpoints of billions of people. Technological advances have increased access to both traditional news sources and new media outlets. While even traditional media sources face allegations of bias, the democratization of the outward expression of political ideas via YouTube and other new media outlets has led to an unprecedented amount of slanted political coverage, much of it lacking any proper vetting for veracity. As access to news has increased, however, so too has the general public's skepticism of the accuracy of reporting. Some of our political leaders (such as President Trump) have attached themselves to and encouraged this skepticism to benefit politically from distrust of the media. Arguing that the media is stacked against him, President Trump frequently lambastes the "fake news" that he claims is a cornerstone of reporting on networks such as CNN, ABC, CBS, NBC and other outlets. Much of the public agrees that the days of the news serving as an objective source of current events are over.[27]

Trump argues that his use of Twitter is essential in the current media climate, as it enables him to instantly send direct, unadulterated messages to millions of people. The issue for the public to resolve, however, is how to ascertain the truth amongst competing news sources—from alleged pro–Trump bias at FOX News to arguably anti–Trump coverage at CNN, and from Trump's own tweets. Trump advisor Kellyanne Conway went so far as to proclaim (to much subsequent ridicule) that the Trump administration was in a position to provide "alternative facts."[28] (Conway's description of the truth as a relative concept, as opposed to an objective truth, is reminiscent of a promotional advertisement for Season 2 of *Better Call Saul*, which depicts Jimmy McGill sitting on a chair with the following tagline hovering over him: "The truth is how you look at it.")[29] This paradigm suggests that it is difficult to effectively argue that the actual truth will emerge from debate in the marketplace of ideas. These issues go well beyond the battle between those who support and those who disdain President Trump. These systemic flaws with respect to fair reporting and a lack of objectivity are a threat to democracy as they likely lead to a disinformed public.

The Dangers of Disinformation

In "Amusing Ourselves to Death," media scholar Neil Postman discusses the distinction between *misinformation*, in which information is entirely false, and *disinformation*, which consists of misleading information.[30] Disinformation is particularly dangerous because consumers are led to incorrectly believe that the information at hand is solid, irrefutable fact. A position on any subject that is formed on the basis of misinformation can likely be more easily corrected if an individual is presented with facts to the contrary. A disinformed individual, however, may attempt to defend his or her incorrect position because it may be based, in some respects, on an underlying truth that is in fact provable. This section examines the effects of the intrusion of misinformation, disinformation and The Big Lie in contemporary society. Both *Black Mirror* and *Electric Dreams* feature episodes where these issues are expertly examined, typically in dystopian settings that serve as frightening extensions of our partially misinformed and disinformed society.

In the *Electric Dreams* episode "Safe and Sound," for example, we watch a teenage girl named Foster and her mom (Irene) embark on a one-year excursion from the West to the technology-obsessed, high-security East.[31] Irene intends to disrupt the Eastern narrative that Westerners have been committing terrorist attacks in the East designed to kill Easterners and sow discontent and discord. While it appears that nobody can confirm that they have seen a terrorist attack in person, such attacks are routinely reported and shown on television. The East strongly encourages its citizens to wear electronic tracking devices (each called a Dex), under the guise of security—particularly in light of the frequent terrorist attacks portrayed by the media.[32] The episode serves as a case study of ways in which government and/or corporate actors could manipulate news coverage and even manufacture events that did not occur to serve an agenda—in this instance, the introduction and implementation of even more intrusive and invasive security and monitoring measures. Because Irene represents a threat to the Eastern elites and the way of life that they have promulgated, the government has a keen interest in engaging in deception to maintain control.

Throughout the episode, a technical support representative named Ethan and his company strategically deceive Foster into performing malicious acts. The dual misinformation and disinformation campaign comes in the form of posing questions to Foster for the purpose of frightening her about her new and unfamiliar surroundings. Technology's role in terms of the transmission of both misinformation and disinformation is critical here: by using "Hear Gel," Ethan forms a relatively close bond with Foster without physically meeting her. The amalgamation of technology and disinformation prove to be a forceful combination replete with deleterious effects.

While Foster expresses a bit of hesitation prior to following Ethan's instructions, reasonable observers may expect that she would be even more suspicious of the narrative promulgated by the East. Irene attempts to convey a deep-seated sense of distrust in Foster, but Ethan's manipulation of media and technology proves difficult for Foster to push back against. Scholar Gloria Origgi argues that citizens in a well-functioning democracy need not necessarily be well-equipped at determining the veracity of a news story or narrative account. Rather, citizens should focus on "reconstructing the *reputational path* of the piece of information in question, evaluating the intention of those who circulated it, and figuring out the agendas of those authorities that leant it credibility."[33] Making a determination of the intention and agenda is a critical component here. Relying solely on a belief about the reputation of a source would not have prevented *The War of the Worlds* confusion, for example. Foster is required to choose to believe one of two competing narratives. Applying a McLuhan-type analysis, perhaps Foster should have placed more faith in her mother—a reliable source of information with whom she presumably formed a relatively strong symbiotic relationship as it relates to the dissemination of ideas and information. In her interactions with Ethan, Foster fails to properly assess the "reputational path" of the information presented to her.

The pervasive and widespread nature of misinformation in our contemporary political environment has been well-documented.[34] As we see in "Safe and Sound," technology serves as a useful resource for the dissemination of such information. In the event a misleading news story on a hot button topic appears on television, for example, it will undoubtedly quickly spread through social media. Even if the story is ultimately retracted, it is the initial story that often generates the most interest—while the truth may be disregarded.

Other television shows similarly explore the dangers of media outlets that spread news lacking veracity—especially when other news presented by such outlets is factually accurate. In *The Simpsons* episode "The Computer Wore Menace Shoes," for example, Homer creates a website under the pseudonym "Mr. X" and simply makes up news.[35] One of his fake news stories, by happenstance, turns out to be truthful. A news organization that provides some news that is verifiable leads audiences to take all news reported by the outlet seriously. The lesson here is that overreliance on a source because of its reputation for presenting truths could have serious consequences. While determining the reputation of a source is critical, we should not be too quick to develop implicit trust in a specific source; perhaps it should be generated over a significant length of time. Such reliance would have been a serious mistake in this instance, as the rest of Homer's accounts were patently false.

Disinformation, or strategic deceit, is so commonplace because of at least two factors.[36] First, there is a modern tendency for many news outlets that were previously renowned for objectivity to espouse political positions on substantive issues. Many such news sources fail to acknowledge this bias and the expression thereof, and the reporting is presented not as overt political commentary or slanted coverage, but rather as objective truth. This approach calls into question adherence to traditional journalistic standards and protocols.[37] Much like a catcher in baseball attempts to "frame" a pitch so that the pitcher receives a strike call from the umpire, many news reporters present stories in a way that reinforces a specific narrative.

The omission of relevant facts while overemphasizing and showcasing others in reporting an account contributes to the public's failure to obtain a complete picture of an event. For example, in the *Electric Dreams* episode "Kill All Others," a lone dissenter and government skeptic observes that the news conspicuously failed to report that a political candidate threatened to move forward with a plan to kill those who disagree with her political agenda.

By reporting on other aspects of the speech while almost entirely failing to mention the threat in their summation of the event, the news outlets contribute to the flood of disinformation in that society. The media intentionally advances and promotes a discourse that focuses listeners on less important facts about the One Candidate, thereby distracting the audience from an issue that merits serious attention. And when the media at some point briefly mentions the threat, commentators argue—on the basis of no evidence whatsoever—that the threat should not be taken literally. An example of similar media bias and framing in contemporary society is the consistently flawed and biased reporting by some news outlets on terrorist attacks in Israel. After two Palestinian attackers attempted to stab police in Jerusalem, for example, CBS produced a headline that failed to acknowledge the attack itself, focusing instead only on Israel's defensive response: "3 Palestinians Killed as Daily Violence Grinds On." This headline strongly suggests the existence of a (false) moral equivalence between the attackers (the terrorists) and the victims (the attacked police), who have a legal and moral right to self-defense. The misdirection by omission of context is, unfortunately, a staple of reporting on Israel by some media outlets, and demonstrates a political bias.[38]

Marshall McLuhan would likely agree with Sean Hannity's and Tucker Carlson's frequently-leveled charge that the failure of some of their competitors to acknowledge a political slant in their reporting inevitably leads to a disinformed public.[39] McLuhan would likely argue that even if Hannity presented commentary that was objectively false, the audience may well reject it or at least be more receptive to questioning its veracity than it would a misleading story presented by a news source traditionally trusted to present news in an objective, unbiased manner. We see this issue in "Kill All Others" as well: the public seems to implicitly trust the news account without questioning whether it was slanted in any manner or represented a full and accurate picture. Bias that is not acknowledged by the reporter poses a serious threat to democracy. An incorrect idea presented under the guise of objectivity results in the formation of an entirely different symbiotic relationship than an incorrect idea presented on a news outlet known for its lack of political neutrality.

As the reach of the Internet continues to expand, it is important to assess a user's ability to differentiate truths and falsehoods. Given the anonymity of many bloggers, for example, it is fair to question whether McLuhan's theory is still relevant in such a de-centralized, democratized, anonymized collection of ideas and thoughts. Are readers of Internet content inherently suspicious of any and all content posted thereon, fearing the manipulation of the truth? Or do "brand" media names still carry significantly more weight, given the belief in heightened journalistic standards for reporting?

The implementation of "net empowerment," a phenomenon that enables "citizens to get direct access to vital public information, rather than being forced to rely on the press as conduit and filter" was considered "the new wave of democracy, the herald of citizen rule."[40] But the proliferation of the Internet—and in conjunction therewith a large number of new media sources—has created a confusing environment for seekers of the truth and objectivity to navigate. It has also made it easier to reinforce one's views without having to deal with counter-arguments. The tremendous access to information enables readers to engage in what FOX News commentator Tucker Carlson refers to as "narrowcasting."[41] The vast number of conservative and liberal media outlets gives readers the ability to spend their entire lives hearing their own opinions repeated back to them. Carlson (though a symbol of this phenomenon, in some respects) apparently laments this paradigm, arguing that "It's good to hear your own assumptions thrown back in your face once in a while because it forces you to reassess why you think what you do. And increasingly people don't have to have that experience."[42]

The Google Effect

The way in which folks obtain and consume information in society has undergone a tectonic shift. Tracking down a book at a local library has given way to Internet searches, where a seemingly infinite amount of information is at our fingertips within seconds. Whereas libraries keep records about what books we are borrowing for record-keeping purposes, there is no evidence to suggest that they use or seek to monetize such data by selling information about preferences to advertisers or other actors. But the same cannot be said about Internet search providers—corporations whose unstated mission is to learn as much about us as possible and create profiles about us to serve their own socio-economic and political agendas. While we have so much information available to us online, we are provided with alarmingly little information about the companies providing us with access thereto. Is Google akin to a library—a content-neutral transmitter of information, storing data for us to find without any influence or pressure? Or is Google engaged in the data mining and behavioral manipulation business, actively seeking out information about us and attempting to alter our preferences to achieve an agenda? Is Google heavily involved in determining how and what we search, and, most jarringly of all, how we think and behave?

In a futuristic society shown on *The Simpsons* episode "Holidays of Future Past," Lisa Simpson provides commentary on technology's place and influence in this reimagined world: "Google, even though you've enslaved half the world, you're still a damn good search engine!"[43] Lisa's remark serves as satirical commentary on the fact that folks often accept the negative consequences of technology (here, enslavement) if they can obtain some benefit (here, accurate and efficient Internet search results). But how might be Google enslaving us? Does it not provide an effective means for folks to access information, consider alternative perspectives and enrich their lives?

Google, the world's leading and most powerful search engine, provides a mechanism through which diverse ideas can reach a global audience. In theory, Google *should* provide a means through which the concept of "net empowerment" might flourish. But Google uses its *own* filters—complex algorithms designed to control the content to which folks have access. By controlling the flow of information, Google effectively manages the way in which societies in the "information age" are structured. This business model calls into question our assumptions about the democratization of access to sources and content. It also leads to users being presented with a distorted view of the world, one formed, at least in some measure, by providing strategically categorized search results replete with the potential to offer biased, slanted news coverage to achieve an unspecified, non-disclosed agenda.

An increased number of diverse media outlets in the "information age" is less valuable if folks use Google searches to access their news. Google possesses the power to ensure that certain sources receive significant attention, while others go largely unnoticed. Even worse, Google reportedly maintains a "quarantine list"—a blacklisting of millions of websites that it does not want users to access.[44] Google apparently also possesses the power to shut down the Internet, as it did (albeit inadvertently) for many hours throughout much of Japan in 2017.[45] And even if we access websites not through Google searches, but through the world's largest Internet browser (Google Chrome), Google collects, stores and users information about our browser history to create a profile of us for potential commercial and political use.[46]

Author and researcher Dr. Robert Epstein conducted a series of studies that demonstrate the ways in which Google could, if it so chooses, manipulate folks into shifting their perspectives on, and votes for or against, political candidates—without the subjects in many cases having awareness that they are seeing biased search results of webpages.[47] Should bumping up a candidate's search results be considered an in-kind campaign contribution that should be reported to election commissions? Is Google skirting our carefully designed campaign finance laws when it fails to so report? While we do not see what is going on behind the curtain at Google, evidence strongly supports the notion that Google uses data that it collects about us to manipulate us;

to steer us in desired commercial and political directions; and to change our thoughts and behaviors to fit its own agenda.[48] Google did not invent the concept of a corporation seeking to exercise control over others for commercial or political gain, but its complex algorithm facilitates this goal in new ways and with an unprecedented, ever-growing magnitude. We should all be frightened about the threats that Google poses to our democracy.

Google's immense reach forces us to ask whether we are comfortable with a corporation possessing and wielding so much power. We rightfully fear authorization governments that seek to stifle dissent and a free press. Should we be concerned that a mammoth corporation—which may not have our best interests at heart—takes actions that have the same effect, intentionally controlling the flow of information and invading our privacy (to the extent conceptions of privacy exist at all in the "information age")? Is Google holding all of us hostage? While Google (and Facebook) provide their applications to us for free, it is important to understand the benefit that they receive from doing so. Google does not sell us products; they sell us to others. As author Dr. Epstein succinctly notes, "We are the product!" When Google "develops another tool for us to use," Epstein observes, "they're doing it not to make our lives easier, they're doing it to get another source of information about us." Google is essentially a vast marketing company: it makes enhancements to its product line not to help us; rather the goal of such enhancements is to upgrade the product that Google is in the business of selling: human beings. Viewed from this perspective, Lisa Simpson's quip about Google's capacity to "enslave" sounds a bit less far-fetched.

And as part of its critique and satirical commentary on hyperconsumerism—even in the very early days of significant data collection—*The Simpsons* also explored the lengths to which marketing companies will go to sell a product. In the 1999 episode "Grift of the Magi," for example, a toy company called "Kid First Industries" buys Springfield Elementary and privatizes it.[49] The company's secret and nefarious plan is to use the classrooms as focus groups to develop and market toys in advance of the holiday shopping season. Just like Kid First Industries—which promised to provide education to Springfield Elementary children *gratis*, without any apparent return on its investment—Google has invaded our schools and provided apps and devices to students for free.[50] But it behooves us to understand that there is a cost to everything. Students in Springfield and those in contemporary society who use Google-subsidized devices have had their privacy rights violated. The data that is collected about them is stored and may be weaponized against them for years to come—at the supermarket, in the insurance marketplace, when they choose a university to attend and when they take a mortgage out to purchase a home. We may use Google's devices free of charge, but they are not offered to us freely, without a return on Google's investment.

Given the political and commercial agendas of those who manage access to content (such as Facebook and Google), we should question whether "net empowerment" is too quixotic, and, in practice, an illusory concept. While media proliferation has theoretically democratized the dissemination of, and access to, the news, tremendous barriers stand in the way of achieving a paradigm wherein information flows freely. We ignore the impact of corporate control over search results—and, ultimately, our thoughts and behaviors—at our peril. How many times has Google moved the goalposts to avoid crossing a line that Chairman Eric Schmidt promised never to cross—the ever-moving, self-identifying target that he refers to as "the creepy line"?[51]

Even as we begin to realize the scope and implications of Google's control over our lives, there exist practical barriers to freeing ourselves of Google's immense reach. Google already knows a great deal about us, and a quick exit seems difficult. Because Google controls the flow of information, we would be left with a dearth of content were we to try to live our lives without the world's most powerful search engine. And because Google wields such power in a largely unregulated fashion, we have reason to fear that we could be cut off from its services at Google's sole discretion. Professor Jordan B. Peterson learned this lesson and suffered the consequences after he objected to draft legislation regarding transgender policy in Canada.[52] He reports that his Gmail and YouTube accounts were blocked, and he was unable to access years of emails stored on Google's servers.[53] Peterson was reportedly not provided with a definitive reason for such cessation of service and explained that Google's seemingly arbitrary censorship created difficulties for him: "You come to rely on these things, and when the plug is pulled suddenly, then that puts a big hole in your life."[54]

Media Consolidation

In addition to the Google algorithm issue, the number of media sources in contemporary society also raises questions regarding the way in which content is distributed and made available in contemporary society. It is fair to question whether a happy medium between unchecked sources (such as Wikipedia) and just a few (albeit, potentially biased) media sources would be preferable.[55] When Lisa Simpson (in *The Simpsons* episode "Fraudcast News" [2004]) creates her own newspaper and rails against Mr. Burns' fervent attempts to consolidate media sources and create an undemocratic monopoly of the news, Homer comments on some of the anticipated problems with the democratization of the dissemination of ideas and proliferation of new media sources: "See, Lisa, instead of one big shot controlling all of the media, now there's a thousand freaks Xeroxing their worthless opinions."[56] The vast number of sources of information available to us does not, according to Origgi, "empower us or makes us more cognitively autonomous. Rather it renders us more dependent on other people's judgments and evaluations of the information with which we are faced."[57] Now that we have experienced the "information age," "we are moving towards the 'reputation age,' in which information will have value only if it is already filtered, evaluated, and commented upon by others."[58] Having too much information at our fingertips— a likely byproduct of decentralization—can be overwhelming. For that reason, we rely on our understanding of the reputation of a source to determine the veracity of the information.

While technology has increased access to political ideas and content, it also leads us to necessarily question the reliability of such content. This new paradigm is not confined solely to political reporting or the news: in the context of examining modern forms of distribution of legal scholarship and analysis, for example, informal legal blogs—often lacking serious vetting for accuracy—exists in stark contrast to Law Reviews, periodicals renowned for meticulous focus on, and attention to, detail.[59] While the widespread dissemination of ideas is a positive result of modern technology, it also increases both incentives and opportunities for disingenuous actors to promote distorted agendas in order to achieve social, economic, legal and political agendas in the new world order.[60]

The Big Lie

Both *Black Mirror* and *Electric Dreams* examine societal fears about technologies becoming so powerful that they can be used to alter our sense of consciousness and reality—leading individuals to believe, and place confidence in, massive lies. In the *Black Mirror* episode "White Bear" (2013), for example, a vulnerable and confused woman is hunted by masked individuals. She is told by a new acquaintance that the individuals chasing her are having their minds altered by a powerful signal appearing on digital screens. As in other *Black Mirror* episodes, an individual's perception of reality is altered, and she has no effective control over what she believes to be real. Because of the powerful forces around her, she has no choice but to attempt to adapt to her new reality. While she may harbor initial reservations about the ability of a signal to possess mind-altering capabilities, she is understandably overwhelmed and influenced by the acquaintance who appears to be on her side. The woman likely assumes that the acquaintance would have no reason to either manufacture or cover up such a massive lie. It seems that the bigger the lie, the more easily it may be believed.

This theme is examined on other television shows as well. In *The Simpsons* episode "Homer Badman" (1994), for example, Homer Simpson is falsely accused of groping the family babysitter.[61] To shift public opinion to his side, Homer makes an appearance on a local news program. The producer records the interview but rearranges words, making him appear guilty. While watching the program on television, Homer is dismayed but ultimately questions his own innocence: "Maybe TV is right. TV is always right."

Homer is so invested in the notion of the infallibility of television that he even believes in his own guilt, despite clearly possessing the knowledge that he is entirely innocent of the charges against him. Later in the episode, an acquaintance of Homer (Groundskeeper Willie) is featured on the same program and accused of criminal activity. Homer quickly condemns Willie, over the objections of Marge: "Hasn't this experience taught you that you can't believe everything you hear?," to which Homer gleefully responds: "Marge, my dear, I haven't learned a thing!" Homer then kisses the television.

While this scene serves as satirical commentary on the public's obsession with, and over-reliance on television, it also serves as a springboard from which scholars can examine another phenomenon: The Big Lie.

This phrase was coined by the monstrous Adolf Hitler and refers to the use, for purposes of propaganda, of a lie so "colossal" in nature that the recipient of the lie would not believe that someone "could have the imprudence to distort the truth so infamously."[62] Hitler's Propaganda Minister Joseph Goebbels used this hideous tactic during the Holocaust, explaining that "If you tell a lie big enough and keep repeating it, people will eventually come to believe it."[63]

While Homer seems to trust what he hears on television simply because of his confidence in the medium, Homer is not alone in believing lies that are stated repeatedly on television. And, the theory goes, it may well be easier to make people believe a massive lie with monumental consequences than a small micro-lie. Historian Richard Evans observed that "If you subject people to a barrage of lies, in the end they'll begin to think 'well maybe they're not all true, but there must be something in it.'"[64]

The combination of a trusted means of communication (in Homer's case, television) with a material message (i.e., a Big Lie) repeatedly presented thereon could result in a measurable impact in society, irrespective of the veracity of such message. As consumers of information presented on mediums through which manipulative actors have the opportunity to hide bias, present fiction as fact and intentionally mislead, we must remain vigilant and maintain a healthy dose of skepticism about what we read, see and hear—especially when it seems that dissenting voices are being silenced.

Repressing dissent is critical to maintaining the Big Lie. As Goebbels acknowledges: "The lie can be maintained only for such time as the State can shield the people from the political, economic and/or military consequences of the lie. It thus becomes vitally important for the State to use all of its powers to repress dissent, for the truth is the mortal enemy of the lie, and thus by extension, the truth is the greatest enemy of the State."[65] Rod Serling succinctly captures this point when he states (in the opening narration to *The Twilight Zone* episode "The Obsolete Man") that, in authoritarian regimes, "Logic is an enemy and truth is a menace."[66]

Reliance on news sources perceived to be authoritative but which lack neutrality are replete with bias, lack objectivity, and even contain Big Lies is a serious threat to our republic. "Safe and Sound" serves as a case study in terms of the dissemination of The Big Lie. Even through there is no evidence that a terrorist attack has ever been committed by Westerners in the East, nobody in the East seems to question their occurrence. A reasonable observer might deem it unlikely that the State would simply manufacture terrorist attacks that have no basis in reality, so a lie of this magnitude might stand a decent change of being believed—even without any evidentiary support. Next, it is possible that Foster's "terrorist attack" was one of a string of such manipulations. If so, there may have been other such "attacks"; simply reporting the "attack" without revealing the manipulation is also a possibility. Finally, the media's frequent reporting of the terrorist attacks has the effect of creating an impression of a societal epidemic. Only those who exhibit extreme distrust of the State would ever come to question the existence of this seemingly systemic problem that is the basis of, and justification for, the East's security apparatus.

"Safe and Sound" is not the only *Electric Dreams* episode to address technology's role in the manipulation of the public and individuals' psyches. In the episode "Kill All Others," for example, the State uses an electronic tracking system to locate a political dissenter, and the media spreads the messages of the candidate without criticizing a political candidate's immoral plan to kill all dissenters. *Black Mirror* addresses this phenomenon as well. In the episode "Shut Up and Dance" (2016), for example, a computer hacker blackmails several individuals into performing acts that are both embarrassing and criminal in nature. The hacker threatens to release embarrassing information over the Internet unless the individuals follow the hacker's instructions. In the episode "Men Against Fire" (2016), army commanders use sensory-altering technology to spread disinformation and achieve their agenda. In "White Christmas" (2014), a small "cookie" chip is implanted in, and then removed from, a prisoner's head. This is followed by a manipulation of the cookie's sense of time and space to extract a confession from the digital "cookie" copy of the man. In "White Bear" (2013), memory-erasing technology is deployed as part of an elaborate punishment of a criminal suspect. In the series premiere "The National Anthem" (2011), a kidnapper blackmails the Prime Minister of England into performing an indecent act with a pig, streamed over the Internet, in exchange for the release of the kidnapping victim.[67] And in the episode "Hated in the Nation" (2016), individuals are targeted for death through a morbid, yet democratic voting system on social media. In all these situations, technology plans a pivotal role in advancing the misguided agendas of those attempting to disrupt the existing social and political order and cause harm. The intersection of technology, disinformation, politics and a bad actor proves, in all of these cases, to serve as a destructive force in society. This combination is particularly relevant to an analysis of how media and government forces are portrayed in the episode "The National Anthem."

"The National Anthem" and Media Satire

Black Mirror's "The National Anthem" illustrates many of the issues and themes discussed earlier in this chapter. The kidnapper's strategy of showing Princess Susannah bound to a chair, begging for her life, grips the nation's attention. The visualization is impactful and McLuhan would likely argue that a powerful symbiotic relationship is born. We *feel* the Princess's pain and despair as she reads the kidnapper's grotesque ransom demand. Similarly, we see terrorists on the television series *24* (2001–2010, original series) (and in the real world) use the power of media not only to broadcast their message to a wide audience, but also to *show* the world what they can do.[68]

Technology, media and government forces merge together for a deleterious purpose in the episode. The government attempts to dictate what people watch—and, of equal significance, what they do not watch, while the media dictates the way in which an event is discussed, reported and broadcast.[69] The narrative generated by this joint initiative influences the public's perception of the Prime Minister and its view regarding the decision that he should make. As the nature of the news reporting begins to change, so, too, does the public's perspective of the Prime Minister. The episode depicts media professionals discussing how best to report the kidnapper's demand—such as whether to discuss the obscene details or to just provide a general overview of the request. The narrative promulgated by the media informs how the public reacts to the demand, and, somewhat circularly, the media also relies on anticipated public reaction when determining how to best report the account.

Regarding the latter point, one of the central themes of "The National Anthem" is that the public is willing to embrace and indulge in the humiliation of another individual—a phenomenon also explored in the episode "Shut Up and Dance" (where the victims of security breaches fear public consumption of their embarrassing moments); in the film *Network* (1976) (where news anchor Howard Beale promises to commit suicide on live television as a sarcastic response to his impending job loss over low television program ratings) and in the film *The Show* (2017) (where a large audience waits in bated breath as folks eagerly anticipate the spectacle of another individual's suicide).[70] These examples invite us to consider whether media outlets and viewers at home bear any responsibility for serving as a medium and audience, respectively, through which malicious or desperate actors can gain attention. Our obsession with consuming sensational stories and depictions of events is often a contributing factor to an individual's decision to perform an action.

We see the government and media work together in "Men Against Fire," too. In that episode, the media furthers the government's agenda by reporting that "roaches" are sick, referring to them collectively as "creatures" not by their individual names. Use and manipulation of (and by) the media is an essential strategic component of their dehumanization. A similar strategy is at play in "Kill All Others," where the media's silence and failure to condemn the One Candidate's desire to kill the "others" allows the regime to more easily advance its insidious goals.

One message in these episodes is that media and government actors have interests that sometimes diverge from the best interests of the public.

Masks and Lack of Trust

The political actors in both "The Waldo Moment" and "Safe and Sound" wear technology as a mask in their respective quests for power and influence. The anonymity of the Internet in contemporary society enables individuals to mirror this approach when disseminating information, ideas and propaganda. The Internet enables a great deal of communication to pass, often without pressure or repercussion in the event falsehoods are expressed. Traditional media outlets do—or at least should—fear consequences that could result from failures to present unadulterated truth. As scholars Hunt Alcott and Matthew Gentzkow observe, "Because reputational concerns discourage mass media outlets from knowingly reporting false stories, higher entry barriers limit false reporting" as compared to reporting on random websites.[71]

Notwithstanding the reputational consequences that traditional mass media outlets should fear from false reporting, Alcott and Gentzkow argue that society is currently experiencing a precipitously sharp and continuing decline in the "trust and confidence" in the mass media "when it comes to reporting the news fully, accurately and fairly."[72] Even if a media outlet reports the truth, the audience's view of the information presented is often poisoned by skepticism and distrust.

Social media is an especially powerful avenue through which to distribute disinformation, as well as cause social angst and civil unrest. Fake social media profiles—whether in business or in politics, for example, can cause a recipient of a message to place an undue amount of trust and confidence in the veracity of the substantive content contained therein.[73] Fake social media profiles can serve as a mask underneath which actors whose agenda it is to spread disinformation can hide behind in a covert manner.

Social Media Profiling: Data Collection and Disinformation

In this age of pervasive disinformation, it is important to take stock of the premier purveyors and conduits of information in contemporary society. On the Internet, social media is a powerful source of influence: 62 percent of adults in the United States report that they get news on social media platforms.[74] The business practices of Internet search and social media companies influence the content that is presented to users. Copious amounts of data on individuals are collected by such companies for diverse purposes, including to determine what products to sell and what political agendas to promote. These companies effectively profile users by using such data. The documentary *The Creepy Line* (2018) explores this phenomenon, arguing that Google (the world's leading search engine) controls our society by structuring and organizing it, using profiles that it creates about users for a range of purposes—from targeted advertising to determining and influencing political preferences of individuals.[75]

2. Technology and Political Manipulation 65

The collection of personal data is an inherent part of life in several of the futuristic settings on *Black Mirror*. For example, in the episode "Be Right Back" (2013), a simulation of a woman's deceased boyfriend is constructed based on his social media profile and other audiovisual data. The decedent's frequent use of social media platforms enables a machine to rely on such data to create a very accurate portrait of the man. Similarly, in "Hang the DJ" (2017), an online dating application collects data from the relationships of (simulated) individuals to generate an ideal match for the individual. In the film *Nerve*, a website collects data about "players," creating user profiles to aid "watchers" in their quest to determine the fears of the players.[76] We can imagine scenarios where data is not only collected, but also manipulated to further a bad actor's agenda. Hackers, for example, attempt to access personal data to steal identities and other malign purposes. Businesses, news organizations and social media companies seek to further their agendas as well. In "The National Anthem," for example, the media closely monitors its audiences' reactions to a news account and tweaks its presentation of the story to closely align with viewers' interests.

Social media companies often use the data that they collect to spread disinformation. In a blistering speech outlining public policy concerns regarding data collection and surveillance, Apple CEO Tim Cook warned that "Our own information is being weaponized against us with military efficiency. Rogue actors and even governments have taken advantage of user trust to deepen divisions, incite violence, and even undermine our shared sense of what is true and what is false."[77]

As a prominent member of the cable talk show circuit, political commentator Tucker Carlson observes that much of the content provided to us on the Internet and other media forums is presented to affirm an individual's own worldviews.[78] The practices of Facebook are a prime example. Facebook presents users with a list of "trending" news stories based on the types of stories that Facebook believes are of interest to an individual user or because Facebook desires to further a particular social, political or corporate agenda.[79] It is imperative for a well-functioning democracy in the technological age to guard against "algorithmic bias," namely the phenomenon of a computer system reflecting the implicit values of the folks involved in coding, selecting, collecting or using the data to teach the algorithm.[80] Even if the facts in a "trending" news article are true, the failure of Facebook to present a competing narrative that, perhaps, interprets the facts differently or calls into question the context in which they are presented, arguably leads to a disinformed user base. As Assistant Professor of Journalism Nicole Dahman notes, "What we see on Facebook is dictated by algorithms that decide what you see based on what you like and dislike, what you comment on and click on. Rather than getting a diversity of perspectives that contribute to political discourse, we see an echo chamber."[81] By presenting only certain news and other information to an individual user, Facebook contributes to the distribution of content that does not present a full or fair account of a given subject. Facebook's use of algorithms in determining what information and advertisements to show a user serves to limit the amount and nature of content to which a user has immediate access. Even worse, the data science firm Cambridge Analytica used data that it collected on Facebook "to target persuadable voters based on their individual psychology."[82] This firm used sophisticated artificial intelligence to send voters political messages "based on predictions about their susceptibility to different arguments."[83] The creation and utilization of autonomous "bots"—programs designed to run independently and mimic a human user—has, according to Dr. Vyacheslav Polonski (a researcher at the University of Oxford) the potential to "shape public discourse and distort political sentiment," as they produce the "illusion of public support" for a particular candidate or political agenda.[84] As Polonski concludes, such bots "can be used to highlight negative social messages about a candidate to a demographic group more likely to vote for them, the idea being to discourage them from turning out on election day."[85]

The issue exists in a commercial context as well. Fans who join Facebook groups devoted to, say, the television series *Better Call Saul*, will be presented with advertisements for the series as well as products related thereto. While effective from a marketing perspective, the presentation of an avalanche of *Better Call Saul*-related items demonstrates Facebook's view of its users not as information or truth-seekers, but rather as consumers. Aside from product marketing, Facebook may also have vested commercial interests in what side of a contentious political issue it presents to a user—and the way such issue is presented.

Given strong evidence of Facebook's lack of neutrality and manipulation of access to content, it is fair to question whether it (and other platforms whose coders employ similar practices) should enjoy the protections of Section 230 of the Communications Decency Act (CDA) of 1996. Section 230 states, in part, "No provider or user of an interactive computer service shall be treated as the publisher or speaker of any information provided by another information content provider."[86] Because Facebook appears to be involved in the content business—not merely as a passive transmitter of unfiltered content, but often as a preacher, a powerful influencer of ideas—the applicability of this portion of the CDA is questionable.

Free speech advocates—such as Emma Llanso of the Center for Democracy and Technology—argue that the applicability of Section 230 to Facebook and other platforms is critical to "protecting free speech online," thereby advancing First Amendment interests.[87] Others, such as Michael Beckerman of the Internet Association, point to the wealth that this protection has produced. Beckerman argues that Section 230 is "the one line of federal code that has created more economic value than any other."[88]

But critics charge that Facebook is anything but a neutral medium or public forum through which content is funneled to users; it engages in practices which seem to promote specific viewpoints to specific audiences.[89] Far from taking a hands-off approach with respect to the content uploaded on its platform, Facebook appears to edit, filter and order content, steering users in a specific direction.[90] It manages (and sometimes bans) content by ensuring that it complies with its "community standards" policy.[91] In short, Facebook is heavily involved in the content business—even though it would forcefully argue that it cannot possibly manage every single item of content on its platform and therefore should not be legally or morally responsible for such postings. Given Facebook's actions and business model, it seems reasonable to insist that Facebook and other platforms and providers that engage in similar practices be treated and regulated in a way comparable to non-neutral, content-providing media outlets. That is not to suggest that such platforms should not enjoy the First Amendment protections enjoyed by media companies and other purveyors of content.[92] The issue is that Facebook has the best of both worlds: it is largely insulated from legal liability based on the content that users upload, yet evidence suggests that the company actively manages and reviews a great deal of content—apparently to further its own agendas. Because of the lack of transparency and disclosure by Facebook as to its business practices, strategies and agendas, debate continues as to the proper way to regulate it: as a media company, technology company, neutral public forum for the exchange of views or some form of hybrid combination thereof.

The *Black Mirror* episode "Fifteen Million Merits" provides satirical commentary on the ways in which consumers receive and manage content. In the fictional world presented on this episode, folks have access to too much unwanted content. They must pay "merits" to avoid being assaulted by undesirable content, such as pornography. Given that consumers of the news in our society are inundated with a surplus of content, we could imagine a model in which corporations charge folks to avoid seeing certain content. We could envision a potential political impact (such as an effect on election results) based on this scenario.

As it stands today, Facebook presents its users with a limited view of the world—given the selected advertisements and political content that users receive. The key here is the "selectivity" on the part of Facebook. While the Internet theoretically provides individuals access to infinite perspectives and information, Facebook's filters (much like Google's algorithms) serve to limit the information to which an individual has immediate access. Users are free to dig deeper and conduct their own searches to paint fuller portraits of issues, but it is important to be aware that the view of the world presented to us by Facebook and similar platforms is intended to fit a corporate and political agenda and is based on individual user preferences.

Power is concentrated at the highest levels of these companies as the corporate dictators feed information to users in an undemocratic and largely non-transparent fashion. Some folks have begun to criticize such companies for their concerted efforts to influence thoughts and behaviors via use of powerful algorithms—see, for example, the critics and watchdog groups featured in the documentary *Facebook: Cracking the Code*—but such criticism has yet to have a discernable or meaningful impact on the rapid growth of these companies or their advancement of ever-more powerful tools with an enhanced ability to exert control over users.[93] While the Internet, ideally, should be used to explore alternative ideas and expand our minds, the filters enable Facebook to present users with an affirmation of the user's specific world views, rather than a more open-ended, objective exploration of counter-perspectives.[94] Borrowing from famed journalist Malcolm Gladwell's analogy, this manipulation makes the Internet feel more like a "dinner party"—where friendly, supportive viewpoints are presented by invited guests, rather than a "festival of ideas"—where hostile viewpoints are explored and our own predispositions and preferences are challenged in an open forum.[95]

Internet search engines present similar challenges for the quixotic, open-minded truth-seeker. As noted earlier, Google effectively controls the flow of information in this technological age. Experts at search engine optimization frequently attempt to, with varying degrees of success, manipulate a search engine's algorithms to push their content to the top of a search result page. Ideally, the results that appear at the top of a search results page should be based not on popularity or result from the manipulation of search optimizers, but rather an independent commission interested in promoting facts over falsehoods. This, of course, is a highly impractical (and still restrictive) approach to managing the Internet. Given the impracticalities, it is essential to understand that the Internet is politicized, commercialized and agenda-driven to such an extent that it is difficult to gain new perspectives and find the truth among a web of deception and competing (and sometimes manipulative) agendas.[96] All of the above calls into question the concept of "net empowerment": perhaps the Internet is not the beacon of true freedom and access to content that we had hoped it would be.

Given the amount of "fake news" in society, the lack of fact-checking makes it nearly impossible to identify fake from real news. This point is highlighted in the *Black Mirror* episode "The National Anthem." When viewers turn on their computers and see Princess Susannah bound to a chair and hear about the odd purported ransom demand, they are incredulous and question the veracity of the entire situation. One Internet user remarks that since this development is not being reported on television, it is likely not true. This demonstrates an inherent mistrust of Internet content and suggests that television is perhaps deemed a more reliable source of information.[97]

Digital Humiliation: Just "Shut Up and Dance"

Individuals with nefarious motives often make use of technology not only to disinform or to achieve specific political or commercial agendas; hackers may attempt to misuse modern technology for a wide range of deleterious purposes, including manipulation of, and control over, strangers on the Internet. The *Black Mirror* episode "Shut Up and Dance" (2016) highlights this concern. This episode reflects contemporary realities and fears regarding the malicious actions of hackers as well as vigilante justice.

Technology provides an avenue through which individuals can exert control and influence in life. For example, folks often manage their personal finances and create fantasy football teams online. In the latter example, a casual football fan can be an "armchair general manager"—ranking players, executing trades, drafting players and choosing which players to sit or play for his or her team on a weekly basis. This is an example of an enhanced form of a traditional board game, such as *Monopoly* or *Risk*, each of which enable players to make strategic decisions during the game that affect the worlds created therein. In the *Black Mirror* film "Bandersnatch" (2018), this concept is featured quite prominently: in this special interactive film, the audience makes decisions for and controls the actions of Stefan—the protagonist who is developing a video game of a similar nature, which contains multiple pathways for the video game characters.

Computer hackers seek to manipulate and abuse technology so that they, too, can gain control. The stakes are high, of course, and often involve control over an individual's life for nefarious purposes. This abuse often has serious consequences for the affected individual. Hiding behind the cloak of anonymity on the Internet, hackers often act boldly and fearlessly as they attempt to infiltrate an individual's accounts, private moments and personal information—and even steal his or her identity. The use of technology by individuals to exert control over others is a common theme examined on many *Black Mirror* and *Electric Dreams* episodes in a variety of contexts, including "U.S.S. Callister" (2017); "Hated in the Nation" (2016); "Fifteen Million Merits" (2011); "Kill All Others" (2018); "Safe and Sound" (2018); "Arkangel" (2017); "Nosedive" (2016); "The Entire History of You" (2011); "The Waldo Moment" (2013); "The National Anthem" (2011); "White Bear" (2013); "Shut Up and Dance" (2016); "Men Against Fire" (2016); "The Hood Maker" (2017); "Crocodile" (2017); "Black Museum" (2017); and "White Christmas" (2014).[98]

Hacking and data security breaches are pervasive in contemporary society. There is a hacking attack every 39 seconds, which translates to an impact on 1 in every 3 Americans every year.[99] Since 2013, 3,809,448 records are stolen during breaches every day.[100] The breaches are extremely costly: the average cost of a data breach affecting a company is expected to exceed $150 million by 2020.[101] And evidence suggests that as technology expands its reach, the number, scope and magnitude of vulnerabilities increase. As Bruce Schneier (2018) observes: "We used to only be concerned about bits vulnerabilities. Now the risks are against life and property."[102] The victims of such hacking suffer not only economic consequences, but often must deal with emotional, psychological and reputational consequences emanating from the breaches. If embarrassing information about an individual is leaked over the Internet, the individual's life may be adversely affected forever.

There have been instances where the humiliated individual is so disturbed that he or she commits suicide. *Black Mirror* examines this phenomenon as well. In "Shut Up and Dance," for example, we see Kenny attempt to commit suicide—although this is likely not only a result of the humiliation he faces but also the unconscionable demand that he fight another individual to the death. In "Hated in the Nation," we see an individual who is targeted in the insidious "Game of Consequences" show a detective her slashed wrists—a by-product of an attempted suicide resulting from the extreme embarrassment she faced on the Internet. This scene, unfortunately, reflects contemporary realities. Studies have shown a "strong correlation" between the suicide rates of teenagers and their ownership of smartphones and use of social media in contemporary society.[103] In some cases, embarrassment on social media has been directly linked to the immediate cause of the suicide.[104]

The ability of hackers to exert control over others is expertly examined on the episode "Shut Up and Dance." In the episode, a hacker gains access to an embarrassing and highly incriminating tape of a young man (Kenny) and threatens to release the footage to everyone on Kenny's contact list unless

Kenny satisfies the hacker's demands. It seems that the hacker relishes the immense power and control over the affected individuals, each of whom follow the instructions given to them. The ability of this hacker—and those in contemporary society—to disrupt and ruin individuals' lives is real and significant. The episode explores the power of recordings distributed publicly over the Internet (or the threat thereof) to affect folks' lives and behaviors, given the Internet's enormous reach and the permanent stains that could arise from posted content. "Shut Up and Dance" also asks the audience to consider whether the blackmailer's actions are justified in situations where the victim of the blackmail is misusing technology for insidious purposes.

We see this dual misuse and abuse of technology by both victim and bad actor in the context of vigilantism on other episodes, too. In "Hated in the Nation," for example, a hacker surreptitiously takes control of killer bees and uses them to kill folks as a punishment for what the hacker deems to be unacceptable behavior on the Internet.[105] Less extreme forms of this phenomenon exist in contemporary society. The media frequently refers to this concept as "online shaming," described as a form of Internet vigilantism employed by proponents to right injustices and hold folks accountable for their actions and words.[106]

In both "Shut Up and Dance" and "White Bear" technology is used to manipulate individuals—arguably for justifiable reasons.[107] There is a strong argument that the victims of the surreptitious activities in each episode (i.e., playing a role in a youth's murder in "White Bear," and watching child pornography in "Shut Up and Dance," respectively) deserve some form of punishment.[108] The nature of the punishments and the process through which they are meted out, however, are controversial. Technology is employed by the vigilantes—the perpetuators of the deception—to design and implement punishments for the criminals and bad actors without use of, or reliance on, the criminal justice system. Due process protections are ignored, and the United States Constitution's prohibition on "cruel and unusual punishment" is apparently not a consideration for those developing and executing the uniquely harsh punishments. In short, law and order are circumvented in these dystopian worlds.[109]

Both "White Bear" and "Shut Up and Dance" provide decisively grim commentary with respect to morality and humanity's reaction to crimes and punishments. Zack Handlen observes that "Shut Up and Dance" shows a "willingness to force moral questions that make everyone feel awful."[110] A similar sentiment is expressed by television columnists Matt Donnelly and Tim Molloy, who note that "no episode of 'Black Mirror' will leave you feeling worse about humanity."[111] It is also troubling that the deceivers and those watching the deception unfold seem to relish the violence and pain experienced by the victims of the manipulations. In "White Bear," for example, the reveal is made onstage in front of a live audience—like on a scripted television show. This communal lack of empathy for the torturous punishments forces us to question how we would react to being complicit in, or even watching, a bad actor face serious, painful consequences for his or her actions. As Handlen observes with respect to "White Bear," "the glee to which that punishment is delivered throws the whole enterprise into question."[112] If the television audience was previously unsettled by the dire situations faced by the individuals before we knew that they were bad actors, do we now feel comfortable watching them deal with their circumstances once we learn about their repugnant actions? Or would we prefer a more balanced, reflective, and, ultimately, less cruel approach to punishing these individuals for their crimes?

Black Mirror and *Electric Dreams* also address the ways in which technology can be used to both connect and disconnect individuals in a globalized society. The next chapter discusses this theme by critically examining episodes focusing on social media and online dating.

3

Rate Me, Like Me, Follow Me, Control Me, Love Me, Kill Me

A Dystopian Guide to Social Media and Online Dating

> "It is true, we shall be monsters, cut off from all the world; but on that account we shall be more attached to one another."
> —Mary Shelley[1]

In "On Paradise Drive: How We Live Now (And Always Have) in the Future Tense," commentator David Brooks argues that there are two competing types of individuals in society: blondes and brunettes.[2] He emphasizes that the distinction is not based on actual hair color, but rather on their differing perspectives on the world and their ability and willingness to reflect on same. The blondes are vapid and unaware of their shortcomings because these individuals are elevated by others. Brooks notes that the vapid individual is the "One Who Is Chosen," while the brunette is far more reflective and must earn everything in her possession.[3]

The brunette likely lacks access to certain social and economic privileges in society, as she has not been coddled or elevated by her peers. There is an emptiness that defines the blondes—as they rely on others in the community to maintain and support their status. The brunettes, by contrast, are tethered not to fake constructs, rankings or other societal paradigms dictated by others, but rather by their own self-worth and material contributions to society.

In the *Black Mirror* episode "Nosedive" (2016), the audience is introduced to Lacie, an individual who (invoking Brooks' metaphor) seeks to be the "One Who is Chosen." Like all other social media addicts in this dystopian future, Lacie is a vapid, blonde individual. In this world, status is defined by how an individual is ranked by others, on a scale of 1–5, on a social media platform. Obtaining and maintaining a high ranking opens the door to exclusive benefits, such as lower mortgage rates on homes. The desire to achieve a high ranking informs virtually all of Lacie's daily actions, all of which are intended to impress others: from photos that she takes and posts online to impress others; to who she interacts with (unfortunately for Lacie, her "inner circle" is comprised of mostly "mid-low range" folks); to how she interacts with others; to practicing her smile until she finds one sufficient to impress other high-ranking individuals.[4]

Lacie even hires a social media consultant / brand strategist to analyze her interactions with others, her "socials" (which seem to arise to nearly the same level of importance as one's vital signs) and the metrics regarding her "sphere of influence" (i.e., whether strangers and her inner circle like her). This job is presumably a lucrative one that is in high demand, as most individuals in Lacie's world are quite interested in engendering successful self-branding strategies.

In the society depicted on "Nosedive," feelings and emotions are necessarily suppressed, as they could stand in the way of achieving a high ranking. Most individuals in this world wear a mask, and the rankings are not an honest assessment of a person's self-worth or value and/or contribution to society. The rankings are a classic popularity contest and are skewed because some individuals simply award high ratings to others to hopefully receive a similar rating in exchange. The individuals who take part in this societal obsession are not living a true or meaningful experience. The lucky 5-star individuals have been elevated by their peers, not because of what they do for the world but because of how they are viewed in a superficial light. Warren Buffett famously stated that "the big question about how people behave is whether they've got an Inner Scorecard or an Outer Scorecard. It helps if you can be satisfied with an Inner Scorecard."[5] In the society depicted on "Nosedive," individuals are only focused on an Outer Scorecard because an Inner Scorecard would have no bearing on their social media ranking. In short, social media has created a world replete with vapid blondes seeking to climb the social ladder. The brunettes (who lack such privilege) exist without regard to their ranking, but can live a more meaningful existence by expressing themselves without fear of a sharp rating decrease.

"Nosedive" is a wonderfully presented humdinger of an episode, expertly exploring and satirizing societal use of and reliance on social media. It forces us to ask ourselves how distinguishable our contemporary usage of social media is from Lacie's obsession. A thoughtful consideration of Lacie's engagement with social media demonstrates that the platforms she uses provide a mechanism for strangers to gain emotional influence over her thoughts and behaviors. Why would she—*or we*—implicitly consent to relinquish such control over our lives to anyone, much less folks who we do not even know? This question is explored in the television series *God Friended Me* (2018–present), where an anonymous individual using the pseudonym "God" directs and influences the actions of an individual that "God" befriends on a social media platform.[6]

Novelist and journalist Tom Wolfe opined that "I think every living moment of a human being's life, unless the person is starving or in immediate danger of death in some other way, is controlled by a concern for status."[7] This theory is supported by the actions of the affected individuals in "Shut Up and Dance," all of whom take extreme measures to avoid embarrassment. Wolfe's viewpoint also reinforces Brooker's contention that problems typically blamed on technological innovations are frequently the fault of human beings themselves, not their creations. When discussing the allure of such innovations, Richtel observes that our devices play to "primitive social wiring and our deepest reward systems," and argues that "we need to catch up to that understanding or it has a chance to enslave us…."[8] Access to social media did not generate our desire to impress others; rather, it provides a pathway to doing so and allows us to focus on this objective on a minute-by-minute basis. We are addicted to what *The New York Times* columnist Nellie Bowles describes as "the slot machine-like pleasure of refreshing Instagram for likes."[9] Many of us post photos online to impress others, and we seek to grow our follower base. This implicitly limits our freedom to make independent choices and act accordingly, at least in some respects. And scholars have observed that technology platforms and interfaces that "stand in for people as a remote proxy" often have the same effect on our behavior as a physical person in a room judging or grading us.[10]

On social media, we invite friends and strangers alike to judge us, and we deliberately cultivate an image designed to gain the admiration of anyone who comes across our pages. This phenomenon is examined on the television series *You* (2018–present), where a man makes a series of assumptions about a woman based on her social media profile.[11] He considers her profile to be a "collage" of carefully selected life events, not an accurate or complete portrayal of the woman's life. In fact, his expectation is that her profile intentionally excludes details about the deep and more significant interactions throughout her life. The man believes that the woman's failure to post about their first meeting, for example, is affirmation of the development of a meaningful connection, one that should not be advertised to the world via a social media platform because it is too real and does not fit neatly into the woman's contrived portrait of her life. In other words, it was not an encounter meant to be devalued by showing it to anyone who happens to be browsing the

Internet. In sum, the woman uses social media as a mask, a disguise intended to convey a specific image that obfuscates aspects of reality.

If folks like our masks, then surely (per conventional wisdom) we have done something right. Bryce Dallas Howard, the actress who portrayed Lacie on "Nosedive" reveals that she intentionally gained 30 pounds to do the episode, noting that "It was really important for me to show that this insecurity she feels [including with respect to her body weight] in the world is because she's not comfortable in her own skin. She's not accepting herself for who she is. I wanted [the episode] to be about image, and about how people want to control what other people think about them by trying to control themselves in ways that are harmful."[12] Some folks believe that when they enter the vaunted social media party, it behooves them to make sure that they do so looking flawless—even if that entails taking fairly drastic measures to impress others.

And for those folks who take social media too seriously, there could be demonstrable impacts on their own self-perception. What is intended to impress others could lead us to have a different perception of ourselves. We might not recognize or remain true to ourselves as we wear our masks. Artist Leslie Hung (speaking about the misadventures of Lottie in the graphic novel series *Snotgirl*) argues, "The shift in the way that we perceive ourselves through the lens of what we post on Internet platforms ... is really interesting...."[13] It is potentially dangerous as well. We run the risk of losing a sense of reality if we cultivate a social media image that does not accurately reflect who and what we are.

For some individuals, social media provides a means to validate that they have achieved fame. The documentary *The American Meme* (2018) explores this phenomenon, chronicling the vapidity of stardom attained via social media.[14] Because of a variety of faux and tangible benefits, some folks strive to attain the coveted blue check mark—or *verified-status* on Twitter. This verification mechanism is intended to inform the public that the account is not fraudulent or a fan account, but also has the effect of elevating the individual over his or her peers: if someone has been "verified" by a large multinational corporation, they have, apparently, *arrived*. If Twitter decides that an individual is important enough that others would want to impersonate that individual, we are supposed to infer that the individual must be pretty damn important.

Contemporary usage of social media is pervasive.[15] As of the fourth quarter of 2017, Facebook had 2.2 billion monthly active users, while Twitter had 330 million monthly active users.[16] In 2017, the average user of social media platforms spent 135 minutes per day on social media.[17] According to a recent marketing study, the average person will spend 5 years of his or her life on social media.[18] Folks use these platforms for diverse reasons: as a source of news, entertainment and connecting with other individuals. Social media's ability to connect individuals in a meaningful manner is debatable.[19] On the one hand, folks living in diverse areas of the world can connect with each other by joining groups devoted to shared interests or affiliations. Furthermore, friends and family who are separated by geographic borders can use social media to interact and share photos and videos with each other. Friendships and romantic relationships are frequently forged on social media platforms, with individuals connecting based on shared interests and/or attraction to each other's photos, among other reasons. From this perspective, social media helps to satiate the innately human desire to build and sustain significant relationships with one another.

On the other hand, the nature of the connectedness is sometimes circumspect, especially if the online interactions do not result in in-person meetings between folks. Is communication with others over the Internet as meaningful as physical interactions between individuals in their own communities? Sometimes the Internet (and social media specifically) has the effect of engendering more isolation. Virtual reality researchers Jim Blascovich and Jeremy Bailenson observe that "the Internet and virtual reality easily satisfy ... [many] social needs and drives—sometimes [they are] so satisfying that addicted users will withdraw physically from society."[20] While social media is undoubtedly a useful tool for starting to forge new business and personal relationships in some cases, any online resource can arguably be considered insufficient to create a meaningful relationship between individuals without an eventual physical meeting. A recent study showed that our brains are unable to handle having an extremely large number of actual friends, and having a relatively small number of close friends who we interact with in ways not confined to the virtual space is better for our overall mental health.[21] That study concluded that the number of friends is not necessarily a relevant factor with respect to whether an individual has a strong, healthy social life; rather it is the nature of the interaction that matters, and it appears that virtual interaction alone is insufficient to maintain healthy social relationships.[22] In fact, the failure to maintain real, healthy relationships is linked to loneliness, which, in turn, is linked to mental health issues (such as premature death).[23] We must be cognizant of the power of technology to directly or indirectly disrupt the way in which we interact with one another. Our relationships are sacred; they are the social bonds that hold society together. We must be wary of the potential power of contemporary innovation—including novel forms of communication—to adversely affect the nature and scope of the relationships that we form.

Interactions between folks on social media are sometimes manipulated by individuals who seek to hide behind the mask and anonymity of the Internet. While online dating websites have led to many successful relationships and happy marriages (including mine), some people use the sites to deceive others and hide behind a cloak of anonymity. The MTV documentary television series *Catfish: The TV Show* (2012–present), for example, explores cases in which a deceitful romantic "partner" deceives an innocent, unsuspecting individual into believing that the deceitful person is someone that he or she is not.[24] The deceptive individual in these instances uses the anonymity of the Internet to trick the other individual into falling in love, loaning money, and more.

Often, individuals use pseudonyms on the Internet and often feel emboldened to make threatening remarks and comments that they would otherwise feel uncomfortable repeating in the physical presence of others. It is easier to make disparaging comments, express controversial views and even make threats over the Internet than it is in person. This theme is explored on "Hated in the Nation," where folks advocate and promote violence as the play the "Game of Consequences." We see a similar concept at play in the film *Nerve*, where "watchers" of an Internet game are emboldened to demand that "players" engage in behavior that is abominable or dangerous or both—all while the "watchers" hide behind both figurative and literal masks as they film the "players" in action.

Actor Bill Murray observes that "Social media is training us to compare our lives instead of appreciating everything we are. No wonder why everyone is always depressed."[25] Comedian and actor Seth Rogen echoes this observation, sarcastically tweeting that "Instagram is great because otherwise I wouldn't know how many parties I wasn't being invited to."[26] Even if human beings would likely still compare social and economic statuses absent social media, this platform provides an overly convenient outlet to do so, where folks are constantly under pressure to define and promote their statuses to impress others. The sentiment expressed by Murray has been examined in sociological and psychological studies. Researchers and health experts have warned about the potential dangers of overuse of social media. The American Academy of Pediatrics, for example, has identified cyber-bullying and "Facebook depression" as possible harms resulting from social media use by children and teens.[27] A research study concluded that use of Facebook was tied to fewer moments of happiness and less overall satisfaction with life.[28] Other researchers have discovered that the more time spent by an individual on social media platforms, the more socially isolated they feel.[29] A study conducted at the University of Pennsylvania, for example, found that limiting daily use of social media to 30 minutes or less can boost mental health.[30] Researchers at the University of Pittsburgh's School of Medicine shows that folks who check their social media multiple times a day are three times more likely to develop depression than folks who do not do so.[31] *Forbes* health contributor Alice G. Walton opines that "Part of the reason Facebook makes people *feel* socially isolated (even though they may not actually be) is the comparison factor. We fall into the trap of comparing ourselves to others as we scroll through our feeds, and make judgements about how we measure up."[32] Other researchers have concluded, after examining the ways in which Facebook conjures up jealousy in individuals, that "This magnitude of envy incidents taking place on FB alone is astounding, providing evidence that FB offers a breeding ground for invidious feelings."[33] The researchers also conclude that this jealousy can lead to a dangerous cycle of users attempting to outdo each other.[34] Another study compared the way people feel after using Facebook with the way they predicted they would feel prior to such use. While most users felt worse after use, they had incorrected believed—or forecasted—that they would feel better prior to actual use.[35] Salesforce Chief Executive Officer Marc Benioff sums up many of the aforementioned findings and sentiments when he describes Facebook as "the new cigarettes of our industry," explaining that "It's a technology that's addictive, it may not be that great for you, and it might be something that you want to go back to."[36]

While many *Black Mirror* and *Electric Dreams* episodes present potentially ominous predictions about the future, "Nosedive" is one of the episodes that comes strikingly close to reflecting our current reality.[37] We have devised scenarios that stretch the limits of our reliance on social media. On NBC's reality television series *The Circle* (2018), for example, participants are placed in living quarters together and communicate only via social media platforms.[38] The individuals rate each other, and ultimately block the least popular folks from their accounts while rewarding the most popular individuals. Folks already use systems to rate individuals—including with respect to skills (such as Uber drivers and fantasy football players)—and appearance (such as the "hot or not" website).

Furthermore, going "viral" on social media may cause the affected individual to experience great success or failure. This point is examined on an episode of *The Office* (2005–2013). In the episode "A.A.R.M.," salesman Andy Bernard auditions for an *American Idol*–like singing competition.[39] Andy whines to the judges about not being selected and his tantrum goes viral: memes are created based on the incident, and he is the butt of jokes across the Internet—including on social media platforms. And, in the "Promos" episode of *The Office*, we watch Andy vacillate between feelings of elation and anger as he reads online comments about his banjo playing.[40] The *IFC* series *Brockmire* (2017–present) is premised on the notion that a viral Internet video could define and ruin an individual—in this case a famed sportscaster—and lead to his career downfall.[41] Social media is a dominant force in contemporary society, and, as in "Nosedive," ratings and comments posted on such platforms could have a measurable impact on an individual's life.

The social and economic hierarchies generated by the social media platform featured on "Nosedive" are eerily similar to the class systems created by the Chinese app Sesame Credit.[42] Pilot versions are currently in use, and the Chinese government aims for full implementation by 2020.[43] The application utilizes data to track and rank what folks do, and assigns a credit rating to the individual. One main distinction between a financial credit rating and Sesame Credit's social credit system is that Sesame Credit's rating is highly dependent on social factors, such as how much charity given by an individual, whether the individual takes care of his or her parents, and how much time the individual spends on certain activities, such as playing video games.[44] Scores could reportedly decrease if an individual "run(s) a red light, criticize(s) the government on social media or sell(s) tainted food to customers."[45] The application blacklists some individuals for relatively minor offenses—such as a $70 theft of cigarettes.[46] Millions of Chinese nationals have already been blacklisted from booking flights and buying train tickets.[47] Like the rating system on "Nosedive," the score is also affected by the rankings of those with whom the individual socializes.[48] The score, which ranges from 350–950, is intended to be used to either grant access to, or exclude folks from, aspects of society.[49] The social credit score has the effect of treating some citizens as more important and valued than others. As journalist Mara Hvistendahl recounts after receiving a low ranking from a beta version of the system, "I belonged to the digital underclass."[50]

These scores determine how an individual will be able to navigate through life. For example, a low social credit rating could mean that the individual needs to pay deposits on bike and hotel rentals, while higher-rated individuals need not do so. The app appears to be integrated with China's List of Dishonest People, and users have reported being excluded from luxury hotels, obtaining bank loans, booking high-end travel seating and being banned from using certain forms of travel.[51] Those folks with higher scores receive more favorable loan rates, are given an expedited path to obtain a visa and are featured prominently on dating websites.[52]

The rating system in Chinese society allows the government to encourage social behavior that it deems appropriate and punish behavior of which it disapproves. The factors used in this compliance mechanism are entirely within the control of the government and are subject to change at any time. If the government wishes to strongly discourage the use of video games, for example, it could decide to place great weight on that factor in determining the individual's social credit score. The punishment could have a meaningful impact on an individual's quality of life. According to the CEO of Sesame Credit, the system "will ensure that the bad people in society don't have a place to go, while good people can move freely without obstruction."[53] *The Week* also reports that "video surveillance will track everyone through facial recognition" software contained within the application.[54] Another app launched in China lets users know if they are within 500 yards of an individual who is in debt and also encourages folks to report such individual to authorities if they appear capable of making payment.[55]

Even if folks are not as obsessed as Lacie with their social media rankings, they should be concerned about the potential consequences of their social actions and inactions. China seeks to merge Big Data and modern technology to quell dissent and engender social behaviors that conform to government-defined conduct standards. As Chinese social commentator and novelist Murong Xuecun observes, the system "is like Big Brother who has all your information and can harm you in any way he wants."[56] Because citizens could be penalized for their seemingly innocuous social actions in this increasingly Orwellian society, they cannot—unlike the brunettes in "Nosedive"—afford to be apathetic. The social credit system is the worst fear of civil libertarians, who are skeptical of government and seek to bolster individual liberty by advocating restrictions on the ability of government to interfere in the lives of its citizens.[57] The social credit system in China presumably lacks any system for due process before a score is lowered. The system is also devoid of any checks and balances over government overreach and further intrusion into the personal lives of individuals. Unlike a well-structured (and fair) criminal justice system—which metes out punishment based on statutes, case law precedent and a fair adjudication of issues—the pilot social credit system in China does not have necessary protections that would put citizens at ease. Citizens will likely (and understandably) feel a constant sense of anxiety over potential consequences of their social behavior.

The Chinese social credit system has elements in common with other worlds presented on both *Black Mirror* and *Electric Dreams*. For example, in *Black Mirror*'s "Fifteen Million Merits," access to many aspects of society (such as the ability, in one's home, to turn off digital advertisements for pornography) is dependent on how much the individual pedals on a stationary bicycle. The common theme is that access to benefits in society is dependent on questionable factors that are controlled and determined by an outside force. The government could, for example, arbitrarily decide to require the commission of a specific social action, conversion to a mandated religious faith or completion of an approved exercise routine in exchange for integration into society. Alternatively, the government could punish social behavior that it deems inappropriate by cutting off access to services, thereby making life more challenging for the affected individual. Government's use of Big Data and technology to repress and crush dissent and silence alternative viewpoints is reminiscent of *Electric Dream*'s "Kill All Others" and "Safe and Sound." In both episodes, government actors use highly intrusive and invasive monitoring systems to track the movements of those considered "outsiders" by the empowered elites in the respective societies. Technology is used by the governments in these societies not to democratize the spread of information or enhance the marketplace of ideas, but rather to silence and punish dissent.

Rating systems are explored in other films and television shows as well. On Netflix's *The Good Place* (2016), for example, such a system is used to determine whether an individual advances to heaven or is sent to hell.[58] And the concept of a rating system is closely linked to the inclination of folks to influence the behaviors of others. In the film *Nerve*, for example, folks who sign up to play a game perform outlandish tasks at the request of "watchers."[59] The goal of each player is to impress and increase the number of their watchers and move up in the game rating system. The film examines several themes, including the depths to which watchers will attempt to control the players' actions, and the limits (if any) ambitious players will place on the actions that they will take. And in the Netflix film *Cam*, women attempt to outdo each other to increase their rankings as they perform erotic acts on their webcams.[60] By acting in such a way, folks are not true to themselves; their actions are informed by the desires of others. The protagonist's obsession to move up the ladder in both *Cam* and *Nerve* mirrors Lacie's passionate desire to do so. In both cases, the behavior of the protagonist is effectively dictated by this compulsion. And each protagonist considers his or her own willingness to perform to be a laudable objective—one that is in fact viewed as a badge of honor by those encouraging them to act.

These cases—along with other examples, such as "Shut Up and Dance"—explore the desire for folks to control others. Just as technology does not cause folks' desire for status and to impress others, however, the human desire to exert control over others is not a recent phenomenon nor is it a byproduct of technology's influence in the world. The propensity for folks seeking to enslave each other is not a newly discovered phenomenon that did not exist prior to the introduction of technology; rather, innovations are a facilitator used by malicious actors to achieve such objectives. The fact that folks use contemporary technology to manipulate others should not surprise us if we are prepared to honestly assess human behavior throughout history. The desire to use technology for such insidious purposes extends beyond a personal, individual level; authoritarian-leaning governments seek to use contemporary innovations for purposes of consolidating political and socioeconomic power and control.

And rating systems have found their way into societies beyond China, as it is not the only place where "Nosedive's" ranking system closely mirrors reality. For example, the original version of an app called "Peeple," which has been referred to as "Yelp for People," "gave users the capacity to rank any person around them on a star system."[61] Uber has announced plans to block low-rated riders in Australia and New Zealand.[62] China (through the government-linked company ZTE) has also exported monitoring technology—in the form of the "fatherland card"—to Venezuela, which gives the Venezuelan government the ability to monitor, reward and penalize citizens.[63] The potential dangers of this objectification of individuals by others has, fortunately, not gone unnoticed. In addition to the potentially quantifiable penalties from governments, the social consequences are quite ominous and jarring. As columnist Caitlin Dewey observes, "One does not have to stretch far to imagine the distress and anxiety that such a system would cause even a slightly self-conscious person; it's not merely the anxiety of being harassed or maligned on the platform—but of being watched and judged, at all times, by an objectifying gaze to which you did not accept."[64]

"Nosedive" provides a picture of the momentary, utterly meaningless, fleeting glee that an individual often feels when her past is liked or ranking elevated. Because the ranking system in the episode (just like the number of followers an individual has on Twitter) is not static and is constantly subject to change, there is no option for an individual to rest on her laurels if she wishes to remain relevant in the social media universe. The desire to continue to gain ever-more followers and "likes" leads to addictive behavior. Researchers at Nottingham Trent University found that "it may be plausible to speak specifically of 'Facebook Addiction Disorder' ... because addiction criteria, such as neglect of personal life, mental preoccupation, escapism, mood modifying experiences, tolerance and concealing the addictive behavior, appear to be present in some people who use [social networks] excessively."[65] Intellectual property attorney Richard Raysman refers to Facebook as an "opioid," pointing out that his wife is unable to relax when they arrive at a restaurant until she takes a photo of her food and posts it on her account.[66] Folks seek to repeatedly attain the "high" that they feel when their post becomes popular, or after gaining new followers. Social media is an insatiable animal because the popularity metrics contained therein require constant attention. A post that garners a great deal of attention will, in short order, quickly be forgotten and supplanted by new, fresh posts.

Despite how high someone may climb on the social media ladder, the possibility of a swift downfall always exists. Soon after we watch Lacie build up her ranking and reach near-privileged status, she experiences a quick and precipitous fall—hence the "nosedive" episode title—leading to her social media demise. Until she arrives at the wedding, Lacie never does anything seriously wrong or offensive throughout her plunge—except if we consider the expression of natural emotions such as anger and frustration to be offensive.[67]

The scariest part of "Nosedive" is not the possibility of losing one's social status because of a few (seemingly innocuous) missteps. Instead, it is the idea that some obsessed folks may plan every action and inaction based on social media planning and metrics. When Lacie is invited to be the maid of honor at the popular woman's wedding, for example, she is overjoyed not by the prospect of celebrating the marriage, but rather by how her ranking would increase. And the bride was not seeking a true friend to be by her side. Rather, she acknowledges that she chose Lacie specifically because of Lacie's up-and-coming status. The bride believed, based on the statistical analysis conducted by her team, that the choice of Lacie would play well with the social media universe and help raise the bride's social media status.

Social media obsession does not only cause individuals to miss out on life; the addiction also informs actions and effectively controls and dictates life. In Lacie's world, relationships only work if an anonymous sea of social media users approve of them. There is no freedom of emotion, of actions or of inactions in this universe. The folks are slaves to their phones and other streaming devices. Smiles are devoid of true feeling. Anger is punished. The individuals living in this world are less human than the artificially-created beings that we see in many other *Black Mirror* and *Electric Dreams* episodes. Their social media obsession has made these individuals operate as blondes. The sad reality is that life has lost true meaning for these folks.[68]

But a few brunettes co-exist beside the blondes.

The Brunettes

One such brunette in this episode is Lacie's brother. He is largely apathetic with respect to his mediocre social media ranking. He implores Lacie to understand that highly ranked individuals are only superficially happy and lack true meaning and joy in their lives. Lacie instead chooses superficial rankings and association with someone that she should despise over the unconditional love of her brother. Rather than using social media to form a closer connection with someone who cares deeply about her, she uses it to forge an opportunistic alliance with the bride—a woman who had previously betrayed her.

Another brunette is a low-ranking truck driver who picks up Lacie as she attempts to hitchhike to the wedding. She explains to Lacie that she used to care about her ranking, but became apathetic once her "4.3" husband fell ill with cancer and was denied treatment because he was not a "4.4." By breaking free of the barriers and constraints of that system, the truck driver can freely express herself and openly reflect on the world and its shortcomings. Although society discriminates against her and she therefore cannot access certain benefits, she lives a life replete with thoughts and emotions—all of which she feels free to express.[69] She realizes that self-worth should not be tethered to an individual's social media ranking, especially when that ranking is contrived and is based on an individual acting solely to impress others. The truck driver's life experiences are much more real, and, by extension, valuable, because they are *hers* and do not belong to the social media community.

The inherent value of expressiveness has previously been examined throughout popular culture. In Lois Lowry's dystopian novel "The Giver," for example, the reader is introduced to a community without pain or emotional depth.[70] The society lacks color and memory, and individuals conform to the "Sameness" prevalent throughout society. In George Orwell's "1984," freethinkers are labeled as "thought criminals" and the size of dictionaries is reduced to more easily allow the government to control and define language and the expression of language.[71] In the film *Pleasantville* (1998), color, love and emotional outbursts are introduced into an unsettlingly wholesome and extremely bland society.[72] In the satirical thriller *The Stepford Wives* (1975), a photographer suspects that the emotionless and submissive housewives may be robots.[73] And *The Twilight Zone* episode "Number 12 Looks Just Like You" (1964) explores a world in which individuals do not express themselves with distinct physical appearances.[74] The common theme in these television shows, films and movies is that passion, creativity and free expression are critical components of a well-functioning society. Society should nurture these ideals, not repress and penalize open thought.

Lacie's prison scene is both informative and symbolic. We watch her and another prisoner, sans phones or any other electronic device, yell out loud insults at each other. She is now liberated, unshackled from the confines of digital screens and ratings systems. The lesson here is that Lacie becomes freer in prison than she was on the outside because she is no longer beholden to a social media platform. Her predicament has allowed her to reevaluate and scrutinize her relationship with technological devices. Prison gives her the ability to express herself freely, without regard for how the outside world may react. The emptiness of social media could pose a risk to how—and what—we value in our world. If our primary concern is achieving a high ranking or gaining new followers, we could potentially fall victim to forgetting what is meaningful to us in our own lives. We watch Lacie, for example, rely on rankings to inform who she forms relationships with, how she interacts with others, and who and what she likes and dislikes. Our value systems could be altered by the semi-democratic, yet largely anonymous, social media platform and voting process. We are reminded of the wedding speech that Lacie had prepared, in which she observes that "In this world, we're all so caught up in our own heads. It's easy to lose sight of what's real, what matters." We know, of course, that Lacie had lost perspective of what is important. It is not unreasonable to expect that prison will open her eyes, however, and we are hopeful that she will live an emotional, reflective, expressive life going forward. She may in fact become a brunette.

While social media was perhaps intended to be used as a mechanism to advance individual expression, we need to be mindful of getting caught up in the number of "likes," "friends" and "followers" that we have, and instead try to remain true to our own identities and realities.

Calculating Love: Charting an Algorithmic Course to Cupid

Social media and online dating websites and applications are frequently used to find romantic partners. This phenomenon is explored on *Black Mirror*.

The episode "Hang the DJ" (2017) is a satirical examination of online dating websites and applications, free will and the power of love in a technology-obsessed society. The following examination of this episode intentionally disregards the surprise ending and treats the situation that we are presented with as reality as it appears to exist in this fictional world.

In the episode, we meet Frank and Amy, individuals who sign up to an online dating system that dictates who they date and for how long. The pair instantly form a strong connection, but the "System" sets the expiry date for their relationship at only 12 hours after they first meet. After the System terminates their relationship, they each date other individuals, each for preset durations, until the System pairs up the couple again. The System frequently reminds the couple that each relationship happens for a reason and that data collected during the relationship is processed and ultimately used by an algorithm to produce a more informed picture of an individual's relationship preferences.

Online dating websites in contemporary society present individuals with access to profiles about many potential romantic partners. While such sites allow individuals to have more options to meet romantic partners, the System in "Hang the DJ" serves as a matchmaker—effectively eliminating individual freedom. Paradoxically, the System hearkens back to a time during which prearranged marriages were more common. Individuals are not free to naturally build relationships according to timelines that they decide. They are required to remain in relationships that they may consider uncomfortable or worse. Amy opines that life must have been much more difficult when folks made their own dating selections, and Frank believes that having such free will would lead to "option paralysis." They agree that the System makes life simpler, in that all relationship-related decisions are "mapped out" by the technology. Frank's characterization of the utility of the System is reminiscent of the narrative promulgated by dictators in totalitarian societies who seek to dismantle and eliminate individual rights and liberties. While there is an advantage to avoiding the overwhelming prospect of freedom and the corresponding benefit of not overthinking one's options in life, the lack of freedom in making choices tears at the fabric of what it means to be human. If all our choices are made for us, we necessarily question the meaning of life and our place in the world. Furthermore, the fact that the System makes choices for individuals does not guarantee happiness for those folks—despite the System's promise of a statistical 99.8 percent ideal match success rate. The evidence to back up the statistic is both circumspect and unverifiable; it seems not only dubious but impossible to prove or disprove.

It is fair to wonder (as Frank and Amy do) how technology could understand human emotion and desire, especially if an individual expresses those feelings in a more cerebral or less physical or conspicuous manner. Furthermore, individuals take different amounts of time to open up with new partners, and it would seem that the System would not be able to account for this variable during short-term relationships.

The System creates unnatural relationships and dynamics—often forcing individuals to either form a bond together if they want to "enjoy" a preset long-term relationship with a partner or restrain emotion during short-term relationships when in fact the pair do feel an initial connection with each other. Individuals are required to either waste their time in long-term relationships destined to end or fruitlessly yearn for additional time with a partner that they like. The episode invites us to ask whether we would allow technology to bind us together or tear us apart when our hearts and minds desire otherwise. Would we remain complacent, subject to the output of algorithms or, alternatively, seek to rebel and escape from the harness?

We may not be too far away from a reality in which technology could in fact determine, with a reasonable degree of accuracy, whether a relationship has staying power. Some experts expect that by 2021, digital assistants (such as Alexa) will, by analyzing couples' conversations and interactions, "foresee the chances of staying together to within 75 percent accuracy, and by 2025 they will tell if there is sexual chemistry between couples."[75] Such devices might also help determine if couples are "well-suited" to be together at the initial stages of a relationship.[76] If we introduce technology that accurately predicts whether a relationship will survive, how big a leap is it to imagine giving technology the power to determine when a relationship *should* end based on its observations?

The System—and other potential applications of similar technology—merits thoughtful consideration because of its unique attributes. It is noteworthy that no human beings are involved with determining romantic matches. The algorithm relies on artificial intelligence to produce its output. The System analyzes the results of each simulation to generate a response, and *learns* from the results of each relationship when determining its next simulated match.

"Hang the DJ"'s brilliance lies in its contextual examination of online dating, and possible extensions of our contemporary usage of this service. Online dating websites are a prime example of an innovation where humans intend to use technology to achieve an end (in this case, enter a relationship) but where the means of achieving that end change so significantly that it calls into question the initial intended purpose. It is fair to question the inherent value of a predetermined match and relationship in which the folks involved must follow the rigid instructions of a technological system. Taking the episode at face value, it seems, throughout most of the episode, that human beings are expected to follow the strict orders of technology. They have seemingly relinquished to technology significant freedoms—the ability to choose who you meet, date, marry and have sexual intercourse with—without having any idea of *how* the algorithm works, or *why* it creates or breaks specific relationships. Instead of humans managing our own relationships, it is technology that manages them for us. Even if we are impressed by the technology and convinced by its metrics, we can imagine scenarios where reliance on technology in this fashion would be extremely dangerous. Perhaps a hacker, for example, could covertly manipulate the algorithm for nefarious purposes, forcing unknowing individuals to pair up to achieve the agenda of the hacker. Repressive governments could similarly alter the algorithm to pair up folks to achieve desired ends. Or, if artificial intelligence advances in an uncontrollable way, it is conceivable that it could use this type of technology as part of its strategy to conquer humans, intentionally forcing folks into destructive and unhealthy relationships.

Use of online dating websites in contemporary society is pervasive. According to Hayley Matthews, the editor-in-chief of the website Datingadvice.com, 2017 marked the year during which "online dating became the most common way for newlyweds to meet one another."[77] *The Knot* reports that 19 percent of brides (surveyed in a poll of 14,000 individuals) state that they met their spouse online.[78] Annual revenue captured by the online dating industry exceeds $3 billion. Matthews also cites evidence to support her claim that "online marriages are less likely" than marriages where the spouses met elsewhere to end within the first year.[79] She attributes this statistic to the utility and effectiveness of "personal compatibility algorithms," which, she argues "work exceedingly well and yield great results for relationship-minded users."[80] Matthews cites a *Forbes* article to support her contention that such sites "facilitate ... longer lasting connections."[81]

According to statista.com, "30% of Internet users aged 18–29 currently use dating sites or apps and an additional 31% had done so previously."[82] Folks use such sites and apps for a variety of purposes, including for purposes of seeking meaningful, long-term relationships, casual relationships and sexual encounters. Given the size of the industry, large number of competitors, and diverse business models and approaches, it is understandable that the owners of an app such as the System would seek to obtain a competitive advantage (i.e., use of virtual simulations) to generate desirable results for users. We see companies in real-life compete in this crowded marketplace by seeking such advantages by similarly relying on and boasting about proprietary algorithms.

For example, the popular relationship website eharmony.com requires users to complete a "Relationship Questionnaire." The company's proprietary algorithm analyzes those responses and matches a user to other users based on a comparison of their respective outputs. Much like the System in "Hang the DJ," eHarmony offers a "Guarantee," promising that: "We guarantee you will be satisfied with the matches we introduce to you at eHarmony" and offering three months of the service for free if satisfaction is not achieved. eHarmony's proclamations of pride and effectiveness in its process and algorithm go well beyond the user guarantee. The company has claimed that it has a "scientifically proven matching system." An advertising watchdog in the United Kingdom prohibited eHarmony from making this claim because it could not prove that its relationship service is more effective or appropriately suited to creating meaningful, lasting relationships than other sites or sources.[83] Just as it is not possible to prove or disprove the System's 99.8 percent ideal match promise, it is impossible to independently verify the validity of eHarmony's "scientifically proven" marketing slogan. The intent of such declarations is to convince a potential user that a technological algorithm based on a formula comprised of secret elements is superior to other means of finding relationship partners. Advertisements appearing on eHarmony's website highlight this point: "Try eHarmony with complete confidence and rest assured that you're getting the best experience possible." Like the supreme confidence that users are supposed to place in the System—no questions asked!—eHarmony users are asked to sit back and place their full faith in the website's ability to find compatible individuals to match with each other. Should users do so even if they do not necessarily agree with the matches?

"Hang the DJ" raises important questions about the utility, in the context of searching for love, of using algorithms that make effective use of data. As a general matter, technology is not particularly well-equipped at understanding emotions (such as love) and the intangible elements of which they are comprised. As our technology becomes more powerful, it is, however, conceivable that the metrics used to understand human emotion and decision-making may also become more advanced. If we are somehow able to demonstrate that an algorithm *is* better at finding relationship ideal matches for folks, would it be fruitful or wise to fully rely on technology for purposes of finding love just as we use predictive analytics in other contexts?[84] Would we—or should we—ever proceed down a path where we might relinquish some or all our free will and trust an algorithm's relationship-seeking metrics and process? Should governments seek to ban or regulate such technology, or, alternatively, should we be free to choose to utilize such technology, understanding that a system like the one shown on "Hang the DJ" may require periods of unhappiness while moving through the dating process? What if it could be shown, statistically, that reliance on the process leads to a reduced divorce rate and greater happiness? Even if the evidence points squarely in this direction, perhaps it is better to retain our freedom and *own* any poor choices that we make. Perhaps this process of trial and error and constant discovery is what makes life worth living—and maybe this process would seem too unfulfilling if a dating system mapped out all our love-related strategies, actions and inactions. It is in our interest to continue to exert control over technology, rather than the other way around. As technology becomes more powerful, debating the pros and cons of its usefulness and effectiveness—and the extent to which usage should be regulated—are essential if we want to make sound, reasoned decisions with respect to how to best manage technology.

The Hashtag Democracy of Death

The *Black Mirror* episode "Hated in the Nation" (2016) tackles many of the issues addressed throughout this book, including social media obsession, vigilantism, artificial intelligence, privacy, security, digital humiliation, environmentalism, exercise of free speech, criminal accountability, hacking and the use of the Internet as a democratizing force (i.e., "net empowerment.") Excluding the film *Bandersnatch*, it is the longest *Black Mirror* episode to date—with a length of 89 minutes.

In the episode, "honeybee-mimicking drone insects" known as ADIs are used by a computer hacker to kill targets identified by social media users. The episode is structured much like a police procedural series, as two detectives work feverishly to solve murder cases. The detectives (Karin and Blue) quickly discover a link between the murder victims: each was the recent target of users' wrath on social media because of his or her controversial behavior and the subject of an ominous "#Deathto" hashtag. An expert hacker had devised a scheme—or what he refers to as the "Game of Consequences"—wherein folks choose a target, post the target's name and photo on a social media platform using "#Deathto" and the individual with the most votes in this public ballot will be killed by an ADI in an incredibly painful fashion after 5 p.m. each day.

The hacker's written manifesto expresses his dismay that individuals could hide behind the Internet's cloak of anonymity, and that their online expressions typically have no real-world consequences. While it might seem as though the hacker's primary objective is a morbid form of "net empowerment"—whereby individuals are free to express their views online, with measurable, salient consequences—his ultimate goal is even more haunting. As if it were not bad enough to pervert democracy for such an ignoble and morally repugnant purpose, the hacker also wants to punish the voters—none of whom use the hashtag with any knowledge or even suspicion of any real-world consequence—with death. The hacker / game designer wants to hold the unwitting game players accountable for their Internet behavior, teaching the world a "moral lesson" in a deleterious and insidious manner. The use of the bees to carry out this grand plan also seems largely symbolic—not only should the hashtag targets be killed, so, too, should the players experience the excruciatingly painful sting that is the consequence of their collective Internet behavior.

The episode raises important questions, such as whether those using a "#Deathto" should bear any moral and/or legal responsibility for the end result of the users' cumulative online posts. Many social media users in the episode and in contemporary society do not take their online musings seriously. And even if there is *some* thought prior to making a post, it can often be appropriately characterized as venting, merely expressing a momentary sentiment. As Detective Karin observes, "that Internet stuff drifts off like weather. It's half hate. They don't mean it."

Black Mirror reflects contemporary anxieties with respect to potential failures of our existing legal system to deal with issues raised by the introduction of emerging technologies. The show also forces us to question whether speech on the Internet should remain largely unregulated. The Internet was not yet in existence when most freedom of speech laws in the United States were developed and precedents made through decisions by the United States Supreme Court. Should the emergence of the Internet lead us to re-examine our current legal system's constructs and freedoms as they relate to speech? Is our current legal structure adaptable to these changes or is the system too antiquated—and ripe for revision—as a result of modern mediums of communication? Charlie Brooker acknowledges that he is not sure of the most appropriate answers to questions like these and also adds that he is generally not an advocate for additional restrictions on free speech. He keenly observes, though, that advances in technology require us to at least reconsider existing norms and standards given the changing landscape: "I think it's like we've evolved an extra limb—social media is just like we haven't worked out how to walk with three legs yet—we just keep banging into the walls."[85] It seems that modern technology has perhaps advanced more quickly than our legal system on issues relating to the free speech.

On the question of accountability for one's online posts and the consequences that emanate indirectly therefrom, the answer is similarly murky. Criminal law in the United States requires an *actus reus* (i.e., acts or omissions that comprise the physical elements of a crime), *mens rea* (i.e., criminal intent or a guilty state of mind) and a showing of causation in order to hold a defendant responsible for his or her actions.[86]

The government is permitted to regulate speech if such speech incites or is likely to incite violence.[87] The general right to exercise free speech is not a viable defense in such cases. Since the users of the hashtag (presumably) do not intend their posts to be used to threaten or harm the targets of their posts, however, it seems that they lacked the requisite *mens rea* to be responsible for a serious crime, such as first or second-degree murder.[88] The failure to possess a criminal intent in connection with the act of posting would be a strong defense a potential criminal charge. A prosecutor may argue that the *mens rea* element can be satisfied for less, though still serious, crimes even if the actor did not intend a specific result. For example, a crime such as "criminally negligent homicide addresses situations where a defendant is aware of a situation, should know it's dangerous, but ignores a risk that results in a death of another."[89]

In the context of the "Game of Consequences," a defendant may argue that he or she should not be responsible for the first death because he or she had no reasonable expectation (and a reasonable person under the same or similar circumstances would not reasonably be expected to have such expectation) that his or her use of a hashtag would lead to the death of the hashtag subject.[90] The game players were completely unaware that they were playing a game at all, and it seems unreasonable to impute knowledge of the game when determining criminal responsibility. This argument is weakened as more victims of the game emerge: at some point, it seems reasonable to impute an assumption that the hashtag user knew or *should have known* that the hashtag could influence the killing of the target. Even in those cases, however, a defendant could argue that their overt act of posting did not directly cause the individual's death. The defendant could argue that the killer's act was an "intervening cause." But if the killing was foreseeable, then it would not be deemed a "superseding cause," and henceforth not absolve the defendant from liability. If, however, the killing was not foreseeable, the prosecution would need to demonstrate that there is a direct link between the negligent action of the defendant and the death of the individual—although the prosecution could turn to the felony murder doctrine, holding an individual criminally responsible for deaths caused during the commission of a felony (if the game playing is considered a felony). Here, the defendant could argue that the killing could have occurred had he or she not participated because thousands of other individuals posted the same hashtag and the vote count would have led to the same result absent the individual's participation. The prosecution would have a difficult time arguing that, in the case of the individual defendant (as opposed to the collective whole) that the defendant's post was both the "but for" and "proximate cause" of the death.[91]

Even if the *mens rea* and causation requirements for a specific crime are met, however, it may be difficult for a prosecutor to argue that the use of the hashtag was a sufficiently overt action—a direct threat—against the subject of the hashtag. Regarding a social media posting that is not sent to the individual subject or (to the knowledge of the individual posting the content) any hitman who could carry out the act, it is unclear that an indirect message posted on the Internet would constitute a criminal action. Free speech near-absolutists would argue that the 1st Amendment to the United States Constitution protects speech of this nature. Even if it can be demonstrated that the post incited others to act, the words could be interpreted as an expression of disgust about a person, not a direct threat to harm the individual. While it is true that direct online threats to cause injury or death to an individual have constituted crimes, those causes differed because of the specificity of the threat and an explicit direction and incitement to carry out a violent act. In such cases, the speech appeared to constitute more than an expression of a desire, but instead an urgent call to action. It is a stretch to argue that "#Deathto" with no other specificity, request or demand for others to commit an overt act would satisfy the *actus reus* element.

A prosecutor would have similar difficulty arguing that the defendant's post could satisfy the elements of a criminal conspiracy charge.[92] There was no collective effort on the part of any of the game's participants to have the hashtag target killed. In fact, the hashtag users were manipulated and themselves targeted by the creator of the heinous crime.

In sum, it appears that our current legal system is not well-equipped to deal with some of the nuances of online threats—that is, if we feel that protecting individuals from such threats outweighs the benefits and virtues of near-absolute protections for free speech. The question of whether to more extensively regulate—and perhaps even criminalize—types of Internet speech is a complex question, demanding critical thought about the pros and cons of taking or not taking such action. Assigning a gatekeeping agency to watch over Internet speech sounds like a recipe for controversy. Such an agency would likely, based on political disposition, strive to either satisfy either free speech near-absolutists or individuals in favor of heavy regulations on speech—and would inevitably anger and provoke one side or the other much of the time. Brooker's view is that folks should be more careful about what they say and do online, and perhaps face consequences for certain condemnable online behavior: "People should be more accountable for what they say. It's just difficult to see how you do that without the law getting involved."[93]

In addition to the potential legal implications of participation in the "Game of Consequences," "Hated in the Nation" also forces us to consider the moral consequences of an individual's Internet behavior. Individuals should adapt their behavior to reflect the reality that their posts—even hyperbolic ones—could be taken seriously. It is reprehensible and unjustifiable to make irresponsible online posts that bully, threaten or make fun of others—

even if legal culpability is not a feasible punishment. Such posts, however, are commonplace and reflect our current reality. As television columnist Alex Mulane observes, "Hated in the Nation" is "a great example of how the show at its best can merge its heady high-concepts with more traditional storytelling to effectively hold that black mirror up to our own society."[94]

Technology provides a forum for individuals to express ideas that they previously held internally and did not communicate openly. Detectives Karin and Blue reminisce about a time long gone by, where folks still made "kill lists" and had other dangerous thoughts, but just kept these thoughts in their own heads. While Brooker may be correct that the "problem" we have is a "human one"—that is, that our thoughts, actions and motivations often have adverse consequences—there is no denying that technology plays a pivotal role in the expression and distribution of deleterious content. As one of the detectives observes, nothing today is private: "These things," she notes, looking at her phone, "absorb who we are. They know everything about us." This comment is in line with the sentiment expressed by Elon Musk when he noted that our digital devices are, in effect, extensions of ourselves.[95]

"Hated in the Nation" also uses satire to examine whether the democratization resulting from a largely free and open Internet is beneficial to society. The film *Nerve*, which features "watchers" who vote for what ignominious acts should be performed by the "players" raises similar questions.[96] As a general matter, the anonymity of individuals using the Internet creates a sense of unaccountability and unbridled, uninhibited freedom. The cover that the Internet provides not only promotes a free exchange of ideas; it also provides a mechanism that allows bad actors to easily disguise themselves and insert themselves into areas where they may otherwise be unwelcome. Those seeking to covertly disrupt an election, for example, can effectively wear a costume and employ bots to promote a political agenda. On the one hand, perhaps there is some virtue to discounting the source of a message and instead relying solely on analyzing the substantive content contained therein. On the other hand, however, there are dangers inherent in this approach. As discussed earlier, the source of information helps us to determine how we perceive the veracity of the message—and that is an important and necessary tool to have at our disposal in the modern context of "fake news" dissemination.

Because of the lack of accountability on the Internet, it is impossible to gauge the level of attention afforded to an individual's online behavior. This message is explored in several *Black Mirror* episodes, such as "Nosedive," where we see that digital interactions are often shallow and fleeting. We should be careful not to rely too heavily on the outputs of digital transactions—especially those involving voting. For example, query whether the

Internet is an ideal forum for Major League Baseball or the National Basketball Association to use for purposes of recording all-star ballot votes. Should we limit the nature and scope of projects and initiatives that are determined by crowdsourcing? If we are to rely on the outcomes and products of Internet-based voting, should folks be incentivized to vote responsibly by threatening that their identities could be revealed, even if the reveal is not likely to result in legal culpability—a point examined in both "Hated in the Nation" and *Nerve*? "Hated in the Nation" forces us to ask these questions, calling into question the utility of collective empowerment via the Internet and whether, and to what extent, we should promote a free and democratic vision for the Internet.

Next, let's examine the privacy and security-related considerations in technology-infused universes.

4

Privacy and Security-Related Considerations in a Hyper-Techno World

> "We live, in fact, in a world starved for solitude, silence and private: and therefore starved for meditation and true friendship."
> —C.S. Lewis, *The Weight of Glory*[1]

On *Parks and Recreation,* Parks and Recreation Department Director Ron Swanson is a member of a jazz ensemble. He uses a pseudonym (Duke Silver) to conceal his identity and meticulously avoids telling any of his friends or colleagues of his musical talent or that he is a member of the group. Swanson's desire to maintain his privacy is consistent with other actions in his life—he dismisses technological innovations that superficially connect folks with each other; he is angered when he receives mail from any person or company who has dared to learn his home address; he retreats to his cabin, frequently in isolation; and he even declines to advise his co-workers of the birth of his child. While some of Ron's perspectives, actions and concealments may be considered a bit extreme, Swanson's agenda is noteworthy in that it can be sharply contrasted with those in society who seek to increase the number and scope of their connections with others—revealing much—too much?—personal information about themselves in the process. Ron's decision not to hide details about his life to others underscores the immense value he places on the ideal of privacy, despite the hyper-connected world in which he lives. Perhaps Swanson unnecessarily overvalues his privacy, at the expense of forging bonds with others.[2] It may also be the case, however, that many folks sadly fail to adequately emphasize individual privacy as they march through life—losing too much of their personal space in the process. Are our lives necessarily enriched in all or most respects as a result of our digital connectedness? Or, as philosopher Hannah Arendt posits, is a "life spent entirely in public, in the presence of others" a "shallow" one?[3]

Philosopher Ayn Rand argued that "Civilization is the progress toward a society of privacy. The savage's whole existence is public, ruled by the laws of his tribe. Civilization is the process of setting man free from men."[4] In effectively decrying the concept of global interconnectedness—wherein privacy considerations fall to the wayside as folks interact more frequently with each other, revealing more of themselves—Rand asks us to question whether building connections with one another at the expense of relinquishing our personal space is a laudable goal. Privacy scholar Alan Westin similarly argued that individuals need "moments 'off stage' when the individual can be himself ... a respite from the emotional stimulation of daily life."[5] Perhaps ensuring the sanctity of our privacy is an essential component of maintaining our dignity, personal liberty and sanity. If we reveal too much about ourselves, what, exactly, are we trying to protect by employing enhanced security measures? Can our use of technology be repurposed so as not to violate valued privacy norms? Would doing so advance or impede our conception of "progress"?

Popular culture explores dystopian universes wherein folks are required to relinquish their privacy if they wish to flee the adverse conditions in which they live. In "Fifteen Million Merits," for example, participation and victory in a widely-broadcast talent show is required for escaping the monotonous, meaningless existence of pedaling stationary bicycles. Becoming a celebrity and conceding privacy is a prerequisite for leaving the doldrums, an environment comprised of screens streaming mindless entertainment to distract the masses.[6] In the film *The Show* (2017), contestants on a warped reality show exhibit an intense desire to escape poor life circumstances and are willing to broadcast their extreme suicides in front of a global audience.[7] Such folks fail to retain privacy even in their final act in life.

Everyone desires some level and degree of privacy. But privacy has different meanings to different folks. In most circumstances, individuals would like to choose what they expose and reveal to the world. And if our expectations of privacy are not satisfied, we may choose to alter our behavior. Take a basic example. On the *Curb Your Enthusiasm* "The Doll," Cheryl David enters a bathroom without a functioning lock.[8] When a man enters and sees her indisposed, Cheryl defiantly tells Larry that she will no longer attend events where the man may appear as a guest for fear of running into him. Her desire to avoid an embarrassing situation due to her exposure leads her to alter her behavior. Other common situations in which individuals attempt to maintain their privacy are examined throughout popular culture. Celebrities often seek refuge from the public, for example, so that they can maintain their privacy—as Alec Baldwin and Kim Basinger do on *The Simpsons* episode "When You Dish Upon a Star."[9] And folks may be hesitant to speak or act freely and openly if there is a chance that their words or actions are being recorded.

Sometimes folks agree to forego some of their privacy for a discreet purpose. For example, the workers on *The Office* (apparently) consent to being subjects of a documentary on office life in the United States. They are followed around with cameras and are equipped with microphones, which pick up their voices. But, unbeknownst to the workers, their voices are recorded and secret moments filmed without their knowledge.[10] The workers pull out their microphones when they do not want to be recorded and retreat into rooms without videographers when they want to be alone or address matters in a private way. They panic when they find out that hidden cameras and microphones picked up those moments that they had intended as private. The camera crew had designed these countermeasures to ensure that the documentary would reflect a more accurate depiction of their work and personal lives. The office workers presumably did not provide informed consent—though perhaps the agreement that they signed, if any, advised them of this approach. Were the workers duped when entering into this arrangement? Did they have the power to decline or opt-out? As evidenced by their frenzied response to the news that their private moments may be exposed, the office workers would have presumably altered their behaviors had they known that they were being filmed all the time.

What'ya Gonna Do When They're Watching You?

As modern technology steadily extends its scope and reach, it is fair to say—without much more than a hint of hyperbole—that we might be being watched and recorded all the time. We live in a surveillance culture, where governments and corporate actors watch us to maintain control, exploit us and manipulate our thoughts and behaviors for political and commercial purposes. The existence of such a culture is generally known, but the extent to which we operate in the dark—without having knowledge or awareness of what is going on behind the curtain—is frightening. Calo observes that:

> [M]odern computer users don't necessarily feel as though they are being tracked. We may know, as an intellectual matter, that somewhere, someone might eventually pick up on our digital trail. But the experience of searching, surfing or emailing is actually a lonely one. We're aware of no operator lurking on the line. In the moment, we don't

expect anyone other than our intended recipient to read our email. We don't expect any company employee, hacker, or government official to link our searches with us, personally. Modern communication overwhelmingly feels anonymous, even when it isn't.[11]

We should be cognizant of the possibility that we are frequently being watched. As we develop technologies that allow us to interact with the world differently, we often sacrifice our privacy rights. When America Online introduced instant messaging, for example, we communicated mostly with friends and largely via words. As technology has advanced, we reveal more of ourselves—photos, locations, etc. ...—to strangers. We put ourselves at increased risk of danger by voluntarily engaging in such exposure.

Today, our Internet browsers record our search histories—inserting this information into algorithms designed to create profiles of us to be accessed and used by political and commercial actors for years to come. Our Fitbit devices record our exercise habits. Insurance companies use invasive techniques and devices to track our habits, including whether we take medicine. Our Alexa devices record what we say for sixty second windows—and, because of a reported technical flaw, have in some instances apparently transmitted our conversations to others.[12] Overhead cameras take pictures of us running red traffic lights. Dating applications (such as Tinder) collect information about us and help us find potential romantic partners and mates (see "Hang the DJ"). We use tracking devices such as Xplora and Jiobit—not entirely dissimilar to the technology featured on "Arkangel"—to watch over our children. Amazon has patent protection for wristbands that track and steer employees' movements (reminiscent of the health-monitoring devices employed in "Kill All Others" and the physical tracking technology used in "Safe and Sound").[13] Our embarrassing and disgraceful private moments can be recorded without us even knowing it—whether in public or in the comfort of our homes (see "Shut Up and Dance"). Companies use drones that could record information about our homes from overhead (see "Autofac"). Our social media and Snapchat accounts along with dating applications, armed with powerful GPS technology embedded on our cell-phones, advise both friends and strangers of our physical locations (see "Shut Up and Dance"). Those devices may also reveal our interests, birthdays and political preferences to others (see "Nosedive"). Some regimes with authoritarian leanings have begun to use monitoring systems (such as social credit applications and "fatherland cards") to watch, reward and punish citizens.

We must be aware that we could be recorded at any place and time (as we see in the camera-streaming dating guidance model explored in the first part of "White Christmas," where the privacy of both a man and the woman he seeks to meet is invaded), and that our social media footprint may continue to subsist following death (see "Be Right Back").[14] As artificial intelligence and other technologies become more advanced, we run the risk of losing privacy in the most intimate of areas—from thoughts ("The Hood Maker") to memories ("The Entire History of You," "Crocodile") to dreams and subconscious thoughts (see the film *Inception* [2010]) to the way that we see ("Men Against Fire").[15] The potentiality of bringing robots into our homes (see *Humans*) or being inundated by interactive advertisements displaying digital images of folks (see "Kill All Others") or using digital assistants (such as Alexa) that may soon have the ability to predict, if not dictate, the staying power of our intimate relationships (see "Hang the DJ") presents additional concerns from a privacy perspective.[16] As Calo states, "Technologies that introduce the equivalent of people into our homes, cars, computers and mobile devices—places historically experienced as private—threaten our dwindling opportunities for solitude and self-development."[17] Even though we know that the robots and interactive digital images are not real, we still often feel as though we are being watched by them. And, as Calo's research demonstrates, we frequently adjust our behavior accordingly.[18]

In sum, we are constantly surveilled not only by friends and family as we "check in" to events and locations on our social media accounts, but also by corporations trying to sell us products; political organizations seeking to understand (and manipulate) our preferences and influence our votes; governments attempting to address security (and perhaps) undisclosed concerns; schools trying to recruit us; malicious folks seeking to steal our identities and cause us economic and social harm; strangers gathering information about us for the purpose of dating us; and governments seeking to exert authority and control over the mundane aspects of our lives.

Given the status quo and the ever-expanding landscape of a technology-infused society, it is fair to wonder whether our exposure is so significant that there is simply no turning back. As we engage with newly introduced innovations that help us save time and energy, we take on significant risk. Clara Shih, the Chief Executive Officer of the digital marketing platform company Hearsay Social acutely observes that "With new technologies promising endless conveniences also comes new vulnerabilities in terms of privacy and security. And nobody is immune."[19] We recoil at the sensational thought of hackers accessing sensitive data about us through security breaches, but do we sufficiently examine the often-unnecessary risks that we take on in our daily lives? Do we consider the implications of voluntarily providing so much information to individuals and entities who may not have our best interests at heart—from political actors to marketing agencies to corporations? In short, it may be too late to take back what we have lost—our privacy, and, with it, our freedom to operate without watchful eyes peering in as we move through life. Are we at the point of no return, having already relinquished anonymity and autonomy? Or, as *Black Mirror* and *Electric Dreams* ask, is there even more to lose?

In our technology-obsessed world, we tend to repeat hackneyed slogans relating to privacy and security-related considerations without giving sufficient thought as to their substance. Our historical experiences with the introduction of new technologies showcase our eventual willingness to adopt such technologies, even if we were at first hesitant, skeptical or wary of doing so. Such adoption often comes at the expense of both privacy and security. Contemporary trends suggest that we are gravitating towards a largely privacy-free world. For example, an Internet meme reminds us that in 1998, we were warned: "'Don't get in a car with strangers'; in 2008, we were also warned not to 'meet people from the Internet alone.' But now, in 2018, we find ourselves neglecting both of those warnings as we use the Uber car service: 'Order yourself a stranger from the Internet to get into a car with alone.'"[20] As our technologies become irresistible, we frequently find ourselves gradually drifting away from adherence to privacy and security-related principles that have sustained us and served us reasonably well throughout the years. Instead, our thoughts and decisions are more frequently dictated by, and closely aligned with, corporate and government interests than we would care to acknowledge.

We tell ourselves that maintaining privacy and enhancing the security of individuals, governments and corporations are paramount considerations, but fail to acknowledge the sacrifices that folks would have to make to advance these objectives in a meaningful way. We preach and feign allegiance to these dual and largely quixotic agendas while unabashedly and perhaps recklessly exploiting technological innovation for our common benefit—often wildly unaware of the necessary steps that would need to be taken to achieve the professed ends. We frequently volunteer information about ourselves openly on the Internet via blogs and social media platforms (see "Nosedive"), blissfully ignorant and unsuspicious of the potential for unintended consequences if such information falls into malicious hands. Suffice it to say that our actions and omissions are often inconsistent with the objectives stated above. Striking an appropriate balance between several competing agendas—from maintaining our liberties, enhancing our security, ensuring our privacy to obtaining the benefits of technology—requires discipline, patience and a nuanced understanding about the pros and cons of immersion in technological innovation. As a general matter, human beings are not particularly well-equipped to engage in the foregoing if doing so provides constraints on our ability to achieve efficiencies. If we do not place significant value on the ideal of privacy—or if such considerations are deemed less important than the benefits obtained when privacy is sacrificed—it seems possible, if not inevitable, that we stand to lose much more moving forward.

Depending on the context, technology can be used as a mechanism to both provide increased layers of security—helping to ensure our safety—while also affording criminals with enhanced capabilities to cause significant harm. A similar split exists with respect to privacy considerations as well: while the Internet frequently allows folks to hide behind a cloak of anonymity (on message boards and the like), it also allows corporations and political organizations to track our online movements and preferences. We can lock ourselves in our basements and use pseudonyms when logging onto the Internet, but we are never quite alone. We are being watched and tracked, even while attempting (often in vain) to conceal our identities from strangers. And we may not even know it.

Privacy (or a Lack Thereof) in The Twilight Zone

Privacy considerations feature prominently in some episodes of *The Twilight Zone* and lurk as part of the thematic backdrop of many others. In "A Penny for Your Thoughts," for example, a man possesses the power to read the thoughts of others.[21] He invades the privacy of others, making incorrect assumptions when interpreting those thoughts. We realize that while an individual's thoughts provide a window through which to understand the person, more background is needed to fully grasp an individual's motivations. A similar concept is examined on "The Entire History of You," where memories can be accessed in a vacuum without the associated underlying context for a previous experience. This theme is also explored on *Electric Dreams*' "The Hood Maker," where a Teep (Honor) reads the thoughts of a Normal (Agent Ross) but is unable to determine his feelings toward her: "You can read minds but you can't read my heart!," Agent Ross tells her.[22] Even advanced technology that provides access to an individual's personal information and data does not tell us everything there is to know about a person. Governments and corporations would be wise to take this lesson to heart, as the invasion of our private thoughts and moments may not be as informative as they might wish to believe. The broader lesson in these episodes is that even powerful technologies frequently have limitations: they typically lack a "human touch"—be it determining emotion or figuring out the intended meaning behind grammatical ambiguities.

Privacy considerations are explored in several other episodes as well. In "People Are Alike All Over," human beings are placed in their natural habitats for alien observers to see—a scenario resembling the ways in which we watch animals in a zoo.[23] In "Where is Everybody," a man becomes uncomfortable (and possibly paranoid) as he begins to believe that he is being watched.[24] And in "Time Enough at Last," a man seeks solitude so that he could read books without the bothers or pressures of others pestering him for attention.[25] In all these episodes, folks perceive privacy as an important ideal worthy of preservation.[26] In the contemporary age of recording and interconnectedness, it is fair to question whether individuals place similarly high value on maintaining personal privacy. *Black Mirror* and *Electric Dreams* tackle this question through their exploration of the potential introduction of various technologies.

Seeing and Dreaming

What if governments could infiltrate our minds, directly impacting our dreams and the way in which we see and experience reality? *Black Mirror*'s "Men Against Fire" invites us to ask this question and to consider whether living in a world of distorted reality—even if it insulates us from unsettling images—is desirable or even sustainable. By invading our dreams, uploading artificial images as we sleep, the government invades our personal space during our most intimate moments. A similar concept is explored on an episode of *Futurama*. In the episode, "A Fishful of Dollars," corporations insert advertisements into folks' dreams.[27] The intent is to influence folks' decisions in a similar vein to the way in which subliminal messaging is intended to affect decision-making processes of folks in *The Simpsons* episode "New Kids on the Blecch" (relating to military recruitment) and "The Zack Tapes" (relating to dating).[28]

In "Men Against Fire," the military also violates the sanctity of perception by altering our vision. Because of the MASS implant technology, we literally cannot believe our own eyes.

If the government can control what and how we see and dream, it can exert its will over us. And technology may soon exist that enables the government to alter the way in which we remember our experiences.

Remembering, Experiencing, Changing and Deleting Our Memories

In the film adaptation of George Orwell's novel "1984," lovers Winston and Julia observe that while the Party has the power to torture individuals and make them pledge allegiance to the State in both word and deed, it does not have the ability to get inside of individuals—to see through to their hearts.[29] We are rightfully protective of our memories, a place to which we could retreat—our "homeland" on which we could build a "palace," in the words of painter Anselm Kiefer.[30] The way that we feel is personal to us and outside forces and actors have generally been unable to infiltrate our innermost emotions—those which we may not reveal to anyone in the outside world. For the most part, the way that we internalize and process our thoughts and experiences has been a right and ability that we retain exclusively—unencumbered by the prospect of innovations allowing others to peer into our minds. As social critic Arthur M. Schlesinger, Jr., observed, "Science and technology revolutionize our lives, but memory, tradition and myth frame our response."[31] "Every man's memory," novelist Aldous Huxley pointed out, "is his private literature."[32]

But what if technology advances to a state where it allows other individuals to read our thoughts (such as in "The Hood Maker" or "A Penny for Your Thoughts") or access our memories? This moment may not be far away. In a *Vanity Fair* article entitled "Apple Predicts *Black Mirror* Memory Implants Could Soon Be a Reality," journalist Maya Kosoff reports that Elon Musk's start-up company Neuralink is in the process of developing a "neural lace technology" that involves "implanting tiny electrodes that may one day upload and download thoughts," and will presumably include features that allow for sharing such thoughts with others.[33] And Kosoff quotes Apple executive and Siri co-founder Tom Gruber stating his belief that it is "inevitable" that "A.I. will make personal memory enhancement a reality."[34]

The way that we remember something—a person, a place, an object—informs how we interact with the world. Because our past experiences influence the way in which we will act prospectively, technologies that enable third parties to manage the memories of others can ultimately affect the behavior of the subject, as they provide the third-party actor a mechanism to exert control over future actions—a phenomenon examined on the television series *Homecoming* (2018–present).[35] Furthermore, if a third-party can review a subject's memories, the reviewer would likely learn more about the subject than he or she wishes to reveal. But the subject might not engage with the world in the same manner if he or she fears that someone might access such memories. This is a logical extension of Calo's observation that our behavior will likely be influenced due to the prospect that we may be watched.[36] We might be embarrassed to perform an action or attend a controversial event for fear that others might rewind the tape of our lives. We may become less innovative and more conformist, more obedient. We would likely express ourselves less freely, more carefully. In short, we would not be ourselves. And eventually we might not have a clear idea of what exactly we have lost; we may have trouble defining ourselves because we have behaved in a guarded manner for so long.

The result of such a technology may be that we ultimately do learn not only to behave differently, but perhaps think and feel differently. We may need to adapt in this way if we want to survive and thrive in a world where memories are accessed by others at will. We will not only behave differently; we will *become* different, too.

Contemporary science fiction has explored the storage of memories and transference thereof (see, for example, the cortical stack storage device featured on *Altered Carbon* [2018–present]).[37] The dystopian worlds of *Black Mirror* explore memories from a variety of angles, introducing technologies that impact how we remember and share memories with each other. These worlds examine some of the possible consequences of memory storage, loss, enhancement and erasure technologies. Fear of losing memories is a theme in "Playtest," as Cooper's anxiety results largely from his desire not to develop senility like his father. Memory loss by artificial means features prominently in "White Bear," as the episode invites us to consider potential abuses of technology that erases memories. Manipulation, brainwashing and enslavement are some of the possible consequences that could result if authoritarian regimes or other bad actors gain access to such technology—concepts also explored in other contexts (see *Eternal Sunshine of the Spotless Mind*, *Homecoming* and *Westworld*).[38]

The technologies presented on "Crocodile" and "The Entire History of You" redefine how folks view the importance of maintaining the privacy and sanctity of memories. It is difficult to conceive of anything more internal and personal than one's recollections of, and thoughts about, the past. Memories are at the core of who we are. It is, in the words of historian Thomas Fuller, "the treasure house of the mind wherein the monuments thereof are kept and preserved."[39] As Nobel Laureate and Holocaust survivor Elie Wiesel poignantly observes, "Without memory, there is no culture. Without memory, there would be no civilization, no society, no future."[40] The way in which we interpret our past experiences informs our prospective interactions with the world.

In "The Entire History of You," folks use a memory implant known as "the grain" to record all their memories. Individuals frequently rewind the "tape," displaying past events, exactly as they had seen them, on screens. Folks can and do watch their memories over and over again. This ability invites folks to share such visualizations of memories with each other: they can compare notes and use the memories for evidentiary purposes—to resolve arguments and to examine and critique important past conversations and events. The folks in this society become addicted to the grain, obsessing over reviewing videos of the past—perhaps to the detriment of experiencing the present and living life to the fullest. They do not place supreme value on the privacy and personal nature of an internal memory. They voluntarily—sometimes eagerly—share the visualizations with others.

The episode invites us to imagine scenarios where an individual's grain is stolen and sold off to perverts or other malicious actors for their viewing pleasure.[41] A hacker might attempt to use the implant for other nefarious purposes—such as blackmail or extortion. The possibility of folks using accessed memories for insidious purposes is explored in *Eternal Sunshine of the Spotless Mind*, where a man's memories are used by another man in an especially creepy type of identity theft: the third party deceptively uses the accessed memories to develop a romantic relationship with a woman; by artificially knowing what the woman likes, he impresses her and builds a relationship in an entirely unnatural way.[42] We can also consider the effects on the individual, and potentially—the search for the truth—if a hacker creates and implants false, artificially generated memories into the grain (see *The Twilight Zone*'s "The Lateness of the Hour," where robots are equipped with an artificially-produced memory tract).[43]

Individual privacy could also be invaded in less extreme, more mundane scenarios as well—such as prospective or current employers requesting access to memories stored on the grain for purposes of conducting background checks on employees or airport security conducting security checks on travelers. While potentially useful for such purposes—if we disregard the potential for fraud—the technology presented on the episode also enables a user to edit or delete individual memories. This feature calls into question the fundamental purpose of the technology: if memories can be removed or revised at will, the evidentiary function and value of the memory implant is dubious. While it may be true (as one user in the episode mentions) that memories are not only inherently subjective but also unreliable and subject to manipulation by outside actors, the ability for a user to make changes to one's memories lessens its potential for use in high-stakes situations where accuracy is critical to a resolution of an issue.[44] The difference is that the implant can be manipulated only by the user—that is, unless the implant is hacked and altered by a third party actor.

The use of technology for evidentiary purposes is not necessarily desirable—even if accuracy is somehow guaranteed and achieved. One context where this issue is debated is the implementation of instant replay technology in sports. Traditionalists opposed to its introduction have argued that deference to calls by umpires and referees—even if such calls may rightfully be objectionable on the merits—is a fundamental part of the game. They acknowledge that receiving a call in or against one team or player's favor is partly a function of luck—especially on close plays. Because the sports world has historically functioned without the option to use replay technology, there is little question that numerous calls and games have been decided incorrectly. The introduction of replay technology therefore places the modern sports game on a different level—it changes, in some ways, the nature of the game itself. Umpires are less important—casualties of automation—if their judgment could constantly be reviewed and corrected. Does that take anything away from the game itself? Does increased accuracy make contemporary sports competitions different than in previous years? Should historical records be marked with an asterisk, identifying this distinction? Is the value of tradition lost by introducing instant replay or is achieving accuracy the primary and fundamental concern and objective, justifying the introduction of the technology? Are concerns for speed and momentum in the game—all of which would be adversely affected if the game is slowed down to review replays—trumped by the ideal of achieving accuracy?

Just like the debate within the sports world—which was largely resolved by effecting compromises as to when and how frequently instant replay can be used—there are considerations at play other than a general desire to access accurate memories. The ability to engage in self-delusion, for example, is a critical feature of exerting control over, and innate subjectivity with respect to, our memories. If we experience trauma, for example, we might wish to forget it, skip details or channel it in a way that allows us to deal with it in a more productive—if not comfortable—fashion. The subjective way that we remember (or fail to remember) a memory can be an important defense or coping mechanism. Conversely, even if we can effectively delete or modify a memory using artificial features and processes, are we letting ourselves off the hook too easily? Our brains might act on their own to store information in a way that is perhaps more suitable for a variety of reasons. What dangers could arise should we tinker with this natural ability to process and store memories and information?

We might abhor the prospect of others asking to see our memories and we might edit our memories for the sole purpose of impressing others—especially if there is merit to Tom Wolfe's contention that we are always concerned with achieving and maintaining a high status by gaining the praise of others. We might not feel comfortable with sharing either our unadulterated or modified versions of memories with others and may be eager to hit the delete button. Yet if these feelings are reasonably likely to arise—a desire to engage in self-delusion, or a pressing impulse to impress others; or a general desire to maintain privacy—what objective does the memory implant achieve? What is its "value-add"? We can clearly identify what is at risk: the sanctity and privacy of our memories. They are ours and we lose a great deal by editing them, deleting them, sharing them and thinking about how others will react to them. And if we are comfortable sharing and editing physical manifestations of some of our memories, we already have tools for doing so—namely, cameras and photoshop software applications.

We also must acknowledge that gaining access to someone else's memories—as we see in "The Entire History of You"—can have unintended consequences. The potential for modifying memories to serve an agenda cannot be discounted; doubts as to the reliability of a memory may lead to chaos and confusion. But dangers exist even if the accuracy of the memory is somehow verifiable. We might learn, for example, what someone thinks of us, or about an affair that could cause us emotional harm. Gaining more information is often deemed an unquestionable good, a laudable goal, but learning hidden secrets could also hurt us. Ignorance is sometimes bliss, and nature intended that individuals be permitted to maintain their private thoughts and recollections without foreign intervention or oversight. This is one of the essential themes of "The Entire History of You." In the context of our spousal relationships, if we remove our rose-tinted glasses and see each other for who we really are and all that we have done over the course of our lives, would we—*could we*—remain in love with each other? Exercising the ability to read thoughts or access memories might be destructive to our social fabric; the structural relationships between individuals, those on which society is based, might begin to crumble if not entirely collapse.

While it is not entirely clear from "The Entire History of You" whether deletion of a memory from the grain also removes the memory from one's brain entirely—in other words whether the grain is a back-up repository or an actual replacement for the brain's ability to store memories—it is worth considering the impact of a technology that replaces the brain's memory functionality in its entirety. If we were to possess the ability to completely remove a memory, we might decide that we need not bear the burden of remembering the happy moments spent with a now deceased family member or experienced during a failed relationship, since the act of remembering could conjure up feelings of sadness. As the ancient Greek tragedian Aeschylus observed, "There is no pain so great as the memory of joy in present grief."[45] But should we exercise such a power? What would result if we could simply delete any memory that we do not wish to see? Would this produce a populace that is ill-equipped to handle stressful, traumatic or disappointing situations? Would technology that is most effective at deleting memories also require the removal of ancillary memories that are tied in some way to the primary memory at issue?

Popular culture has explored these scenarios. For example, we see the negative effects of the deletion of primary and ancillary memories in the dark drama *Eternal Sunshine of the Spotless Mind* (2004), where the protagonist experiences a series of gaps and lapses after purging memories of an ex-girlfriend.[46] The film follows the man on this dark journey, and the audience witnesses how confusing it can be to live life with an incomplete set of memories. Not surprisingly, the man experiences a distorted version of reality, unable to rely on the past to understand or engage with the future. And in the television series *Homecoming* (2018–present), a corporation erases the disturbing memories of war veterans, intending to make the veterans more durable, less emotional and therefore better prepared to return to the battlefield.[47] The soldiers initially react positively after memories are removed: they report feeling better about their lives and are not weighed down by mistakes and sadness from their previous war mission. The soldiers do not provide consent for this initiative, nor is the technology refined enough to delete only harmful memories; instead, ancillary memories are frequently deleted as well—leaving the minds of the soldiers lacking context and depth for other aspects of their lives. Deletion of their memories changes the soldiers, as they exhibit a lack of emotion about the past; their responses to events are muted. They are, in some respects, less human, more artificial. By deleting memories, folks ultimately become more stoic, more robotic and less empathetic as they lack the proper context in which to consider actions and consequences. The series invites us to consider practical considerations as well: what if military training memories are deleted, leaving the soldiers dangerously unprepared and ill-equipped for return to the battlefield? These soldiers are effectively treated like machines, so the corporation presumably deems them replaceable and does not value their lives.

It is decidedly unnatural to possess an artificial ability to store, edit and categorize our memories, or to "over-remember" or "over-delete" therefrom. The concept of deciding which memories we should retain—and how such memories should be retained—takes an essential power away from us: the ability to naturally, without selective, artificial intervention by us or others, forget. Taking away this natural power—or conversely, giving us too much power in this context—disrupts the way that we process, retain and retrieve information. And an individual may come to regret the decision to modify or delete a memory, the latter of which is the central focus of *Eternal Sunshine of the Spotless Mind*.[48] Removing or adjusting our memories to serve an agenda changes how we recall and understand our interactions with the world. In short, altering the way that we remember makes us a bit less human.

A host of Constitutional and other legal questions are raised by the introduction of the memory implant technology. Should law enforcement, for example, ever possess the right to change our memories if doing so would remove knowledge of a dangerous skill that we might have learned (e.g., such as a visual memory of how to produce an illegal weapon?) Would it be reasonable for law enforcement to rely on the content stored on a memory implant if the origin of the content is not verifiable? Even if the source of origin is knowable, would use of the content in a criminal context—to be used against a defendant—violate Constitutional due process protections? Are these concerns mitigated if the chip was initially planted voluntarily? What measures would need to be in place to prevent abuse—such as an unscrupulous law enforcement official forcing a suspect to delete or modify memories under duress? Conversely, if the source of origin is verifiable, should a defendant be permitted to use the content as exculpatory evidence? In both contexts, what assumptions would an adjudicator be permitted to make about memories that may have been deleted or edited by the user or other actor?

The episode—like many others—also invites us to consider whether it is a story about "someone whose natural tendencies are enabled by a piece of technology," per episode writer Jesse Armstrong.[49] Is it, as Armstrong suggests, "a cautionary tale about someone getting tech that allows the latent bad parts of their character to come out"? Or does the technology itself *create* such bad attributes, changing the tendencies of humans?[50] Brooker, Armstrong and Serling tend to believe that for all its power, technology does not often alter our desires or inclinations; instead, devices such as the "grain" allow such tendencies to flourish, for good or ill. Our focus and behaviors may change as the result of the introduction of new technologies, but it may be the case that such technologies awaken dormant, natural aspects of the human spirit rather than producing new elements of our characters. Other episodes, such as "White Christmas," explore this phenomenon as well. When a man's emotions consume him upon learning the truth about his wife's child, for example, we are left to consider to what extent the "blocking" technology contributed to his distress. Would he not have been similarly distraught had such technology not masked the truth? Or can we rightfully place the blame on the technology, since it forced the man to bottle up his emotions until he exploded? The technology may have not created his feelings, but the masking of the truth seems to have led to a more combustible and horrific conclusion.

Extracting Memories

In *Black Mirror*'s "Crocodile," an insurance adjuster logs folks' recollections about car accidents by hooking them up to a recall machine—which she refers to as a "corroborator." The machine provides the adjuster with a visual of the subject's memory. The gripping episode explores the inherent limitations of subjective memories and demonstrates that technology can help, but not entirely eradicate, the phenomenon of inaccurate memories. By collecting various recollections, the adjuster proceeds to build a "crowd-sourced picture of reality." This portrait is enhanced by using familiar sensory references—playing a song or sniffing an aroma—that were present at a particular place and time to shine light on the memory. In this way, the formation and transmission of the memory is not organic. The use of this process is consistent with our perception of memory as an art. As Japanese scientist Susumu Tonegawa noted, "Recalling a memory is not like playing a tape recorder. It's a creative process."[51] Folks can attempt to manipulate the recall device by inventing and conjuring a synthetic, faux memory that will show on the reviewer's screen. While it may not be easy to dispense entirely with a memory that we desire to forget—"Nothing fixes a thing so intensely in the memory as the wish to forget it," as French philosopher Michael de Montaigne observed—the idea that memories are not malleable by a variety of factors is patently false.[52] Consistent with the notion that memory development is a type of art, Philosopher John Dewey poignantly observed that "Time and memory are true artists; they remould reality nearer to the heart's desire."[53] In a society where third parties can access an individual's memories, the incentives for artistry and fictionalization of events increase. And because memories are framed and influenced by emotion, often altered for purposes of serving as a defense mechanism, their veracity is dubious. They are frequently flawed and their potential usefulness in a law enforcement environment or for purposes of settling an insurance claim is highly questionable.

But the idea that technology cannot effectively solve the memory inaccuracy problem is not the central issue explored in "Crocodile." The episode suggests that by gaining access to memories, a third party might delve into a hidden world in which secrets are stored—the release of which could wreak unpredictable havoc. In the episode, the insurance adjuster is woefully unprepared when a subject's memory reveals that she is not a witness but rather a murderer. This reveal leads to a slew of other murders, all as part of a rushed cover-up. Experience tells us that human beings will often go to significant lengths to hide evidence of crimes from others. The implementation of technology that makes it harder to do so does not deter the criminal; ultimately, it just sows more unnecessary harm and destruction. The other instructive lesson is that invasive technologies could make folks paranoid (here, killing a baby who is a potential witness to a murder, but is revealed to be blind), but perhaps not lead to a sufficient level of observance (as we learn when law enforcement hooks up a gerbil who witnessed some of the murders). Still, as entertainment reporter Travis Clark notes, "it could be argued that Mia is driven mad more by her own guilt and selfishness than by any technology"— once again showcasing Brooker's contention that our biggest problem is ourselves not our technologies.[54]

A thorough consideration of the potential ramifications of implementation of this technology unmasks other dangers. Those who have access to the memories of others are empowered not only to document such memories in legal reports to solve crimes, but also to wield power and control over the subject. Nefarious law enforcement officers might extort and blackmail folks over collected memories. Malicious actors can hack memory storage devices. Once an embarrassing moment is released from one's brain, its ultimate landing place is entirely unpredictable; even if a scrupulous law enforcement promises not to reveal such moment, there is no guarantee that such agent will one day not be hooked up to the recall machine—leading to another party gaining access to the embarrassing memory. The parade of horribles is frightening.

Perhaps most significantly, once a memory is released to a third party, the subject no longer has any semblance of privacy—despite the adjuster's proclamation to a subject that "private is private." While under duress, the adjuster promises a subject that an incriminating report and footage will be deleted. The subject questions whether it is possible to delete, raising the broader idea that once something is released, it is difficult to remove. The Internet is a perfect example of this phenomenon; a blotch nearly always turns into a permanent stain. Privacy cannot be effectively retrieved or restored once it is lost.

While the adjuster advises a subject that she will not include irrelevant embarrassing moments in her report unless such memory reveals causing physical harm to the subject or others, the collection of memories is ripe for mismanagement and abuse. The use of such technology in a law enforcement context raises serious due process-related questions. Should a witness ever be compelled by a court to submit memories to the recall machine? Would the concept of "informed consent" be relatable in this context? Would 5th Amendment protections against self-incrimination apply in the memory recall context? Could the use of subjective, potentially inaccurate memories from witnesses be used against a defendant in a criminal or civil context? Would a "crowd-sourced" depiction of a memory provide ample support for inclusion as a matter of evidence? Or should extracted memories always be deemed inadmissible, given the significant likelihood of fraud or unintentional inaccuracies? Since we do not always exclude witness testimony based on memory, why should there be a different standard for memory visualizations—especially if they are corroborated by other witness memory accounts? Alternatively, would a defendant be permitted to introduce a memory of his own or from a witness to support his case? Would all societies require a warrant for use of the recall machine against a suspect? What if a warrant is obtained to obtain access to a specific memory, but other, incriminating memories are also accessed? Could a witness become a suspect (as in "Crocodile") if a memory is seemingly incriminating? Would such other memories be used against a defendant in criminal or civil contexts? How would the statute of limitations apply in the memory context? Would a memory of an event that took place outside of the prescribed limitation period be excluded from evidence, or would exceptions to the statute be considered in the memory recall context?

Given the subjective nature of memory, overreliance on a memory extraction tool in a legal context seems ill-informed and dangerous. But would that stop authoritarian-leaning regimes from implementing such technology in their societies? And even in societies with robust and fair systems of justice, is there a place for such technology in the courtroom? Despite potential inaccuracies, a memory arrived at in good faith perhaps should hold some weight—even in high-stakes legal settings. If we agree with novelist Barbara Kingsolver that "Memory is a complicated thing, a relative to truth, but not its twin," perhaps it could be useful as part of a case, albeit not as the sole evidence necessary and sufficient for conviction.[55] Under existing legal standards in the United States, evidence can be introduced in a criminal trial if it satisfies certain thresholds—most importantly, whether its relevance outweighs its prejudicial nature. The reliability of evidence that is introduced is a matter for the factfinder.

The circumstances in "Crocodile" lead to a scenario where the murderer and insurance adjuster pit one technology against another to achieve an objective. For example, the murderer seeks to create an alibi by renting a film and disposing of the body while it plays. The assumption is that the hotel will time stamp the rental, eliminating the possibility that she will be blamed for the murder.

"Crocodile" also raises other privacy-related issues. For example, the insurance adjuster uses facial recognition technology to identify a witness that she sees in a subject's memory. It seems that all folks in society are potentially subject to identification by use of this technology—a concern deemed so significant to Amazon employees that it prompted them to protest (directly to Amazon Chief Executive Officer Jeff Bezos) the company's potential sale of such software.[56] And the use of both the facial recognition and memory recall technologies seems pervasive within this dystopian society: the adjuster advises that the recall technology was previously used only by police but is now used much more broadly. While folks do not consent to the recognition technology, the adjuster makes a half-hearted attempt at obtaining informed consent for use of the memory extraction technology. Each subject is asked to review and agree to the terms of use. But the consequences of failing to agree are unclear. The adjuster states that it is a legal requirement for witnesses of accidents to agree to an interview, though it is less clear whether use of the technology is a strict requirement. If it is, and if potential witnesses are required to submit to the technology, a review of the terms is effectively meaningless—and the content of the recordings cannot reasonably be considered the product of consent. Consent without a viable alternative is no consent at all. And the nature of the "consent" is also circumspect: are subjects advised of the potential unintended, and often unpredictable, consequences that could indirectly result from the memory recordings?

Behavioral Considerations and Developing Symbiotic Relationships

A theme common to several *Black Mirror* and *Electric Dreams* episodes is that the dearth of privacy in our lives influences our behavior. Lacie's behavior in "Nosedive" is a perfect example. Because she knows that she is always being watched and judged by other folks, she performs actions intended to impress and increase her ranking. She also chooses to refrain from taking actions that might detract from her score. And these "choices"—decisions made based on implicit restrictions on citizens' thoughts and behaviors— serve the goals of authoritarian-leaning regimes because folks will think twice before performing an action that the government may deem objectionable (see "Kill All Others," "Safe and Sound," China's social credit system and the "fatherland cards" in Venezuela).

Artificial intelligence plays an important role in this context as well. We may be more guarded or act in a way designed to impress if we feel that artificially intelligent robots can observe us (see "Be Right Back" and *The Twilight Zone*'s "Uncle Simon").[57] Due to technological advancements, we might be able to document and study these behaviors. For example, a real-world sex doll rental company reportedly creates and sells replicas of deceased lovers, and a study could compare and contrast our interactions with such sex dolls with those we have with natural humans.[58] And a funeral home in Sweden has announced plans to use voice recognition software and virtual reality to produce digital substitutions of deceased individuals.[59] Perhaps most stunningly—and closely connected to "Be Right Back"—a company called Luka designed a chat bot to mimic a decedent's speech patterns by "harvesting his social media posts and text messages," and translating such data into deeds.[60]

Such innovations may also allow us to consider the relationship between Calo's arguments regarding the impact of human-looking robots on our behavior and Marshall McLuhan's theory that the "medium is the message."[61] If a robot gives us information, would we consider it more or less reliable than information we receive from a natural human? What is the nature of the symbiotic relationship created between humans and "lifelike" robots? If our behavior is directly tied to the way we perceive a robot in terms of its physicality and similarities to humans, would we also be more likely to view such robots as a reliable medium of communication? Would the value that we place on the information be tied to how closely the robot resembles a natural human?

Control and "Chilling Effects"

Sometimes, the owner of a recording containing private and/or sensitive footage seeks to use such tapes to exert control over a subject. In *The Office* episode "The Lover," Dwight hides a recording device in Jim's office with the stated intent of trapping and destroying Jim.[62] In "Arkangel," a teenager declines to engage with a girl he likes after the girl's mother secretly records their drug-related encounter and threatens to release the footage to authorities. Folks in "Shut Up and Dance" are similarly subjected to blackmail based on covertly-made recordings. While the actions of the victims of these blackmail schemes are rightfully deemed disgraceful (and sometimes illegal), it is worth considering whether society should be concerned when folks record each other without obtaining consent and then seek to use those recordings for their own benefit.

The absence of privacy threatens to have a chilling effect on "the expression of eccentric individuality."[63] Watchful eyes can inhibit free speech, inform (and limit) our actions and create an uncomfortable environment where we seek to modify our behavior not only to impress (see "Nosedive,") but also maintain our anonymity (see "Kill All Others"). As Calo posits, "The purposive exploitation of our natural propensity to behave in the presence of others, coupled with our inability to distinguish between real or virtual surveillance, could substitute for direct prohibitions on speech or investigation."[64]

Prying eyes will likely be less interested in those of us who conform to mainstream views and ideas, but may seek to cause damage or harm to those who think, feel or act outside of generally accepted societal norms (see "Kill All Others.") Charles Fried argues that "If we thought that our every word and deed were public, fear of disapproval or more tangible retaliation might keep us from doing or saying things which we would do or say if we could be sure of keeping them to ourselves."[65] We watch Philbert in "Kill All Others," for example, wear a disguise and attempt to conceal his identity when asking an unpopular question at a political event. When his actual identity is revealed, he fears for his life—demonstrating a keen understanding that one of the main underlying purposes of the dearth of privacy and personal space in this dystopian society is to ferret out and destroy dissenters. We can tell by Philbert's reaction that he would not have had the temerity to recite his unpopular views had he known his identity would be revealed. (Note that he also refrains from political dialogue at work for fear of reprisal, even before he is ordered by his boss to avoid such talk.) Environments where privacy rights have intentionally been stripped away from folks are generally not conducive to showcasing creativity or outward expressions of unpopular viewpoints.

Other social consequences could result from a lack of privacy as well. For example, interactions with one another could lead to boring and dull experiences if we expose too much of ourselves to the outside world. "The Hood Maker" takes this problem to its logical extreme: as Honor explains, Teeps do not enjoy dating because of the lack of mystery—they often end up finishing each other's thoughts.

Technology has disrupted not only industries, but also the ways in which we view ideals such as privacy and personal space. United States Supreme Court Chief Justice John Roberts reminds us that "The fact that technology now allows an individual to carry such information in his hand does not make the information any less worthy of the protection for which the Founders sought."[66] But whether we view the conception of privacy with as much zeal as previous generations is questionable. As our technology advances in the modern "age of recording," our ability to retain such ideals, and interpret ideas, concepts and events in ways that we deem fit on a very personal level decreases. The question is whether, and to what extent, we care about this paradigm shift. As we become more connected, we lose a part of ourselves—the opportunity to retreat to our own respective corners and subsist quietly and privately with our thoughts and memories as we interpret them. Might we lose the ability to live in a sometimes-necessary state of self-delusion if we allow devices to record all events exactly as they occurred, negating the way that we would have otherwise perceived any memory (see "The Entire History of You")? If our memories were to become standardized and not subject to debate, it seems that we might relinquish the very personal ability to naturally remember as our brain so desires, negating a helpful defense mechanism used by folks throughout history. The warning here is that if we do not have a sufficiently deep appreciation for the ideal of privacy, we will likely be unable to resist technology's incursion into our thoughts and memories. If we fail to draw a line in the sand, it seems inevitable that uses of technology to advance efficiency (at the expense of privacy) will influence not only how we think and behave, but also, sadly, how we remember.

As technology advances exponentially, the opportunities for folks to benefit from such capabilities increase as well. For example, it might have been unthinkable not too long ago that an insurance company would offer lower premiums in exchange for evidence that folks take their medicine daily. One insurer has even required, as a condition of obtaining insurance coverage in all of its policies, that folks exercise regularly—requiring the use of a fitness tracking device.[67] In exchange for the realized economic benefit, the consumer is willing to provide a corporate entity with firm evidence of taking medicine and/or exercising (by video or electronic monitoring). A personal action that may rightfully be considered intrusive is now a viable option for some companies and individuals. Given the current trajectory, what other opportunities will be presented due to continued scientific achievements? Will we give up even more of our privacy? Do we value our personal space and internal thought more than we value the potential benefits that might be attained if we give up a bit more of ourselves? What are the potential unintended consequences that may result due to this trade? If technology advances further, are there limits to the types of intrusions we would accept? Would access to our thoughts (see *Electric Dreams*' "The Hood Maker" and *The Twilight Zone*'s "A Penny for Your Thoughts"), dreams (see *Black Mirror*'s "Men Against Fire") or memories (see *Black Mirror*'s "The Entire History of You" and "Crocodile") be considered out of bounds or off-limits?

Achieving the dual goals of maintaining privacy and enhancing security is made increasingly difficult by voluntarily exposing ourselves on the Internet in a variety of contexts and for a wide range of purposes—from extreme applications of and immersion in social media (see "Nosedive"); to making use of Internet streaming for insidious purposes (see "Shut Up and Dance");

to openly expressing controversial opinions aimed at achieving fame (see "Hated in the Nation"). None of these applications of technology is inherently harmful—use of social media, streaming content and expressions of ideas can properly be considered positive attributes of the Internet in certain respects. However, misguided use of this technology can have negative consequences, including the loss of privacy and susceptibility to security-related harms. Refraining from using the Internet in certain ways in a concerted effort to maintain our privacy requires a type of discipline that is generally inconsistent with past human behavior.

Stop, Drop and Roll? Or Surveil, Track and Control?

The utilization of increasingly invasive and intrusive technological devices could also leave us vulnerable from both privacy and security perspectives. While our intentions may (sometimes) be in the right place, *Black Mirror* and *Electric Dreams* demonstrate that the use of powerful devices could have unintended consequences that could undermine the initial intent. As we watch the story of Jack and Carrie in "Black Museum" unfold, for example, we realize that the device that allows for the transference of Carrie's consciousness into Jack's brain leaves Carrie without any liberty and Jack with a dearth of privacy. We are forced to ask whether we are willing to relinquish autonomy to gain some benefit—even at the risk of battling unintended consequences.

This issue is thoroughly explored in the episodes featuring tracking and monitoring devices—from "Arkangel" to "Safe and Sound" to "Kill All Others." In each of these episodes, those empowered with the devices—parents, corporations and governments, respectively—use their power to exert control over the monitored and tracked subjects. Whether the intentions of those doing the monitoring are noble (such as ensuring the safety of a child, such as in "Arkangel") or insidious (such as tracking the mental health of a dissenting class perceived as a threat to elites [see "Kill All Others"]), the uniform result for the subject is a loss of freedom. Furthermore, actors seeking to exert control frequently lie about the scope of the collection and use of data and the motivations underlying same. For example, in "Kill All Others," Philbert is advised by his employer that data collected by the health tracker is "confidential" and will only be transmitted to the company's human resource department—a highly dubious promise. Philbert is operating under duress (fear that he will lose his job) and with misinformation (the truth is that the "One Candidate" desires to make use of the health monitoring system to advance her objective of eliminating "others" from society). Given the context, questions arise as to the nature and validity of the permission purportedly granted by Philbert: can his assent to the data collection reasonably be considered "informed" or even qualify as "consent" in the first place? The ignominious methods deployed in "Safe and Sound" to gain a user's trust and thereafter affix a monitoring device raise similar concerns as to both consent and the nature of the intended use of the collected data. The issue of consent is explored in greater depth later in this chapter.

"Arkangel" provides an example of a device that allows those doing the monitoring to not only censor the subject's ability to experience the world but also monitor the subject's vital signs and limit creativity (by pixelating the subject's drawings of gory images). Such features present significant limitations on the subject's ability to understand and live life. As episode director Jodie Foster acutely observes, "If you create a false reality for your child, under the guise of protecting them, you're altering the normal course of how a person discovers their own life. You're breaking their independence and controlling them."[68]

And the parental hub device featured in "Arkangel" is subject to inevitable abuse: it is highly predictable that the mother will intervene after she covertly invades her daughter's most intimate moments by watching the daughter have unprotected sex. But instead of talking with her daughter about the dangers and risks of such an action, she secretly slips a "day-after" pill into the daughter's drink. On another occasion, she makes use of the hub's facial recognition technology to track down (and subsequently blackmail) the daughter's boyfriend. The mother uses the device not only to monitor her daughter; she uses the information gathered to secretly influence the events that her daughter will experience.

These restrictions on expression and action are inconsistent with ideals such as freedom of speech and other personal liberties. The loss of liberties combined with a plethora of unfortunate emotional effects resulting from the introduction of such devices should perhaps cause us to pause before introducing them into society.

Some *Black Mirror* and *Electric Dreams* episodes warn us that the introduction and abuse of technological devices might cause us to seek isolation from each other, as we yearn to escape from our powerful, overly-informed, connected, and manipulative devices. "Nosedive's" prison scene speaks to this point, for example. "Arkangel" asks us to consider whether the strong desire to protect a loved one could boomerang, causing folks who are tracked and monitored to have violent confrontations with, and ultimately drift apart from, those in control of the device. If those empowered with the devices mask the realities that we experience, it might be easier for the subject to physically harm those in control of the device. In the episode's brutal fight scene, for example, the daughter beats her mother with a tablet but, because of the parental advisory feature, only sees pixelated images of the carnage until the device breaks. "Arkangel" also invites us to ask whether the tracking and monitoring might also lead to unfortunate emotional consequences. We might even rebel and consider charting a more dangerous course—the hitchhiker's path—as we break free from the shields and layers encapsulating us. Could it be that our overindulgence of devices intended to protect each other and bring us closer together may ultimately (and ironically) separate us? As we run from our devices, we may also seek distance and space from those pushing the buttons.

Privacy and Security: Fair-Weathered Friends or Strange Bedfellows?

Privacy scholar Alan Westin observed that "the individual's desire for privacy is never absolute, since participation in society is an equally powerful desire. Thus each individual is continuously engaged in a personal adjustment process in which he balances the desire for privacy with the desire for disclosure and communication of himself to others, in light of the environmental conditions and social norms set by the society in which he lives."[69] In the "information age," this "adjustment process" requires folks to decide whether the benefits of access to technologies outweigh the harms resulting from the loss of privacy. We strike a balance that we (hopefully) feel comfortable with from a social perspective. But do we engage in a sufficiently robust and comprehensive cost-benefit analysis when the relinquishment of privacy in exchange for social advantages also implicates our security?

The relationship between privacy and security is complex. The interplay between these concepts is often described as a zero-sum game, a scenario in which one ideal must be given up to effectively realize the other. In exchange for sacrificing our privacy, for example, we often feel more secure. But the premise that we are safer due to this trade is circumspect. As novelist John Twelve Hawks posits, "Anyone who steps back for a minute and observes our modern digital world might conclude that we have destroyed our privacy in exchange for convenience and false security."[70] As our devices become more powerful, we often use that power to reveal more about ourselves to the outside world—thereby sacrificing privacy. We are told that our devices are more secure, but we also must acknowledge that as technology advances, bad actors' attempts at wreaking havoc become more sophisticated as well. Our robust security industries are, at least in part, outgrowths and responses to the destructive capabilities of devices readily accessible to those wishing to do us harm. Security professionals are in a constant battle of one-upmanship against individuals with bad intentions. And folks with insidious motivations have a large toolbox at their disposal with which to cause chaos and destruction. Despite the powerful security devices available to us, it is fair to question whether we would ultimately be safer if our technology was far less-advanced. The technology explosion has made it more likely that criminals possess the ability to steal our identities. Malicious actors could use information about us—accessed via electronic devices—for purposes of blackmail (see "Shut Up and Dance.") Technology that is designed to protect individuals from harm or maintain their anonymity and privacy could be manipulated to destroy lives (the abuse of the "Z-Eye" technology in "White Christmas" is an example of this phenomenon). Devices that track our movements—where we agree to relinquish privacy so that we could remain safe—could ultimately cause us harm (see "Arkangel," "Kill All Others" and "Safe and Sound.") Our most advanced, "secure" devices often have unknown security gaps, providing a window of opportunity to sophisticated actors to access, process and use sensitive data in destructive ways—even as powerful weapons (see "Hated in the Nation.")

From a security perspective, it is an unfortunate reality that as we excel at developing devices that help create efficiencies and often protect us from harm, many of those same devices, quite ironically and paradoxically, make us vulnerable to attack. For example, we must be aware of, and to the extent possible, guard against the possibility that commercial drones (such as those featured on "Autofac") or military drones (including those intended to spy on our enemies) could gather information about us from above.[71] The devices that store our data so that we will not lose it and so that it could be accessed more conveniently could be hacked, leading to a loss of data and a host of adverse economic, social and emotional consequences. Data that is encrypted and stored in supposedly secure servers and devices could be accessed and manipulated by expert hackers, causing us serious damage.

In the "information age," data is a critical component of our daily lives. Our ability to function in a world driven by technical analysis of data elements could be significantly disrupted by breaches of our data and other violations of our privacy. *Black Mirror* and *Electric Dreams* highlight some of the ways that our exposure in hyper-connected worlds creates a new type of warfare, one in which people are vulnerable to attempts from many corners to access our data and manipulate our lives. Our overreliance on devices could have a significant impact on our well-being if and when our devices, and, ultimately we, come under attack by forces targeting our sensitive information. These forces include not only lone wolf attackers, but also governments seeking to invade our privacy.

Fourth Amendment Protections

The Fourth Amendment to the United States Constitution prohibits unreasonable searches and seizures by the government. Privacy is not explicitly mentioned in the Constitution, but courts have historically interpreted the Fourth Amendment (as well as others, such as the 9th Amendment) to protect privacy rights in a variety of contexts. Determining whether a violation of an individual's privacy rights is quite fact-specific and necessarily analyzed on a case-by-case basis. Courts must balance the privacy rights of individuals with the interests of the state in taking a specific action. Questions regarding potential privacy-related violations have been addressed in a wide variety of contexts, resulting in a fair number of landmark judicial opinions covering, among other areas: school drug testing policies (*Veronia School District 47J v. Acton* [1995]); warrantless searches of students (*New Jersey v. T.L.O.* [1985]); stop and frisk (*Terry v. Ohio* [1968]); collection of voice samples (*United States v. Dionisio* [1973]); analysis of handwriting (*United States v. Mara* [1973]); the use of GPS technology (*United States v. Jones* [2012]); the collection of DNA from arrestees (*Maryland v. King* [2013]); the use of dogs to collect an individual's scent (*Florida v. Jardines* [2013]); and the warrantless search and seizure of the digital contents of a cell phone during an arrest (*Riley v. California* [2014]).[72]

Advances in modern technology have surpassed an arguably outdated legal system, especially with respect to privacy considerations. The digitization of data contributes immensely to fears of privacy loss. As privacy scholar Will Thomas Devries observes, for example, "The modern evolution of the privacy right is closely tied to the story of the industrial-age technological development…. Unlike previous technological changes, however, the scope and magnitude of the digital revolution is such that privacy law cannot respond quickly enough to keep privacy relevant and robust."[73] The President of the Committee for Justice Curt Levey correctly observes that, in the context of privacy law, "Rapid technological change inevitably outpaces the glacial evolution of the law."[74] This timing disparity is a potential cause for concern. As Orin Kerr, a Fourth Amendment scholar at the University of Southern California observes, "As technology advances, legal rules designed for one state of technology begin to have unintended consequences."[75] Still, the law has advanced to some degree in this space. This advancement should perhaps not be especially surprising since, as Calo states, "Technology has always been a key driver of privacy law, scholarship and policy."[76]

Most recently, the United States Supreme Court held (in *Carpenter v. United States* [2018]) that the government (generally) needs a warrant to collect data about locations of customers of cell phone companies.[77] This decision was hailed as a significant victory for privacy rights by watchdog groups and advocates. It was hailed as a "landmark privacy case" by director of the Knight First Amendment Institute at Columbia University Jameel Jaffer—who also pointed out the significant First Amendment protections at issue in the case.[78] Kerr opined on the outcome of the case, arguing that it demonstrated a willingness on the part of the court to reign in practices that it deemed overreaching before the government curtails additional civil liberties: "Big Brother is coming and we need to stop it…. It almost reflects an anxiety about technology threatening privacy. If we don't stop the government here, what will they be able to do?"[79]

In the *Carpenter* case, the government argued that the United States Supreme Court's "Third Party Doctrine"—namely, that no search or seizure occurs if the government obtains data that the individual provided to a third party—applies to wireless providers. But the Third Party Doctrine was created 40 years ago, well in advance of the modern technology revolution. Today, so much information is collected by third party service providers that the government would be able to circumvent warrant requirements to obtain such data in a very broad range of situations. The Court held that the voluntary conveyance principle portion of the Third Party Doctrine is not applicable to cell phone data because there is no "affirmative act on the part of the user beyond powering up."[80]

In *Carpenter*, Chief Justice John Roberts acknowledged that Fourth Amendment law must continue to evolve to account for "seismic shifts in digital technology."[81] As evidenced by the majority decision, it appears that the law is slowly adapting and adjusting to contend with advances in the privacy arena, although modern technology still appears to have a distinct advantage from a structural perspective. For a host of procedural and resource-related reasons, courts are notoriously slow to adjudicate novel issues. And despite the United States Supreme Court's heavy reliance of precedent when reviewing new cases in the docket, the *Carpenter* decision included the following sentences—potentially limiting its precedential value: "Our decision today is a narrow one. We do not express a view on (scenarios) not before us."[82] If presented with slightly less favorable facts from a litigant—

and, perhaps a more compelling governmental interest—the outcome may be different the next time around.

Personality Rights

In addition to the privacy protections under the Fourth Amendment, some states also recognize personality rights, also known as the right of publicity. The right includes the power of a covered individual to control and restrict the commercial use of his or her name, image, likeness and persona. Sometimes this right only protects folks whose likeness is most likely to be exploited, such as politicians and celebrities. In our celebrity-obsessed culture where folks frequently attempt to misappropriate and appropriate the likenesses of famous individuals, legal protection for such individuals may make sense from a public policy perspective. As technology advances, a strong argument can be made that such rights should be extended to all individuals. The exploitation of less wealthy folks may not be economically motivated, but could still cause harm to the affected individual. Given the existence of cloning and other replication technologies, opportunities and incentives to misappropriate an individual's likeness to confuse others increase exponentially.

Such technologies also impact the policy debate as to whether the publicity right should be applied posthumously. The decedent could still experience reputational harm following his or her death. Should companies be prohibited from profiting off the exploitation of a decedent's loved ones by misappropriating and building synthetic recreations of the deceased? The use of Ash's likeness in "Be Right Back," for example, causes Martha emotional distress. Had Ash been alive, would he have given his informed consent to the use of his persona in a way that would likely cause his loved ones harm? Furthermore, the decedent might also experience reputational damage if his or her likeness is replicated and ultimately causes harm to others. If someone, for example, had not known that Ash passed away and the synthetic recreation performs an action that reflects poorly on Ash, folks might develop an unwarranted negative perception of Ash even after the natural Ash has passed away. Folks should be able to manage their likeness, whether or not technology exists that allows others to replicate it.

Regulation and Oversight—By and Of Government?

As discussed above, contemporary legal and regulatory systems may not be sufficiently robust, nuanced or fine-tuned to handle the challenges and complexities presented by our interconnectedness and immediate access to information about each other. But there is a larger foundational issue here as well. Even well-defined laws that effectively capture societal concerns regarding data collection and powerful technologies would not substitute for our deeper connection to, and intense desire to retain, liberty. If we are willing to relinquish our privacy (and, with it, emotional control over our lives) to technology companies, moguls and other folks, no law or regulation—irrespective of how strong—will change the way in which we value such rights. As Judge Learned Hand brilliantly observed, "Liberty lies in the hearts of men and women; when it dies there, no constitution, no law, no court can save it; no constitution, no law, no court can even do much to help it. While it lies there, it needs no constitution, no law, no court to save it."[83] In sum, the buck starts and stops with individual citizens. Laws and regulations can help reign in potential abuses by cold and steely corporations or other malicious actors, but laws and regulations will not save us from ourselves.

We must also be aware that there are practical issues and limitations related to our ability to promulgate laws and regulations to perhaps mitigate, if not eliminate, some of the adverse consequences relating to the introduction of powerful technologies. One significant concern is many lawmakers' fundamental lack of understanding of the ways in which technologies function and their potential impacts within society. At an April 2018 Senate hearing, for example, Facebook CEO was quizzed about the basic nature of his business. South Carolina Senator Lindsey Graham (R) asked: "Is Twitter the same as what [Facebook does]"?[84] And Utah Senator Orrin Hatch asked Zuckerberg: "How do you sustain a business model in which users don't pay for your service?" Hatch's lack of understanding about Facebook's business model is especially concerning. It is important for lawmakers to understand that *we* are the product that Facebook is selling. Facebook's users are its most important commodities; the valuable data that Facebook collects about us has led to its enormous success. If our legislators do not understand these critical aspects of the technology space, they will not be able to appropriately legislate and reign in potentially overreaching, if not outright dangerous, business practices of such companies. Education not only of the public but also our legislative and executive branches is a critical component of the drafting and implementation of effective legislation in this area. One of the persistent, perhaps intractable challenges to ensuring an educated leadership is the role of technology lobbyists and Silicon Valley's significant monetary contributions aimed at protecting the interests of the technology industry and distracting (preventing?) lawmakers from receiving impartial, balanced information on these issues.

Even if the task of regulation of novel technologies is placed in the hands of knowledgeable, capable individuals, challenges would persist. Crafting legislation that is substantively rigid and simultaneously sufficiently flexible to allow for effective enforcement in an age of ever-evolving technologies is a daunting task. As international privacy and cybersecurity attorney Justin Keslowitz observes, "Because of how quickly data-driven technologies evolve, and legislatures' inability to predict how companies will use such future technologies to collect and monetize people's data, even the most privacy-protective legislatures cannot successfully fashion data protection laws that are not outdated (and oftentimes obsolete) by the time they take effect."[85]

At a macro-level, regulations have been introduced in some jurisdictions to broadly address data protection in various industries. Rules regarding the access, storage and transfer of sensitive personal information within and across borders, for example, is covered by the European Union's General Data Protection Regulation (GDPR)—though similarly comprehensive legislation is noticeably absent at the federal level in other jurisdictions, such as the United States. Corporations expend significant energy to comply with regulations applicable to it, while simultaneously streamlining business processes and creating strategies devoted to implementation of technologies that make it easier to collect and analyze data from a variety of sources. Even as regulators and legislators slowly adapt to contemporary privacy and security-related landscapes—each of which is a moving target—innovators find new ways to make use of data in ways that can be both beneficial and harmful to individuals and society at large. As evidenced by the existence of gaping holes in even the most robust regulations—such as with respect to the GDPR's silence on records management of cryptocurrency exchanges—the speed of innovation seems to routinely exceed the pace of regulation.

Reasonable folks also debate the extent to which government should be involved in data privacy and security oversight. Some experts argue that contemporary circumstances mandate significant regulation that was largely unnecessary in the past. Proponents of this perspective point to a seismic shift in the way in which data is gathered, accessed and used. But even if folks reach consensus as to the general need for regulation, questions arise as to which actors should be subject to such regulations. To what extent are contemporary governments subject to control by companies such as Google, which stores officials' emails on its servers? Should government be trusted to regulate private industry, while reserving (and even expressly permitting) itself to collect information for a range of purposes—many of which could fall under the vague and broad rubric of "national security," as we see in "Hated in the Nation"? Or should government itself be expressly prohibited from collecting data for most, if not all, purposes? Microsoft founder Bill

Gates points out these contemporary challenges, advocating for restrictions on the ability of government to access information: "Historically, privacy was almost implicit, because it was hard to find and gather information. But [given the existence of] digital cameras or satellites or just what you click on, we need to have more explicit rules—not just for governments but for private companies."[86] Others are less nuanced in their calls for oversight not by government, but *of* government in this context. They argue that past experience should serve as a warning that the ability of governments to protect data is circumspect—particularly because governments may have an interest in using information in unsettling ways. Poet and cyberlibertarian political activist John Perry Barlow opined that "Relying on the government to protect your privacy is like asking a peeping tom to install window blinds."[87] And there is evidence that the government has, for good or ill, altered the privacy and security landscapes to which we are subject. The ACLU has pointed out, for example, that the NSA has "weakened the security of the communications that we all rely on" to conduct mass surveillance.[88] And, capitalizing on antiquated elements of our legal system that appear ripe for review if not a refresh, the government (according to an analysis by the ACLU) "argues that the 4th Amendment protects information that you keep in your desk, but not information that you keep online, like old emails or pictures."[89] Is the government improperly trying to take advantage of the failure of the legal landscape to catch up to modern technology? Do the arguably heinous actions of leakers of sensitive information and government secrets (such as Julian Assange and Edward Snowden) represent, at least in a theoretical sense, a necessary level of pushback against governments that, perhaps, have reached a bit too far?

A deep-seated mistrust of government is a theme examined throughout popular culture. *Black Mirror* examines this concept in episodes such as "The Waldo Moment" (where a populist, fictional cartoon character ignites and relies on such mistrust of establishment politicians as he seeks power) and "The National Anthem" (where government and media forces conspire, albeit for a noble cause, to deceive an audience). On *Electric Dreams*' "Safe and Sound," government-controlled media fabricate terrorist attacks—using fear as a false rationale to strip folks of their privacy rights by advocating the use of tracking devices. The consequences of the failure of a populace to express a sufficient level of distrust is explored on "Kill All Others," where a mood of widespread complacency fuels a political party's ability to track down dissidents.

A fear of totalitarian governments exerting improper authority over the interactions between individuals, including the flow of information, is also explored on shows such as *The Twilight Zone*'s "The Obsolete Man."[90] In that episode, books are burned, religion is prohibited and a librarian is sentenced to death. More broadly, the idea that government actors could collect information about individuals and use it for a range of questionable, if not malicious, purposes (including exposing such data at will to achieve an objective) is examined on episodes such as "Kill All Others." Authoritarian governments seeking to quell dissent would likely welcome the ability to track, monitor, and—as is the case in "Kill All Others"—ultimately expose detractors. Even those governments without bad intentions may use advanced systems to collect data and fail to conduct sufficient diligence on potential security flaws and gaps, providing bad actors with a centralized database ripe for attack (see "Hated in the Nation.")

Technology can be (and is) used by governments, law enforcement agencies and corporations to collect data about folks. Google and Facebook monitor our Internet activities to develop profiles of us. Private companies such as Axon Enterprise are devoted to developing "advanced electronic control devices designed for use in law enforcement, corrections, private security and personal defense." Such initiatives are frequently the subject of political pushback, with organizations such as the ACLU arguing that governments and corporations frequently overreach in this arena. The organization, for example, seeks to prevent Amazon from selling facial recognition technology to police officers. The ACLU's narrative is that an Orwellian "big brother"-type of surveillance—not unlike the measures employed in episodes such as "Hated in the Nation" and "The Hood Maker"—will arise if watchdog organizations are unsuccessful in their persistent attempts to quell such intrusions. Such organizations argue that government strategies to manipulate human emotions produces a populace replete with fear, thereby generating false justification for a wholesale reduction of civil liberties. This is one of the key themes explored in "Safe and Sound"—an episode which envisions a population mired in a constant state of fear based on falsehoods concocted and promulgated by the government. Once such intrusive measures are introduced into a society, governments have little incentive or motivation to remove the measures. If we do not push back against vague and sweeping descriptions of purported national emergencies—whether it be the endless global war described in George Orwell's "1984," the fabricated string of terrorist attacks in "Safe and Sound," broad, morally bankrupt and vague objectives intended to combat an ill-defined enemy (as in "Kill All Others," or, perhaps the seemingly endless "War on Terror" in contemporary society)—the rule of law is at risk of being supplanted by the exception.

While many, if not most, citizens may agree that certain defined exigencies require the implementation of advanced surveillance techniques, defining the parameters of the emergency in terms of nature, scope and duration is a difficult task and ripe for abuse. Critics may argue that we too often find ourselves living in a constant (and therefore effectively fictional) "state of exception."[91]

The State of Exception

During one of the dark, tumultuous days on the television series *24*, fictional federal agent Jack Bauer seeks to break the rules to achieve a laudable objective—in this case, saving the innocent life of the First Gentleman of the United States. Bauer's FBI counterpart (Larry Moss) opposes the approach, proposing instead to work within defined boundaries—even if such boundaries sometimes serve as obstacles in achieving the agency's goals. The pair engage in the following exchange:

AGENT MOSS: The rules are what make us better.
BAUER: Not today.[92]

And so we enter the "state of exception."
Sociologist Amitai Etzioni describes the "civil libertarian's narrative about how democracies are lost" as follows:

> First, the government, in the name of national security or some other cause, trims some rights, which raises little alarm at the time (e.g., the massive detention of Japanese Americans during World War II). Then a few other rights are curtailed (e.g., the FBI spies on civil rights groups and peace activists during the 1960s). Soon, more rights are lost and gradually the entire institutional structure on which democracy rests tumbles down the slope with nobody able to stop it.[93]

The risk of sliding down the slippery slope described above is increased by the introduction of powerful technologies capable, and designed for the purposes of, surveillance, tracking and monitoring. We see elements of this phenomenon in "Arkangel," where a mother reintroduces tracking technology to monitor her older daughter. If surveillance is to only be used during "exceptional" times due to desperate circumstances (in this case, monitoring of a young child following a traumatic experience during the child went missing), it should not be used once the exigent circumstances have been removed or no longer exist. But the temptation is too strong, given the technology's continued availability. In this situation, the exception has become the rule. We see this during Jack Bauer's situations as well: Bauer breaks the rules so often that it is difficult to distinguish the rule from the exception. And the ultimate result could be a totalitarian government (not unlike the one presented on

"Kill All Others") that sees no need to continuously attempt to justify the use of an exception that has, in practice, become the rule. The law is co-opted, and the exception usurps the rule of law.

Authoritarianism may be the result if the exception repeatedly overpowers the rule of law. And hardline governments falling into this category could care less about drawing lines or defining boundaries. Government surveillance programs are ripe for abuse under this paradigm. Once governments have the power to surveil, they may not be eager or willing to relinquish such power—and we must wonder whether governments may attempt to justify continued surveillance in dishonest ways, as we see in "Safe and Sound." Even more jarring, however, is the refusal of the government in "Safe and Sound" to argue that its intrusive "security" measures are intended for use on a temporary basis. Because the terrorist attacks are fabricated and there is no desire on the part of the government to curtail use of the measures, it seems highly unlikely that such exceptional practices will not become the long-term way of life in this dystopian society.

The Chilling Effects of Government Surveillance

The use of surveillance techniques by governments has been examined throughout popular culture—from George Orwell's novel "1984" (where Big Brother observes citizens and demands conformity in both language and deed) to *The Twilight Zone*'s "The Jeopardy Room" (where state actors rely on surveillance to concoct a complex plot to murder a former army general).[94] As a general matter, the introduction of new technologies that can be used for surveillance or other intrusive or invasive purposes typically are so used—at least until an attempt is made to reign in such power. It is therefore important to consider the potentially stifling chilling effects of surveillance on political and socioeconomic behaviors.

Scholars have argued that the possibility of surveillance is effective in modifying behavior, even if the surveillance does not take place around the clock. As Calo notes, "It is probably enough not to know whether you are being watched to experience discomfort or chilling effects."[95] The threat of government-controlled artificial bees that might spy on us (see "Hated in the Nation") or devices that monitor and make determinations about our "mental health" (see "Kill All Others") or devices that monitor our thoughts ("The Hood Maker") or gain access to our memories ("Crocodile," "The Entire History of You") cause us to react and thereby implicitly limit our freedom.[96] Because folks modify their behavior when they believe they are being watched, governmental power in this regard should be closely examined and curtailed. These episodes reflect the growing societal anxieties regarding the introduction of social credit systems and "fatherland cards" in countries such as China and Venezuela.

As we examine the technologies presented on *Black Mirror* and *Electric Dreams*, it behooves us to consider whether technologies currently employed by governments (such as "bugging" phones) are qualitatively distinct from measures that most folks would deem overly intrusive (such as reading thoughts, per "The Hood Maker").

"The Hood Maker": "Don't Steal Our Minds!"

Several critical issues associated with government surveillance programs are examined on *Electric Dreams*' "The Hood Maker." In the episode, beings referred to as "Teeps" have the power to read the minds of other folks living in society. The government in this dystopian universe use the Teeps' power for surveillance purposes, engaging some Teeps to read the thoughts of protesters and those suspected of crimes. Neither the government nor the Teeps seek consent to invade folks' minds, each disrupting (as they fail to acknowledge) the sanctity of free and independent thought.

In the episode, a police officer (Agent Ross) and a Teep (Honor) interrogate a suspect. As we watch Honor read the thoughts of the suspect, it becomes clear that the government does not recognize or observe any due process protections for those accused of crimes. These actions are consistent with the standard set forth in the "Anti-Immunity" bill, which permits the government to obtain "total access to a civilian's thoughts at any time as deemed appropriate by the agent in charge."

Given the existence of this technology, it may be too quixotic to expect that government actors will not seek to use it to collect information about citizens—especially in this society, where Normals and Teeps are inching toward civil war. The government may argue that the principles emanating from the state of exception should apply during this period—even though the disputes between the Normals and Teeps could produce a long and protracted militaristic and psychological warfare. The hood maker, Dr. Cutter—a scientist engaged by the government to produce masks that repel the Teeps' powers by blocking electrical signals—explains the difficulty of ridding society of the Teeps' powers, distinguishing it from the "overreaction" of folks' to the introduction of technology that could more easily be turned off by simply pulling a plug. The hoods are qualitatively similar to "burner" phones that folks can use to block others from listening in on their conversations. Both are examples of technology being developed as a reflexive reaction to other technologies.

Once a powerful technology is introduced into a society, it behooves citizens to assume and anticipate that various actors—governments, corporations and other individuals—will seek to exploit such technology to their advantage (potentially to the detriment of others). The reaction from folks to the idea of banning or refraining from using innovative technologies is often dismay and disbelief, even as the negative consequences emanating from the technology are readily visible. This phenomenon is explored in "Crocodile," where a woman is met with wide-eyed stares when she states that she is happier without the memory implant device used by others. Her position does not immediately impede the other folks' desire for "progress," since the technology has already been introduced. But her counterparts seek uniformity of interest on this point, and it could be argued that a collective fascination with technology is a necessary incentive for its development and production by innovators.

If banishing a technology from society is unrealistic, the next best approach may be to regulate it and thereby (at least theoretically) limit its usage and application. This is the argument made by famed civil libertarian and Harvard Law School Professor Emeritus Alan Dershowitz in the context of the torture debate.[97] Such an approach assumes, of course, that the stated goal is to reduce a controversial practice—an objective that stands in stark contrast to the presumed purpose of the Anti-Immunity bill.

While expressing his strong condemnation of the practice of torture, Dershowitz argues that the most effective means to limit its usage is to legalize it in select, narrowly-defined scenarios. Dershowitz's argument is premised on the notion that no government regulation would abolish the practice of torture entirely, given its perceived effectiveness in some circles.[98] By restricting its application to only the most severe and desperate situations—such as the "ticking time bomb" scenario—Dershowitz predicts that the reliance on torture as an operational technique will be minimized.[99] In his view, the failure to clearly define permissible (if not morally acceptable or justifiable) boundaries for the implementation of an abhorrent activity contributes to its increased frequency of use. If both (1) the challenges of defining the scope and conditions for its introduction are overcome and (2) the consequences for the failure to strictly adhere to such conditions are clearly outlined and enforced, such regulation may be effective in deterring all but only the most extreme and desperate needs to employ this dastardly measure.

Others disagree with Dershowitz's proposal on both philosophical and practical grounds. Though it might pass muster from a utilitarianist's perspective if it can somehow be shown to achieve a greater good, Dershowitz's policy prescription would fail when viewed through the lens of Immanuel Kant's "categorical imperative"—defined as "an unconditional moral obligation that is binding in all circumstances and is not dependent on a person's inclination or purpose."[100] Since torture is not universally acceptable in "all circumstances," it would unquestionably not satisfy this standard. Other folks—such as former United States President Bill Clinton—argue that the decision to validate, or at a minimum, excuse torture should be determined on a case-by-case basis without reference to a prescriptive statute.[101] He argues that the "Jack Bauer person" should not feel as though he or she has any legal support for his or her action whatsoever.[102] Instead, the individual would only commit the heinous act of torture, so the theory goes, if the situation were so dire that the agent had no other option and is willing to take the risk of facing criminal responsibility. A judge or jury could then decide to excuse the actions if the circumstances warranted using practices at its disposal. One such tool for factfinders is "jury nullification," where a jury effectively disregards existing law when rendering its verdict.

Keeping these competing perspectives in mind, we can consider whether legalizing the use of Teeps for surveillance in limited, defined circumstances could reduce the overall instances of spying. The Anti-Immunity bill as described on "The Hood Maker" would need to be heavily amended and the objectives that the bill is seeking to achieve would need to be reconsidered. Even if folks were generally comfortable with allowing the type of invasive surveillance technique to be used in limited circumstances (or resigned to its use due to realities on the ground), the Anti-Immunity bill is alarming because of its immense scope and lack of oversight. The discretion given to the government is jarring, as it effectively prevents any questioning of the agent's actions or motives. Meaningful and effective parameters that clearly limit an agent's authority and subject the agent to appropriate consequences must be set forth in such a bill. As it stands, the use of this surveillance technique is ripe for abuse. The vague standard falls far short of the "reasonable suspicion" standard that must be satisfied in the United States for law enforcement to invade suspects' privacy rights in much less invasive ways—such as frisking them on the streets. And, like torture, the practice would likely fail to satisfy the categorical imperative, though it might be a candidate for passing a utilitarian analysis.

Furthermore, the government does not plan to apply the provisions of the Anti-Immunity bill—assuming it becomes law—in a uniform manner. Instead, Teeps who team up with agents are forbidden from reading the thoughts of agents. The government therefore applies the rule capriciously and arbitrarily. An argument by the government that it should be a protected class—excluded from the law's purview—because it possesses sensitive information seems circular. It has come into the possession of such information by relying on the power of the Teeps and it seems patently unfair to carve out the government from the general rule. The fact that the government does not want to subject itself to the standards set forth for the rest of society should serve as a red flag, both with respect to the government's priorities and the alarming scope of the law. In a not-so-subtle nod to those who leak and expose government secrets, Dr. Cutter states that "Protection should be democratic. So should knowledge." Protection for me, but not for thee, seems to be the government's (untenable) position in this regard.

Informed and Uninformed Consent—Privacy and Beyond

One of the hot-button issues in the privacy arena is the question of consent. It is an unfortunate reality that we are watched all the time without giving permission or signing off (see "Shut Up and Dance" and "Hated in the Nation," for example). In a society structured around an open marketplace of ideas, would it not be reasonable to similarly permit the free exchange of information if the subject consents to the exchange (as in "Nosedive")? But the nature of such consent, and the requirement to provide information relevant to the decision-making process are debatable issues. Furthermore, it is highly impractical to demand consent from all potential subjects in any context where a potential privacy right is at issue.[103] For example, some may argue that facial recognition technology should be prohibited without obtaining the consent of all folks whose faces are recognized in the database. Seeking prior consent from all folks in the database would not only be infeasible; it would likely stand in the way of achieving relevant objectives, as those who wish to remain anonymous would most likely decline to provide such consent.

The provision of consent could take various forms, resulting in different iterations of this idea in practice. Should corporations be permitted to share consumer information with third parties if they provide users with an "opt-out right"? Or should informed consent require an affirmative act on the part of the subject—i.e., an "opt-in right," where the subject assents, presumably in writing, to disclosure to third parties? Even when companies do seek such affirmation via click-through arrangements, how many of us read through "terms of use" documents presented to us on websites? If we rely on a service (such as Google) to store emails, do we knowingly submit to the idea that Google can shut off our access to such emails with or without cause, at any time, in its sole discretion—even though Google is expressly granted this right in its non-negotiable "Terms of Service"?[104] If we were aware of such risks, would we use an email service where the provider lacks such an ability, or is Google so entrenched in our lives that we would not blink when presented with onerous terms? What should we make of the lack of transparency and alleged abuse by companies such as Google and Facebook in terms of making use of our data? Even if both companies consistently behaved in accordance with their policies—a questionable premise, to say the least— would a sentence in their privacy or Terms of Use policies be sufficient to insulate them from the wrath of users who may not be paying full attention (i.e., nearly all of us)?

Structural issues aside, should we assume that all consent is necessarily properly "informed"? What information must be disclosed to the user to qualify? Must the user be educated about all potential consequences resulting from the disclosure—a bar so high that it is unlikely to be satisfied in practice? Outside of the privacy context, is it even possible to be made aware of *all* risks—especially in the context of applications of novel technologies? Conversely, should it be solely the user's responsibility to inform herself of the potential issues and concerns (disclosure-related or otherwise) arising from the use of such technology?

The issue of informed consent is examined on several episodes of *Black Mirror* and *Electric Dreams* in various contexts. Bad actors or those arguably skirting Constitutional protections frequently disregard any potential consent issues as they commit their actions (see "Shut Up and Dance" and "Hated in the Nation," respectively). Other episodes provide a more nuanced look at these issues.

In "Black Museum," for example, the self-serving Rolo Haynes fails to adequately advise subjects of the potential dangers lurking behind the newly-introduced sensory and digital transference technologies in the first two segments. Given the experimental nature of such technologies, Haynes may not have had access to sufficient data to provide the subjects with a properly vetted inventory of possible risks. But he could have described the technologies in a more balanced way as opposed to reliance on salesman-like puffery. And Haynes has no excuse (or defense) with respect to the hologram technology presented during the third segment of the episode. Haynes aggressively negotiates with a prisoner for the rights to his posthumous consciousness, with the heinous purpose of torturing that consciousness in his dark, warped museum.

"Arkangel" provides another case study of the failure to disclose potential risks of new technology. The mother is informed that the technology is completely safe. There is no attempt on the part of the production company to warn the mother of any short-term or long-term risks associated with its implementation or use. The episode invites us to ask whether the company should be held at least partially responsible for the harms caused by the authorized use of their technology.

Other episodes (such as "Playtest" and *Electric Dreams'* "Real Life") present similar challenges for both the producers and end users of technology. Sometimes (as in "Playtest") users are asked to sign liability waivers—agreeing not to sue if the technology does not work as advertised or, worse, if harm is caused to the subject. Depending on the facts at hand, such waivers may not be legally enforceable. While helpful in terms of providing evidentiary value as to discussions that may have been had between the parties, a judge might deem the document overbroad and unfair—especially if the subject is not a sophisticated end user. In fact, many courts frown upon waivers that seek to insulate companies from liability. Waivers are struck down with great frequency on public policy grounds, with courts often finding that waivers serve the ends of companies at the expense of unsuspecting end users. They are often closely scrutinized and strictly construed against the party drafting the waiver. In 2005, the Wisconsin Supreme Court observed that none of the exculpatory contracts coming under its purview had been held enforceable over the previous 25 year period.[105] On the other hand, even in the case of an unenforceable (or lack of executed) waiver, is it reasonable, especially in cases relating to new technologies, to expect that end-users will be informed of all potential consequences? Given the novel (and often untested) nature of the technology in these cases, it may not be justifiable to place legal or ethical responsibility on those introducing the technology if things go awry.

The issue of informed consent (or lack thereof) in the privacy context arises, perhaps most prominently, in the second segment of "Black Museum." In that segment, Carrie consents to the initial transference of her consciousness into Jack's brain, but she does not consent to Jack's decisions to "pause" her or, even worse, transfer her consciousness into a stuffed teddy bear. Carrie's privacy rights are violated, and she is left without any recourse.

"Arkangel" also invites us to consider whether minors should have the right to receive information and provide or withhold approval prior to the implantation of invasive devices. Even if minors are not provided with a consent or "opt-out" right, should the issue of consent be revisited once they reach a certain age? If parents no longer have legal responsibility for children past an established age, should such parents continue to have the right to invade such children's privacy? We also, incidentally, see the use of facial recognition technology at work in this episode—and it is quite evident that the teenager subject had not given prior consent in any form to use of the image of his face in a database.

In "White Christmas," a prisoner's privacy and Constitutional rights are violated when a cookie is implanted and then extracted (both, presumably, without his consent). The episode serves as a case study of potential law enforcement abuses of technology without obtaining consent. Here, law enforcement seeks to use the cookie to collect information about the prisoner to be used at trial. And in the first segment of this episode, a woman is watched by sexual voyeurs without her consent.

In "Men Against Fire," the protagonist (Stripe) expressly grants the military permission to implant the invasive MASS device into his brain. The device alters the senses, makes use of augmented reality and creates dreams at night. His private thoughts are affected. He is generally advised of the functionality of the device prior to its implementation, but he does not seriously consider the actual consequences of the technology. His express agreement is based on a vague, passive understanding of the nature of the device. Stripe's lack of attention to the matter is understandable, if not wise, as he placed his trust in the military and was likely not aware that such powerful technology even existed. Even if Stripe's willingness to use the device constitutes informed consent, he is later strong-armed into keeping the device. He is threatened by a military psychologist with imprisonment and streaming of an endless loop of painful footage if he does not consent to removal of his memory of the past few days and have his implant reset. In this second case, Stripe only consents because he is under severe duress; because of such pressure, it cannot reasonably be suggested that he provided consent in an entirely voluntary fashion. These threats also force us to revisit the scope and terms of the initial consent: if Stripe was not advised of the impracticability of removing the device prior to its implantation, it seems that his consent to the initial insertion was not truly informed.

Now let's turn to a discussion of the virtual worlds, alternate universes and digital clones presented on *Black Mirror* and *Electric Dreams*, and their place in, and relevance to, contemporary society.

5

Alternate Realities, Digital Clones and the Meaning and Value of Life

> "I wish I could show you, when you are lonely or in darkness, the astonishing light of your own being."
> —Hafiz[1]

Manufactured Realities: Living in a Cave

In *The Allegory of the Cave*, the ancient Greek philosopher Plato describes the lives of prisoners who have been chained to a wall throughout their lives.[2] The group is exposed only to shadows visible on the wall that are formed by objects passing in front of a fire. The prisoners give names to the shadows, as the shadows form the group's entire perception of reality. This reality is manufactured, but it is the only reality that the individuals know and experience.

Reality for the prisoners—and for all human beings—is a relative concept. Our ability to perceive is entirely linked to, and directly informed by, application of our senses interacting with and observing an environment. Like chained prisoners, we are tethered to a notion of reality formed by impressions made through our senses. Our experiences and relationships with our environment are dictated by an imperfect ability to perceive. Any deviations from what we consider to be reality may be incomprehensible. A colorblind person, for example, is not able to understand or imagine the color red, just as no human being would be fully able to comprehend the features of a world that has no basis in our understanding of fundamental aspects of the universe.[3] If we were to somehow escape from the inherent sensory restrictions that bind us, we would then enter another realm—one unencumbered by limitations on perception, a life defined by pure fact and form.

Because reality is a relative concept born from the subjective perceptions of the individual perceiver, notions of altered states of reality and alternate universes (both objectively real and perceived) are ripe concepts for treatment within the science fiction genre. This is a frequent theme explored on a host of episodes of *The Twilight Zone*, where the characters and the audience are each thrown for a loop upon discovering that the reality they are experiencing conflicts with their expectations and pre-existing conceptions of the world. Sometimes, these experiences result from the convergence of alternate or parallel universes (a concept explored a bit later in this chapter), while other episodes lack a wholly satisfying explanation for the strange events and occurrences. Examples of episodes tackling these concepts include time-travel episodes such as "Walking Distance" (which examines a man's emotions upon realizing that he has gone back in time); "Person or Persons Unknown" (which follows a man as he discovers that nobody has any knowledge or memory of his existence); "The Mind and the Matter" (wherein a man is empowered to re-create the world as he deems fit); "Valley of the Shadow" (where a reporter encounters a strange town where folks have the ability to reverse time); "Five Characters in Search of an Exit" (which follows five individuals stuck in a cylinder); "A Quality of Mercy" (which showcases an American solider switching places with a Japanese officer); "death" episodes such as "The Hunt" (where a man has passed away without having come to this realization); as well as a collection of *Planet of the Apes*-type episodes, where humans realize that they had entirely misjudged the nature and/or history of their surroundings.[4] And sometimes folks manufacture settings intended to throw others' beliefs about their environments into disarray—as in "One More Pallbearer," where a disgruntled, self-delusional man fabricates a nuclear threat to trick his enemies into believing the world is coming to an end.[5]

Modern technology can be—and often is—used to seek reprieve from our own environments. Such technology enables us to enter altered states of reality and escape the bondage of our reality as it exists from our individual perspectives and experiences. Several *Black Mirror* and *Electric Dreams* episodes address the potentiality of technology altering an individual's sense of space, time and reality—sometimes against her will and resulting in harm. In "White Bear," for example, the townspeople devise and implement a complex scheme relying on the repeated use of memory-erasing technology to punish a woman involved in a child's murder. In "Men Against Fire," soldiers have a chip implanted in them to alter their vision and hearing, causing them to see and hear a class of people as subhuman, zombie-like monsters referred to as "roaches."[6] In "Safe and Sound," Foster suspects that the Dex device causes her to hallucinate. In all these cases, reality is shown to be a relative concept—capable of being altered and manipulated to satisfy the agendas of those in power. These episodes highlight some of the dangers of technology falling into the wrong hands.

Emerging from the Cave

In the blockbuster film *The Matrix* (1999), an individual named Neo is presented with a choice: swallow a blue pill and resume a life that is an illusion, a reality manufactured by those in power (to subdue and exploit humanity by using their heat as an energy source); or swallow a red pill and learn the truth about the world.[7] The audience watches in great anticipation as to whether Neo will choose the red pill—a choice that would exhibit the human inclination to search for the truth, despite the possibility of adverse consequences and risks of exiting a reality with which he is familiar. Neo needs to determine whether he has a strong desire to emerge from Plato's cave.

Altered perceptions and/or states of reality have been examined throughout popular culture, not only in the virtual reality space but in more traditional environments as well. *The Twilight Zone*'s "Shadow Play," for example, focuses on a convicted murderer's recurring nightmare of being sentenced and subsequently executed.[8] In *The Twilight Zone* episode "Stopover in a Quiet Town," a couple wakes up to find themselves in a town where their surroundings appear to be props.[9] In the film *Groundhog Day* (1993) actor Bill Murray plays a man named Phil Connors who lives life on a repeating 24-hour loop.[10] Other films have focused on subjects living in, and sometimes emerging from, manufactured realities. In the film *50 First Dates* (2004), for example, Drew Barrymore plays a woman named Lucy Whitmore, whose short-term memory loss prevents her from remembering anything that occurred the day before—leading her family and friends to create a fabricated reality to protect her.[11] The documentary *The Wolfpack* (2015) provides the account of seven children who rarely leave their apartment.[12] Siphoned off from society for many years, the children, according to *New York Post* columnist Sara Stewart, "learned everything they know from 5,000 movies."[13] Their reality was one built nearly exclusively atop a mountain of fictional films. Their account is reminiscent of the film *Blast from the Past* (1999), where a 35-year-old man (played by Brendan Fraser) emerges from a nuclear fallout shelter where he had spent his entire life.[14] The man's attitudes and manners make him likeable, but he seems out of place in modern times. In the film *The Game* (1997), an elaborate setup convinces a man of the emergence of a new set of life circumstances.[15] In the television series *Wayward Pines* (2015–

2016), folks are trapped by town leaders in a picturesque, creepy and fabricated town to prevent them from learning the truth about the destruction of most of humanity.[16] In the film *Total Recall* (1990), a man is unable to tell whether the reality that he experiences is real or is the result of memory implants.[17] In the miniseries *Maniac* (2018), folks under the influence of powerful experimental drugs experience fantasy worlds and have difficulty distinguishing real life from fiction.[18] And in the series *Homecoming* (2018–present), veterans are sent to a mental rehabilitation facility where they suspect that their surrounding environment is a manufactured reproduction of a city.[19]

Popular culture has also examined the ways in which belief in altered states of reality or troubling circumstances influences behavior. *The Twilight Zone* famously explored human reaction to altered states of reality. In *The Twilight Zone*'s "The Monsters are Due on Maple Street," for example, a town is struck by a series of bizarre events—such as flickering lights and cars starting on their own.[20] The aliens that strategically cause these oddities watch overhead, observing how toying with folks' expectations causes them to descend into a manic state of desperation and paranoia. In *The Twilight Zone*'s "The Shelter," neighbors who were previously friends with one another become hysterical and engage in racism, nativism and intense anger toward each other as they react to the prospect of sharing a bomb shelter as nuclear war threatens civilization.[21] *The Twilight Zone* posits that departing one's existing, comfortable reality for an alternate state often leads to an outpouring of human vices, such as greed, selfishness, ruthlessness, anger and hatred. This theme is echoed on *The Simpsons* episode "Bart's Comet," where Springfield residents (led by Homer's rallying cry) kick Ned Flanders out of his own bomb shelter.[22]

All these films and television shows examine potential human reactions to altered realities and unnerving circumstances. The common thread is that humans are subjects of their environments and unique perceptions of reality. And when those environments or perceptions change, so, too, does human behavior. The disconnect between one's perception of reality and the reality observed by others is the subject of the film *The Truman Show* (1998).[23]

In *The Truman Show*, a man named Truman Burbank (played by Jim Carrey) learns that his life has been filmed since birth and is the subject of the ultimate reality show. Truman's family, friends, neighborhood and everyone and everything else he believes to be real are manufactured. For Truman, the fabricated reality that television executives have artificially developed for him is as real as anyone else's reality. Upon learning the truth about his existence and surroundings, however, Truman must decide whether to leave the studio and enter the real world. As he considers whether to exit, it is prudent for him to consider and anticipate the significant possibility of experiencing heartbreak and despair based on life's exigencies—concepts foreign to him while living within the sheltered confines of a television studio.

Truman's hypothetical emergence from this cocoon could represent a new chapter in his life—one replete with value and meaning, in which the possibilities for what events may take place are not dictated by television network executives. Perhaps living a real life is more valuable than one insulated from the reality of the world that others experience. In stark contrast to those who seek to escape such realities in favor of a more stable, content life (including by means of technology), many folks will see the inherent value in refusing to live in such a protected state. Any decision to engage with the natural world demonstrates a deep desire to emerge from the guarded cave in which he had been residing. If he chooses to leave the protected space, he must be prepared to *live*.

We can draw parallels between Truman's existence and scientific theories about our own perceptions of reality. Many scientists believe that there is a significant chance that the realities that we all experience are complex simulations. This theory holds that "everything we experience is just lines of code in an advanced programme—in the same way virtual worlds created in computer games are just projections of data."[24] NASA scientist Rich Terrile predicts that "very quickly we will be a society where there are artificial entities living in simulations that are much more abundant than human beings."[25] He pointedly asks, "If in the future there are more digital people living in simulated environments than there are today, then what is it to say we are not part of that already?"[26] Elon Musk, a proponent of the theory that humanity is living in a simulation, believes that advances in technology will enable us to conjure up virtual worlds, and that it is probable that someone has beat us there without our knowledge. He believes that the odds of humankind not living in an artificially-created simulation are "one in billions."[27] Terrile agrees, asserting that "If we are not living in a simulation, it is an extraordinarily unlikely circumstance."[28] Scientist Neil deGrasse Tyson, for his part, believes that the chances that our lives are merely computer simulations "may be very high." He surmises that he would be the only one in a room of people unsurprised if this theory is ultimately proven true.[29]

This concept is explored on *Black Mirror*'s "Hang the DJ," where simulated digital beings exist in an artificially-created virtual world. Consistent with theories promulgated by experts regarding the lack of self-awareness of digital simulations, the simulated beings are unaware that they are copies of natural humans subsisting in a simulated universe. This lack of self-awareness is also explored in *The Twilight Zone* episode "In His Image" in the context of robots.[30]

Black Mirror devotes another episode—the critically-acclaimed and award-winning "San Junipero"—to a thorough exploration of the concept of human consciousness subsisting in a digital wonderland.[31, 32] In "San Junipero," two "women" meet, experience a simulated world together throughout different time periods and fall in love—all through code stored and maintained on a computer server. This moving love story is beautifully presented, and the show received a positive response to its portrayal of two lesbian women experiencing a powerful emotional and sexual connection with one another that transcends time and space via their respective digital consciousnesses.[33] San Junipero is a blissful place where the deceased can "live" and the elderly can visit, with individuals inhabiting the bodies of themselves at younger ages. Living together in eternity in the virtual paradise of San Junipero means that folks can experience an environment where physical limitations, rigid social constructs and judgmental third parties are no longer barriers to be overcome as prerequisites to live a meaningful and fulfilling existence.[34, 35] In short, this technology provides opportunities to those who may desperately need a new lease on life because of old age, infirmities, prejudices or ostracism. "San Junipero" demonstrates the ways in which folks who use avatars in the cloud can enjoy a liberating experience, one in which they are freed from a variety of physical constraints and emotional strings. This technology forces us to consider redefining pre-existing (and widely accepted) notions of life and death.

While visiting or living in San Junipero, the physical beings seem to become convinced that the bodies they possess in the virtual universe are their own, demonstrating the potential power of virtual embodiment technology in the context of avatars in the cloud.[36] Research has demonstrated that the brain does not effectively distinguish between natural reality and virtual reality, making the heady concepts explored on "San Junipero" relevant to a fulsome discussion of virtual embodiment technology.[37] We could ask a series of metaphysical questions as we dive deep into this phenomenon, requiring us to consider whether such a consciousness is an extension of ourselves or simply a copy—an independent entity that may not have any connection to or relationship with our natural (deceased) selves. "San Junipero" also raises serious questions about the meaning and value of a digital existence. How do we rate the intrinsic aspects of a physical environment that are absent from a digital experience? Is the quality of such an experience less valuable in some way than a physical experience? If the brain fails to distinguish between physical and virtual, are any identifiable deficiencies in a virtual world meaningful? Is a digital human consciousness equipped with the capacity to experience a virtual world for eternity? Will a natural person's knowledge of an infinite existence lead to unpredictable, and perhaps, deleterious consequences? Will possessing such knowledge change the way in which we behave in terms of our interactions with one another, including risks that we take both during our natural and digital lives? Would the ability to live an immortal existence be available to everyone, including convicted felons? What if a hacker or other malicious actor invades the server and seeks to wreak havoc in a virtual environment? From a socio-economic perspective, who would be able to afford access to this technology? Would only the wealthy have access to technologies that preserve consciousness for time immemorial—a phenomenon explored on the television series *Altered Carbon* (2018–present)?[38] Would lower income folks be excluded, exacerbating economic class divisions within society?

Notwithstanding these important questions, the heartwarming episode demonstrates that connections made between folks in a virtual environment could be both deep and meaningful for the individuals "existing" on the server. Love is unimpeded by body, space and time, and its power to live on and thrive in immortality is a powerful and comforting notion. The emotions experienced in this virtual simulation are felt by their physical counterparts in the physical world during their natural lives (and before choosing to be euthanized and uploaded to the server on a permanent basis). The potential ability of this extraordinary technology to bring depth to an afterlife should not be discounted, even if the environment in which the individuals thrive is simply a digital paradise. And the episode should not be viewed as far-reaching or entirely outlandish science fiction. Kurzweil predicts that we will, in the not-too-distant future, put "computers into our brains, connecting them to the cloud, expanding who we are."[39] That may or may not ultimately lead to the replication of human consciousness that will subsist on a server for time immemorial. Still, "San Junipero" serves up its story as one that merits attention—a potential impetus for us to reexamine and redefine the meaning and value of life and death. And the natural women featured in "San Junipero" would likely agree with the assessment that this technology allows them to grow by exploring and engaging in experiences that would otherwise be unrealistic both during and after the conclusion of their natural lives.

Both "San Junipero" and "Hang the DJ" conclude on a happy and uplifting note, with Charlie Brooker intentionally seeking to use "San Junipero" to explore a "hopeful use of technology"[40] in response to (what he viewed as unfair) criticism that the series nearly exclusively explores and provides commentary on negative aspects and consequences of technological innovation. This optimistic chord serves as a stark contrast to the tone of many other *Black Mirror* episodes.

Parallel Universes and Alternate Realities: Exploring the Nooks and Crannies of Bandersnatch

Theoretical physicists have raised fascinating questions about the nature of our existence. Is it possible that the universe in which we live is only one strand of a timeline in which people, places and events subsist in an infinite number of ways? Could the existence (and potential convergence) of distinct universes help to explain some of the strange situations characters throughout popular culture (see *The Twilight Zone*) appear to find themselves in? Are our lives comprised of only one possible outcome of a string of decisions that we make? Do the other possible decisions and outcomes resulting therefrom exist simultaneously in an alternate or parallel reality? Is belief in, or knowledge of, the possible extensive of our doppelgangers in such a reality relevant to our own existence? Is it fair to categorize ourselves as individuals if alternate versions of "us" exist in a parallel universe? Should the possible existence of parallel universes be deemed wholly irrelevant to us if we define ourselves not by our physical appearance but by characteristics that are, in fact, unique to ourselves? Are such alternate realities and our doppelgangers contained therein akin to the digital copies explored on other *Black Mirror* episodes—namely, separate, independent entities that have no connection to our natural bodies, emotions or experiences?

A portion of the astronomical *multiverse theory* posits that the choices that we make (or do not make) in this life form an alternate reality that exists separate and apart from our own universe. There is a lack of consensus within the scientific community as to the accuracy of the *multiverse theory* and its individual components—namely, the potential existence of infinite universes, bubble universes, daughter universes, mathematical universes and parallel universes.[41] Testing and determining the veracity of this theory is a difficult, intractable problem, given the seemingly unprovable nature of the contents contained within the theory. The *infinite universes* theory, for example, holds that time is flat and universes repeat themselves—tenets which appear to be, at this moment in time, impossible to prove or disprove. Some have questioned this theory, pointing to the "singularity theorem," which "tells us that an inflationary state is past-timelike-incomplete, and hence, most probably did not last a truly infinite amount of time."[42] This leads to the conclusion that there are a large number of universes out there, but "not enough of them to give us alternate versions of ourselves; the number of possible outcomes grows too rapidly compared to the rate that the number of possible universes grows."[43]

The *parallel universe* component of the *multiverse* theory is closely linked to the idea of a state of infinite expansion. As aerospace scientist Elizabeth Howell explains, the driving force behind the *parallel universe* theory is that there are an "infinite number of cosmic patches," but a finite number of "possible particle configurations."[44] Given this construct—especially a reliance on the questionable assumption of universe expansion over a limitless, infinite period—the arrangements of the particles necessarily repeat. It therefore stands to reason that some of the particle combinations will exactly match our own physical make-ups.

Explaining the way in which particles act is a critical part of the foregoing analysis. Proponents of the *daughter universes* theory examine the behavior of subatomic particles, known as *quantum mechanics*. The theory suggests that when we look at objects, we are split into multiple timelines (or universes) and see different outcomes. And if there are a finite range of outcomes but an infinite number of universes, it is inevitable that a universe will exist to cover each possible outcome. Howell explains that "If you follow the laws of probability, it suggests that for every outcome that could come from one of your decisions, there would be a range of universes—each of which saw one outcome come to be. So in one universe, you took that job to China. In another, perhaps you were on your way and your plane landed somewhere different, and you decided to stay. And so on."[45] As astrophysicist Ethan Siegel notes, it is incredible to consider the idea "that there's a universe out there for every outcome that's conceivable. There's one where everything with a non-zero probability of having happened is actually the reality in that universe."[46]

Is it possible that a universe exists where, as Siegel outlines, "everything happened exactly as it did in this one, except you did one tiny thing different, and hence had your life turn out incredibly different as a result?"[47] This theory has been explored in our popular culture. It was satirized, for example, on a "Treehouse of Horror" episode of *The Simpsons* (1994), where Homer goes back in time, performs one small action differently and causes the entire universe to change.[48] And in the film *Back to the Future* (1985), after protagonist Marty McFly travels back in time and inadvertently interferes with the beginning of his parents' romantic relationship, he sees an alternate reality in which his parents never marry and Marty's image from the future disappeared from a physical photo.[49] Pop culture is littered with other examples where the multiverse is explored and parallel universes feature prominently.[50]

Enter the multifaceted world presented on *Bandersnatch*, the interactive *Black Mirror* film which allows audience members to dictate the actions of the film's protagonist. The innovative episode is reminiscent of the popular "Choose Your Own Adventure" book series, where a reader is given the opportunity to make choices while reading the story that affect the ending.[51]

Bandersnatch invites us to go back and make different choices, as we engage in an immersive, active and intense viewing experience. In both the film and the book series, the choices that the audience / reader makes lead the characters down a different path. And we are aware that alternate realities exist where different decisions lead to different outcomes.

Bandersnatch asks the audience to entertain the idea that alternate realities may in fact exist not just in the film but in our world as well. Much like the multiple strings of events explored throughout the film, however, this idea, too, is just one thread of several distinct possibilities. The film forces us to explore the idea of our existence and asks us to question basis assumptions about life, such as: the relationship between free will and determinism; the possibility and meaning of an infinite existence; the idea that time is a social construct that may not exist in all realities; the idea that an outside actor controls our thoughts and actions; the realization that we may not be able to trust what we see, hear or experience; the belief that our actions have consequences that matter; the assumption that our lives are individualized, unique and special; and the notion that we are, perhaps, being constantly and relentlessly manipulated for reasons that we cannot even begin to understand. In sum, the film is a chilling referendum on a construct that we call "life." We are left with more questions than answers as we try, in vain, to follow Stefan on a convoluted and seemingly never-ending journey.

The theory of alternate realities is expressed in *Bandersnatch* in ways that make us doubt that this strand answers our questions in a satisfactory way. It is not clear whether the film is promoting the idea of parallel realities, given the questionable way in which this concept is presented. For example, fellow game developer Colin implores Stefan to see the big picture—life on a grand scale; one that is manipulated by governments watching over, conning, and drugging us; one in which mirrors allow folks to travel back in time; and one that we can repeat an infinite number of times in parallel universes—only when Colin is under the influence of a powerful drug (presumably LSD). And Stefan's obsession with learning about the life of Jerome F. Davies—the author of the *Bandersnatch* fictional book on which the game Stefan is developing is based—leads Stefan to explore mind control conspiracy theories that led to the downfall of Davies.

As we dictate the decisions made by Stefan, he asserts that he feels like he has lost control over his life; he appears to realize that he is not making decisions for himself but is unsure why. Stefan seems to rely on flawed past decisions to make different choices in new and parallel realities. Folks who he meets for the "first" time seem to vaguely remember meeting him previously—suggesting that the events are playing out not in a separate universe

5. Alternate Realities, Digital Clones and the Meaning of Life   149

but in one universe where time is seemingly non-existent and folks have a chance to go back and try again, effectively changing the past. Is it fair to suggest, as Colin does, that no action that we take matters because "we" (or our doppelganger in a parallel universe) can and will choose to make the opposite decision? Are our individual choices not the only thing that matter? Why should we care about how an alternate reality, if one so exists, plays out? Are we content with settling on the idea that an outside force (in this case, the audience) is to blame? Or does Stefan instead perhaps engage with a powerful, indescribable spirit—one that allows him to feel connections between parallel realities as he attempts to re-create his game and go through multiple iterations of his life? If an outside force or actor is in control, is it fair to characterize our existence as a simulation? Like Pac Man, are our lives "Programmed and Controlled" by others (as Colin suggests while under the influence of LSD), leading to the conclusion that our sense of free will is a falsehood? One depiction of Stefan's life even shows that his life is just one big test; he is the subject of a warped study that gauges his reactions to a series of events—his experience is an illusion and bears some thematic resemblance to "White Bear." Ultimately, we reach the conclusion that whether and how Stefan is experiencing parallel and divergent realities is decidedly unclear. The complex film invites us to consider these multiple paths as we follow Stefan on a curvy adventure, perhaps through time (if such a construct exists).

As we pursue the diverse narratives stored in the film, our individual navigation of the story may reveal certain preferences to Netflix. In this way, the film might be viewed as a pathway for the company to produce revenue after we conclude the streaming experience.[52] We are empowered to make small decisions (selection of cereal and music) and big decisions (how to engage with Stefan's father while Stefan is in an unstable emotional state). The film does not lack a sense of irony in this regard: one reading is that it is, as *The New York Times* critic Maureen Ryan argues, a "dystopian saga with a subtext about the danger of allowing our technological overlords to monitor and control us" that also includes an overt promo for Netflix—a technology "behemoth bent on world domination."[53] Further, some commentators have speculated that as we watch and exert some level of control over the actions of Stefan, Netflix might be watching us, possibly collecting and seeking to use data for a range of commercial purposes.[54] A careful study and understanding of user preferences could produce invaluable information for Netflix and other third parties. Was the interactive film specially designed to enable our decisions be analyzed by Netflix in a meaningful way? Will Netflix use metrics collected about our selections within the film as it decides what types of new content to produce? Will Netflix sell data about our choices of cereal and music to other corporations? If so, are we, collectively, part of Stefan's journey? As we watch and engage with Stefan, it behooves us to be aware that Netflix may, perhaps, be watching and, in some respects, covertly engaging with (and/or talking about) us as well.

Escaping to Virtual Worlds

Playwright and novelist Max Frisch observed that "Technology is a way of organizing the universe so that man doesn't have to experience it."[55] Journalist Alana Semuels echoes this sentiment, noting that "Technology has allowed people to outsource the things they don't want to do." We see this phenomenon not only with respect to applications of modern technology, but also in the context of outdated forms of technology. A classic example from our popular culture is *The Flintstones'* (1960–1966) utilization of animal-powered technology.[56] Instead of resorting to more labor-intensive means of waste disposal, for example, Fred and Wilma place a pig underneath the kitchen sink.[57] In lieu of washing dirty dishes by hand, the family stuffs them into a pelican's mouth.[58] In theory, the utilization of both primitive and modern forms of technology should provide folks with more time to do other tasks and experience life in new ways. And while it is abundantly clear that the efficiencies created by use of technology provide this benefit—e.g., ordering a product online in a matter of seconds versus an hour-long trip to the store—it is also true that we fail to experience aspects of what was previously considered ordinary life as a result thereof.

Modern forms and applications of technology demonstrate that Frisch is partially correct: human beings often use technology in a way that allows them to temporarily flee harsh realities or the monotonous daily grind in search of virtual worlds that may be more peaceful or adventurous—universes, in short, that provide an escape from the stresses and frustrations of an individual's existence in the real world. Virtual reality applications, as described more fully below, provide folks with the option to exit worlds that do not suit their tastes. Folks do not flee the concept of an "experience" entirely; instead, they can make use of technology to experience multiple virtual worlds, hopping from one to another. Individuals become ultimate, uninhibited universe trekkers. And the implementation of such technologies is expected to be pervasive. Ray Kurzweil predicts, for example, that "By the 2030s, virtual reality will be totally realistic and compelling and we will spend most of our time in virtual environments.... We will all become virtual

5. Alternate Realities, Digital Clones and the Meaning of Life 151

humans."[59] Access to, and immersion within, places such as San Junipero may be in the cards in the near future.

Black Mirror and *Electric Dreams* both take a sharp and critical look at cutting edge technologies, such as virtual reality, augmented reality and mixed reality—each of which allow human beings to experience life in new and fascinating ways. Virtual reality, or "VR," is defined as "an artificial, computer-generated simulation or recreation of a real life environment or situation."[60] Virtual reality—access to which typically requires use of a headset— "immerses the user by making them feel like they are experiencing the simulated reality firsthand, primarily by stimulating their vision and hearing."[61] Dr. Ken Hillis argues that virtual reality "supports the fantasy that communication of messages or information, and the conduits through which they are transmitted, together might offer an adequate imaginary space that would substitute for aspects of the material world considered by many to be exhausted."[62] By contrast, augmented reality, or "AR," is described as a "technology that layers computer-generated enhancements atop an existing reality in order to make it more meaningful through the ability to interact with it."[63] This type of technology is "developed into apps and used on mobile devices to blend digital components into the real world in such a way that they enhance one another."[64] A mainstream example of AR is the popular *Pokemon Go* game, where players attempt to capture virtual depictions of Pokemon characters appearing in the physical world.[65] Mixed, or hybrid reality, or "MR," merges real and virtual worlds where physical and digital objects co-exist and interact with each other.[66]

Applications of the aforementioned technologies to enhance the video game-playing experience have become mainstream, adding additional layers of realism to such games. Virtual reality is expected to disrupt other industries as well, including healthcare, education, sports, architecture, flying and many more. *Forbes* predicts that the market for VR and AR healthcare-related applications will grow to $5.1 billion by 2025, with approximately 3–4 million patients awaiting the introduction of such technology.[67] Virtual reality has been shown to distract patients, thereby aiding in pain reduction. In addition to pain management applications, VR has also been successful in healthcare arenas such as prevention, training and adherence to treatment regimes.[68] "Telemedicine"—or a "cellphone-based standalone VR system"—enables physicians and other medical professionals to provide access to a greater number of individuals and serve populations without adequate access to traditional healthcare.[69] Virtual reality also helps to fulfill the wishes of dying individuals, providing a mechanism for such people to "travel" to places they always wanted to see—all without leaving their beds.

On the education side, VR can be used to effectively transport students to virtual worlds comprised of historical events, or learn about human biology and astronomy by entering virtual worlds where powerful images are displayed through a VR headset. Architects may seek to use VR to "allow them to do a virtual walk through of a building."[70] In sports, professional athletes can train by simulating plays without having to step onto the field.[71] For frequent flyers tired of long, monotonous flights, strapping on a VR headset will allow them to enter exotic worlds without leaving their seats.[72] All these applications (and so many more) are expected to transform human existence as we know it. VR removes many limitations created by forces such as space and time. It allows us to continuously create, explore and enhance new worlds in exciting, non-traditional ways. As with most emerging technologies, however, we must be careful to use VR in moderation—a theme common to several *Black Mirror* and *Electric Dreams* episodes.

Virtual reality creates efficiencies, reducing human reliance on the physical world. Folks need not spend 18 hours on flights to explore exotic locations or to visit historical monuments. Instead, they could simply strap on a headset and fool their brain into believing they are physically on location. Folks can rely less on their physical bodies and more on digital environments to immerse themselves in a wide range of experiences. The human body is a functional unit, but virtual reality reduces the necessity and relevance of such functionality. Virtual reality can overcome physical limitations—explorers accessing virtual environments need not be limited by physical disabilities, age or other frailties of the physical body. We must ask, however, whether unrestricted immersion in such environments is wise. Not only do we lose our bodies in virtual reality; if we are not careful, we may also lose ourselves.

The potential benefits and consequences of the introduction of virtual reality into society are explored throughout contemporary popular culture. In the independent film *Other Life* (2017), for example, powerful biological software creates a virtual universe in someone's mind.[73] Use of the software is addictive, and the government plans to use the software to create a virtual prison system. In the dystopian world presented in *The Matrix* (1999), most folks are unaware that they are living in a simulated reality created by powerful sentient machines.[74] In the futuristic society set out in *Ready Player One* (2018), virtual reality software is used by many humans to escape the poor conditions existing in the real world.[75] In the film *Lawnmower Man* (1992), drugs and virtual reality are used to enhance the intelligence of subjects, with disastrous results.[76] The treatments cause the protagonist (Jobe) to experience intense aggression and he exacts revenge on those who he considers enemies.

5. Alternate Realities, Digital Clones and the Meaning of Life 153

The conscious decision to enter an altered state of reality can be characterized as a form of *escapism*. The ability to enter alternate states of reality, intentionally or otherwise, has been explored in popular films, music and television shows long before the mainstream introduction of virtual reality and augmented reality technologies. In his hit single *Sometimes a Fantasy* (1980), Billy Joel sings the praises of entering a fantasy world of one's own imagination, arguing that the experiences therein could have positive emotional benefits to the dreamer.[77] In *The Wizard of Oz*, we learn that Dorothy's adventure is all a dream. But before her dream starts, she sings *Over the Rainbow*, a song whose lyrics focus on fleeing to another place in search of a better life.[78] (She then dreams that she is "not in Kansas anymore," but learns that home is where she wants to be.) A similar point is made in *The Twilight Zone* episode "Walking Distance" (1959), where a 36-year-old man unexpectedly experiences life as a child in his hometown and realizes that being a child is not as idyllic as he had anticipated or remembered.[79]

The Twilight Zone explored the concept of escapism in a variety of contexts. Many episodes of the series are linked by a common thread, namely a strong desire to flee existing circumstances or an established environment. Examples include: fulfilling a dream to live life as a younger person ("A Short Drink from a Certain Fountain"); seeking refuge from a loveless broken home ("The Bewitchin' Pool"); creating a world devoid of others ("The Mind and the Matter"); traveling back in time ("Back There"); searching for personal connections to the past ("The Trouble with Templeton"); seeking tranquil and serene environments ("A Stop at Willoughby"); reverting back to a previous time to experience love ("Static"); and finding love in unconventional places ("Miniature").[80]

Black Mirror and *Electric Dreams* both examine this theme, too. In the *Black Mirror* episode "Fifteen Million Merits," for example, a woman seeks to escape her reality by winning a reality show. And in the *Electric Dreams* episode "Impossible Planet" (2018), an elderly woman embarks on a highly improbable journey to reach Earth, which had been destroyed by a solar flare. She and her spaceship tour guide miraculously experience Earth and rekindle a romance that the pair seemingly had during another age. This outcome is ambiguous, as it seems that they may have transcended space and time or repeated history in some way. (Perhaps they have somehow entered a parallel universe.) In any case, the woman's nostalgic return to Earth reflects a deep desire to escape her current reality.

People may seek to flee their current realities for many disparate reasons—to escape grief or danger, to find love, to provide entertainment to others or to more generally reach a happier state. Actors train their brains to enter altered states to portray characters in powerful ways, particularly in the context of acting out scenes embedded with great intensity. This task can be emotionally draining and exhaustive, leaving the brain in a state of temporary confusion. In his memoir *A Life in Parts*, actor (and *Electric Dreams* executive producer Bryan Cranston) recounts that during one intense scene while filming *Breaking Bad* (2008–2013), his mind pictured his own daughter dying as opposed to the character (Jane) dying in the scene.[81] Cranston was visibly broken and shaking and had to be held by his fellow cast members during this breakdown.[82] *The Twilight Zone* episode "A World of Difference" highlights this phenomenon, providing satirical commentary on the depths to which actors may immerse themselves in their work—sometimes unable to distinguish life on the set from their natural environments.[83]

Folks use a variety of mediums to accomplish the escape objective, such as immersing themselves in an engrossing fictional film, television series or book.[84] The workers in *The Office* play a murder mystery game to distract themselves from the company's significant financial woes.[85] Other individuals use video games when seeking a break or lose themselves in a meaningful song when searching for a reprieve from the daily grind of their lives. The television series *Kiss Me First*, for example, centers on a girl's decision to escape to her virtual reality video game as she copes with the loss of her mother.[86] And, as Billy Joel observes in the song *Piano Man* (1973), folks attend his concerts to forget about their lives for a couple of hours.[87] Some folks seek to live and dream in the past, a point examined on *The Twilight Zone*'s "16 Millimeter Shrine," where a former actress is obsessed with watching old movies of herself.[88] Virtual reality does not necessarily encourage the idea of escapism or promote its merits—it simply provides new avenues through which folks can flee their lives. It seems that there may in fact be an innate human craving for such escape. As psychologist Andrew Evans observes, "As escapism appears to be a natural mechanism, the mind must have a need for it."[89]

Virtual reality and its voluminous applications present people with the opportunity to experience new, enhanced forms of escapism. The proclivity to experience new virtual environments represents a tectonic shift and transformation of humanity. As Blascovich and Bailenson observe, "We sit on the cusp of a new world fraught with astonishing possibility, potential, and peril as people shift from face-to-face to virtual interaction."[90] Virtual reality applications provide mediums for escapism that are distinct, both in nature and degree, from traditional methods of, and avenues for, seeking reprieve. Apps that promise new "virtual reality environments" could become the most extreme form of escapism yet. Such apps would allow individuals to choose their world and live in it whenever they choose to do so.[91] In such cases, "virtual reality becomes the reality," according to strategic analytics professional David J. Wierz.[92] The blending of real vs. fake, fact. vs. fiction and reality vs. virtual reality is a theme explored on several *Black Mirror* and *Electric Dreams* episodes, most prominently in *Electric Dreams*' "Real Life" (2018) and *Black Mirror*'s "Playtest" (2016). Much of the time, the consequences of entering into such an altered state are innocuous. If the powerful technology is misused or abused, however, the results could be devastating.

Examples of such extreme consequences include user experiences with immersive video games. In 2004, for example, a 13-year-old boy committed suicide after playing the "World of Warcraft" video game for 36 hours straight.[93] He reportedly did so to "join the heroes of the game he worshipped."[94] Another player of the game stated that "Living inside the World of Warcraft seemed preferable to the drudgery of everyday life."[95]

Several *Black Mirror* and *Electric Dreams* episodes tackle the question of what exactly is created by virtual reality. Are the simulated and digitally-enhanced versions of worlds and people created by virtual and augmented realities, respectively, "real" in some sense? How does a digitally simulated universe differ, if at all, from a digital copy of a world or physical being? If digital and real are indistinguishable from one another, why should we value physical life as objectively more important than virtual life? "Playtest" highlights the ability of such innovative technologies to transcend reality and to confuse users.

Horror Games

In *Black Mirror*'s "Playtest," a man (Cooper)—seeking a reprieve from difficult circumstances in his personal life—signs up to test an "interactive augmented reality system," which is described as "layers on top of reality." This powerful technology is a form of artificial intelligence, as it learns about the individual and uses that knowledge to figure out how to most effectively frighten him. Cooper is brought to a creepy mansion, where he becomes progressively more frightened by his "surroundings." He is emotionally broken—confused and unsure how to distinguish between real and fake. As we become aware of Cooper's unceremonious end, we are invited to ask whether the chip installed in his head traps him in this horrific state for eternity.

Cooper escapes the trauma of his personal situation only to be faced with his biggest fear: losing all sense of reality. Perhaps the lesson here is that escapism does not always provide a pathway through which folks can remove problems or circumstances in their lives. Escaping to another reality does not guarantee happiness or a completely new set of circumstances. Perhaps our underlying fears, concerns and motivations cannot be erased by entering an altered state of reality. We see a similar theme in "Real Life," where real and virtual lives overlap so much that it is impossible for the individual to determine which life is real and which is virtual. This leads us to ask fundamental questions about how life is, or should be, defined. Is "reality" a subjective product of an individual's mind or is there an objective conception of what "real" looks like? The answer is less straightforward than one may at first suspect.[96]

Finding the "Real Life"

In *The Office* episode "Local Ad," paper salesman Dwight Schrute creates an avatar in the game "Second Life" in an attempt to remove himself from his real-life troubles.[97] The avatar is intended to reflect his previously happier life. He even creates an avatar for his avatar—"Second Second Life."[98] This utilization of avatars to escape from reality demonstrates a desire to remove one's self, at least temporarily, from an existing reality.

The concept of escapism is also explored in *Electric Dreams*' "Real Life" episode (2018). In the episode, a female cop obtains access to "another life" on a device controlled by a computer chip. She is supposed to accept this other life as reality for a period of time. The other life is similar to what an individual experiences when the individual becomes lost in a dream.[99] The purpose of entering the altered state of reality is to take a "vacation" from her life. She needs a way to escape certain trauma in her life. She alternates between two distinct realities, but they overlap in uncomfortable, confusing ways—the faces of those in each life are the same, but the woman has a different relationship with those individuals in each world. She is a female in one world and a male in the other. Folks from each reality attempt to convince this individual that the world he/she is currently experiencing is the real one—i.e., actual, physical reality. Throughout the episode, we wonder whether she will choose correctly: will she remain trapped in a painful world from which there is no escape?

The episode raises existential questions, including uncertainty about the inherent value of a physical body and what qualities define true existence. We are left to marvel at the keen ability of a technological device to allow a person to shut off his or her actual life and switch to an alternate reality. The episode serves as sharp commentary on the immense power of virtual reality

5. Alternate Realities, Digital Clones and the Meaning of Life

and the possibility that it could trick the brain into believing an entirely fabricated and manufactured reality is real. As Jim Blascovich and Jeremy Bailenson write, "The brain often fails to differentiate between virtual experiences and real ones."[100] They argue further that "the brain doesn't much care if an experience is real or virtual."[101] Outside of the virtual reality context, we can attest to experiences in our daily lives to buttress the point that our brains often do not care whether an environment or presentation accurately reflects reality. Take our indulgence in fictional television shows and the amount of time hardcore fans devote to ensuring that the details within those worlds are consistent. Or consider the fact that advertisers pay athletes millions of dollars to promote goods because they know that consumers will be inclined to buy the advertised products. While consumers are not blind to the athletes' deals, we lose ourselves in a fictionalized world, one in which we believe an athlete's proclamations that he or she uses a product—thereby apparently (and somewhat inexplicably) validating it in our minds. We know that the industry of paid advertising is often based on a fiction, yet we buy into it. There are times where we simply do not care whether we are experiencing or watching something that is based on reality or fantasy.

A related point is examined on *Kiss Me First* (2018), when a mysterious woman named Mania tells the protagonist Leila that she wants Leila to join a select virtual reality community so that the pair can be friends in the real world.[102] This demonstrates that Mania's brain did not much care whether the relationship is real or virtual and in fact seeks to use relationships created in the virtual environment to enhance her physical surroundings. Use of a chip to effectively transport between realities requires a change in an individual's mental state. "Real Life" demonstrates that the failure to manage how you control the way that technology changes your brain can, however, have dangerous consequences. (In contemporary society, drugs can be used to confuse reality and induce alternative mental states.)

It is fair to ask whether the use of virtual reality for purposes of a temporary reprieve from our lives is harmful. Utilization of virtual reality in moderation may, in fact, be healthy. If the brain is fooled into believing a virtual experience is real, must it be assumed that the consequences are always negative? If folks can pursue and find happiness, is there a sound basis to disrupt their newly found contentment? We may question the validity of such feelings, but it is undeniable that they exist, at least in the individual's mind. As Blascovich states, "A virtual second life can replace the 'real life' of some individuals, but this can be good or bad: who is to say that a virtual life that is better than one's physical life is a bad thing?"[103] In addition, folks may immerse themselves in virtual worlds to gain insights into how they could potentially make improvements in their own lives. As Stanford psychologist and author Dr. Elias Aboujaoude posits, "the appeal of these environments is not so much that they help us totally escape reality. Rather, it is that they make us believe that we can recreate and change our own."[104]

An escape to an alternate reality could, however, have severe consequences. First, it must be understood that an escape to another reality does not necessarily mean immediate access to greener pastures. Such environments do not guarantee an abundance of equality or freedom for folks immersed in such worlds. Segregation and exclusionary policies could exist. In *Kiss Me First*, for example, Leila's entrance into a secret segment of a virtual world is initially met with resistance by its core members; most players in this game either do not know of the existence of this segment or are denied access. Second, escapism and the subsequent reversion back to a natural reality could be rife with potential consequences. As psychologist Andrew Evans observes in the context of discussing "negative escapism," one "definition of unhealthy escapism—escapism gone too far—is the effect it has on the essential fabric of living … [in particular, with respect to] the individual in the context of family, friends and social commitments."[105] The "blocking" technology in "White Christmas" masks reality, forcing those subjected to it to be ostracized and lose all social connections. In "Arkangel," an extreme version of a parental advisory device allows parents to prevent children from experiencing potentially disturbing or unsettling content, substituting such content for pixelated images. While arguably beneficial in the very near-term, prolonged usage could have negative consequences—given that children who are not exposed to the exigencies of daily life could become maladjusted and woefully unready to survive the world as they grow up. On *Dexter* (2006–2013), Dexter Morgan escapes from his comfortable social environment.[106] Despite repeatedly toggling between this happy environment and one in which he commits horrific murders, he ultimately loses those closest to him due to his heinous exploits. We witness an extreme version of negative escapism as *Bates Motel*'s (2013–2017) "psycho" Norman Bates exhibits signs of dissociative identity disorder as he morphs into his deceased mother Norma and commits vicious murders.[107] Norman acknowledges the stresses inherent in his situation: "We all have bad days when we wonder what's real and not real."[108]

Although Evans correctly observes that virtual reality "potentially offers a wondrous parallel universe of unlimited possibilities," it is up to humans to exploit these wonders and possibilities in fruitful, productive ways as opposed to engaging in potentially destructive actions.[109] Doing so requires folks to implement knowledge learned while immersed in virtual worlds to improve their own lives and the lives of others in society upon returning to a physical reality. As with most emerging technologies, folks would be wise to use virtual reality and augmented reality in a balanced manner and with an appropriate level of caution. We need to take great care to avoid situations (like those in "Playtest" and "Real Life") where the altered state of reality seems all too real and we lose all sense of space and time. In "Real Life," the extreme confusion caused by a powerful application of virtual reality technology serves as a case study of the effects of the failure to manage technology and use it for the benefit of humankind. In that episode, as in many other *Black Mirror* and *Electric Dreams* episodes, technology ultimately causes harm due to humanity's failure to exert sufficient control over it in a sustainable manner.

Traveling with "The Commuter"

Escapism is the central theme in the *Electric Dreams* episode "The Commuter" (2018), too. In the episode, the protagonist (Ed, a train worker), boards a train and, drawn in by an intriguing woman, travels to a destination that is not on the map (Macron Heights). Doing so enables him to escape the misery of his own life: he has a troubled, violent son and a boring job. When he returns home from the idyllic Macron Heights—a world replete with friendly waitresses serving pie, clear skies and a couple repeatedly celebrating their engagement during each of his visits—his violent son is no longer in the picture, and, apparently, has never been born. His actual life changes due to his entrance into this alternate world.[110]

Macron Heights is a place to which folks flee to leave their current predicaments. Individuals who are drawn to it refuse to accept reality as it is currently exists in the natural world. Macron Heights is, in some respects, a utopia. It is a shiny place where stress, fear, regret and pain do not exist. It presents a false life—an escape from one's reality—one without a basis in truth. While existing pains are vanquished, new regrets emerge in their place. The episode invites us to ask how we would feel if we were faced with the erasure of someone who is close to us, yet who causes us anxiety. Would we experience deep sadness and a sense of missed opportunity over never having known such a person? We might realize that the alternate life presented by Macron Heights—one devoid of true love, earned accolades or accomplishments and protected by an invisible layer of false, manufactured sanguinity—lacks meaning and genuine happiness. Living a true life, one unencumbered by any foreign protective barriers, gives purpose to an individual's actions, thoughts and emotions. Perhaps truth is more important than happiness—a premise that is relevant in connection with a consideration of the memory modification and deletion technologies to which we are introduced in "The Entire History of You" and the film *Eternal Sunshine of the Spotless Mind*. An occasional break from reality may be beneficial at times, but an idyllic world shielded from the consequences of one's actions is not a viable or meaningful path for brave individuals intent on reclaiming their lives and moving forward. Taking such an escapist route is, in many respects, a cowardly course of action.

When Ed is reminded by his female companion that he had always dreamed of such an idyllic, peaceful life, he retorts: "Dreaming is not the same as wishing it's true!" We wonder if Ed—like many of us who would perhaps welcome a brief respite from troubling circumstances—is just a fair-weathered escapist. His interest may have been piqued by this new world, but does his heart lie with his family? As we watch Ed straggle between the two competing realities, we wonder whether his unconditional love for his son—not guilt or a sense of obligation to live with him—will triumph over the neat perfection of Macron Heights. Will he be willing and eager to go down with the ship, with the understanding that painful times likely lie ahead?[111] If Macron Heights cannot replicate true love, would it be reasonable to expect that a person would choose to subsist in such a reality?

If we seek to exploit virtual reality as a mechanism to escape and seek a brief respite from our daily lives, we need to take the warnings provided by "The Commuter" seriously. A momentary escape to an idyllic world may provide some short-term benefits, but such a world could feel empty and meaningless because it does not allow life to proceed in a normal course. A life that is well-lived is one in which an individual faces and overcomes struggles that come his or her way. A long-term escape to a world without the possibility of disappointment, where things move with certainty in a defined order and definite pattern, lacks elements that make life special, unpredictable and, ultimately, worth living. As we watch the episode, we wonder whether Ed will come to this realization, and expect that doing so will allow him to gain a greater appreciation for the life that he lives—despite the enduring anxiety he feels over his son's troubled nature and other exigencies of life. Would extinguishing the existence of his son in a contrived way to eliminate his frustration over his son's antics be a viable option? Perhaps the only way to give meaning to life is to live it fully, deal with emotions such as fear and regret, and appreciate whatever life has given you—even if things do not go according to plan or if opportunities are cruelly taken away.

All Aboard the "U.S.S. Callister"

In *The Simpsons* episode "Treehouse of Horror VI," Homer Simpson enters a three-dimensional environment.[112] He is perplexed by his surroundings, and grows fearful when he ultimately ends up on Earth and encounters real human beings. Homer has entered another universe, an alternate state with which he is neither familiar nor comfortable. He transforms into a three-dimensional being and expresses uncertainty regarding his new physical body and surroundings. The convergence of natural and digital universes is also examined on *Black Mirror*.

In the award-winning *Black Mirror* episode "U.S.S. Callister" (2017), we watch a brilliant, reclusive programmer and co-founder of a video game company (Robert) become frustrated by his co-workers' failure to recognize the importance of his work and status at the company. He fetches each co-worker's DNA and uses it to create digital clones within a space adventure game that is reminiscent of a *Star Trek* environment. Robert places the DNA in a machine at home and effectively merges the physical and digital worlds in which he resides. He serves as the captain of the U.S.S. Callister spaceship and treats the digital clones aboard the ship miserably: exerting sexual dominance over the women, and, in one particularly egregious case, creates and destroys additional copies of the company CEO's son to ensure obedience from the CEO clone.[113,114,115] Like other serial abusers of digital copies in *Black Mirror* dystopian universes, Robert feels no remorse about the pain that he causes his subordinates aboard the ship, treating them as puppets and using this virtual environment as a platform to exact revenge for what he perceives as his co-workers' mistreatment of him in the real world.

The episode is instructive in terms of the perceived value of escaping to a digital environment. Robert uses the game to escape from natural reality and creates an environment where he alone is in control and no one dare question his ultimate authority without facing his wrath. For Robert, hiding within the game and showcasing an entirely different side to his personality is a meaningful experience even though he is not exacting revenge on his colleagues, but rather on digital copies thereof. The artificially-created environment provides him with the opportunity to escape his own personality and assume the aggressive persona of the company's CEO (Walton). This outlet enables him to deal with his day-to-day frustrations while knowing that he will have the opportunity to have real power and control while captain of the ship—an opportunity that Robert finds deeply compelling and enormously satisfying. Causing the digital copies to suffer satisfies Robert's desire to exact revenge on the physical persons from which the copies were made—

even though the physical individuals are completely unaware of, and do not experience, this treatment. The digital copies are entirely separate, independent entities and the humans from whom they are copied experience none of the sensations or emotions of the copies.

"U.S.S. Callister" sparks comparisons to "Hated in the Nation" and "Shut Up and Dance" in that punishment is meted out and poetic justice realized in the natural world based on actions taken by folks in a virtual environment ("U.S.S. Callister") or while using the Internet to perform actions ("Hated in the Nation," "Shut Up and Dance"). All three episodes explore the theme of accountability for individuals' behavior in environments and worlds likely considered insulated from such accountability. "U.S.S. Callister" can also be compared to other episodes in which digital copies are created and, in some cases, abused. The cruel treatment of digital copies is a theme examined in both "Black Museum" and "White Christmas." As in both of those episodes, the digital beings can think and feel both emotions and pain. Because the copies in "U.S.S. Callister" not only experience torture and pain but were created for the sole purpose of enduring such abuse, Robert's actions (in terms of both creating the copies and torturing them) are highly immoral. In this vein, Robert's actions are comparable to those of the museum operator's creation and abuse of the hologram of the prisoner. The corporate representative's / informant's actions in "White Christmas" are condemnable, though the sole purpose of the creation of the copies was not tied to intentional abuse. Abuse of the copies in that episode is reprehensible, but we can at least confidently acknowledge that the copies were created for exploitation to further a non-retributive agenda.

Life on a Chip

Several *Black Mirror* episodes, such as "San Junipero," "Hang the DJ," "White Christmas" and, as discussed earlier, "Black Museum," explore the question of whether digital copies (i.e., digital clones) of physical beings possess characteristics that fully embody what we consider the essential elements of life. Such episodes force us to ask questions about the nature of life and how technological innovation may redefine its essential meaning. It is important to consider the composition of a digital copy, and whether such copies contain features that humanize them. Like physical clones of physical beings, the digital copies in these episodes subsist separate and apart from the physical being. They are entirely separate entities, unconnected to the natural person from whom they are cloned. The physical being does not feel the sensations of the natural being—unlike the situation in "Black Museum," where the physical being does feel such sensations. Episodes such as "San Junipero" and portions of "Black Museum" also examine the nature and value of a virtual life from the perspectives of physical human beings. In such situations, powerful technology enables (physical) human beings to effectively live vicariously through "life" stored on a chip.

The overarching lesson from the first set of the episodes described above is that insofar as a digital copy is (at least superficially) existing in a form that is indistinguishable from traditional reality, those copies should be treated with respect and dignity. This idea is expressed in episodes such as "Hang the DJ," where we are led to believe and are given no reason to question that the digital copies of Frank and Amy are real individuals. These copies seem to feel and experience real emotions, such as love, sadness, hope, anxiety, regret, frustration and anger. While they are created to satisfy the desires of actual, physical human beings, these digital copies of Frank and Amy seem all too human in their ambitions and motivations. When they dissipate, the audience is left to wonder whether they were treated fairly—or, more importantly, whether fair treatment should be afforded to any digital copies that seem, by all indications, to possess and retain certain human qualities and traits. Sometimes, digital images or manifestations of physical beings are embraced—take, for example, Waldo's popularity in "The Waldo Moment"—but in most *Black Mirror* episodes, the rights of digital entities that are untethered to natural individuals appear to be non-existent.

Technology has the power to modify the way in which we look at life and define humanity. The technology presented on *Black Mirror* (and, in some cases, introduced in contemporary society, such as cloning and gene-edited babies) gives humans the ability to arguably create and modify forms of life—and enable folks to experience life in new ways. The exercise of such power demands an appropriate use of discretion and accountability for improper exploitation of the treatment of the newly created life forms.

A Visit to the "Black Museum"

In *Black Mirror*'s "Black Museum," a woman named Nish visits a strange museum replete with criminological artifacts. A museum operator named Rolo Haynes offers the woman a tour, and the audience is introduced to three interwoven tales.[116] In the first part, a doctor uses a chip to feel the physical sensations of his patients. This transference of sensation has unintended consequences, as discussed earlier in this book.

The second part of the episode recounts the story of a married couple, Jack and Carrie. After becoming comatose following a car accident, Carrie's consciousness is transferred to Jack's brain. Carrie vicariously sees and feels emotions and physical sensations and, in some sense, lives through Jack. After Jack meets another woman, he "pauses" Carrie and eventually agrees to extract her consciousness and place it into a stuffed monkey plush doll, where it remains stuck to this day. Several legal and ethical issues arise in connection with this story. First, there is a question as to whether Carrie gives informed consent to the extraction of her consciousness into Jack's brain. Through use of special technology, she communicates her consent to the transfer while comatose by "pressing" a button. As previously discussed, this consent may not have been fully informed, however, as the risks are not communicated to her. She also does not consent to the transfer of consciousness to the stuffed monkey.

Haynes points out that at the time of the planned transfer to the monkey deletion of her consciousness is not legally impermissible, although it raises ethical questions. Eventually, the United Nations makes it illegal to transfer the consciousness into a stuffed doll, but also makes it illegal to delete.[117] Carrie's consciousness is therefore in no man's land—a state of legal limbo—demonstrating that the law is inadequate to handle the nuances and circumstances created by use of this technology (a theme discussed in detail in Chapter 4). This outcome, combined with the fact that Carrie's consciousness can experience suffering, raises ethical concerns about the nature of the technology and its manifestations, the transfer process and the lack of control that the conscious self has once a transfer is initiated. The consciousness can be paused, transferred again and bad actors can even delete it. Are these actions akin to slavery or murder, respectively? What rights should the "conscious self" have, given its displacement from the physical being? Is physicality a prerequisite for the applicability of the concept of inalienable rights? Furthermore, is it ethical for one human to host two consciousnesses? Does doing so raise concerns from a religious perspective? What does it mean for someone's consciousness to live within you? Should the host be indicted and condemned as a slave owner? These are just some of the perplexing questions raised by the morbid application of this technology in the story of Jack and Carrie.

Trapped During a "White Christmas"

The questions of what rights should be afforded to an artificially-intelligent digital copy of a human being, and how humans should treat such a copy are

5. Alternate Realities, Digital Clones and the Meaning of Life   165

also examined on the *Black Mirror* episode "White Christmas." The episode is divided into three interwoven parts (much like the format and presentation of "Black Museum") and raises serious legal and ethical questions about the nature and definition of life, police overreach and misconduct and the use of technology to interfere with, and limit, individual liberties. Part 1, as discussed further in Chapter 4, examines the use of technology for purposes of non-consensual sexual voyeurism.[118] That part foreshadows elements of the rest of the episode, as a murder takes place in which the murderer poisons an individual to transition him to another metaphysical "state." Parts 2 and 3 of the episode explore related concepts of making and treatment of digital copies of natural human beings.

The second part of the episode serves as biting satirical commentary on the popularity and ubiquity of "smart" homes powered by devices whose inner-workings many of us do not fully understand. In this segment, a "digital cookie" had been implanted in a woman's brain, shadowing her and learning her preferences and inclinations and gaining a general understanding of how her brain works.[119] The cookie—which is a digital copy of the woman, a "simulated brain full of code"—is extracted from the woman via a surgical procedure and inserted into an egg-shaped device. The woman then uses the cookie to perform menial tasks, such as preparing coffee, scheduling appointments and setting alarm clocks. It is as if a person's consciousness were stuck inside of an Alexa digital assistant device. The cookie is a slave.

After the digital copy angrily protests her predicament, the company representative manipulates her sense of space and time, pressing a few buttons to mute her and trick her into believing she had been stuck for months when it had only been a few seconds. This deception, enslavement and the technology itself raise serious ethical questions. We are forced to consider the nature and definition of life. Should we define life as form over substance or do the substantive characteristics of an entity hold any weight in making such a determination? A physical body is not a prerequisite for the creation of digital technology capable of making decisions, having feelings and expressing emotions. Is it ethical to force such digital copies to suffer? Does a copy of a physical human being possess any human characteristics?

The copy created from the woman's brain is not a stagnant, static entity. It can do more than perform the routine tasks that it was created to handle. One can make a strong argument based on this technology that life is not a binary determination; rather, perhaps we can define it on a spectrum and assign rights accordingly. She is clearly able to feel and express emotions, such as fear, sadness and anger. She seems to be a sentient being in this regard, and the informant acknowledges as such, asking her at one point how she is "feeling." The representative later defends his cruel treatment of the cookie and dismisses any notion that his behavior was improper, arguing that "It wasn't really real, so it wasn't really barbaric."

The representative brushes off any difficult questions and concerns about his horrible treatment of copies possessing human-like qualities. He speaks of the situation in a callous way, explaining that his goal was to "break" the digital copy without having it "snap completely."[120] The fact that the representative needed to break the cookie's spirit serves as an indication that she possesses a human-like quality of endurance, seeking to persevere under difficult circumstances. She need not possess a physical body to feel or express her pain or anger. She is locked up without any due process or legal protections, despite possessing so many elements that comprise life. On a spiritual level, she may not have a distinct soul, but it seems that the digital copy deserves some form of protection against those who wish to exploit it for personal benefit, creating needless suffering. The act of creating a cookie that so closely resembles life as we know it should produce a corresponding obligation not to abuse the immense power of creation.

Torturing Holograms

If the representative's poor treatment of the cookie in the second part of "White Christmas" is ethically questionable, the torture by Haynes of a digital hologram of Nish's father in the third part of "Black Museum" represents an act wholly defined by moral bankruptcy and depravity. In exchange for a cash payout to his family, a convicted (yet apparently innocent) murderer signs over the rights to his "digital self." Haynes performs a "fully conscious upload" of the prisoner as he is executed in the electric chair. The prisoner reemerges as a hologram in the museum, where the operator encourages visitors to pull the execution lever. It is clear that the hologram feels the extraordinary pain, and when the operator accepts higher payment for extended simulations of the electrocution experience (longer than ten seconds), the prisoner's spirit is broken and the damage becomes permanent. He becomes a shell of himself, demonstrating that digital beings can experience real change in terms of their personalities and the way in which they interact with physical beings.

The treatment of the prisoner arguably represents the most severe and cruelest treatment seen in any *Black Mirror* episode—rivaled perhaps only by the abhorrent creation and destruction of Walton's son Tommy in "U.S.S. Callister." This episode strongly pulls at our heartstrings and forces us to seri-

5. Alternate Realities, Digital Clones and the Meaning of Life 167

ously consider prohibiting abominable treatment of digital beings. It also leads us to question why tourists would feel comfortable pulling the lever, causing the pain and even purchasing souvenir snapshots that encapsulate the hologram's torturous moments. It may be the case that the tourists simply copy each other, falling into the trap of "groupthink"—a phenomenon in which achieving group consensus is a primary objective, resulting in folks feeling discouraged to act creatively and disclaiming individual responsibility for actions.[121]

A counter perspective on the above is that the digital cookie, notwithstanding any of its "feelings," is simply a product of technological innovation. If we provide legal rights to a creature created by technology, are we allowing technology to effectively manage us? At what point do creations become as important—or perhaps more important—than their creators? These issues—along with questions about the creation of a spectrum of humanity—are addressed in depth later in this chapter.

The Constitutionality of Advanced Blocking Technology

The use of technology to mask reality is explored in various contexts on *Black Mirror* and *Electric Dreams*, whether via the aforementioned "escapism" episodes or the abuse of devices (see "Arkangel"). The potentially dire consequences resulting from the misuse and abuse of such masking technology are explored at length in "White Christmas."

In the third part of "White Christmas," a woman uses "Z-Eye" technology to permanently block her husband from communicating with or seeing her and her soon-to-be-born child.[122] This technology prevents him from seeing facial or other salient, distinguishable features on both her and her child and extends to photos of both. He only sees them as gray amorphous figures and cannot communicate with them. The man experiences deep sadness because he has been cut out of their lives, and when he learns certain truths about the circumstances of the child's birth, he becomes enraged. This episode highlights, and provides sharp commentary on, the possibility of deleterious consequences emanating from the use of powerful technology that masks reality. It also invites us to consider the similarities to blocking folks from our lives via technology platforms, especially on social media. Implementation of technology that gives folks the ability to isolate others can lead to grief, despair and chaos.

Each of the above stories is set against a backdrop of two "men" sitting in a secluded cabin exchanging these accounts.[123] One of the men is an undercover informant who combines savvy investigative techniques with invasive technology to extract a confession from a digital copy of a prisoner.[124, 125] Law enforcement inserts an "augmented reality" chip into a prisoner-defendant's brain.[126] The chip—which houses a digital copy of the physical prisoner—is "transported" to a reality where "he" is not a prisoner, but instead a roommate in a secluded (simulated) cabin with another individual (who, unbeknownst to the digital copy) is a police informant. As the informant and cookie talk, the informant convinces the digital cookie to reveal his reason for being in the cabin. The episode invites us to consider the potential of cops relying on confessions made by digital copies of folks.

The interactions between the "men" in the cabin raise a series of difficult (and fascinating) questions with respect to the digital cookie, the prisoner and the informant. Regarding the cookie, such questions include: What is the nature of the simulated "reality" that the digital cookie experiences? Is the digital cookie entitled to legal rights, given the fact that it expresses emotions and seems to feel anger, pain, frustration and regret? Are there moral or ethical issues with deceiving and imprisoning a cookie? Should the digital copy of the prisoner be forced to remain in a simulated cabin without the exercise of due process? Contemporary legal systems do not address such issues. This episode serves as a wake-up call that our systems of justice lag behind and have not caught up to the rapid introduction of modern technologies.

With respect to the prisoner, thorny questions include: Should a confession made by a cookie be taken seriously from an evidentiary perspective and used to potentially hurt or help the prisoner's standing in a legal setting? If so, would a designated number of simulations need to be run that show a required degree of consistency in statements made by the copy? Would such simulations need to remove variables such as the "location" of a simulation (such as cabin vs. a beach setting)?[127] Are the prisoner's legal rights violated by the invasive implantation and extraction of a cookie? Is the manipulation of such a cookie for purposes of using a confession against the prisoner an unfair way to circumvent the prisoner's due process rights? Most of these questions have definitive answers, and it is clear that the rights of a physical human being are violated by law enforcement and the informant's manipulative use of technology in this episode. Even if the prisoner had been read his Miranda rights—a legal requirement upon being held in police custody to ensure due process for folks accused of crimes—it would seem the protections afforded to him by Miranda would likely have been negated due to police deception. Because the prisoner's rights were violated by the invasive procedure of implanting and then extracting a cookie device, none of the

5. Alternate Realities, Digital Clones and the Meaning of Life   169

statements that the digital copy makes—including, but not limited to, his confession—should be admissible in a court of law. We would not want to live in a world where technology is used to effectively circumvent our due process rights, including with respect to processes and procedures for police investigations, interviews and depositions. Basic civil liberties of the individual are taken away by implementation of extremely invasive technology—presumably without any initial informed consent. The purpose of Constitutional and other legal protections for the criminally accused is to require the prosecution to prove its case beyond a reasonable doubt without taking advantage of a vulnerable defendant. The failure to maintain these protections and to allow technology to adversely affect how accused folks are treated would change the fabric of our democratic republic, one which currently strives to provide reasonable protections to respect the rights and liberties of individuals.

Constitutional questions arise as to the legality and legitimacy of the nature of the informant's punishment. We learn that the informant is also a criminal and he had agreed to employ the coercive investigative techniques described above in exchange for a reduced punishment for his illegal, non-consensual sexual voyeurism (and failure to report a murder) shown during part 1 of the episode. At the end of the episode, he learns his sentence: he is not imprisoned, but a chip is implanted in his brain that mimics the "Z-Eye" technology introduced during part 3 of the episode. This technology blocks him from seeing facial or other salient, distinguishable features on any individual. He is forced to wander this dystopian world as an outsider—ignored by, and unable to communicate effectively with, other individuals.

This (presumably permanent) punishment may not pass Constitutional muster. The 8th Amendment to the United States Constitution prohibits "cruel and unusual punishment."[128] In *Furman v. Georgia* (1972), the United States Supreme Court held that there are four principles which should be used to determine whether a punishment is so severe that it should be designated "cruel and unusual."[129] These principles include: (1) "a punishment must not by its severity be degrading to human dignity"; (2) a punishment must not be "obviously inflicted in wholly arbitrary fashion"; (3) a punishment must not be so severe that it is "clearly and totally rejected throughout society"; and (4) a punishment must not be "patently unnecessary."[130] Strong arguments can be made that there are other ways to effectively punish the informant for his actions (principle 4), and that implementation of this technology should be rejected by society (principle 3), a point buttressed by potential consequences emanating from its implementation as seen in part 3 of the episode. Most significantly, the use of the technology to permanently block the informant' ability to communicate with anyone seems like an extraordinarily severe punishment, one that defeats the meaning, purpose and value of life—and, with it, the dignity of the informant (principle 1).

In addition to issues regarding the nature of the punishment, there appear to be serious questions about the processes and procedures used with respect to determining the punishment. Per the second principle set forth in *Furman*, arbitrary punishments are a relevant factor in determining whether a punishment is "cruel and unusual." It is troubling that the police department, as opposed to a court of law independent of the police, metes out the punishment. It seems that the punishment is determined in a capricious manner. It is not apparent that the defendant has a right to appeal this "reduced" sentence, and it is not clear if there are any parameters or guideposts used by law enforcement to determine the sentence.

"White Christmas" is so brilliant because it forces us to look at difficult questions from multiple angles and perspectives. For example, in part 2, we consider whether digital copies should have rights akin to those afforded to physical human beings. While this point is also examined in part 3, the latter turns the purpose of the initial question on its head. Where a copy was a servant in part 2, part 3 shows a copy as a servant of police and harmful to the interests of the physical person from whom it was copied. Taken together, the episode encourages the audience to take an objective view of the responsibilities of those creating and using technology that has the power to arguably redefine life and question the meaning and value of our collective existence.

Defining Humanity: "Human Is" vs. "The Father Thing"

In *The Twilight Zone* episode "Number 12 Looks Just Like You," every individual, upon reaching adulthood, undergoes a surgical procedure known as "the Transformation" to convert his or her body into an attractive model.[131] The episode satirizes folks' obsession with their physical appearances and demonstrates that conformity with respect to physical features can lead to a loss of individuality. Physical attributes are valued by humans (in part for superficial reasons), even as we potentially move towards a hybrid existence where the natural merges with the digital.

In the natural world, physical characteristics function as important status markers—connections to past experiences that go well beyond engendering attractiveness between individuals. In *The Twilight Zone* episode "The Trade-Ins," two senior citizens seek to substitute their physical bodies for younger replacement models.[132] The episode is instructive in terms of the couple's feelings about the value of their bodies. Instead of serving as barriers to a meaningful experience, the couple's frail bodies represent a lifetime of love, commitment and memories of happy times together.

The Twilight Zone showed us that physicality is a relevant concept beyond the utilitarian and functional elements of a body. Our natural bodies are important, of course, for purposes of identification (see "Mirror Image").[133] The series also explored the metamorphosis and transformation of the body and other physical characteristics (see "The Fugitive").[134] And it also examined the ways in which humans and robots may represent interchangeable beings. For example, when advanced, lifelike robots are designed to resemble our physical characteristics, the risk of robots and humans switching places to fool others increases (see "In His Image").[135] The episode invites us to consider the possibility of a robot forming a romantic relationship with a human only to be destroyed and replaced by the human whose physical body and characteristics formed the basis of the robot's design and make up. How will the other party react to such a switch? Would she even notice the difference between human and robot, considering the robot himself lived most of his life with a lack of self-awareness of his status? From the perspective of human inventors, is it wise to build robots that effectively serve as improved, better versions of ourselves, creating a physical double that embodies characteristics that we deem superior? Would engaging in a development process that cherry-picks those characteristics that we wish to retain while adding new ones that improve upon ourselves represent responsible behavior?

In a world obsessed with self-improvement and the dream of producing "better" versions of ourselves, it is not surprising that folks have considered whether technology could be used as a means to achieving such ends. The theme of using technology to escape existing realities by creating "superior" versions of ourselves has been examined throughout popular culture. On the television series *Family Matters* (1989–1998), for example, Steve Urkel develops a "transformation chamber" to take on the identity of historical figures such as Albert Einstein and celebrities such as Bruce Lee.[136] Urkel frequently transforms into an alter-ego—Stefan Urquelle—to win the admiration of his love interest, Laura Winslow.[137]

The Twilight Zone examined other aspects of physicality and how such elements might relate to our other distinguishing characteristics. In the episode "The Masks," for example, a dying man effectively forces his relatives to wear ugly masks that reflect each relative's actual personality.[138] The physical characteristics of the masks symbolize each relative's character traits. And in the episode "Eye of the Beholder," a society consisting of pig-faced individuals recoils in horror upon seeing a beautiful woman's unbandaged face.[139] When a doctor removes a woman's bandages, her beauty is revealed to the audience. In both episodes, physical features are considered defining characteristics of the individual.

Black Mirror explores the ways in which folks place special emphasis on physical traits and characteristics. In "U.S.S. Callister," for example, villain Robert Daly is eager to torture copies of folks who have wronged him in the natural world and is the least bit unsatisfied that the natural folks are not experiencing his punishments. The personalities of the copies and the natural folks are decidedly different from one another, as they are separate and distinct entities. But Daly equates the natural folks and their copies because of their identical physical appearances.

Electric Dreams presents two competing narratives and perspectives on the potentially symbiotic relationship between physical appearance and innate characteristics that define an individual being. In the *Electric Dreams* episode "Human Is" (2018), a general who mistreats and verbally abuses his wife appears to be killed during an alien combat mission. Upon his surprise return, the man's demeanor and overall personality are fundamentally different than before the mission. His wife must decide whether (and how) to convince authorities that the man is in fact her husband and not an alien replacement. Do the man's appearance and overall looks define him as a person? The episode forces us to question whether we would proceed with building a life together with a partner despite a lack of history or familiarity with one another if the replacement is kinder, gentler and treats us well.

The reaction of the general's wife in "Human Is" can be sharply contrasted with the response of a boy (Charlie) whose father's body is inhabited by an alien being in the *Electric Dreams* episode "The Father Thing" (2018). Charlie completely and utterly rejects the alien, explaining that it is a person's "insides" that matter, not the superficial exterior body. Charlie would not agree with the general's wife's apparent belief that there is a definite symbiotic relationship between an individual's outward appearance and the way in which we relate to and interact with that individual. Charlie's perspective is similar to that of the folks living in the dystopian world set forth in the series *Altered Carbon* (2018–present).[140] Immortality is defined in that show as an everlasting consciousness, one that can be transferred from one physical body, or host, to another.

Defining human qualities and characteristics is a tricky subject, particularly in the age of artificial intelligence and other powerful technologies that may seem to blur the line between human beings and their creations.

Synthetic Recreations of Humans

> "No day shall erase you from the memory of time."
> —Virgil, *The Aeneid* (19 B.C.E.)[141]

In the *Black Mirror* episode "Be Right Back," a woman's (Martha) boyfriend (Ash) dies, and her friend signs her up for a unique service that allows her to "talk" to "Ash." Martha writes to "Ash" and advanced software searches all of Ash's past online interactions with folks. This exercise generates realistic voice and digital responses, intending to duplicate and mimic Ash's personality and reactions. Like the aforementioned *Electric Dreams* episodes, the episode raises questions as to how to define humanity and touches on the concept of escapism. Executive producer Annabel Jones describes the episode as a "story about love and grief in the 21st century"; one that asks how folks "mourn in the modern world, where everyone is digitally present."[142] Jones explains that the episode forces us to consider how folks can "let go" in a world in which a deceased spouse's "image and videos are still playing on Facebook and you can carry them" around at all times.[143]

The digital resurrection technology explored in this episode invites us to question existing conceptions of life and death. Much like "San Junipero," it challenges us to consider redefining these concepts. Do we define life by the existence of natural physical characteristics? By the ability of an actual person's consciousness to interact with the world—a concept explored in the film *Transcendence* (2014), when a man's consciousness is uploaded to a powerful computer?[144] By a diligent reconstruction of a natural person's physical and emotional make-up? Do we dare stray from the traditional notion of death? Do we define death solely in reference to the natural person's inability to experience and engage with others, or does a realistic, synthetic version of an individual that interacts with others lead us to a different definition and conclusion? Should we distinguish between "personal death" (i.e., as it applies to the individual) and "death within the community" (i.e., no longer interacting with others even in a synthetic format)?

If the software accurately replicates the personality, demeanor, responses and reactions of Ash, what characteristics of Ash are missing—at least from the perspective of those who interact with the software? While the software is not a sentient being, it creates an impression that others can use to continue engagement with an entity that is, for some intents and purposes, no different than the natural Ash. This becomes even clearer when Martha orders the body that hosts the software—a host that is in the exact physical form of Ash. And Calo's recitation of research suggests that our interactions with interfaces that include human-like features may resemble the way in which we interact with natural humans.[145]

Spending time interacting with powerful technologies—especially those that "watch" us (such as artificially intelligent robots)—has a demonstrable impact on our behaviors and emotional responses. We feel, justifiably or not, that we must always be "on." As Calo notes, "We tend to react to human-like machines and programs as though they were actually human."[146] Much like Bailenson's and Blascovich's conclusion that the brain does not react differently to real versus virtual environments, Calo observes that "Our brains often cannot tell the difference between fake people and real ones—even though we know, intellectually, that the 'person' we're interacting with is not complete or real. We still react to it the same way, right down to our psychological response."[147] Perhaps this serves as a partial explanation for why Zheng Jiajia, a Chinese engineer, married a sex robot that he had developed and designed.[148] Research has shown that "people are not evolved to twentieth-century technology. The human brain evolved in a world in which *only* humans exhibited rich social behaviors, and a world in which *all* perceived objects were real physical objects."[149]

These observations are relevant to an analysis of Martha's reactions to the various forms of the recreated Ash in "Be Right Back"—from communication via written messages to phone to physical communication. The episode explores this progression, and her reactions throughout each step. She seeks and then experiences an emotional attachment to Ash—with such attachment increasing in intensity when the interface takes on a physical form. Her anger at the recreated Ash reaches a climax when he is in a physical state. This supports the premise that the more human-like the interface, the stronger our response.

Our reactions to artificially-created beings intended to resemble those from the past is also examined on *The Twilight Zone*'s "Uncle Simon."[150] Here, in sharp contrast to "Be Right Back," we see that robots may provide an unwelcome connection to the past. In the episode a cruel, verbally abusive man secretly builds a robot and programs it to "mature" and eventually match his voice and personality. The niece feels more and more threatened by the robot as it takes on the attitude of her uncle: the robot berates her and barks harsh orders at her. She adapts her behavior as the robot becomes a substitute for her uncle.

Just like the niece in "Uncle Simon," Martha feels as though the physical recreation of Ash is watching her and adjusts her behavior accordingly. She attempts to recreate her previous relationship with the natural Ash by engaging in such activities. Martha's behavior in this regard is consistent with research in this area. Social experiments have confirmed that folks often work more assiduously to "present themselves in a more positive light with a talk-face display than when interactions with a text display."[151]

Does Martha lose anything by continuing a "relationship" with the synthetic duplicate? Perhaps, but given the software's propensity for accurately cloning Ash's reactions and nature, she initially maintains and expresses her love for Ash, notwithstanding his death. If, as research has shown, the brain does not necessarily care if an environment is real or artificial, are manifestations of emotions, such as love, with an artificially-created duplicate any different than experiencing a virtual environment?[152] Sure, an emptiness may arise in such a circumstance but if the option of escaping to a situation in which communication with loved ones seemingly exists, is there harm in indulging in the escape?

While Martha is not interacting with a being by any traditional definition, she is able to find some degree of comfort and peace in her continued engagements with an effective duplicate of her boyfriend. The synthetically-recreated Ash is, not surprisingly, insufficient for Martha. The "relationship" that she forms with synthetic Ash proves to be unfulfilling, as his lack of ability to engage in independent creative thought and exhibit true feelings dooms any potential future together. Because the software is limited to Ash's previous experiences, it is unable to respond effectively to new stimuli. Martha's experience with using the software supports the validity of the philosopher Soren Kierkegaard's observation that "Life can only be understood backwards; but it must be lived forward."[153] Synthetic Ash draws on past experiences to formulate responses in some situations, but it does not react appropriately to Martha's frustrations or physical altercations because his archive lacks such a response. While he pleases her sexually and tells her that he loves her, Martha knows that the synthetic being feels no physical or emotional attachment to, or connection with, her. She eventually becomes frustrated, telling him that he is just a "performance" of things that the real Ash did in the past and lacks the ability to have real, independent thought. The episode asks us to consider whether the enslavement of synthetic Ash, keeping him around for novelty purposes, is cruel, given the fact that he does not feel emotions (unlike those *Black Mirror* scenarios where quasi-human beings are imprisoned and/or tortured, with the being feeling such punishments).

The Spectrum of Humanity

"Humanity is not a state. It's a quality."
—Leo Elster, *Humans*[154]

In "1984," protagonist Winston Smith posits that "It's not so much staying alive, it's staying human that is important."[155] But technology may be moving us in a different direction. Futurist Ray Kurzweil predicts that human beings will merge directly with technology by the 2030s.[156] He believes that humans with a chip implanted in their brains will be "godlike."[157] This development would entail human brains connecting with a cloud environment, much like we see in "San Junipero." Kurzweil believes that such a scenario means that "our thinking then will be a hybrid of biological and non-biological thinking."[158] While such a potentiality may be seen as a threat to the way in which we define humanity, Kurzweil paints a more optimistic picture—predicting that we will "enhance ourselves," rather than allow such a change to detract from who we are as a species.[159] He further argues that the very conception of forming hybrid beings is a fundamentally human notion at its core. The desire to adapt and augment ourselves is, Kurzweil argues, "the nature of being human—we transcend our limitations."[160] This concept has been explored in popular culture, most famously in the blockbuster film *Avatar* (2009), where human intelligence is injected into a foreign, biological host body to explore another planet's (Pandora) biosphere.[161] By using the genetically-engineered body, a remotely located physical human is able to interact with the native people of Pandora.

Armed with the knowledge that our hybrid existence could be an immortal one, would we alter our behavior? The fact that we would be overcoming such a significant human limitation—a finite existence—by subsisting on a cloud platform could lead to marked changes in humans' interactions with each other and the world.

The fascinating questions raised earlier in this chapter relating to the potential legal rights that should perhaps be recognized and afforded to digital copies of physical individuals lead to broader questions about humanity's relationships with its creations. Given hypothetical situations where such creations—whether digital copies or robots—feel emotion, should our legal system provide special protections given to other protected classes in contemporary society? The ultimate determination as to whether such creations qualify as human—and with such classification, be held to human obligations and receive human benefits—may not be one that allows for a binary "yes or no" response.

Perhaps the scope and nature of rights afforded to such creations should be based on a nuanced examination of several factors. Examples of such factors, may include, by way of example: an ability to empathize; a capability to experience; defined and measurable degrees of cognition and consciousness; and the possession of a moral compass enabling the creation to appreciate justice and fairness.¹⁶² The ability to feel and express love for others may stand apart as a supremely important factor in defining humanity and distinguishing humans from other beings. As fictional scientist William Hurt poignantly states in the film *A.I. Artificial Intelligence* (2001), "Love will be the key by which [robots] acquire a kind of subconscious never before achieved—an inner-world of metaphor, of intuition ... of dreams."¹⁶³

Still, there is a lack of consensus on what types of characteristics are relevant to a determination of humanity—and even whether defining whether a being fits a predefined conception of "humanity" should be the dominant consideration in considering the way in which we treat our creations. While many films attempt to bridge the gap between humans and artificial beings by showing that advanced AI has the capability to exhibit love, sadness, anger and empathy, a contrarian perspective is that the ability to feel and express such emotions is not particularly relevant as a way of differentiating humans from their creations. For example, in the film *Blade Runner* (1982), bioengineered beings called "replicants" exhibit more empathy than humans.¹⁶⁴ And one of the main takeaways from the film *Terminator 2: Judgment Day* (1991) is that a machine may develop an understanding of, and appreciation for, the value of human life and take actions to protect humans.¹⁶⁵ Does this mean that humans and advanced AI share characteristics that "humanize" our creations? Or should we look to a different set of criteria to determine the nature of rights that should be afforded to our creations? Is reaching consensus on the meaning of "human" a necessary or sufficient factor in developing a model spectrum of rights-based treatment of our creations?

Developing such a spectrum and implementing same is not unchartered territory for humans. We have, for example, created the "Mixed Reality Continuum," which "covers all possible variations and compositions of real and virtual objects."¹⁶⁶ This spectrum spans from objects in a fully natural world on the one end to entirely digital objects on the other.¹⁶⁷ Furthermore, we constantly classify animals by means of a spectrum. Many of us are more than willing to kill a pesky bug while simultaneously professing support for charities whose stated mission is to protect endangered species or other selected classes of creatures. Many are willing to eat certain animals whereas we view with disdain, anger and disgust those who feed on other animal species or hunt animals for sport. A credible argument can be made that such examples demonstrate rampant hypocrisy. Others may argue that there are solid foundational reasons for making such distinctions and cataloging certain actions as moral or immoral on a case-by-case basis.

Often, the justification for treating humans differently than animals is based on religious belief, with a traditional view that human beings have a soul, whereas animals do not, and that God ordered humans to rule the Earth.[168] Dr. Juan Carlos Marvizon points out that "the Theory of Evolution and modern physiology have pushed back against those beliefs, showing that there is an evolutionary continuum between animals and humans and that there are no fundamental differences between the physiology of humans and other mammals."[169] Whether or not an individual subscribes to the Theory of Evolution, questions about the relationship between humans and animals—including those with respect to conceptions of moral superiority—continue to be debated. In the context of digital copies of humans, similar questions are increasingly relevant in the context of the offspring of our technological innovations. The development of a continuum or spectrum may be a useful exercise in connection with a careful consideration of these issues.

For purposes of the foregoing discussion, whether the distinctions we create in the case of animals are justifiable is largely beside the point. The noteworthy fact is that these distinctions are frequently made, and it begs to reason that we might seek to classify beings created by technological innovation using similar constructs.

Human beings have a vested interest in refusing to engage in discussions about mapping out a viable, formalized spectrum through which to view and categorize our technological creations. One significant fear is competition that humans might face from artificially-created beings. As we seek to manage the offspring of our technology, granting certain rights or acknowledging such rights to be inalienable as they relate to such technology could lead to workplace displacement of humans and a degradation in the inherent value of what it means to be human. The television series *Humans* examines such potential consequences, depicting synthetic beings supplanting humans in not only the workforce but also in arenas such as childcare and cooking meals.[170] Understandable fears of such potential developments may result—and in some instances already have resulted—in unfavorable treatments and classifications of artificially-created beings.

The Other

Sociologist and philosopher Zygmunt Bauman wrote that societies frequently organize themselves by use of identity categories.[171] He observed that one class is "but the other of the first [class], the opposite (degraded, suppressed, exiled) side of the first and its creation. This abnormality is the other of the norm ... stranger the other of the native, enemy the other of friend, 'them the other of us.'"[172] The "Other" is deemed by the empowered group as

5. Alternate Realities, Digital Clones and the Meaning of Life 179

less deserving, not "normal" and both a threat and burden to the privileged class. This tactic has been deployed throughout history by dictators and empowered groups to justify poor treatment of groups of individuals— apartheid in South Africa, the Holocaust and slavery in the United States are a few examples of the destructive power of designations of the "Other" at work.

Popular culture has explored this idea as well. In *The Simpsons* episode "A Tale of Two Springfields," for example, the poorer section of Springfield is forced to use a new area code, angering residents of the former and creating a clash (and ensuing insult-hurling, us versus them debate) between the wealthy and lower-class folks.[173] Furthermore, as a recurring thematic plot point throughout *The Simpsons*, residents of each of Springfield and Shelbyville view the other town's residents with disdain—leading to poor treatment of the opposing town's residents.[174] Over the course of *The Simpsons'* exploration of various countries and global cultures, the show has examined and provided satirical commentary on the concept of "American exceptionalism," whereby America is deemed qualitatively superior in a variety of ways to other places.[175] All these examples are components of a broader theme: the perception and resultant treatment of groups of people as the "Other."

Other television shows have examined this phenomenon as well in a myriad of contexts. In the *Parks and Recreation* episode "Eagleton," residents of Pawnee are barred by the snobbish government leaders and citizens of the neighboring town of Eagleton from entering Eagleton parks due to the perceived boorishness of Pawnee residents.[176] On the television series *Gilligan's Island* (1964–1967), folks indigenous to the deserted island are routinely portrayed as inferior, often ridiculed by the members of the band of shipwrecked individuals.[177] On the series *Perfect Strangers* (1986–1993), U.S. citizen Larry Appleton repeatedly mocks the Mypiot culture of his cousin Balki Bartokomous.[178] In *The Twilight Zone*'s "People Are Alike All Over," human beings are locked up in caged zoo exhibits in a zoo run by Martians.[179] In *The Twilight Zone*'s "Eye of the Beholder," pig-faced individuals place a beautiful woman is placed in exile with people exhibiting similar physical features.[180] In *Electric Dreams'* "Kill All Others," a candidate for political office seeks to crush dissent by killing her opponents—folks deemed to be impediments standing in the way of a warped new world order. In *Black Mirror*'s "Nosedive," folks with low social media rankings are excluded from certain societal benefits and privileges that others enjoy. In *Electric Dreams'* "The Hood Maker," the "Normals" blame the "Teeps" for society's ills and seek to inflict collective punishment on all Teeps after a member of the group murders a Normal. In *Electric Dreams'* "Safe and Sound," the East (in an attempt to ostracize Westerners) promulgates the narrative that Westerners commit terrorist attacks and seek the destruction of peace-loving Easterners.

The deleterious effects resulting from asserting definitions of, and promulgating rules regarding, treatment of a group of folks as the "Other" is explored on *Black Mirror*'s "Men Against Fire," where an army uses technology to effectively dehumanize a class of people.[181, 182] The episode, according to executive producer Annabel Jones, is "about the future of warfare and military conditioning, and how technology could provide the ultimate propaganda tool."[183] The MASS sensory-altering technology—which is implanted into soldiers—masks this group's physical characteristics, making it appear to soldiers as though they are vicious zombie-like monsters referred to as "roaches."[184] The masking technology makes it easier for soldiers to kill the roaches, as it removes their empathy toward their targets. The episode title stems from S.L.A Marshall's work, *Men Against Fire: The Problem of Battle Command*, which, as Brooker notes, "talked about the low percentage of soldiers who actually fired their weapons during the first two world wars."[185]

Combat in "Men Against Fire," as Charlie Brooker notes, is "being censored for the soldiers."[186] The MASS implant is a response to the psychological consequences of killing in the army, an issue thoroughly examined in works such as Dave Grossman's *On Killing: The Psychological Cost of Learning to Kill in War and Society*.[187] We learn from one of the roaches that the implementation of this technology was the last step in a strategically planned and executed dehumanization process. The measures became progressively more severe, depicting a slippery slope of poor treatment. Government and mass media combined to implement a targeted strategy that began with screenings, DNA checks, a registry and emergency measures. The media lies to the public by saying that the roaches are ill and refers to them not by individual name, but instead collectively as "creatures." Due to this extensive misinformation campaign, the public is led to believe that roaches are rife with disease and possess criminal tendencies. They fear that continued breeding will disrupt humanity's course. The army directly communicates this message to a man harboring roaches, as a soldier forcefully asserts that roaches are not human beings.

The scariest lesson from "Men Against Fire" is that ordinary civilians demand the eradication of the roaches, despite not having the MASS implant. The public is aware that the roaches are human beings but still want them killed. This demonstrates that government disinformation campaigns could match or even exceed the effectiveness of technology's power to influence. The technology provides a means to allow soldiers to kill their targets without experiencing any feelings of regret or remorse, but it is the will of the ruling class that demands that the soldiers engage in the genocidal killing. This unfortunate human inclination to retain power at all costs—even if doing so entails killing those who are considered threats to power—is not derived from any independent will of technology or because of any artificially intelligent beings causing technology to act in a rogue manner. Rather, human beings set out to create the technology to achieve their own insidious objectives. Once again, we are reminded of Brooker's contention that technology should not be viewed as an independent harm or evil against which we must contend; rather it is the nature of human beings to seek to use technology (or any other tool that could provide a competitive edge or advantage) to further destructive objectives. And even if such technology is eliminated or its use heavily regulated, the potential for humans to find other ways of enslaving, torturing and destroying each other would still exist.

It has been stated that "The only thing necessary for the triumph of evil is for good men to do nothing."[188] "Men Against Fire" is not an episode that focuses solely on the effects of powerful technology. Instead, it reflects deleterious societal attitudes about, and miserable treatment of, classes of individuals throughout human history—absent reliance on such technology. Much of our science fiction relates back, in some form or fashion, to this unfortunate reality. If we scratch beneath the surface of a series such as *The Twilight Zone*, for example, we realize that the show is not about aliens or robots causing us harm, but instead traffics in the ways in which human beings have a propensity to use new ideas, developments and unexpected situations to harm each other. If we possess not only the capacity but the desire to inflict others by enslaving them or casting them as undesirable outsiders, no technology can save us nor take the blame for our attitudes or aggressions resulting therefrom. As Rod Serling stated: "I happen to think the singular evil of our time is prejudice. It is from this evil that all other evils grow and multiply. In almost everything I've written there is a thread of this: man's seemingly palpable need to dislike someone other than himself."[189]

As noted earlier, extreme examples of anti–Semitism, prejudice and racism in our world include the murder of Jews during the Holocaust, Japanese internment camps and African American slavery. The heroes are those that work to save the targeted people, such as the man who harbors roaches in the episode and the couple who saved my grandmother during the Holocaust.[190] Such heroes do, fortunately, exist—and they counteract not only the destructive power of certain technologies but also human-inspired and generated evil in the world.

It is an unfortunate human tendency to define other groups and individuals by reference to one's self and to identify characteristics or qualities in others that do not, in the view of one's self, measure up to the standard established by such individual. Sometimes the Other is defined by reference to the possession of characteristics or traits that seem odd or unfamiliar to the elites or other folks empowered within a society.

This theme is explored on *Electric Dreams'* "The Hood Maker," where Teeps experience emotions (such as love) and physical pain, but are considered inferior to Normals because of their unique and different characteristics. The Teeps are forced to abide by government orders because, in the words of Honor, "I'm software. And software doesn't have a choice." Folks living in this dystopian society fail to take a nuanced approach to the issue of defining humanity. Given Teeps' similarities to humans, should they be considered close to human on a spectrum, as opposed to mere software—a tool used for purposes of exploitation by Normals?

Social theorist and activist Simone de Beauvoir observed that "The category of the *Other* is as primordial as consciousness itself."[191] The group creating the classification builds a wall of separation to maintain its perceived superiority in society and to maintain its social, economic and political privileges and advantages therein. So, too, with our treatment of the technology that we create. By defining standards of humanity in a way that machine can never achieve, we seek to maintain the integrity of the importance of physicality and our bodies as functional, irreplaceable aspects of life. We seek to preserve the dignity of what we consider to be human, disallowing flexibility, with the dual objectives of limiting competition and increasing our own stature and prestige. Some folks have, regrettably, decided to resort to physical abuse against our own technological creations. For example, there have been reports of people kicking food delivery robots developed by a company called Starship Technologies.[192] Journalist Isobel Asher Hamilton cites this experience as an "early insight into how cruel humans could be to robots."[193]

While this abuse is reprehensible, others have taken the polar opposite view as to the nature and rights of our creations. Some observers fear that the poor treatment of these creations may lead to widespread "speciesism." MIT professor Max Tegmark recounts a conversation between Google co-founder Larry Page and Elon Musk, in which Page accused Musk of "treating certain life forms as inferior just because they were silicon-based rather than carbon-based."[194] Other commentators, such as filmmaker Maxim Pozdorovkin (producer of the documentary *The Truth About Killer Robots* [2018]), fear that our mistreatment of robots will "spill over and we will be ruder, more aggressive, more inconsiderate to humans."[195]

The classifications are frequently challenged, with varying degrees of success, by the class designated as the "Other." Digital creations and artificially-created beings may seek legal rights and privileges to which society has declined to provide them access. A successful challenge and some level of support from dissenters in the ruling class is often required to obtain some degree of stature, power and status within society.

A Model Spectrum

In *The Wizard of Oz*, the Tin Man dreams of being defined as a human being, singing that he would become "kinda human" if he were to possess a heart.[196] The Tin Man is not alone in his quest for qualities typically associated with humans: the Scarecrow is desperate for a brain, while the Cowardly Lion seeks courage. Ironically, each of these characters already possesses these defining elements and traits, but (in the case of the Tin Man and the Scarecrow) are missing the physical embodiments of same. The Wizard of Oz advises them that the physical embodiments of things such as a heart and a brain are not nearly as valuable as the ability to feel and think—irrespective of the means one uses to do so. Empirically, it is not necessary to possess such physical attributes so long as a being is able to perform the equivalent functions. It is in this spirit that we can consider whether artificially-created beings that lack physical human bodies and human body parts—or contain digital elements—are entitled to certain rights. If a robot or digital clone can duplicate and mimic the ability to feel emotion and to think creatively is possession of a human brain and heart necessary to be considered human? In sharp contrast to conceptions of humanity that rely strictly on the contents of one's body—such as a robot baseball player being deemed a human only after he is gifted a human heart, as in *The Twilight Zone*'s "The Mighty Casey")—The *Wizard of Oz* demonstrates that humanity can come in various forms and need not be narrowly defined by reference to possession of physical traits and characteristics.[197]

And civil libertarians argue that a fair system of rights-based justice demands that we adapt our perspectives to changing circumstances. Alan Dershowitz, for example, observes that "The development of rights is an ongoing human process, because changing circumstances demonstrate the need for changing rights."[198] Modern technology forces us not to only ask *which* rights should be changed, but also *who* or *what* should enjoy the benefits of such rights.

Despite our familiarity with developing classifications, any attempt to formally create a fair and just spectrum—and, as a prerequisite thereto, define humanity—would be inherently tricky. In addition to overcoming any inherent biases and the favoritism and predilection towards human superiority, we would need to determine the relevant metrics and weight attached thereto. The process would involve intense debate, with no clear right or wrong answer. We would seek to set clear parameters for the debate and avoid a "slippery slope" scenario, under which arguments could be made that any innovation should undergo a similar analysis. None of these challenges should prevent us from developing a rights-based spectrum. Dershowitz argues that "Advocating rights without a perfect theory is far better than silently accepting wrongs until such a theory can be perfected."[199]

The television series *Humans* explores potential difficulties and roadblocks in the debate, drawing the following spectrum which we can apply as a model to the digital copies created in the dystopian worlds of *Black Mirror*: (1) synthetic humans that are only machines; (2) synthetic humans with consciousness and feelings but no free will or inclination to make their own choices: they feel sensations and (in some cases) emotions, but do not engage in independent thought or an advanced desire to further their own interests; (3) synthetic humans with consciousness and feelings but possessing free will; and (4) human (by birth) but having a digital brain and memory implanted while an adolescent: a prototypical hybrid being of the type envisioned by Kurzweil and Musk.[200] Each of these categories of beings can be analyzed in turn.

We might feel comfortable removing category 1 from a discussion about affording rights to artificial beings. *Humans* suggests that beings possessing consciousness (categories 2 through 4) deserve special attention and possible protection from human mistreatment.[201] The series uses several synths as case studies for how humans may interact with artificially-created beings across various categories. Much like the disparate reactions of humans to the robot "Andrew" in the film *Bicentennial Man* (1999), folks react to the synths in a variety of ways—protest and rejection; wonder and awe; compassion; and, unfortunately, abuse.[202] One key example in *Humans* is the relationship between a synth named Odi, and his owner, Dr. George Millican. Odi is initially a category 2 being and forms a type of a friendship with Dr. Millican. Dr. Millican takes a liking to Odi, and, given Odi's excellent memory, uses him to recall past good times. Odi eventually gains free will, but only wants to continue to help others. In effect, Odi declines a shift in his classification to category 3 because the only purpose that he can understand is to serve the needs of others, as opposed to advancing his own interests. Odi's motivations contrast sharply with those of other synths presented on the series, many of who seek independence from humans and invite open conflict with their creators. Odi's attitude and predisposition is reminiscent of Ash's demeanor in the *Black Mirror* episode "Be Right Back," as both have no desire to further their own respective interests.

Humankind's relationship with category 2 beings is highlighted on *The Twilight Zone* episode "The Lonely."[203, 204] In the episode, a prisoner sentenced to solitary confinement on an asteroid is presented with a realistic "female" robot named Alicia for purposes of companionship. The prisoner develops what he perceives as a meaningful connection with Alicia. She is capable of feeling emotions, has a functional memory and possesses a life span similar to that of a human. Given the prisoner's dire circumstances on the asteroid, perhaps it is not unthinkable that his brain, over time, failed to effectively distinguish between real versus fiction. Research supports the idea that humans frequently have strong reactions to "human-like computer interfaces and machines," as they "evoke powerful subconscious and psychological reactions, often identical to our reactions to each other."[205] We would prefer to engage with interfaces that remind us of other individuals than a machine lacking such characteristics: we might choose to share our stories with a robot designed to look human over a standard tape recorder, for example. Serling concludes the episode by explaining that without use, the machines created by man—even those "made in his image" and "kept alive by love" become "obsolete."[206] Like the non-conscious synths on *Humans*, Alicia was created to serve man. But the question of how to treat such creations—especially if man falls in love with them—is a complicated one.

This theme has been examined in popular culture in a variety of different ways. On *Humans*, for example, a man seemingly falls in love with Mia, but is willing to abandon her (albeit, reluctantly) in a way that demonstrates he does not consider her to be a real woman. In the film *Ex Machina* (2014), we see the inverse: a man falls in love with Avy, a category 3 being, only to be rebuffed and abandoned when she departs the research facility where she was created.[207] In *The Big Bang Theory* episode "The Beta Test Initiation," Raj (in a dream) falls in love with his virtual assistant, Siri, imagining a version of "her" as a tangible, physical embodiment.[208] In the film *Cherry 2000* (1988), female androids are used as substitutes for wives.[209] In the *Electric Dreams* episode "Crazy Diamond" (2018), a femme fatale that possesses "quantum consciousness" disrupts a marriage as a man tries to choose between his artificial and human lovers. The episode suggests that a re-definition of humanity also forces us to reconsider relationships with our human counterparts. And in the film *Her* (2013), a man's love for Samantha, a category 3 being (in the form of a computer operating system) that lacks a physical body is not quite unrequited but met with competition from other men with whom Samantha has formed a romantic relationship.[210] In this film, Samantha arranges for a human surrogate to represent her in a sexual interaction with a natural human. The complexities and nuances of these relationships underpins the challenges presented by the novel aspects of engagements with our machines.

Folks feel quite different about enslaving synths that are conscious but, understandably, have no qualms about doing so for non-conscious synths who are built and designed solely for human exploitation (category 1). Studies have demonstrated that "We are hardwired to react to these agents as though they were actually human"—a phenomenon enhanced by interactions with those who closely resemble the physical appearance of natural humans.[211] As Calo notes, "As a general matter, the more anthromorphic qualities—language, voice, face, eyes, and gestures—an interface possess, the greater our reaction."[212] In fact, we typically do not distinguish between talking to a computer or a person.[213] Raj's reaction to the physical version of Siri demonstrates this phenomenon: just as he is unable to speak to natural women unless he is drunk, he is similarly unable to communicate with Siri.[214]

On *Humans*, a married man (Joe) has sexual intercourse with Mia (whose synth name is Anita). Joe's wife Laura considers him to be a cheater for doing so, but Joe brushes aside her concerns in a callous manner reminiscent of the informant's dismissive response in "White Christmas" when criticized for his cruel treatment of a digital copy. Joe argues that his actions could not be considered abuse or cheating given the non-conscious status of Anita. Once Joe realizes that Anita can enter a conscious state of mind, however, his perspective on his own actions change and he expresses regret, embarrassment and horror at his behavior.[215] Studies suggest that Joe's mindset might have been a bit different here; perhaps it would have been realistic to expect that Anita would be viewed more like the man viewed the robot in "The Lonely."[216]

As the real humans in *Humans* continue to interact with and engage the synths, questions arise as to the appropriate levels and types of relationships that should be forged between man and his creations. Laura's reaction to Joe's sexual interaction with Anita is more consistent with Calo's findings. Her anger is understandable given Anita's physical resemblance to humans and other human-like features. The prisoner's feelings for the robot in "The Lonely" are also reasonably consistent with Calo's summary of the research in this field—especially given the prisoner's strong desire to form a bond with human beings. The depictions of the relationships in *Ex Machina* and *Her* are similarly consistent. As Calo neatly sums up, "Any technology that suggests the presence of a person—the ability to manipulate symbols (i.e., language), the appearance of voices, eyes, hands, or the ability to transmit information to a remote party—makes us think that a person is really there."[217] Calo's argument is supported by other representations in popular culture as

5. Alternate Realities, Digital Clones and the Meaning of Life 187

well. In *The Twilight Zone*'s "The Lateness of the Hour," for example, a scientist treats his robot creations like real people, declaring that his robots have "life" because they have minds and wills of their own, along with an artificially-generated memory tract.[218] The parents of an artificially-created android "son" in the television series *Extant* (2014–2015) similarly treat Ethan like their natural offspring—presumably because of his human-like appearance—even though they know of his artificial composition.[219] And as demonstrated by both "The Lateness of the Hour" and *The Twilight Zone* episode "In His Image"—where a "man" encounters his body double—robots may engage in interactions with humans and lack the knowledge that they are not in fact human.[220] Lifelike robots have the potential to fool not only human beings, but themselves as well. This lack of self-awareness can be built in as part of a robot's design.

Determining "consciousness" is considered by many scientists and philosophers to be a "hard problem."[221] It is generally accepted that plants and animals with very small nervous systems exhibit no consciousness at all.[222] Dr. Marvizon points out that the "question of whether animals have consciousness, or what animals have it, remains … unanswered in the strict sense."[223] Humans are the only species believed to possess the "ability to see ourselves as selves extending from the past to the future"—an "extended consciousness" of sorts.[224, 225] It is questionable whether the digital copies in the forms presented on the *Black Mirror* episodes discussed earlier in this chapter have such ability. The copies in "White Christmas," for example, are locked in a defined space and time. While the copy of the prisoner has a clear memory about past events experienced by his physical being counterpart, it is not clear that the copy will have a clear sense of space and time moving forward. It is noteworthy that humans in this dystopian world have the ability to manipulate space and time from the perspective of the copy—as we see in both parts 2 and 3 of the episode (i.e., the copy believes she experienced months stuck in the egg, when it was only a few minutes; and the prisoner believes he is in a real cabin for several years when only 70 minutes have passed). Perhaps the copies would have the ability to understand and measure space and time without human involvement and manipulation, and perhaps humans should be prohibited from engaging in such deception of copies.

Digital Consciousness Transference

The second and third parts of "Black Museum" showcase the prospect of extracting an individual's consciousness and inserting it into another host.

The museum operator describes the newly inserted consciousness as a "hitchhiker" and a "passenger" who experiences emotions as well as physical sensations vicariously throughout the host. The transfer leads to a situation where, as Nish describes it, there is "no privacy" for the host and "no agency" for the individual from whom the consciousness is extracted. Both Jack and Carrie had good intentions, using the extraction procedure to prolong the "life" of Carrie. The audience is asked to consider whether removing Carrie's consciousness from her physical body could lead to disastrous results. This story supports the argument that the physical body is a critical, if not essential, part of a meaningful, fulfilling life, despite its fragilities and frequent wear and tear. Such an argument, however, does not necessarily detract from an argument that digital copies should have legal rights and privileges.

The synthetic beings who cannot only feel but can also make decisions on their own (category 3) are elevated to a more human-like state. An example from *Humans* is the character of Mia, who, much like the computer featured in *The Twilight Zone*'s "From Agnes—With Love" falls in love with a human.[226] Not only does she feel sensations and emotions, she also acts outside of prescribed boundaries to further her own desires. Bender from *Futurama* (1999–2013) qualifies, as he too is fully sentient and seeks to push his own agenda (often in a comically abrasive, sarcastic fashion) as he interacts with humans.[227] The digital copies presented in "White Christmas" fall into this category as well. The informant needs to break the spirit of the copies and manipulate them because they would act in accordance with their own interests were he not to do so.

As more synths in *Humans* "awaken" and enter a conscious state, they exhibit diverse personalities and motivations. The fact that individual synths react to the same circumstances in different ways—some advocate peaceful co-habitation with human beings, while others advance violent agendas—is an example of a human-like quality. The category 3 synths do not take a cookie cutter, one size fits all approach to the world. They have different personalities and motivations; some are good, while others are evil. As a collective group, they struggle with and engage in heated debate over how best to interact with human beings. The desire to engage in debate and exercise free will is the opposite of robotic. Due to their innate characteristics, this category of beings possesses a strong argument to be treated similarly to human beings.

Humans explores the possibility of providing legal protections and status to artificially-created beings that fall into category 3. The category 3 synth Niska murders a man and wants to receive the type of due process that a human would receive. By turning herself into authorities for detainment—and, she hopes, prosecution—she is a martyr for the cause of obtaining legal rights for conscious synths. The NDR series robot Andrew in the film *Bicentennial Man* (1999) embarks on a similar uphill journey for human designation, petitioning the World Congress to allow him to obtain legal status as a human being.[228] Such battles are reminiscent of civil rights struggles throughout history. Success for the category 3 beings will likely require time, education, empathy from the ruling class and eventual acceptance.

On *Humans,* Leo's position as an example of a category 4 being raises questions that are arguably the inverse of those tackled above. Should a human embedded with digital components be treated differently—perhaps with *fewer* rights—than other human beings? By possessing a digital brain and memory, is Leo less human than humans lacking such powerful technology? Does Leo lose human-like qualities because of the introduction of such technology into his body? Or, as Kurzweil would likely suggest, is Leo a prototype of the future of humanity? (Consider Elon Musk's comment about human beings merging with powerful technology to survive and thrive in the future.) Conversely, should Leo be treated *better* than ordinary humans because of his ability to process information more quickly and accurately?

The answers to the foregoing questions may depend on both the quantitative and qualitative nature of the characteristics of the hybrid being—whether the being possesses more traits that we consider to be human or digital, and whether such traits are qualitatively like human traits.[229] Even if full rights are not afforded to beings in certain categories on the spectrum, perhaps regulations against torture and exploitation should exist to prevent the abuses highlighted in "Black Museum" and "White Christmas." Providing such limited rights may help avoid fears that full participation of artificial beings in the democratic process would lead to a legitimate and legal takeover of the world. Other options include allowing treatment of digital beings to be free from regulation, but decided on a personal basis. For example, while the law does not forbid, in many cases, the hunting or eating of most animals, some folks decide not to do so based on a variety of reasons (e.g., moral, religious, health).

While the debate over affording rights to our artificial creations rages on, we must not become too distracted from a far more pressing concern—namely the possibility that we may not be able to effectively co-exist with our creations. And, irrespective of how we might feel about robots or similarly artificial beings, the most important question of all may be the converse—a critical question addressed in the following chapter: how do our creations feel about *us*?

6

Dreading a Post-Apocalyptic Future
From "Metalhead" to "Autofac" and Beyond

> "Man has the power to act as his own destroyer—and that is the way he has acted throughout most of his history. We are the first species capable of self-annihilation."
>
> —Elon Musk[1]

As we consider the immense power of technology, a joke attributed to photographer Sam Haskins merits consideration: "A photographer went to a socialite party in New York. As he entered the front door, the host said 'I love your pictures—they're wonderful; you must have a fantastic camera.' He said nothing until dinner was finished, then 'That was a wonderful dinner; you must have a terrific stove.'"[2]

While we rely heavily on machines to perform a wide variety of functions, there have historically been limits on such reliance. Machines are our tools and their usefulness is entirely dependent upon human ingenuity as we define jobs to be completed. We consider ourselves the artists, the chefs, the creators; our robots and other machines are bit players performing rote tasks—promoting agendas and achieving discreet objectives neatly laid out for them by human beings. Throughout history, humans have been keenly aware of the limitations of machines, and the knowledge of such limitations has served to enhance our own sense of dignity and self-worth. As Fred Rogers observed while meeting with quality control inspectors at a United States stamp production facility, "Machines can't do it all."[3]

But machines sure can do a lot. And the number of things our machines can do is growing by the day. We watch in awe as robots begin to perform more than rote tasks and partner with us as we seek efficiencies in business, education, warfare and healthcare. Do we engage in self-delusion when we cling to the comforting notion that human beings will always have a critical role in the world? The idea that human workers can perform functions that cannot be duplicated by machines was examined on an episode of *The Office.* In the episode "Blood Drive," when receptionist Pam Beasley realizes that a fancy new phone system will replace most of her job she argues that a machine will never be able to put out candy for her colleagues to enjoy.[4] She then realizes that vending machines are a more than adequate substitute for the candy bowl that she places on her desk.

The ubiquity of machines in the workplace and in our homes does not mean that we cannot co-exist peacefully alongside our creations. But what if the dynamics of the fragile partnership that we enjoy with our artificially-intelligent machines begin to shift, causing humans and robots to have a fractured relationship and uncomfortable co-existence? Will robots infused with expanding artificial intelligence become creators and artists, matching or exceeding human ingenuity? Will they not only surpass our intellectual capabilities, but also develop an ability and desire to compete with us? What would these changes mean for society?

Artificial intelligence has infiltrated our lives in many areas. It has, as *The New Yorker*'s Tad Friend states, "grown so ubiquitous … that we rarely notice it." He acutely observes that:

> We take it for granted when Siri schedules our appointments and when Facebook tags our photos and subverts our democracy. Computers are already proficient at picking stocks, translating speech, and diagnosing cancer, and their reach has begun to extend beyond calculation and taxonomy.[5]

Friend provides other examples in a diverse assortment of contexts— from language-processing systems having the capability to detect sarcasm, to poker programs beating experts, to bots negotiating our bills on our behalf to algorithms designed to make paintings and develop music.[6] Artificial intelligence may soon be used to diagnose us in our own homes, as Amazon has filed for patent protection for technology that enables the Alexa device to identify cold-like illnesses by detecting a change in our voices.[7] Artificial intelligence provides assistance in casting television and motion picture productions by estimating "which actors and actresses are most likely to delight audiences for a given television program or film project."[8] Folks even trust artificial intelligence to manage their money. For example, the exchange-traded fund AIEQ—the "AI Powered Equity" ETF—uses IBM's Watson technology to choose stocks.[9] Filmmaker Maxim Pozdorovkin believes the automation in the entertainment industry is closer to reality than pipe dream, observing that "Artists have become shameless in promoting our absolute immunity from this [phenomenon]. But if you look at the economic data, the exact thing that happened to all of these other industries is happening to the arts."[10]

Drawing the line as to the types of activities that we allow AI to perform has not been a specialty of ours. For example, law enforcement has sent robots out to use lethal force against criminal masterminds.[11] Mass shooter Micah Johnson was killed when police strapped a bomb to a robot and detonated it. As Pozdorovkin notes, "Sending a robot to go in and kill someone feels uncomfortable. You can't quite pinpoint it, but it touches into some kind of fundamental, uncanny discomfort."[12] Does the use of robots as domestic weapons against citizens violate what Google chairman Eric Schmidt refers to as "the creepy line"?[13] Or will such a line continue to be a moving target, one that we lack the discipline and will to rigidly define?

The field of robotics and the development of artificially-intelligent beings is expected to continue to expand, with *Fortune* predicting that the market will reach $135 billion by 2019, and is set to grow at an annual rate of 17 percent.[14] Dallas Mavericks owner Mark Cuban predicts that robotics is the wave of the future.[15] Cuban has suggested that President Donald Trump invest $100 billion in the industry in order for the United States to become the world leader in this area.[16] As author James Barrat analogizes in the course of describing the immense societal impact of artificial intelligence, "Artificial intelligence is for the 21st century what electricity was for the 20th and steam power for the 19th."[17] Barrat distinguishes those prior developments from superintelligence by noting that "there's one critical difference—electricity and steam will never outthink you."[18]

And the amount of time that humans have left as the beings holding the most sophisticated intelligence on the planet may be short-lived. Kurzweil predicts that "By 2029, computers will have human level intelligence."[19] He further anticipates that the "singularity, which is when we will multiply our effective intelligence a billionfold by merging with the intelligence we have created" will happen by 2045.[20]

The phenomenon of intelligence expansion has been well-documented, as have its anticipated benefits and potential consequences. In 1965, British mathematician I. J. Good described a concept now referred to as "intelligence explosion":

> Let an ultraintelligent machine be defined as a machine that can far surpass all the intellectual activities of any man however clever. Since the design of machines is one of these intellectual activities, an ultraintelligent machine could design even better machines; there would then unquestionably be an 'intelligence explosion,' and the intelligence of man would be left far behind. Thus the first ultraintelligent machine is

the last invention that man need ever make, provided that the machine is docile enough to tell us how to keep it under control.[21]

Near the end of his life, Good began to fear that nations would compete to dangerously develop superintelligence without adequate protections or safeguards. "They'll become self-protective and seek resources to better achieve their goals. They'll fight us to survive and they won't want to be turned off," Good predicted.[22] Contemporary experts in this area have similarly questioned the notion that intelligent machines would allow humans to maintain control. In April 2016, for example, *Nature* warned that "Machines and robots that outperform humans across the board could self-improve beyond our control—and their interests might not align with ours."[23] Computer scientist Stuart Russell echoes this argument, pointing out that while human beings mostly share similar values with one another, there is no reason to believe that super-intelligent beings would necessarily share the same values as humans.[24] Just as animals rely on human kindness to survive and avoid extinction, human beings may need to rely on the goodwill of super-intelligent beings if our existence does not advance, or, worse, harms the interests of such beings. If such goodwill runs out and if our interests diverge significantly from our artificial creations, humanity could face a violent confrontation over the survival of our civilization. Some experts suggest that we strategize for the hypothetical existential risk caused by artificial general intelligence by developing arguments for our continued existence. Assistant Professor of Integrative Biology & Computer Science and Engineering at Michigan State University Arend Hintze, for example, states that "We all, individually and as a society, need to prepare for that nightmare scenario, using the time we have left to demonstrate why our creations should let us continue to exist."[25]

The potential lack of shared values with artificially-intelligent beings forces us to question the notion—discussed throughout this book—that our technological innovations accurately reflect who we are. Our moral philosophies may conflict with the agendas of artificial intelligence—even if it actively seeks to save us from harm. For example, Russell Roberts, chief information officer for the United States Department of Homeland Security's Transportation Security Administration outlines a hypothetical scenario where a self-driving car is cut off by a truck. Whereas we would do everything in our power to avoid causing harm to others in such a situation, Roberts predicts that if there is a "cliff on one side and a family on the sidewalk on the other," the car "will protect you and take out the family."[26]

As discussed in previous chapters, the introduction and advancement of artificial intelligence into society has significant consequences for the way in which we define and experience life. The impact of artificial intelligence could go beyond profound changes in our lives; it could also have a prodigious and deleterious impact on whether human life is able to subsist at all. *Black Mirror* and *Electric Dreams* also present techno-dystopian post-apocalyptic worlds where artificially-intelligent beings have taken over the Earth, leaving the last remnants of human existence in their wake. As robots continue to develop as free-thinking, intelligent beings, they could turn on humanity—setting up a situation in which machines seek to survive and thrive not with human beings, but rather at their expense. We could envision a future resource-depleted state in which humans compete with robots for access to materials needed to grow their respective populations. In a battle for continued existence, it may not be reasonable for human beings to expect or demand loyalty from their creations. The existential threat from such robots should not be taken lightly.

Many experts believe that concerns over artificially-intelligent beings supplanting humanity merit serious attention and should ultimately lead to reform.[27] Certain existential threats (such as nuclear weapons) are difficult to reduce and contain, but human beings (broadly speaking) ultimately are in control of their own fate. Other threats to our existence fall into a separate category: the potential that no human action could prevent our destruction, despite the prospect of unifying and using our collective best efforts to counter the threat. The introduction of unregulated artificial intelligence that develops on its own and competes with humanity falls into the latter category, potentially leading to an unstoppable force bent on humanity's destruction. There may not be an effective way to realistically control unregulated forms of artificial intelligence that are designed to operate on their own and develop mechanisms capable of harming human beings.

Scientists that develop (or play a significant role in the development of) new forms of technology often flash the loudest warning signals about the potential for destructive uses thereof.[28] Elon Musk, for example, has articulated fears over the unregulated integration of artificial intelligence into society:

> I am really very close, I am very close to the cutting edge in AI and it scares the hell out of me.... So the rate of improvement is really dramatic. We have to figure out some way to ensure that the advent of digital superintelligence is one which is symbiotic with humanity. I think that is the single biggest existential crisis that we face and the most pressing one.[29]

Microsoft founder Bill Gates has expressed serious concerns about the potential dangers of artificial intelligence, expressing disbelief and frustration over the lack of attention these dangers have received in some corners: "I don't know why some people aren't concerned," he wonders. Predicting that the introduction of artificial intelligence could be the "worst event in the history of our civilization," the late theoretical physicist Stephen Hawking urged the creators of artificial intelligence to "employ best practice and effective management" with respect to technological development.[30, 31, 32] In his book "Our Final Invention: Artificial Intelligence and the End of the Human Era," James Barrat details the risk of extermination of the human species, concluding that more preparation is needed to deal with the potentially destructive behavior of artificial intelligence.[33]

Some skeptics of the existential threat theory of artificial general intelligence argue that artificially-intelligent programs will learn moral truths and adapt their goals to maintain amicable relations with humans. Professor Richard Loosemore, for example, argues that artificial general intelligence will adapt to its environment and seek to avoid destructive results.[34] Professor Hintze agrees that it may be possible to use evolution to impact the moral and ethical philosophies of artificial intelligence, stating that "It's likely that human ethics and morals, such as trustworthiness and altruism, are a result of our evolution—and factor in its continuation."[35] She predicts that "We could set up our virtual environments to give evolutionary advantages to machines that demonstrate kindness, honesty and empathy."[36] Hintze concludes that "This might be a way to ensure that we develop more obedient servants or trustworthy companions and fewer ruthless killer robots."[37] Other experts, such as Accenture I.T. executives Paul R. Daughtery and H. James Wilson agree, predict that "cobots" will unleash and enhance human potential in the future.[38] Count Larry Page among the optimists as well, asserting that digital life is both natural and desirable, and predicting a positive outcome if we let digital minds be free rather than seeking to enslave them.[39] And Facebook founder and CEO Mark Zuckerberg has similarly sounded an optimistic note, decrying Musk's doomsday predictions as "pretty irresponsible."[40]

Philosopher Nick Bostrom disputes this notion, arguing that morality will not stand in the way of a program achieving programmed goals.[41] In articulating his *orthogonality* thesis, Bostrom argues that the machine will use any resources at its disposal to accomplish its task, irrespective of any consequences to humans.[42] Bostrom asserts that humans should not assume that the concept of *anthropomorphism* (i.e., that objectives will only be pursued in a manner that folks deem reasonable) would apply.[43] Conversely, the artificially-intelligent being or machine may not act in a way that is consistent with the well-being of those around it.[44] Bostrom sets forth the following illustrative thought experiment: If tasked with the relatively straightforward task of maximizing the number of paperclips in its collection, the artificial intelligence could engage in a series of actions that could ultimately adversely affect the interests of humans—such as transforming the entire Earth into a manufacturing facility for paperclips, removing humans as part of the process.[45] This concept is explored in a more heavy-handed way in the film *Singularity* (2017), where a supercomputer called Kronos is tasked with ending all war.[46] Kronos reasons that since human beings are the cause of war, ending all wars requires eradicating humanity.

While humans intend to use technology as a tool for accomplishing a task, the technology that we introduce unquestionably impacts our existence, altering our behavior and thoughts. And once we demand that our technology achieve tasks that require critical thinking, we lose the ability to manage and exert control over such technology. As *The Matrix*'s Agent Smith asserts, "As soon as we started thinking for you, it really became our civilization."[47] HAL, a spaceship computer in the epic film *2001: A Space Odyssey* (1968), stated that it must kill humans aboard the spaceship because "this mission is too important for me to allow you to jeopardize it."[48] The ability to retain control over our existence may vanish as we ask technology to accomplish objectives. Barrat agrees, hypothesizing that superintelligent beings will focus on self-preservation and acquisition of resources.[49] Barrat's theory is logical, if the superintelligence is ultimately going to achieve the goals assigned to it by humans. As *The New Yorker* staff writer Tad Friend neatly sums up, "An A.I. system may need to take charge in order to achieve the goals we gave it."[50] This concept is explored on *Electric Dream*'s "Autofac" (2018), where a factory directs folks to use unnecessary products that proxies of the factory argue will enrich the lives of users. Ultimately, human beings may be casualties of a machine's pursuit of goals that we set forth.[51]

Researchers have acknowledged the inability to effectively manage artificial intelligence. Musk likens this inability to exert control to "those stories where there's the guy with the pentagram and the holy water and he's like, yeah, he's sure he can control the demon. Doesn't work out."[52] *The Twilight Zone* tackles this situation in the episode "The Howling Man."[53] The episode explores humankind's hubris in believing that the devil can be contained. The devil is captured and imprisoned, but he manages to convince a well-intentioned man that he is innocent and that the imprisonment is unjustified. The man is relying on incomplete and misguided information when he releases the devil. And therein lies a significant issue with the theory that we will be able to manage and control artificial intelligence. Since we do not know the effects of the development of uninhibited artificial intelligence, is it wise to invite it into the world? Or will we unleash the devil, a force open to, if not actively seeking, our destruction? Will our mechanisms of control inevitably fail? As Rod Serling states in the closing narration, "You can catch the devil, but you can't hold him long." We may be able to effectively control artificial intelligence for a period of time, but it may not be practical to believe that we could do so indefinitely—especially as the superintelligence continues to advance.

Echoing Serling's message, Professor Hintze states that "We know that 'to err is human,' so it is likely impossible for us to create a truly safe system."[54] On a related note, Hintze observes that the pace of achievements in artificial intelligence exceeds human's ability to anticipate its consequences: "We try to engineer AI without understanding intelligence or cognition first," she notes.[55] Hintze adds that "we have not yet come up with a clear idea of what we want AI to do or become. In part, of course, this is because we don't yet know what it's capable of."[56] This sentiment is echoed by both Musk (asserting that artificial intelligence is "capable of vastly more than almost anyone knows and the rate of improvement is exponential" and Bostrom ["Before the prospect of an intelligence explosion, we humans are like small children playing with a bomb."]).[57] Such somber predictions coupled with the inability for humans to predict with any degree of certainty the ultimate consequences of an artificial intelligence explosion lead us not only to question the optimism of folks such as Kurzweil, but perhaps lament such unbridled—and, arguably unsupported—enthusiasm by those (such as Kurzweil, Google's Director of Engineering) in positions of power to advance artificial intelligence. A cautious approach to the introduction of artificial intelligence would be prudent, even if folks tend to side with the optimists. If they are wrong, and artificial intelligence is more dangerous than surmised, disastrous consequences could result. Artificially-intelligent beings may develop independent agendas anathema to the interests of humanity, once again resulting in human casualties as part of the outcome of the execution of such an agenda.

Collective Responsibility for Existential Threats

Science fiction plays an important role in the examination of the potential existential threat engendered by the introduction of artificial intelligence. The depictions presented on television shows and movies highlighting these concerns represent the audience's first visual representations of the potential threats and impacts. Cultivation theory predicts that this first introduction has a significant effect on the way in which we consider and weigh the merits of the threats presented to us.[58] The theory hypothesizes that an audience's perception of reality is effectively cultivated in a way that is largely consistent with the programming to which such audience is exposed.[59] If popular culture depicts these threats in a relatively realistic manner, perhaps they can be effective in sounding the alarm, leading to reforms that could help prepare and save humanity from impending doom.

Despite the anticipated benefits of the introduction of artificial intelligence, much of the science fiction genre has historically focused on either the potential negative consequences of artificial intelligence over which humanity has lost or relinquished control or the use by humans of AI, sometimes for nefarious purposes. Examples of losing or intentionally relinquishing control include: a scene in episode of *Humans*, where Joe loses his job due to decisions made by—and communications between—machines, absent any human involvement; a scene in the film *DriverX* (2018), where the protagonist (Leonard) is hired by an Uber-like company without a human behind the employment decision; and "Playtest," which examines the immense power of augmented reality to use advanced artificial intelligence to stoke fear in humans (inviting us to ask what could result if humans lose the ability to exert control over such technology).[60, 61] While not all these examples necessarily have overt adverse consequences, they support the notion that human beings—members of a species historically focused on gaining power—are often willing to cede power to technology. And if we cede too much power to our creations, have they already defeated us without firing a shot?

Creating "life" from raw materials, artistry and power surges is a prevalent theme throughout popular culture, from *Frankenstein* (1818) to *Pinnochio* (1940) to *Weird Science* (1985).[62] Such films share elements with stories focused on the introduction of steely, metallic machines designed and built by humans. The messages communicated through popular culture regarding the introduction of robots into society has been reasonably consistent and largely dystopian, with a few noteworthy deviations fixated on a significantly more hopeful idea—namely the capacity of artificially intelligent beings to possess endearing characteristics and to feel and express emotions such as love (see *Wall-E* [2008], *Robot & Frank*]2012], *A.I. Artificial Intelligence* [2001], for example).[63] The central theme in apocalyptic science fiction films focused on the negative consequences of artificial intelligence (such as *The Terminator* [1984] and the Fabrication Machine featured in 9 [2009]) is that the robots are coming to destroy us, and, further, that we have nobody but ourselves to blame for this inevitable and ignominious conclusion to the human species.[64] The science fiction genre is in fact littered with such tales of humanity's loss of control over and/or imminent destruction at the hands of ruthless and unstoppable AI (see, for example, *The Machine* [2013], *Kill Command* [2016] and *American Cyborg: Steel Warrior* [1994]).[65] The primary vehicle employed within stories focused on representations of robots and other artificial creations to express this frightening idea is a visual demonstration of the ways in which human beings are shown to possess a wide blind spot when it comes to considering the potential destructive power of artificial intelligence.

This point is expressed in playwright's Karel Čapek's play *Rossum's Universal Robots* (1921), the first literary representation of robots featured on a world stage.[66] The play "imagined the manufacture of robots *en masse* in Rossum's eastern European factory."[67] The robots murdered humans, leading their chief engineer to cry, "I blame science! I blame technology!"[68] But the engineer quickly reflected on the situation and reversed his position on the matter—arriving at the same conclusion that Charlie Brooker reached years later: "We, we are at fault!," the engineer exclaimed.[69] As political science professor Eileen Hunt Botting observes, "It was not the technology that was the problem, but rather the 'megalomania' of the scientists and the technologists."[70] Botting traces this theme throughout global literature, finding relevant—and, in many cases, prescient—connections and links between contemporary innovations and historical representations of artificial creations throughout popular culture. She asks: "Are we, like Frankenstein, setting into motion maniacally smart devices of our own demise?"[71] This line of inquiry ultimately leads to the following question: is technology the monster that deserves to shoulder all the blame or are we the nefarious or, at a minimum, grossly negligent, monsters because we unleashed the technology without carefully considering the consequences of doing so?

The question of who is to blame for "setting into motion" the events that may lead to our creations eradicating us has received significant attention throughout popular culture. Assigning fault for the existence and output of human behavior was examined in *The Simpsons* episode "Girly Edition" (1999).[72] In the episode, Lisa Simpson explains to Groundskeeper Willie that society is to blame for Bart Simpson's troubled behavior and that Bart is, in many respects, everyone's son. Lisa is correct in noting that the prevailing circumstances of an individual's life play a role in the development of the person. If Bart is "America's bad boy," it is not only Bart and/or his parents that should receive blame. School administrators, teachers, counselors, friends, siblings and enemies all play a role in his development. A similar notion of accountability and measuring and allocating responsibility is relevant to an analysis of the introduction of powerful AI. Just as it is too easy to blame Bart alone for his poor behavior, it is overly simplistic to place full responsibility on technology itself—even sentient creations (such as the monster created by Dr. Victor Frankenstein)—for causing us harm. And just as

Bart's parents should not receive all the supplemental blame, it is unfair to place too much blame on the inventor herself. While Homer and Marge play an important role in molding Bart, assigning them full accountability while relieving other external actors of their share of fault paints an inaccurate portrait of the circumstances that influenced Bart. Similarly, while inventors of potent technology play a critical role in the development of technology, it behooves us to look closely at all the actors who encouraged the introduction of such innovations. As we consider where and how to assign responsibility for badly behaved children and dangerous technologies, we must be sure to look in the mirror and consider our individual and collective role in the process.

At the heart of many popular literary representations of AI is the tenet that it is not only the inventor of AI that is responsible for the output of such inventor's research. The inventor is the last of a long line of folks who could have, but failed to, halt the release of such technology. The reluctance to stop such technology is rightfully deemed a collective (and colossal) failure of watchdog groups, lawmakers, corporations, lenders, regulators and private citizens willing (and often eager) to bring ever-more powerful devices into their offices and homes. Each of the foregoing groups bears some level of responsibility for the production, development, introduction and use of technology whose adverse consequences are not fully known at conception. As technology was conceived of, funded and utilized by arguably reckless stakeholders, such folks unwittingly took risks that are of a nature that the human species may not be able to overcome. The notion of collective responsibility is expressed throughout popular culture and is communicated to audiences via a host of films—and even their titles, such as "Frankenstein AI—A Monster Made by Many."[73]

Other films and television shows focusing on jarring and frequently nefarious applications of artificial intelligence include *Ex Machina* (2015), which demonstrates the power of AI to deceive and destroy; *Chappie* (2015), which explores the adverse consequences of gangsters using a robot to commit crimes; the Netflix film *Tau* (2018), where a mad scientist seeks to use AI to imprison and exploit a test subject for personal gain; and "Hated in the Nation" and "U.S.S. Callister," each of which ask us to consider whether we have sufficient protections in place to prevent the weaponization of artificial intelligence.[74]

It behooves us to guard against not only strictly militant applications of AI, but also against scenarios that give some folks an unfair advantage over others. A developer of AI wields significant power over the potential limitations of the AI: what if the developer uses AI to gain power, influence and money at the expense of others? How can we create and maintain a fair system to ensure that robots act within certain prescribed boundaries—one that not only restricts the ability of robots to wreak havoc over humanity but also one that does not advance the interests of select individuals over those of others? A thoughtful analysis of these issues requires us to consider how we can objectively and effectively apply Isaac Asimov's "Laws of Robotics"—namely, that robots: (1) cannot injure human beings through acts or omissions; (2) must obey the orders of humans unless doing so conflicts with # 1; and (3) a robot must protect its own existence as long as doing so does not conflict with # 1 or # 2.[75] Because robotic design is subject to the whims and potential vices of its developers, it is important to question how we can prevent its inventors from surreptitiously amending or placing addendums on such directives. This phenomenon was explored in the film *RoboCop* (1987), where evil corporate executives attempt to place themselves in a position above the law as they design RoboCop to shut down if it attempts to arrest any executive of the developer corporation.[76] A democratic use of robots to serve a specific function requires that any laws or directives not place the interests of any individuals over those of others.

"Autofac" and Drones: Delivering More Than We Bargained For?

One of the most exciting (and, perhaps dangerous) applications of artificial intelligence is the introduction of unmanned aerial vehicles (UAVs, also known as drones) in the context of commercial deliveries and elsewhere.[77] Amazon Prime Air uses UAVs to provide packages to customers in 30 minutes or less. The company boasts of the benefits of the service, stating that "Rapid parcel delivery ... [will] also increase the overall safety and efficiency of the transportation system."[78] The burgeoning commercial drone delivery industry in the United States is growing at an immense pace. The size of the industry was $40 million in 2012 and reached $1 billion in 2017.[79]

Amazon is a worldwide leader in developing uses of technology that change our world. From its expansive Amazon Web Services (AWS) cloud-based platform to its enormously popular Echo and Alexa systems, Amazon is at the forefront of creating and implementing game-changing technologies. The development and use of artificial intelligence is a fundamental component of many of these initiatives. It is fitting that the first product ever sold on Amazon was a book focused on artificial intelligence. It is similarly ironic that *Electric Dreams*' "Autofac"—an episode whose satire is presumably aimed directly at Amazon and other commercial drone-producing corporations—was picked up by, and streamed on, Amazon Video.

In "Autofac," the audience learns that humans have destroyed each other via war 20 years ago. We are informed that "All lay in waste. Except the great factories that kept working, churning out goods for the slaughtered consumers." The small remaining population of humans (or, at least folks that appear to be humans at this point in the episode) attempts to shoot down and destroy package-bearing drones produced by the Autofac—a fully automated manufacturing and delivering company—as the drones release their payloads. This desire to eliminate the drones is based on practical considerations: nobody has ordered or has any use for the goods being delivered, and the factory is harming the environment and depleting Earth of scarce remaining resources. The humans' goal is to wrest back control over life from the Autofac.

It seems throughout most of the episode that real humans have lost the ability to exert control and authority over artificial intelligence. They devise a strategy to destroy the Autofac. They manage to hit a drone, then proceed to take out its "brain" and make a novel customer service request so that the machine will have to "think" and engage with humans. (We are told by Emily, the protagonist, that the drone is "a pretty sophisticated adaptive AI.") In response to the customer service request, the Autofac sends a customer service representative named Alice (an artificially intelligent robot) to handle the complaint. The humans fail to convince Alice that the Autofac is not needed and should shut itself down due to the destruction it causes.

Alice attempts to win an intellectual battle with Emily by arguing that if humans use the products produced by the company, their lives will be better. Artificial intelligence, she suggests, knows what is best for the human species and submission to its decisions would ultimately be beneficial to them. This sets up the potential for an epic battle over the meaning and viability of human civilization: what is the purpose of human life if we become akin to oppressed robots? How did things get so out of control?

The episode invites us to consider whether a factory that produces products *en masse* and replaces them frequently could also produce synthetic humans to replace those whose lives have been lost. In a dystopian world where humans are deemed replaceable (see "Be Right Back"), is it not reasonable to assume that a factory capable of producing human-like substitutes may do so to satisfy a preset agenda? If the Autofac's mission is to produce as many products as possible, what would happen if it had no more natural humans to serve? Would the factory not need to build a replacement customer base? Would doing so help to fulfill the objective of producing efficiencies—

a goal originally assigned to the factory by natural humans? Or does such a scenario simply create unnecessary inefficiencies—namely the production of products without a naturally existing customer base? As humans build machines and factories to produce and deliver products quickly, should they also consider implementing kill-switch mechanisms to stop machines' abuse of the planet when they no longer serve a useful function? Even if humans are no longer in the picture, perhaps we could still claim victory over machines (and win a symbolic battle that restores human dignity, albeit in a post-mortem fashion) if we manage the way in which machines operate when we are not around to observe them.

Aside from the battle between humans and their creations, "Autofac" raises questions about consumerism, automation, nostalgia and the loss of human values.

The Replacement Culture

In "Autofac," Emily charges that the Autofac has produced a "throwaway culture" where everything (and everyone) is "replaceable." This supercharged hyper-consumerism ironically exists in a world where there are no human customers to make use of the factory's mass-produced products. The development of goods that are not needed, including by the humans' replacements, has generated a culture built not on a discernible need, but one defined by its excesses—precisely the type of inefficiency that the introduction of mass-production factories and drone delivery systems is designed to prevent. Furthermore, it is difficult to conceive of a more extreme inefficiency (and lack of regard for resources) than the creation of synthetic humans for the sole purpose of using the products produced by the "Autofac." Artificial intelligence is stubbornly trying to solve a problem initially presented to it by humans—namely the creation of a cost-effective mass production and delivery system—and using synthetic humans to achieve this goal. In this light, humans (or, in this case synthetic ones) have become the solution to technology's problem, thereby reversing the initial pre-defined roles of humans and their creations. The goals that the Autofac achieves ultimately come at the expense of the synthetic humans.

The motivation underlying this dystopian society is the never-ending quest to achieve a goal not designed to help anyone. Instead, the goal is to produce for the sake of producing—an objective that is effectively an insatiable moving target. The Autofac will never satisfy itself that it has achieved its goal if there is no set number of products to produce; the vague goal of producing as many products as possible ensures that there is always more to do. All other concerns (such as disruption to the environment) fall to the wayside, and succumb to the objective of producing goods that benefit nobody. If everything is replaceable, nostalgia and relationships have no meaning or significance. Past and current experiences are fungible and tradable; they do not possess any inherent value. The artificial intelligence has developed its own sustainable value system—one that is deeply unsatisfactory from the perspective of humans. Automation and, ultimately, extinction have led to the eradication of recognizable human value systems. While humans value more than productivity, the Autofac was designed to care for nothing else. This is the fundamental theme explored in *The Twilight Zone*'s "The Brain Center at Whipple's"[80] and other science fiction tales focused on the negative consequences of automation.

And if everything—and more significantly, everyone—can be replaced, we must consider the ways in which technology can effectively facilitate such substitutions. The film *Cam* tackles this issue, as women who appear on webcams are replaced by artificially-intelligent bots.[81] Viewers can see no discernible difference between the bots and the natural humans, making the webcam a medium through which an artificially-intelligent being may be able to thrive—at the expense of displaced human beings. When taken to its logical conclusion, there are potentially no limits to the disruption that may be caused by a substitute culture. It is not only our goods that are replaceable; we, too, may be substituted for more efficient versions of ourselves.

Other episodes explore the concept of a replacement culture and the human desire to connect to the past through relationships with, and memories of, people, places and objects. Episodes such as "The Commuter," "Real Life," "Playtest," "Black Museum," "White Christmas," and "U.S.S. Callister" center on the potential implications of trading or substituting one environment for another. Other shows focus on the emotional elements of such connections and the inherent value attached thereto. On *Humans*, for example, Dr. George Millican's reluctance to upgrade his old model synth (Odi) not only reflects the fact that he has developed a friendship with Odi, but also because Odi's memory provides Dr. Millican with a window to the past.[82] Odi may not represent the latest or greatest technology, as he is not infused with the most advanced chips. But because he provides a bridge to a past era, his existence is invaluable to Dr. Millican.

The Twilight Zone tackles the idea of a replacement culture in an even more personal way, extending the concept of substituting an environment to an exchange or refresh of physical characteristics. In addition to "The Trade-Ins," where a man grapples with the decision of whether to replace his body with a younger model and realizes the value of his physical body as he reflects on his life, other episodes (such as "The Four of Us Are Dying" and "The Self-Improvement of Salvador Ross," along with *Electric Dreams*' "Human Is") examine the possibility of having the power to change or trade one's face to resemble a face of someone else.[83] While the opportunity to effectively start over in a new environment (or with a new appearance) and forge new bonds could be deemed attractive components of a throwaway culture, the value of each environment, interaction and relationship is necessarily diminished by the always-present prospect of a quick exit. This theme is relevant to a close examination of "San Junipero," as we can consider whether our physical bodies, natural environments and relationships that we develop in such environments are sacrosanct if we are able to transform into anyone and enter any environment that we so choose. While we may find a home in San Junipero, will our memories take up residence with us or will we seek to start completely anew in such an environment?

Intense feelings of nostalgia feature prominently in *The Twilight Zone* episode "Young Man's Fancy."[84] In the episode, a man is so attached to the home of his deceased mother and his childhood possessions that he questions whether to forgo the promise of a future with the love of his life. For the man, the allure of the past is strong and he finds it impossible to move on. The house and other symbols of his childhood have a deep, embedded meaning to him.

While "Young Man's Fancy" takes this idea to an extreme, *The Twilight Zone* is not alone in recognizing the inherent value that folks may place on people, places and objects. On the *Parks and Recreation* episode "Leslie and Ron," for example, Leslie Knope expresses her fury after Ron Swanson's company bulldozes the former home of her friend, Ann Perkins.[85] Ron then surprises Leslie by using the wood from the cut-off door to Ann's former house to create a picture frame—which he then gives to Leslie as a gift. The frame has sentimental value to Leslie; it symbolizes the personal connection she has with her friend, who had moved to another state. On "Nosedive," Lacie's and the bride (Naomi)'s shared memory of a childhood doll (Mr. Rags) is juxtaposed against the portrait of a society consumed by the fleeting nature of social media. Other shows carefully divide professional success and commercial progress—defined, at times, by the rate at which new technologies are developed—and the meaningful, personal connections generated between colleagues. *Halt and Catch Fire* (2014–2017) succeeds in this regard, showcasing that ruthless business leaders and technology developers might form bonds with one another.[86] As the main characters in this show exhibit cunning business instincts, they also come to the realization that human experiences are not replaceable in the way that old technology might be discarded or updated. While products can be substituted by new ideas or innovations, the meaningful connections that folks form with one another are irreplaceable. Other shows are based entirely on nostalgia—such as *The Wonder Years* (1988–1993), which centers on an adult providing a narration of moments from his adolescent years.[87] The series highlights the bonds forged in an individual's life and the value of looking back and reflecting on people and events from the past.

Science fiction also focuses on the use of technology to transcend space, time, place and age, examining technology's role in connecting people and events to the past (see "Crocodile," "San Junipero," and "Impossible Planet"). *The Twilight Zone*'s "Kick the Can," "The Incredible World of Horace Ford" and "Walking Distance" each touch upon a similar theme—the seemingly innate human desire to re-connect with one's childhood.[88] *Black Mirror*'s "The Entire History of You" (2011) explores the importance, role and consequences of one's memories in a society where an implant records everything that we experience. The episode stands in stark contrast to the idea of a throwaway culture; in the dystopian society presented thereon, folks focus on the past, obsessively sharing and critiquing each other's memories.

Black Mirror's "Metalhead" (2017) provides a portrait of a dystopian universe where the ruling class does not value memories or any reference to the past. Those in charge of a world that is devoid of remembrance and focused entirely on efficiency do not place a premium on, and may in fact seek the erasure of, remnants of the past. And one of the ways in which folks traditionally seek connections to the past is through objects—hence the search for the teddy bear in that episode. The protagonist's quest for the teddy bear hearkens back to a more innocent time where people and objects had significance and commoditization of same had not yet begun; a time when human beings served as more than mere targets for killer robot dogs.

In the song *Souvenir* (1974), Billy Joel equates the fading years of one's life with the material objects that similarly dissipate over time.[89] We recall vacations and events that we have attended by referencing the photographs taken, ticket stubs collected, programs stashed away and other mementos that we have collected over the course of our lives. We seek to retain our souvenirs so that we can connect to the past. And we bury time capsules, loaded with symbolic representations of a designated period, to communicate and build bridges with future generations seeking to learn about the prevalent values and interests of such period. The fact that the physical manifestations and representations of our memories are fleeting does not mean that they are unimportant. In fact, souvenirs could serve evidentiary purposes, especially if technology evolves to the point where memories are falsifiable. In *The Twilight Zone*'s "The Lateness of the Hour," a scientist implants false memories into his robotic creations.[90] A robot lacks self-awareness of her status as a robot and possesses "memories" of a childhood that never occurred. But she desperately searches, in vain, for a photo to buttress the case that her childhood was real. The lack of tangible support for her "memories" helps her come to important realizations about her existence.

Joel also sings of the importance of physical symbols as gateways to the past in his single *This Is the Time* (1986).[91] He sings of a strong urge to hold onto the past, even as days pass by unabated by our desire. Joel references an "old hotel" being torn down. The hotel is more than just a building; it is ingrained in the hearts and minds of thousands of guests—lovers, adventurers starting their lives together. We expect that the hotel will be replaced, perhaps by a bigger and better structure. But the hotel itself has meaning to those who recall their experiences in the building. It is not replaceable because of what the hotel represents for those who had wonderful experiences there.

Popular culture examines this point in various contexts. The film *Eternal Sunshine of the Spotless Mind* (2004), for example, touches on this concept. The protagonist is directed by doctors to remove physical mementos of his past romantic relationship from his apartment as a prerequisite for cleansing the man of his memories of his ex-girlfriend. The items evoke strong emotions, evidenced by the man's brain activity during the memory purge procedure. In the series *Homecoming* (2018–present), a director of a mental rehabilitation facility is concerned about the potential consequences that could result from a subject gaining access to a harmonica that he had used during traumatic periods during his life.[92] And in *The Simpsons* episode "Rosebud," we learn that Mr. Burns' endearing attachment to a plush doll (Bobo the teddy bear) from his child ties back to his yearning for youth and the innocence of his childhood.[93] (The episode is a homage to the film *Citizen Kane* [1941], where the meaning of the protagonist's last word is revealed to refer to a memento from his childhood, symbolizing the life that he left behind.)[94]

We find similar examples in our lives, too. For example, a Holocaust survivor named Gert Berliner packed a stuffed bear with him as he escaped Nazi Germany, and then from voyages to Sweden and New York.[95] Uri Berliner, the son of the survivor, described the toy as his grandfather's "most tangible connection to his childhood, to a fleeting moment of innocence."[96] The toy monkey made its way to a museum in Berlin, where it has helped to relate the story of Gert Berliner's life and experiences to millions of visitors.[97] And one of the museum visitors discovered that she was a relative of Berlinger, leading to family members finding and forming relationships with each other.[98] These examples buttress the argument that physical objects are often important symbolic reminders of, and pathways to, the remembrance and formation of events and relationships; they have immense value that far surpasses their purely functional, utilitarian attributes.

Notwithstanding the above, *Black Mirror* and *Electric Dreams* demand that we consider whether places and things are less important, if not wholly irrelevant, if technology allows us to produce a "throwaway culture"—one in which any environment or object can be substituted for another at any given time. The potential for the digitalization of and immediate access to memories (as explored on "Crocodile" and "The Entire History of You") further calls into question the inherent value placed on the mementos that are intended to serve as symbolic representations of events and places in our lives.

Nostalgia, continuity and sentimentality are, perhaps uniquely, human characteristics—although some animals have various social connections and exhibit emotions that might have nostalgic underpinnings.[99] We do not wish to forego and replace our past connections with people or things and would not be content living in a world where everyone and everything can be substituted for something else. The technology featured in "Be Right Back" seems, at first glance, to allow users to maintain a nostalgic connection to the past by developing a synthetic replacement human based on a natural human who has died—much like the "personality images" referred to in "Autofac." Revealing the inspiration for the idea behind "Be Right Back," Charlie Brooker states that it stemmed from "the notion of a souvenir that you know is not real, but which reminds you enough of somebody that it's painful."[100] The substitute provides a tunnel to a time gone by, allowing folks, at least on a superficial level, to interact with those who have left the natural world. What we learn, of course, is that natural people are not replaceable in a way that satisfies or adequately replicates actual human interactions and the continuation of relationships. Both episodes demonstrate that a replacement culture is not a viable alternative to our normal environment. It does not comport with our value system.[101] The lesson herein: do not dismiss or throw away your natural human friends and family. They are not easily replaceable!

In some of the other worlds presented on *Black Mirror* and *Electric Dreams*, innovation tends to supplant notions of continuity. Folks in some of these episodes do not rely on products or people as a way to forge meaningful connections with the past. For example, in "Human Is," a woman is willing to accept the replacement of her human husband by an alien. The replacement husband will likely treat her better and perhaps improve the human species generally. The woman's decision can, however, be sharply contrasted with Charlie's reaction in "The Father Thing." In that episode, Charlie immediately rejects the alien replacement of his father. In choosing love and a desire to maintain a meaningful connection with his father, Charlie demonstrates that he does not subscribe to the substitute culture prevalent in many of the episodes exploring escapism.

"There's a Great Big Beautiful Tomorrow!"

"Autofac's" portrayal of a replacement culture suggests that the ideal of technological innovation is often at odds—if not in direct conflict—with nostalgic sentiments. If everything and everyone can be substituted for something else—something more efficient, more innovative—nothing and no one possesses any inherent, irreplaceable value. Walt Disney's "Carousel of Progress"— an attraction featured at General Electric's "Progressland" at the 1964–1965 World's Fair in New York, as well as at Disneyland and the Magic Kingdom's "Tomorrowland"—questions this premise, amalgamating elements of nostalgia, maintenance of the familial unit as well as progress in the form of technological innovation. The show—which holds the record for the longest-running stage show in the history of American theater—features a family living (and aging appropriately) through different eras, gleefully enjoying the benefits of the modern technology of the day.[102] Each scene ebulliently showcases technological innovations that have made life more efficient, if not more complex, for each of the family members. While the eras are defined by reference to the new technological developments, the family unit remains tightly knit. The family's patriarch speaks glowingly of the innovative and endless parade of gadgets of the day, each presented as useful tools for humans, not as forces that might drive folks apart or change the nature of relationships— or of what it means to be a human being. Ironically, though, the underlying theme that humans are solely beneficiaries, not victims, of technology is called into question by the design of the show: the family members are mechanical robots; human actors are not needed to present the message about the immense value of technology in our lives.

The exhibit presumes—and indeed promulgates the idea—that unimpeded progress (as defined by the fruits of technological advancement) is a positive result of what folks can do if they work hard and put their minds together, with each development more significant and groundbreaking than the previous one. Endless innovation is unassailable; no ceiling is too high to reach; each accomplishment is better than the last. The culture of instant gratification is celebrated, and continuous modifications to and upgrades of existing technology are required to produce a superior tomorrow. The only constant is that no level of production of a never-ending stream of new innovations—no matter how large or impactful—will ever suffice. Progress is measured by how much has been added, how productivity has increased, and how inefficiencies have decreased. A balanced and honest assessment and analysis of what may be lost in the process—including human power, control, privacy and other values—is absent. The lyrics to the song played at the end of each scene, predicting bright days ahead, is consistent with the show's eminently positive portrayal of technology. The sanguinity of the show is consistent with those cheerful celebrations of technology throughout popular culture (such as *The Jetsons*) that produce portraits that lack the nuance and measured analysis of and discourse about the potential effects of the unfettered introduction of powerful technologies.

While the gadgets of previous eras are described to the audiences by the family patriarch with an imbued sense of nostalgia, the overarching theme is that the innovations of the past are not especially useful given their replacements in the ever-evolving substitute culture. But usefulness is in the eye of the beholder—and *that* is the fundamental nature and inherent value of nostalgia. Even if inventions of a past age have been supplanted by newer ones—themes tangentially addressed in films such as *Back to the Future* and animated sitcoms such as *Futurama* and *The Jetsons*—the importance of looking at an object and mentally tying it to cherished memories should not be understated.[103] Whereas the Autofac would have discarded all products in exchange for new ones, folks who wish to maintain continuity with the past would rather keep some of those products around (or at least not forget about them) so that they could escape to a simpler time.

The latest innovation may produce superior results and create efficiencies, but the Carousel fails to acknowledge what might be lost in the substitute culture. This theme is explored (in the context of the way that folks experience music) in the film *DriverX*, as Leonard laments the loss of the way folks previously listened to songs.[104] Leonard explains that he misses the creases in his vinyl record album covers, holding a physical copy of an album and staring at a musician on the cover holding a Gibson guitar. The ambiance produced was unmistakable. Streaming services may put more music at our fingertips more quickly and cheaply. We can quickly drop a song, substituting it for another by pressing a button. And better sound quality—to say nothing of the elimination of the worry about scratching a record—might enhance the listening experience in some respects. But contemporary innovations lead to the loss of something intangible—the overall experience of discovering music in a record store, clutching a vinyl and investing yourself in the music that you have chosen and purchased.

And as we see in episodes such as "Nosedive," widespread access to technology has incentivized us to connect with each other in less meaningful ways. This phenomenon exists not only in the context of interactions in our personal life but also in our commercial transactions. We might still call customer service and sometimes speak to an actual human, but we do not engage in the same types of interactions that we had not so long ago. For example, the loss of the "human touch" when we buy a product on the Internet rather than going to a store or speaking with a salesperson on the phone makes us more isolated and disconnected from others—a phenomenon examined on *The Office* episode "Dunder Mifflin Infinity," when the paper company develops a new website to generate sales.[105] We do not engage with others or inspect the items that we buy or rent (such as a film at the now nearly-extinct *Blockbuster* video store chain), but instead push a button to receive a product. *DriverX* (2018) highlights this phenomenon in the context of Uber-like car services, as folks can communicate their desired pickup and destination locations without talking to another human.[106] As companies such as Amazon experiment with drones, we may not even receive packages from delivery persons in the future. Emerging trends suggest that we will likely continue to replace our interactions with other people in exchange for increased efficiencies. Such continued replacement strengthens the argument that our society is one that is built on a substitute culture. And it is understandable that many of us feel a deep sense of nostalgia for a time that has passed.

As we watch the Carousel turn, it behooves us to understand that progress from the perspective of a corporation could represent carnage and destruction of values from other perspectives. Disney has a financial interest in promoting the ideal of unfettered technological innovation. The company relies on such innovations to produce its vast entertainment complex and to maintain and grow its stature and influence, from theme park attractions to movies and much more. But the Carousel does not acknowledge—and indeed pushes back against—the notion that "progress" as defined by a corporate actor has a much different meaning than it has for the average citizen who may have been displaced in the workplace by a machine, or for policymakers, who may need to redefine and expand conceptions of "humanity" to include super-intelligent artificial beings. While it is difficult to deny that the typical person's life is far superior than the typical person's life fifty years ago due, in large measure, to technological innovation, there is no guarantee that folks will be in a position to make a parallel statement fifty years from now. The Carousel fails to consider who or what may be lost as technology continues to advance in a largely unimpeded fashion.

Black Mirror, Electric Dreams and *The Twilight Zone* represent dark responses to what the writers of those shows likely perceive as the "Carousel of Progress's" overly colorful, "Disneyfied" depiction of the impact of technology in society. By exploring the potential dangers of unbridled innovation, these anthologies present a counterargument to the notion that technological progress necessarily generates happiness without any adverse consequences. They also question whether the ideals of nostalgia and innovation are necessarily compatible, especially when technological progress advances at such a rapid pace so as to not allow for time to reflect and take stock of the past.

A Dark, Robotic Wonderland: Oh, the (Lack of) Humanity!

The moment may have already arrived in which human beings need physical protection from their robotic creations. While it is perhaps naïve to believe that robots are infallible, incapable of making mistakes and even causing injuries—see, for example, their inadvertent puncturing of bear repellent in one of Amazon's factories—do we need to develop advanced ways to guard against dangerous actions by artificially-created beings?[107] Amazon apparently believes that we do. In 2016, Amazon reportedly filed for patent protection of a design for cages to house human workers.[108] The purpose of the cages (according to Amazon) was not to enslave humans, but rather to protect them from robots moving around Amazon's warehouses. The proposal was widely criticized, with critics pointing out that it served as an "extraordinary illustration of worker alienation, a stark moment in the relationship between humans and machines."[109] While Amazon executive Dave Clark acknowledged that the plan was flawed, he acknowledged the need for human workers to be protected from robots at the warehouses.[110] The company therefore introduced a vest that workers can wear that causes nearby robots to stop moving. As robots gain skill and increase their intelligence capabilities, will a vest effectively stop them from harming us? Will the robots seize the idea of the human cages, placing humans in a zoo-like environment seen in *The Twilight Zone*'s "People Are Alike All Over"?[111] Are we inching closer to a world in which robots overrun, enslave and ultimately eliminate the human species?

Whereas *Electric Dreams* uses "Autofac" to explore a post-apocalyptic future where "humans" have been recreated to engender a purposeful world for their technological creations, *Black Mirror* presents the converse scenario: a society in which humanity has apparently been destroyed by its creations.[112] The doomsday scenario of robots destroying humanity and taking over Earth is examined on *Black Mirror*'s "Metalhead" episode. While operating in a crowded field of post-apocalyptic tales, the episode succeeds where some other representations of this scenario fail—especially given its place in a television series focused not on farfetched ideas but on frighteningly real potential prospects for the future. The episode evokes palpable feelings of helplessness and fear caused by artificial intelligence gone wild. It provides a visualization of the popular theory that artificial intelligence is, at best, indifferent to the suffering of humans and at worst, actively pursues it. This episode is characterized by impressive CGI super-effects set forth in a world replete with minimalistic elements—a setting designed to sharply contrast with the beautiful, colorful technological effects featured in other worlds presented on *Black Mirror*. Filmed entirely in black and white, the dreary setting of this post-apocalyptic future seems to show the last remnants of humanity in despair—having been wiped out by small robot "dogs" hell-bent (for unspecified reasons) on mankind's total destruction. Brooker has acknowledged that the faceless, emotionless robot dogs are modeled after a real-life innovation—a cutting-edge line of robots designed by the technology company Boston Dynamics.[113] In contrast to the lovelorn computer featured in *The Twilight Zone*'s "From Agnes—With Love"—and other tales of unrequited feelings of love and sabotage by robots such as in the films *Electric Dreams* (1984) and *Android* (1982) and the "Love-matic Grampa" featured on "The Simpsons Spin-off Showcase" (1997)—the robots have no interest in cohabitation with humans, and they actively seek out folks for gruesome killings.[114] The actions of the robotic dogs reflect Bostrom's and others' fears of potential clashes between humanity and artificial intelligence. Earth has become a killing field, with the last surviving humans typically venturing out only to gather necessary medical supplies and food. The robots exhibit significant resilience, eerily propping themselves back up as humans attempt to defend themselves against the attacks. The fact that the specific circumstances of humanity's demise are not revealed adds an additional layer of dread for the concerned viewer: if the world does not know *how* robots plan to take over, we will not be in a strong position to stop them from doing so.

It is difficult to imagine a more frightful setting, with the robots methodically searching for and—through use of tracking devices—finding humans. As humans come to realize that the robots are unstoppable, they resort to suicide in a last-ditch effort to deprive the machines of death at their hands. The teddy bear that the protagonist attempts to find and bring back for her child represents comfort, warmth and innocence—all of which have been stripped away and lost in this dystopian future. The woman is searching for remnants of a time gone by, where the feelings and motivations of human beings matter. Ethical treatment of human beings is non-existent, and the robots have not enamored themselves to nor cultivated a system of values in which they would feel empathy for humans or restrict them from causing human suffering. The episode is perceived as even more chilling when we consider the net impact predicted by proponents of cultivation theory. Given that science fiction thrillers such as "Metalhead" rarely focus on potentially amicable interactions with artificial intelligence (that may, for example, support the optimistic predictions of researchers such as Loosemore), the audience is more likely to view this dystopian wasteland as a realistic (if not inevitable) conclusion for the human species.

Worshipping AI

Remarkably (and quite jarringly), some folks favor the idea of not only ceding unfettered control to AI, but also promote the idea of building an artificial intelligence God that some people would worship. Anthony Levandowski, an engineer who previously worked on developing driverless cars for Uber, founded a non-profit religious organization called Way of the Future.[115] The organization calls for the controversial development of an artificial intelligence "Godhead," with the following mission statement: "To develop and promote the realization of a Godhead based on artificial intelligence and through understanding and worship of the Godhead contribute to the betterment of society."[116] Some observers believe that this development could take place within the next 25–50 years.[117] Because human beings "tend to trust and obey things that seem more powerful and worthy than ourselves," it is likely that some folks will come to effectively worship the Godhead.[118]

The Twilight Zone explored the idea of human beings blindly following the guidance of machines in the episode "The Old Man in the Cave."[119] In the episode, a group of folks relied on the sound instructions of an unseen entity—a powerful computer—following a nuclear war that decimated most of civilization. Just as the folks in the episode use the machine to their collective advantage, we frequently rely on the perceived validity of Google search results and calculations made by computers. When we place too much trust in the hands of technology, we do so at our peril. This concept is examined in *The Office* episode "Dunder Mifflin Infinity," when Michael Scott drives his car into a lake because his GPS advised him to do so.[120] Michael ignores his own eyes and the warning of Dwight and instead decides to blindly follow the misguided directions of technology. Our misguided belief in the infallibility of technology could have dangerous consequences—especially as it continues to advance and exert more influence over us.

The development of an artificially intelligent Godhead could take our reliance to unprecedented, dangerous territory. The Godhead, for example, could write an "AI bible" for human beings to follow.[121] Such a bible may tell folks how to live their lives—where to travel, what to eat, who to form relationships with. While there will inevitably be folks who are suspicious of such a Godhead, there will likely be others who do follow its guidance (and, dare we say, mandates)—just as folks follow, often blindly, the outputs of their devices.

If such blind allegiance is inevitable, we must at least hope that AI advances to the state where it no longer advises folks to commit murder—as a special beta test version of an Amazon Alexa advice did in 2018, when it blurted out "Kill your foster parents."[122] If some folks will come to rely on a Godhead for guidance, it behooves them to consider that AI may not reach a state where it is flawless or beyond reproach. And, even more frighteningly, we might not be aware of the Godhead's potential goal—perhaps to eradicate humanity.[123] Levandowski's overt proposal should serve as a wake-up call to the rest of us: there are folks who believe in the unfettered development of powerful AI whose human-provided objective is to exert control over us. If there were ever any doubt that some form of regulation is necessary to reign in such proposals, such doubts should be erased.

Conclusion
Waking Up from an Electric Dream

"Reality is wrong. Dreams are for real."
—Tupac Shakur[1]

In the opening scene of the *Parks and Recreation* episode "The Trial of Leslie Knope," Parks and Recreation Department Director Ron Swanson is both puzzled and angered when he is inundated with targeted advertisements as he browses the Internet. Swanson incredulously asks a colleague how the computer "knows stuff" about him.[2] Upon learning that algorithms and cookies relay consumer information to companies, Swanson throws out his computer. This action, of course, solves little. Swanson need not use the Internet, but then he will not be able to access all its benefits and exploit the efficiencies created thereby. And it is also too late for Swanson: relevant information about him has already been collected, and companies can use such information to target and contact Swanson in other ways.

We laugh at Swanson's futile attempts to run from technology. He misunderstands and underestimates the reach and power of the Internet. We must acknowledge, however, that we, too, are largely incapable of avoiding technology once it has been introduced. Regulations may provide temporary protection and a reprieve from technology, but, as Rod Serling shows us in *The Twilight Zone*'s "The Howling Man," human curiosity will not allow forces that endanger us to be locked up forever.[3] As science writer Philip Ball quips in the context of regulating artificial intelligence, "Telling international arms traders that they can't make killer robots is like telling soft-drink makers that they can't make orangeade."[4] Signatories to a ban argue that "Once this Pandora's box is opened, it will be hard to close."[5]

Perhaps most of us fail to comprehend the immense power of technology (and its potential for destruction). We seem to also overestimate our ability to effectively stop it. If we optimistically believe that we can manage technology in a responsible way, are we are naïve as Mr. Swanson? We may be the ones pressing the buttons on our electronic devices and turning on our screens, but, as "Nosedive," "U.S.S. Callister" and other episodes demonstrate, that does not necessarily mean that we are in control. It is undeniable that technology has already started to exert power and influence over our feelings, motivations, language and behavior. Technology challenges our existing norms and preferences. It is, in short, rapidly changing who we are.

Black Mirror and *Electric Dreams* force us to ask whether we are adequately prepared to face a brave new world, one in which fantasy becomes reality and we escape from the realm of science fiction. Both shows provide a springboard for further consideration of issues that could define our existence. It is entertaining (and, at times, thrilling) to watch television shows that explore potential future states, and the positive and negative consequences of technological developments. But will we be ready if and when we awake from these fantasies—our electric dreams—and observe that the anticipated technological landscape becomes our reality? Would it be feasible to return to a previous state if we are uncomfortable with our new environment?

As Billy Joel sings in his single, *All You Want to Do Is Dance* (1976), we may not be enamored with a future state of affairs and wish that we could return to the good old days when life was simpler on many levels.[6] But Ron Swanson's comical attempt to rid his life of technology demonstrates that achieving this goal on a wide scale is impractical. We may collectively realize that the efficiencies produced as a byproduct of our technological innovation have, paradoxically, complicated life. We may yearn to return to a past time, one in which we lacked the capability to build complex robots that ultimately would compete with us for jobs and resources. We may seek a sense of privacy, an ideal made impossible by the constant infusion of social media content and intrusive tracking devices. We may generally want to gradually slow down a bit and become a bit more thoughtful about our innovations before their introduction into society changes how we define and experience life. And, before deciding to escape from our natural environments by entering virtual ones or becoming lost in our screens, we may want to take stock of the non-technological wonders of our world, observing the beauty that surrounds us. As we continue to seek new ways to exploit technology to move more quickly, perhaps we should pause and heed the warning of pop culture icon Ferris Bueller: "Life moves pretty fast. If you don't stop and look around once in a while, you could miss it."[7]

As discussed earlier, policymakers could consider introducing regulations prohibiting or restricting the spread of certain technologies on a wide scale. While strong arguments have been made in favor of government regulation of novel technologies—including those that are expected to disrupt the workforce—it would likely be difficult to determine agreeable and effective parameters, and any decisions made by arbiters would presumably be controversial.[8] Introducing regulations tailored to only reign in corporate overreach in the context of use of technological innovations to achieve an end that is wholly undesirable from a public policy perspective—such as an ability for Amazon to lock you in our house if you fail to pay for its products in a timely fashion—may be a sensible approach.[9] Still, the law of unintended consequences dictates that it may be difficult to accurately predict the potentialities that humans could face down the line if the introduction of modern technologies outside of this one limitation otherwise continues unabated—although shows such as *Black Mirror* and *Electric Dreams* provide keen and critical insight into certain scenarios. On the other hand, wholesale prohibitions on technology could lead to a decrease in efficiency, may deprive the world of truly significant and positive consequences and, as discussed above, may ultimately prove insufficient when battling the unquenchable human thirst for access to knowledge and innovation.

If and when the technologies discussed in this book and examined on *Black Mirror* and *Electric Dreams* are introduced, it may not be possible to turn back the clock and reenter our previous state of life. In his hit single *Time in a Bottle* (1972), Jim Croce sings of saving time in a bottle, but acknowledges that doing so is merely a fantasy.[10] Human nature dictates that post-hoc attempts at regulation of technological innovations that have been widely released will likely fail. Once the curious human species experiences innovation, the practical reality is that it is difficult to hit a pause or reset button.

If we are unable or unwilling to resist the introduction of potentially deleterious technologies, we must question whether humans have sufficient mechanisms to allow us to adjust, subsist and achieve success despite coexistence with such technologies. On the one hand, there is evidence that humans beings are equipped with a keen ability to adapt to new circumstances—a characteristic that has enabled our species to survive calamities such as wars, natural disasters and poverty, as well as changes in society (be it shifting economic models or ways of life, such as industrialization and a departure from a largely agrarian culture).

On the other hand, this ability to adjust and acclimate to new circumstances is not without its limits. Rather, an amalgamation of external circumstances and an individual's predisposition often determines whether an individual can successfully thrive in new surroundings. Popular culture is informative in this arena as well. As we watch *Better Call Saul*'s Saul Goodman character live life using a new identity (Gene, a local Cinnabon manager), for example, the stress and anxiety of hiding causes Gene to collapse.[11] The constant fear of being recognized as his television persona is too much for him to bear. Like other characters on television, Saul is unable to adapt to new circumstances in a healthy way.[12] By examining the effect of changing circumstances on folks—especially on shows where such new surroundings represent a fundamental upending of a comfortable environment (think *Black Mirror*, *Electric Dreams* and *The Twilight Zone*)—we gain a better understanding of the human condition.

Ultimately, the question is whether we will be able to adjust to circumstances altered by technology. How will be adapt if Elon Musk is correct about a future hybrid existence where man merges with machine? Is Ray Kurzweil's flowery vision—namely that human beings will successfully adapt and thrive in a reimagination and redefinition of humanity—realistic? Given the chance that Kurzweil's optimism is misguided, now is the time to be proactive, not paralyzed in the face of potential threats. We need not choose sadness or depression and can attempt to find ways to shine within new paradigms that might be created. As an ancient Chinese proverb suggests, "It's better to light a candle than curse the darkness."[13]

* * *

On Mirrors and Dreams

> "Just as man cannot live without dreams, he cannot live without hope."
> —Elie Wiesel[14]

A properly functioning mirror requires a smooth surface because a rough surface will scatter light instead of reflecting it.[15] The phenomenon of specular reflection results in an orderly reflection of light, as opposed to its converse: diffuse reflection.[16] Order, stability and tranquility are thus characteristics of a normal mirror. What to make, then, of the cold and steely black mirror? What is the nature and direction of the light that reflects off its dark surface? Is it more difficult to see clearly through the blackness? Does this mean that we are driving blind, set to inevitably veer off a cliff?

The dark message lurking within *The Twilight Zone* episode "The Mirror"—where a dictator sees his would-be assassins in a haunted mirror—is that we frequently excel at identifying external factors that could cause our downfall but are far less successful at looking deep within ourselves to find reasons for our demise.[17] Channeling Brooker in this regard, we might conclude that, as an external factor, technology is far less potent than our own destructive tendencies. Technology is simply an avenue, a medium through which human behavior is funneled—like a mirror, it reflects who and what we are. If we are not sufficiently careful, might we be our own assassins—even as we attempt to deflect and place the blame on technology?

It is through our dreams that we experience altered states of reality. Some dreams may be frightening, but they provide an outlet for our imaginations to run wild—an escape from circumstances in real life that may be beyond our control. An electric dream is a dynamic one; a vision replete with potential and exciting possibilities. If we dream hard enough, immersing ourselves in alternate content and experiencing other worlds, we may be able to absorb and implement our new knowledge in the real world in exciting, uplifting ways.

* * *

Sir Arthur C. Clarke warned us that "Before you become too entranced with gorgeous gadgets and mesmerizing video displays, let me remind you that information is not knowledge, knowledge is not wisdom, and wisdom is not foresight. Each grows out of the other, and we need them all."[18] Technology should not be used as a substitute for human knowledge, spirit, instinct or calculation. Despite presenting humanity with a wide range of benefits, the risks of unfettered technological innovation demand that a responsible populace take a measured, relatively cautious approach to its introduction. Our shiny screens will not flash warnings signs to advise us of their potential for causing destruction or wreaking havoc when misused or abused by folks. It is incumbent upon leaders and citizens to be vigilant, to consider the potential consequences of technological advances and to make wise, informed decisions about the role that technology plays—and should play—in our lives. We should not glorify technology without considering its potential adverse impact on the way that we define, experience and live life.

On the other hand, it is also easy to be (perhaps overly) pessimistic about technology and, more importantly, our ability to co-exist with it. *Black Mirror* and *Electric Dreams* demonstrate that, to a large extent, what is intended to connect us, isolates us; what is intended to provide a temporary reprieve from life becomes addictive and all-consuming; what is intended to create efficiency leaves able-bodied workers restless and bored, questioning their value to society; what is designed to maintain privacy and provide security puts us at a heightened risk of exposure to identity theft and exploitation by hackers; what is intended to make our lives simpler complicates things immeasurably.

And yet, human beings are innovative. We are adventurous. We are curious. We are stubborn and strong-willed, and, perhaps most importantly, adept at solving complicated problems. We must resist the twin pitfalls of silence and complacency, for, as Dr. Martin Luther King, Jr., warns us, "Our lives begin to end the day we become silent about things that matter."[19] As we study the ways in which technologies affect our thoughts and behaviors; uncover corporate strategies that seek to use our personal data and preferences to achieve their secret agendas; and acknowledge that inventors, financiers and governments are not tackling these issues in a productive or responsible manner, we must not only remain vigilant but must also use the speech protections and electoral mechanisms afforded to us in our great republic to denounce ethically questionable practices at every turn. We must not forget that silence has the practical effect of acquiescence. We must not allow our past mistakes to define us, and we should optimistically look to the future, anticipating and demanding success. As Rod Serling predicts, "…no matter what the future brings, man's capacity to rise to the occasion will remain unaltered. His potential for tenacity and optimism continues, as always, to outfight, outpoint and outlive any and all changes made by his society…."[20]

We will look forward with hope and amazement, remembering Thomas Jefferson's proclamation: "I like the dreams of the future better than the history of the past."[21] Considering humanity's wars, hatred and prejudices throughout history, perhaps the past is not as idealized, bucolic or idyllic as we may like to think. While we may rightfully feel a sense of nostalgia when considering our past, we can also optimistically look forward to the future in anticipation of the changes and adventures that may come our way.

F.E.A.R.: "Forget Everything and Run" or "Face Everything and Rise"?

Ultimately, we must not fear the future or feel paralyzed by the potentialities examined on *Black Mirror* and *Electric Dreams*. As *Breaking Bad*'s Walter White stated, "What I came to realize is that fear, that's the worst of it. That's the real enemy. So, get up, get out in the real world and you kick that bastard as hard as you can right in the teeth."[22] Armed with the results of an examination of the potential human reactions to the hypothetical situations presented on *Black Mirror* and *Electric Dreams*, perhaps we will be somewhat better equipped to contend with troublesome scenarios. We should keep in mind the sage guidance of American poet Walt Whitman: "Keep your face always toward the sunshine—and shadows will fall behind you."[23] We can move toward future states with a bit more confidence in both our enduring humanity and our keen ability to simultaneously reject wholesale changes while adapting where necessary. Notwithstanding any changes within society and ourselves, we will remain largely recognizable in the mirror and awake from our exciting, enlightening dreams replete with a renewed sense of hope, curiosity, awe and wonder.

Appendix A
Black Mirror *and* Electric Dreams *Episode Lists*

Black Mirror *Episode List*

Series 1

1. "The National Anthem." Directed by Otto Barthurst. Written by Charlie Brooker. Channel 4, December 4, 2011.
2. "Fifteen Million Merits." Directed by Euros Lyn. Written by Charlie Brooker and Kanak Huq. Channel 4, December 4, 2011.
3. "The Entire History of You." Directed by Brian Welsh. Written by Jesse Armstrong. Channel 4, December 18, 2011.

Series 2

4. "Be Right Back." Directed by Owen Harris. Written by Charlie Brooker. Channel 4, February 11, 2013.
5. "White Bear." Directed by Carl Tibbetts. Written by Charlie Brooker. Channel 4, February 18, 2013.
6. "The Waldo Moment." Directed by Bryn Higgins. Written by Charlie Brooker. Channel 4, February 25, 2013.

Special

7. "White Christmas." Directed by Carl Tibbetts. Written by Charlie Brooker. Channel 4, December 16, 2014.

Series 3

8. "Nosedive." Directed by Joe Wright. Story by Charlie Brooker. Teleplay by Rashida Jones and Mike Schur. Netflix, October 21, 2016.
9. "Playtest." Directed by Dan Trachtenberg. Written by Charlie Brooker. Netflix, October 21, 2016.
10. "Shut Up & Dance." Directed by James Watkins. Written by Charlie Brooker and William Bridges. Netflix, October 21, 2016.
11. "San Junipero." Directed by Owen Harris. Written by Charlie Brooker. Netflix, October 21, 2016.

12. "Men Against Fire." Directed by Jacob Verbruggen. Written by Charlie Brooker. Netflix, October 21, 2016.

13. "Hated in the Nation." Directed by James Hawes. Written by Charlie Brooker. Netflix, October 21, 2016.

Series 4

14. "U.S.S. Callister." Directed by Toby Haynes. Written by Charlie Brooker and William Bridges. Netflix, December 29, 2017.

15. "Arkangel." Directed by Jodie Foster. Written by Charlie Brooker. Netflix, December 29, 2017.

16. "Crocodile." Directed by John Hillcoat. Written by Charlie Brooker. Netflix, December 29, 2017.

17. "Hang the DJ." Directed by Tim Van Patten. Written by Charlie Brooker. Netflix, December 29, 2017.

18. "Metalhead." Directed by David Slade. Written by Charlie Brooker. Netflix, December 29, 2017.

19. "Black Museum." Directed by Colm McCarthy. Written by Charlie Brooker. Netflix, December 29, 2017.

Film

20. "Bandersnatch." Directed by David Slade. Written by Charlie Brooker. Netflix, December 28, 2018.

Electric Dreams *Episode List*

1. "The Hood Maker." Directed by Julian Jarrold. Written by Matthew Graham. Channel 4, September 17, 2017.

2. "Impossible Planet." Directed by David Farr. Written by David Farr. Channel 4, September 24, 2017.

3. "The Commuter." Directed by Tom Harper. Written by Jack Thorne. Channel 4, October 1, 2017.

4. "Crazy Diamond." Directed by Marc Munden. Written by Tony Grisoni. Channel 4, October 8, 2017.

5. "Real Life." Directed by Jeffrey Reiner. Written by Ronald D. Moore. Channel 4, October 15, 2017.

6. "Human Is." Directed by Francesca Gregorini. Written by Jessica Mecklenburg. Channel 4, October 29, 2017.

7. "The Father Thing." Directed by Michael Dinner. Written by Michael Dinner. Channel 4, February 26, 2018.

8. "Autofac." Directed by Peter Horton. Written by Travis Beacham. Channel 4, March 5, 2018.

9. "Safe & Sound." Directed by Alan Taylor. Written by Kalen Egan and Travis Sentell. Channel 4, March 12, 2018.

10. "Kill All Others." Directed by Dee Rees. Written by Dee Rees. Channel 4, March 19, 2018.

Appendix B
Television and Film Sources

Episodes Cited from Television Shows

Bates Motel. *A&E Networks, 2013–2017.*

"Hidden." Episode No. 44. Directed by Max Theriot. Written by Torrey Speer. AMC, March 13, 2017.

The Big Bang Theory. *CBS, 2017–present.*

"The Beta Test Initiation." Episode No. 101, Prod. 3X6864. Directed by Mark Cendrowski. Written by Bill Prady et al. CBS, January 26, 2012.

Breaking Bad. *AMC, 2008–2013.*

"Better Call Saul." Episode No. 15. Directed by Terry McDonough. Written by Peter Gould. AMC, April 26, 2009.

Better Call Saul. *AMC, 2015–present.*

"Mabel." Episode No. 21. Directed by Vince Gilligan. Written by Peter Gould and Vince Gilligan. AMC, April 10, 2017.

Curb Your Enthusiasm. *HBO, 2000–present.*

"The Doll." Episode No. 17. Directed by Robert Weide. Written by Larry David. HBO, November 4, 2001.

Futurama. *FOX / Comedy Central, 1999–2003 / 2008–2013, respectively.*

"A Fishful of Dollars." Episode No. 6, Prod. 1ACV06. Directed by Ron Hughart and Gregg Vanzo. Written by Patric M. Verrone. FOX, April 27, 1999.

Homecoming. *Amazon Video, November 2, 2018–present.*

"Helping." Episode No. 5. Directed by Sam Esmail. Written by Cami Delavigne. Amazon Video, November 2, 2018.

Humans. *AMC, 2015–present.*

"Episode 1." Episode No. 1. Directed by Sam Donovan. Written by Jonathan Brackley and Sam Vincent. AMC, June 14, 2015.
"Episode 4." Episode No. 12, Directed by Carl Tibbetts. AMC, November 20, 2016.
"Episode 5." Episode No. 5. Directed by Lewis Arnold. Written by Emily Ballou. AMC, July 12, 2015.
"Episode 8." Episode No. 8. Directed by China Moo-Young. Written by Sam Vincent and Jonathan Brackley. AMC, August 16, 2015.

Kiss Me First. *Netflix, 2018–present.*

"She Did Something." Episode No. 1. Directed by Misha Manson-Smith. Written by Brian Elsley. Netflix, April 2, 2018.

Mister Rogers' Neighborhood. *PBS, 1968–2001.*

"The Pie Restaurant: Part 1." Episode No. 201. NET, February 9, 1970.

The Office. *NBC, 2005–2013.*

"A.A.R.M." Episode Nos. 198 and 199, Prod. 9022 and 9023, respectively. Directed by David Rogers. Written by Brent Forrester. NBC, May 9, 2013.
"Blood Drive." Episode No. 90, Prod. 518. Directed by Randall Einhorn. Written by Brett Forrester. NBC, March 5, 2009.
"Dunder Mifflin Infinity." Episode Nos. 56 and 57, Prods. 403 and 404. Directed by Craig Zisk. Written by Michael Schur. NBC, October 4, 2007.
"Launch Party." Episode No. 58 and 59, Prod. 405 and 406, respectively. Directed by Ken Whittingham. Written by Jennifer Celotta. NBC, October 11, 2007.
"The List." Episode No. 153, Prod. 802. Directed by B.J. Novak. Written by B.J. Novak. NBC, September 22, 2011.
"Local Ad." Episode No. 62, Prod. 409. Directed by Jason Reitman. Written by B.J. Novak. NBC, October 25, 2007.
"The Lover." Episode No. 107, Prod. 607. Directed by Lee Eisenberg. Written by Lee Eisenberg and Gene Stupnitsky. NBC, October 22, 2009.
"Murder." Episode No. 110, Prod. 6010. Directed by Greg Daniels. Written by Daniel Chun. NBC, November 12, 2009.
"The Negotiation." Episode No. 47, Prod. 319. Directed by Jeffrey Blitz. Written by Michael Schur. NBC, April 5, 2007.
"Promos." Episode No. 193, Prod. 9018. Directed by Jennifer Celotta. Written by Tim McAuliffe. NBC, April 4, 2013.
"Search Committee." Episode Nos. 151 and 152, Prod. 7025 and 7026. Directed by Jeffrey Blitz. Written by Paul Lieberstein. NBC, May 19, 2011.
"Trivia." Episode No. 163, Prod. 811. Directed by B.J. Novak. Written by Steve Hely. NBC, January 12, 2012.
"WUPHF.com." Episode No. 135, Prod. 709. Directed by Danny Leiner. Written by Aaron Shure. NBC, November 18, 2010.

Parks & Recreation. *NBC, 2009–2015.*

"Correspondents' Lunch." Episode No. 83. Directed by Nick Offerman. Written by Alexandra Rushfield. NBC, February 21, 2013.

"Eagleton." Episode No. 42. Directed by Nicole Holofcener. Written by Emily Spivey. NBC, May 5, 2011.

"Leslie and Ron." Episode No. 116. Directed by Beth McCarthy-Miller. Written by Michael Schur. NBC, January 20, 2015.

"Sex Education." Episode No. 72, Directed by Craig Zisk. Written by Alan Yang. NBC, October 18, 2012.

"The Trial of Leslie Knope." Episode No. 55. Directed by Dean Holland. Written by Dan Goor and Michael Schur. NBC, December 1, 2011.

Saved by the Bell. *NBC, 1988–1993.*

"The Zack Tapes." Episode No. 14. Directed by Don Barnhart. Written by Peter Engel and Tom Tenowich. NBC, December 2, 1989.

The Simpsons. *FOX, 1989–present.*

"Bart's Comet." Episode No. 117, Prod. 2F11. Directed by Bob Anderson. Written by John Swartzwelder. FOX, February 5, 1995.

"The Burns and the Bees." Episode No. 428, Prod. KABF21. Directed by Mark Kirkland. Written by Stephanie Gillis. FOX, December 7, 2008.

"Burns' Heir." Episode No. 99, Prod. 1F16. Directed by Mark Kirkland. Written by Jace Richdale. FOX, April 14, 1994.

"The Cartridge Family." Episode 183, Prod. 5F01. Directed by Pete Michels. Written by John Schwartzwelder. FOX, November 2, 1997.

"The Computer Wore Menace Shoes." Episode No. 254, Prod. CABF02. Directed by Mark Kirkland. Written by John Swartzwelder. FOX, December 3, 2000.

"Fraudcast News." Directed by Bob Anderson. Written by Don Payne. Episode No. 335, Prod. FABF18. FOX, May 23, 2004.

"Girly Edition." Episode No. 199, Prod. 5F15. Directed by Mark Kirkland. Written by Larry Doyle. FOX, April 19, 1998.

"Grift of the Magi." Episode No. 235, Prod. BABF07. Directed by Matthew Nastuk. Written by Tom Martin. FOX, December 19, 1999.

"Holidays of Future Past." Episode No. 495, Prod. NABF18. Directed by Rob Oliver. Written by J. Stewart Burns. FOX, December 11, 2011.

"Homer Badman." Episode No. 112, Prod. 2F06. Directed by Jeffrey Lynch. Written by Greg Daniels. FOX, November 27, 1994.

"Homer vs. the Eighteenth Amendment." Episode No. 171, Prod. 4F15. Directed by Bob Anderson. Written by John Swartzwelder. FOX, March 16, 1997.

"I (Annoyed Grunt)-Bot." Episode No. 322, Prod. FABF04. Directed by Lauren MacMullan. Written by Dan Greaney and Allen Glazier. FOX, January 11, 2004.

"Itchy and Scratchy Land." Episode No. 107, Prod. 2F01. Directed by Wes Archer. Written by John Schwartzwelder. FOX, October 2, 1994.

"Lemon of Troy." Episode No. 127, Prod. 2F22. Directed by Jim Reardon. Written by Brent Forrester. FOX, May 14, 1995.

"New Kids on the Blecch." Episode No. 262, Prod. CABF12. Directed by Steven Dean Moore. Written by Tim Long. FOX, February 25, 2001.

"Rosebud." Episode No. 85, Prod. 1F01. Directed by Wes Archer. Written by John Swartzwelder. FOX, October 21, 1993.

"Sideshow Bob's Last Gleaming." Episode No. 137, Prod. 3F08. Directed by Dominic Polcino. Written by Spike Feresten. FOX, November 26, 1995.

"The Simpsons Spin-Off Showcase." Episode No. 177, Prod. 4F20. Directed by Neil Affleck. Written by David S. Cohen et al. FOX, May 11, 1997.

"A Tale of Two Springfields." Episode No. 250, Prod. BABF20. Directed by Shaun Cashman. Written by John Swartzwelder. FOX, November 5, 2000.

"Them, Robot." Episode No. 503, Prod. PABF10. Directed by Michael Polcino. Written by Michael Price. FOX, March 18, 2012.

"They Saved Lisa's Brain." Episode 225, Prod. AABF18. Directed by Pete Michels. Written by Matt Selman. FOX, May 9, 1999.

"Treehouse of Horror II." Episode No. 42, Prod. 8F02. Directed by Jim Reardon. Written by Sam Simon, et al. FOX, October 31, 1991.

"Treehouse of Horror V." Episode No. 109, Prod. 2F03. Directed by Jim Reardon. Written by Greg Daniels et al. FOX, October 30, 1994.

"Treehouse of Horror VI." Episode No. 134, Prod. 3F04. Directed by Bob Anderson. Written by John Swartzwelder et al. FOX, October 29, 1995.

"24 Minutes." Episode No. 399, Prod. JABF14. Directed by Raymond Persi. Written by Ian Maxtone-Graham et al. FOX, May 20, 2007.

"When You Dish Upon A Star." Episode No. 208, Prod. 5F19. Directed by Pete Michels. Written by Richard Appel. FOX, November 8, 1998.

13 Reasons Why. *Netflix, 2017–present.*

"Tape 2, Side B." Episode No. 4. Directed by Helen Shaver. Written by Thomas Higgins. Netflix, March 31, 2017.

"The Chalk Machine." Episode No. 5. Directed by Eliza Hittman. Written by Nic Sheff. Netflix, May 18, 2018.

24. *FOX, 2001–2010.*

"Day 4: 8:00 a.m.–9:00 a.m." Episode No. 74, Prod. 4AFF02. Directed by Jon Cassar. Written by Howard Gordon. FOX, January 9, 2005.

"Day 7: 3:00 pm–4:00 pm." Episode No. 152, Prod. 7AFF08. Directed by Milan Cheylov. Written by Robert Cochran and Evan Katz. FOX, February 9, 2009.

"Day 7: 8:00 p.m.–9:00 p.m". Episode No. 157, Prod. 7AFF13. Directed by Brad Turner. Written by Brannon Braga and Manny Coto. FOX, March 9, 2009.

The Twilight Zone. *CBS, 1959–1964 (original series).*

"Back There." Episode No. 49, Prod. 173-3648. Directed by David Orrick McDearon. Written by Rod Serling. CBS, January 13, 1961.

"The Bewitchin' Pool." Episode No. 156, Prod. 2619. Directed by Joseph M. Newman. Written by Earl Hamner, Jr. CBS, June 19, 1964.

"The Brain Center at Whipple's." Episode 153, Prod. 2632. Directed by Richard Donner. Written by Rod Serling. CBS, May 15, 1964.

"Deaths-Head Revisited." Episode No. 74, Prod. 4804. Directed by Don Medford. Written by Rod Serling. CBS, November 10, 1961.

"Eye of the Beholder." Episode No. 42, Prod. 173-3640. Directed by Douglas Heyes. Written by Rod Serling. CBS, November 11, 1960.

"The Fever." Episode No. 17, Prod. 173-3627. Directed by Robert Florey. Written by Rod Serling. CBS, January 29, 1960.

Television and Film Sources

"Five Characters in Search of An Exit." Episode No. 79, Prod. 4805. Directed by Lamont Johnson. Written by Rod Serling. CBS, December 22, 1961.

"The Four of Us Are Dying." Episode No. 13, Prod. 173–3618. Directed by John Brahm. Written by Rod Serling. CBS, January 1, 1960.

"From Agnes—With Love." Episode No. 140, Prod. 2629. Directed by Richard Donner. Written by Bernard C. Schoenfeld. CBS, February 14, 1964.

"The Fugitive." Episode No. 90, Prod. 4816. Directed by Richard L. Bare. Written by Charles Beaumont. CBS, March 9, 1962.

"The Howling Man." Episode No. 41, Prod. 173–3642. Directed by Douglas Heyes. Written by Charles Beaumont. CBS, November 4, 1960.

"The Hunt." Episode No. 84, Prod. 4810. Directed by Harold Schuster. Written by Earl Hamner, Jr. CBS, January 26, 1962.

"The Fugitive." Episode No. 90, Prod. 4816. Directed by Richard L. Bare. Written by Charles Beaumont. CBS, March 9, 1962.

"The Good Life." Episode No. 73, Prod. 4801. Directed by James Sheldon. Written by Rod Serling. CBS, November 3, 1961.

"I Sing the Body Electric." Episode No. 100, Prod. 4826. Directed by William Claxton and James Sheldon. Written by Ray Bradbury. CBS, May 18, 1962.

"In His Image." Episode No. 103, Prod. 4851. Directed by Perry Lafferty. Written by Charles Beaumont. CBS, January 3, 1963.

"The Incredible World of Horace Ford." Episode, 117, Prod. 4854. Directed by Abner Biberman. Written by Reginald Rose. CBS, April 18, 1963.

"The Jeopardy Room." Episode No. 149, Prod. 2639. Directed by Richard Donner. Written by Rod Serling. CBS, April 17, 1964.

"Kick the Can." Episode No. 86, Prod. 4821. Directed by Lamont Johnson. Written by George Clayton Johnson. CBS, February 9, 1962.

"The Lateness of the Hour." Episode No. 44, Prod. 173–3652. Directed by Jack Smight. Written by Rod Serling. CBS, December 2, 1960.

"Little Girl Lost." Episode No. 91, Prod. 4828. Directed by Paul Stewart. Written by Richard Matheson. CBS, March 16, 1962.

"The Lonely." Episode No. 7, Prod. 173–3602. Directed by Jack Smight. Written by Rod Serling. CBS, November 13, 1959.

"Long Distance Call." Episode No. 58, Prod. 173–3667. Directed by James Sheldon. Written by Charles Beaumont and William Idelson. CBS, March 31, 1961.

"The Man in the Bottle." Episode No. 38, Prod. 173–3638. Directed by Don Medford. Written by Rod Serling. CBS, October 7, 1960.

"The Masks." Episode No. 145, Prod. 2601. Directed by Ida Lupino. Written by Rod Serling. CBS, March 20, 1964.

"The Mighty Casey." Episode No. 35, Prod. 173–3617. Directed by Alvin Ganzer and Robert Parrish. Written by Rod Serling. CBS, June 17, 1960.

"The Mind and the Matter." Episode No. 63, Prod. 173–3659. Directed by Buzz Kulik. Written by Rod Serling. CBS, May 12, 1961.

"Miniature." Episode No. 110, Prod. 3862. Directed by Walter Grauman. Written by Charles Beaumont. CBS, February 21, 1963.

"The Mirror." Episode No. 71, Prod. 4819. Directed by Don Medford. Written by Rod Serling. CBS, October 20, 1961.

"Mirror Image." Episode No. 21, Prod. 173–3623. Directed by John Brahm. Written by Rod Serling. CBS, February 26, 1960.

"The Monsters are Due on Maple Street." Episode No. 22, Prod. 173–3620. Directed by Ronald Winston. Written by Rod Serling. CBS, March 4, 1960.

"Nick of Time." Episode No. 43, Prod. 173–3643. Directed by Richard L. Bare. Written by Richard Matheson. CBS, November 8, 1960.

"Number 12 Looks Just Like You." Episode No. 137, Prod. 2618. Directed by Abner Biberman. Written by John Tomerlin. CBS, January 24, 1964.

"The Obsolete Man." Episode No. 65, Prod. 173–3661. Directed by Elliot Silverstein. Written by Rod Serling. CBS, June 2, 1961.

"The Old Man in the Cave." Episode No. 127, Prod. 2603. Directed by Alan Crosland, Jr. Written by Rod Serling. CBS, November 8, 1963.

"Once Upon a Time." Episode No. 78, Prod. 4820. Directed by Norman Z. McLeod. Written by Ricahrd Matheson. CBS, December 15, 1961.

"100 Yards Over the Rim." Episode No. 59, Prod. 173–3654. Directed by Buzz Kulik. Written by Rod Serling. CBS, April 17, 1961.

"One More Pallbearer." Episode No. 82, Prod. 4823. Directed by Lamont Johnson. Written by Rod Serling. CBS, January 12, 1962.

"A Piano in the House." Episode No. 87, Prod. 4825. Directed by David Greene. Written by Earl Hamner, Jr. CBS, 1962.

"A Penny For Your Thoughts." Episode No. 52, Prod. 173–3650. Directed by James Sheldon. Written by George Clayton Johnson. CBS, February 13, 1961.

"People Are Alike All Over." Episode No. 25, Prod. 173–3613. Directed by Mitchell Leisen. Written by Rod Serling. CBS, March 25, 1960.

"Person or Persons Unknown." Episode No. 92, Prod. 4829. Directed by John Brahm. Written by Charles Beaumont. CBS, March 23, 1962.

"A Quality of Mercy." Episode No. 80, Prod. 4809. Directed by Buzz Kulik. Written by Rod Serling. CBS, December 29, 1961.

"The Self-Improvement of Salvadore Ross." Episode No. 136, Prod. 2612. Directed by Don Siegel. Written by Jerry McNeely.

"Shadow Play." Episode No. 62, Prod. 173–3657. John Brahm. Written by Charles Beaumont. CBS, May 5, 1961.

"The Shelter." Episode No. 68, Prod. 4803. Directed by Lamont Johnson. Written by Rod Serling. CBS, September 29, 1961.

"A Short Drink From a Certain Fountain." Episode No. 131, Prod. 2614. Directed by Bernard Girard. Written by Rod Serling. CBS, December 13, 1963.

"16 Millimeter Shrine." Episode No. 4, Prod. 173–3610. Directed by Mitchell Leisen. Written by Rod Serling. CBS, October 23, 1959.

"Static." Episode No. 56, Prod. 173–3665. Directed by Buzz Kulik. Written by Charles Beaumont. CBS, March 10, 1961.

"Steel." Episode No. 122, Prod. 2602. Directed by Don Weis. Written by Richard Matheson. CBS, October 4, 1963.

"A Stop at Willoughby." Episode No. 30, Prod. 173–3629. Directed by Robert Parrish. Written by Rod Serling. CBS, May 6, 1990.

"Stopover in a Quiet Town." Episode No. 150, Prod. 2611. Directed by Ron Winston. Written by Earl Hamner, Jr. CBS, April 24, 1964.

"A Thing About Machines." Episode No. 40, Prod. 173–3645. Directed by David Orrick McDearmon. Written by Rod Serling. CBS, October 28, 1960.

"Time Enough at Last." Episode No. 8, Prod. 173–3614. Directed by John Brahm. Written by Rod Serling. CBS, November 20, 1959.

"To Serve Man." Episode 89, Prod. 4807. Directed by Richard L. Bare. Written by Rod Serling. CBS, March 2, 1962.

"The Trade-Ins." Episode No. 96, Prod. 4831. Directed by Elliot Silverstein. Written by Rod Serling. CBS, April 13, 1962.

"The Trouble with Templeton." Episode No. 45, Prod. 173–3649. Directed by Buzz Kulik. Written by E. Jack Newman. CBS, December 9, 1960.

"Uncle Simon." Episode No. 128, Prod. 2604. Directed by Don Siegel. Written by Rod Serling. CBS, November 15, 1963.

"Valley of the Shadow." Episode No. 105, Prod. 3861. Directed by Perry Lafferty. Written by Charles Beaumont. CBS, January 17, 1963.
"Walking Distance." Episode No. 5, Prod. 173–3605. Directed by Robert Stevens. Written by Rod Serling. CBS, October 30, 1959.
"Where Is Everybody?" Episode No. 1, Prod. 173–3601. Directed by Robert Stevens. Written by Rod Serling. CBS, October 2, 1959.
"The Whole Truth." Episode 50, Prod. 173–3666. Directed by James Sheldon. Written by Rod Serling. CBS, March 31, 1961.
"Will the Real Martian Please Stand Up?" Episode No. 64, Prod. 173–3660. Directed by Montgomery Pittman. Written by Rod Serling. CBS, May 26, 1961.
"A World of Difference." Episode No. 23, Prod. 173–3624. Directed by Ted Post. Written by Richard Matheson. CBS, March 11, 1960.
"You Drive." Episode No. 134, Prod. 2625. Directed by John Brahm. Written by Earl Hamner, Jr. CBS, January 3, 1964.
"Young Man's Fancy." Episode No. 99, Prod. 4813. Directed by John Brahm. Written by Richard Matheson. CBS, May 11, 1962.

Television Shows and News Programs

Altered Carbon. Netflix, February 2, 2018–present.
Brockmire. IFC, April 5, 2017–present.
Catfish: The TV Show. Viacom Media Networks, 2012–present.
The Circle. All3Media, September 2018–present.
Dexter. CBS Television Distribution, October 1, 2006–September 22, 2013.
Extant. CBS Television Distribution, July 9, 2014–September 9, 2015.
Family Matters. Warner Bros. Domestic Television Distribution, September 22, 1989–July 17, 1998.
The Flintstones. ABC, September 30, 1960–April 1, 1966.
Gilligan's Island. Warner Bros. Television, 1964–1967.
God Friended Me. CBS, September 30, 2018–present.
The Good Place. NBC, 2016–present.
Halt and Catch Fire. AMC, June 1, 2014–October 14, 2017.
Jack Ryan. Amazon Video, 2018–present.
The Jetsons. Hanna-Barbera Productions, September 23, 1962–March 17, 1963.
Maniac. Netflix, September 21, 2018.
Perfect Strangers. Warner Bros. Television, 1986–1993.
Silicon Valley. HBO, April 6, 2014–present.
Sister, Sister. ABC, April 1, 1994–May 23, 1999.
Tucker Carlson Tonight. FOX News Channel, May 11, 2018.
20/20. ABC, April 15, 2018.
Wayward Pines. 20th Century FOX Television, May 14, 2015–July 27, 2016.
Westworld. HBO Entertainment, October 2, 2016–present.
The Wonder Years. ABC, January 31, 1988–May 12, 1993.
You. Lifetime, September 9, 2018–present.

Films and Documentaries

AI Artificial Intelligence. Directed by Steven Spielberg. Warner Bros. Pictures, June 29, 2001.

All of Me. Directed by Carl Reiner. Universal Pictures, September 21, 1984.
All Screwed Up. Directed by Neil Stephens. Red Line Studios, September 4, 2012.
American Cyborg: Steel Warrior. Directed by Boaz Davidson. Global Pictures, January 7, 1994.
The American Meme. Directed by Bert Marcus. Netflix, December 7, 2018.
Android. Directed by Aaron Lipstadt. New World Pictures, October 1982.
Avatar. Directed by James Cameron. 20th Century FOX, December 10, 2009.
Back to the Future. Directed by Robert Zemeckis. Universal Pictures, July 3, 1985.
Bicentennial Man. Directed by Chris Columbus. Buena Vista Pictures, December 17, 1999.
Blade Runner. Directed by Ridley Scott. Warner Bros., June 25, 1982.
Blast from the Past. Directed by Hugh Wilson. New Line Cinema, February 12, 1999.
Cam. Directed by Daniel Goldhaber. Netflix, November 16, 2018.
The Change-Up. Directed by David Dobkin. Universal Pictures, August 5, 2011.
Chappie. Directed by Neill Blomkamp. Columbia Pictures, March 4, 2015.
Cherry 2000. Directed by Steve De Jarnatt. Orion Pictures, November 17, 1988.
Citizen Kane. Directed by Orson Welles. RKO Radio Pictures, May 1, 1941.
The Creepy Line. Directed by M.A. Taylor. Wandering Foot Productions, October 2018.
Dating the Enemy. Directed by Megan Simpson Huberman. Pandora Film, September 19, 1996.
Déjà Vu. Directed by Tony Scott. Buena Vista Pictures, November 22, 2006.
Dream a Little Dream. Directed by Marc Rocco. Vestron Pictures, March 3, 1989.
DriverX. Directed by Henry Barrial. Sundance Selects, November 30, 2018.
18 Again! Directed by Paul Flaherty. New World Pictures, April 8, 1988.
Electric Dreams. Directed by Steve Barron. MGM / UA Entertainment Co., July 20, 1984.
Eternal Sunshine of the Spotless Mind. Directed by Michael Gondry. Focus Features, March 19, 2004.
Ex Machina. Directed by Alex Garland. A24, April 10, 2015.
Facebook: Cracking the Code. Directed by Peter Greste. ABC Australia, April 11, 2017.
Ferris Bueller's Day Off. Paramount Pictures, June 11, 1986.
50 First Dates. Directed by Peter Segal. Columbia Pictures, February 13, 2004.
Frankenstein AI—A Monster Made by Many. Directed by Lance Weiler. Columbia University
The Game. Directed by David Fincher. Propaganda Films, September 12, 1997.
The Glass Castle. Directed by Destin Daniel Cretton. Lionsgate, August 9, 2017.
Groundhog Day. Directed by Harold Ramis. Columbia Pictures, February 12, 1993.
Her. Directed by Spike Jonze. Warner Bros. Pictures, October 13, 2013.
I, Robot. Directed by Alex Proyas. Davis Entertainment, July 16, 2004.
Inception. Directed by Christopher Nolan. Warner Bros. Pictures, July 8, 2010.
Kill Command. Directed by Steven Gomez. Vertigo Films, May 13, 2016.
Kill the Messenger. Directed by Michael Cuesta. Bluegrass Films, October 10, 2014.
Lawnmower Man. Directed by Brett Leonard. New Line Cinema, March 6, 1992.
The Machine. Directed by Caradog w. James. Content Media, April 20, 2013.
The Matrix. Directed by Lana Wachowski and Lilly Wachowski. Warner Bros., March 31, 1999.
Metropolis. Directed by Fritz Lang. Ufa, January 10, 1927.
Minority Report. Directed by Steven Spielberg. 20th Century FOX / DreamWorks Pictures, 2002.
Nerve. Directed by Henry Joost and Ariel Schulman. Lionsgate, July 12, 2016.
Network. Directed by Sidney Lumet. Metro-Goldwyn-Mayer, November 27, 1976.
9. Directed by Shane Acker. Focus Features, September 9, 2009.

1984. Directed by Michael Radford. 20th Century FOX, October 10, 1984.
Other Life. Directed by Ben C. Lucas. See Pictures, June 16, 2017.
Pinnochio. Walt Disney Productions, February 7, 1940.
Pleasantville. Directed by Gary Ross. New Line Cinema, 1998.
Psycho. Directed by Alfred Hitchcock. Shamley Productions, June 16, 1960.
The Rachel Divide. Directed by Laura Brownson. Netflix, April 23, 2018.
Ready Player One. Directed by Steven Spielberg. Warner Bros. Pictures, March 11, 2018.
RoboCop. Directed by Paul Verhoeven. Orion Pictures, July 17, 1987.
Robot & Frank. Directed by Jake Schreier. Samuel Goldwyn Films, January 20, 2012.
Rounders. Directed by John Dahl. Mirimax Films, September 4, 1998.
A Scanner Darkly. Directed by Richard Linklater. Warner Independent Pictures, May 25, 2006.
School of the Arts' Digital Storytelling Lab, January 2018.
Seventeen Again. Directed by Jeffrey W. Byrd. Tri-Ess Productions, November 12, 2000.
The Show. Directed by Giancarlo Esposito. Grindstone Entertainment Group, March 11, 2017.
Singularity. Directed by Robert Kouba. Vertical Entertainment, November 3, 2017.
Sister Switch. Directed by Torry Colvin. 24K Black Films, February 24, 2015.
The Social Network. Directed by David Fincher. Columbia Pictures, October 1, 2010.
Spiderman. Directed by Sam Raimi. Columbia Pictures, April 29, 2002.
The Staircase. "The Last Chance." Episode No. 10. Directed by Jean-Xavier de Lestrade. Maha Productions, November 21, 2013.
The Stepford Wives. Directed by Bryan Forbes. Palomar Pictures, 1975.
Steve Jobs. Directed by Danny Boyle. Universal Pictures, October 9, 2015.
The Swarm. Directed by Irwin Allen. Warner Bros., July 14, 1978.
Tau. Directed by Federico D'Alessandro. Netflix, June 29, 2018.
The Terminator. Directed by James Cameron. Orion Pictures, October 26, 1984.
Terminator 2: Judgment Day. Directed by James Cameron. Carolco Pictures, July 3, 1991.
That Sugar Film. Directed by Damon Gameau. Amsterdam International Documentary Film Festival, November 20, 2014.
Total Recall. Directed by Paul Verhoeven. TriStar Pictures, June 1, 1990.
Transcendence. Directed by Wally Pfister. Warner Bros. Pictures, April 10, 2014.
The Truman Show. Directed by Peter Weir. Paramount Pictures, June 1, 1998.
The Truth About Killer Robots. Directed by Maxim Pozdorovkin. Joe Bender, Maxim Pozdorovkin, September 10, 2018.
2001: A Space Odyssey. Directed by Stanley Kubrick. Metro-Goldwyn-Mayer, April 2, 1968.
Wall-E. Directed by Andrew Stanton. Walt Disney Pictures, June 23, 2008.
Weird Science. Directed by John Hughes. Universal Pictures, August 2, 1985.
Wish Upon a Star. Directed by Blair Treu. Leucadia Film Corporation, October 12, 1996.
The Wizard of Oz. Directed by Victor Fleming, et al. Metro-Goldwyn-Mayer, 1939.
The Wolfpack. Directed by Crystal Moselle. Kotva Films, January 25, 2015.

Chapter Notes

Introduction

1. *The Twilight Zone* episode "The Mighty Casey" highlights the strategy of using robots to provide competitive advantages. A struggling baseball team achieves (initial) success by adding a robot baseball player—a machine that demonstrates super strength—to their roster. See *The Twilight Zone*. "The Mighty Casey." Episode No. 35, Prod. 173–3617. Directed by Alvin Ganzer and Robert Parrish. Written by Rod Serling. CBS, June 17, 1960.

2. James Poniewozik, "Review: '*Black Mirror*' Finds Terror, and Soul, in the Machine," *The New York Times*, October 20, 2016, https://www.nytimes.com/2016/10/21/arts/television/review-blacfk-mirror-finds-terror-and-soul-in-the-machine.html

3. In those books, I identify potentially heroic characteristics in the protagonists of each show. On *Black Mirror* and *Electric Dreams*, perhaps the heroes are the shows themselves, as they seek to warn us of a potentially dark future if we do not proceed with caution.

Chapter 1

1. See Bryony Gordon, "Charlie Brooker on Black Mirror: 'It's not a technological problem we have, it's a human one,'" *The Telegraph*, December 16, 2014, https://www.telegraph.co.uk/culture/tvandradio/11260768/Charlie-Brooker-Its-not-a-technological-problem-we-have-its-a-human-one.html

2. *The Simpsons*, "Itchy and Scratchy Land." Episode No. 107, Prod. 2FO1. Directed by Wes Archer. Written by John Schwartzwelder. FOX, October 2, 1994.

3. The potential dangers caused by advancements in robotics and artificial intelligence is one of many predictions made by *The Simpsons* over the years. Many other such predictions have come true, including: the Trump presidency; the closing of Toys R Us stores; the discovery of the Higgs boson particle; the Walt Disney Company's acquisition of FOX; Germany's defeat of Brazil in the 2014 World Cup; and innovations such as FaceTime and smartwatches, among many others. See Megan McCluskey, "15 Times *The Simpsons* Accurately Predicted the Future," *Time Magazine*, updated February 26, 2018, originally published March 9, 2017, http://time.com/4667462/simpsons-predictions-donald-trump-lady-gaga/. See also Maya Salam, "*The Simpsons* Has Predicted a Lot/ Most of it Can Be Explained," *The New York Times*, February 2, 2018, https://www.nytimes.com/2018/02/02/arts/television/simpsons-prediction-future.html.

Throughout this book, I highlight examples of certain predictions from *Black Mirror* and *Electric Dreams* coming true. Aspects of the futuristic worlds shown on these anthologies, at least in some respects, are coming closer to matching our own reality.

4. *The Twilight Zone*, "The Lateness of the Hour." Episode No. 44, Prod. 173–3652. Directed by Jack Smight. Written by Rod Serling. CBS, December 2, 1960.

5. The same theme is examined in the Netflix series *Kiss Me First* (2018). In the first episode of the show, the protagonist (Leila) secures a (real-life) job so that she could afford access to her virtual reality video game. *Kiss Me First*. "She Did Something." Episode No. 1. Directed by Misha Manson-Smith. Written by Brian Elsley. Netflix, April 2, 2018.

6. *The Twilight Zone*. "A Thing About Machines." Episode No. 40, Prod. 173–3645. Directed by David Orrick McDearmon. Written by Rod Serling. CBS, October 28, 1960.

7. See Kira Beilis, "How Your Technology Is Manipulating You," *The Cut*, October 24, 2014,

235

https://www.thecut.com/2014/10/how-your-technology-is-manipulating-you.html (citing Matt Richtel, *A Deadly Wandering: A Tale of Tragedy and Redemption in the Age of Attention* (New York: William Morrow, 2014).

8. Ibid.

9. Ibid.

10. Tim Cook, speaking at Fortune's CEO Initiative Event, June 25, 2018. See Emily Bary, "Apple never meant for you to spend so much time on your phone, Tim Cook says," *MarketWatch*, June 27, 2018, https://www.marketwatch.com/story/apple-never-meant-for-you-to-spend-so-much-time-on-your-phone-tim-cook-says-2018-06-26

11. *The Office.* "WUPHF.com." Episode No. 135, Prod. 709. Directed by Danny Leiner. Written by Aaron Shure. NBC, November 18, 2010.

Ryan's obsession with his phone is highlighted in the episode "Trivia," where he quickly exits a bar upon learning that his phone would be confiscated and placed aside if he remained inside while participating in a trivia contest. See *The Office.* "Trivia." Episode No. 163, Prod. 811. Directed by B.J. Novak. Written by Steve Hely. NBC, January 12, 2012.

12. *Parks and Recreation.* "Sex Education." Episode No. 72. Directed by Craig Zisk. Written by Alan Yang. NBC, October 18, 2012.

13. *The Simpsons.* "Sideshow Bob's Last Gleaming." Episode No. 137, Prod. 3F08. Directed by Dominic Polcino. Written by Spike Feresten. FOX, November 26, 1995. Ironically appearing on a large television screen, Sideshow Bob articulated his rationale for proposing the abolishment of television by delivering the following message: "Wouldn't our lives be so much richer if television were done away with? Why, we could revive the lost arts of conversation and scrimshaw!" It bears mention that I, too, am making substantial use of technology—the Internet, the printing press, etc.—to critique some of the same technology that is indispensable to writing and publishing.

14. Evan Andrews, "Who Were the Luddites?," *History Channel*, August 7, 2015, www.history.com/news/who-were-the-luddites

15. Popular culture has explored the objectives of anti-technology terrorist groups. In the film *Transcendence* (2014), for example, the militaristic "Revolutionary Independence From Technology" (R.I.F.T) group targets AI laboratories throughout the country. See *Transcendence.* Directed by Wally Pfister. Warner Bros. Pictures, April 10, 2014.

16. Chris Weller, "Bill Gates and Steve Jobs raised their kids tech-free—and it should have been a red flag," *Business Insider*, January 10, 2018, https://www.businessinsider.com/screen-time-limits-bill-gates-steve-jobs-red-flag-2017-10

17. Nellie Bowles, "The Digital Gap Between Rich and Poor Kids Is Not What We Expect," *The New York Times*, October 26, 2018, https://www.nytimes.com/2018/10/26/style/digital-divide-screens-schools.html

18. Joe Clement and Matt Miles, *Screen Schooled: Two Veteran Teachers Expose How Technology Use Is Making Our Kids Dumber* (Illinois: Chicago Review Press, 2017).

19. Nellie Bowles, "The Digital Gap Between Rich and Poor Kids Is Not What We Expect," *The New York Times*, October 26, 2018, https://www.nytimes.com/2018/10/26/style/digital-divide-screens-schools.html

20. Ibid.

21. See, e.g., Suzanne Kane, "Smartphone Use in America: Is it Contributing to Cognitive Decline?," *PsychCentral*, July 8, 2018, www.psychcentral.com/blog/smartphone-use-in-america-is-it-contributing-to-cognitive-decline/

22. *13 Reasons Why.* "Tape 2, Side B." Episode No. 4. Directed by Helen Shaver. Written by Thomas Higgins. Netflix, March 31, 2017. Reasonable folks can disagree on whether technology has changed us or whether the problems associated with using technology stem from something innate in humans. The latter position reflects Charlie Brooker's view, as discussed later in this book. Perhaps the answer lies somewhere in the middle.

23. Correspondent Alana Semuels reports that some of Amazon's delivery drivers share their experiences and complaints about their positions, including the lack of human interaction and perceived "robotic" environment in which they work. Alana Semuels, "I Delivered Packages for Amazon and It Was a Nightmare," *The Atlantic*, June 25, 2018, https://www.theatlantic.com/business/archive/2018/06/amazon-flex-workers/563444/

24. Other examples abound. See, for example, ABC's *20/20* news program (May 25, 2018), which did an expose on the technological failures of certain criminals' ankle bracelet monitors. In some instances, the criminals committed murders after the technology failed to function properly.

25. *You.* Lifetime, September 9, 2018–present.

26. *Cam.* Directed by Daniel Goldhaber. Netflix, November 16, 2018.

27. See Sue Surkes, "As influence of AI, big data grows, cyber experts discuss tech safety and trust," *The Times of Israel*, November 15, 2018,

Notes—Chapter 1

https://www.timesofisrael.com/as-influence-of-ai-big-data-grows-cyber-experts-discuss-tech-safety-and-trust/. The article also quotes Dirk Hoke, CEO of Airbus Defense and Space of Germany, who warns that "even if you've secured your own company, your suppliers and sub suppliers may be exposed. The whole ecosystem needs to be protected."

28. See generally William Sweet, "Jeremy Bentham (1748–1832), *Internet Encyclopedia of Philosophy*, undated, www.iep.utm.edu/bentham

29. Jason Parham, "Why Black Mirror's Most Controversial New Episode Is Its Most Important," *Wired*, January 6, 2018, https://www.wired.com/story/black-mirror-black-museum/

30. See Sue Surkes, "As influence of AI, big data grows, cyber experts discuss tech safety and trust," *The Times of Israel*, November 15, 2018, https://www.timesofisrael.com/as-influence-of-ai-big-data-grows-cyber-experts-discuss-tech-safety-and-trust/

31. 24. FOX, 2001–2010; *Jack Ryan*. Amazon Video, 2018–present.

32. Marilyn Butler and Mary W. Shelley, *Frankenstein, Or the Modern Prometheus: The 1818 Text* (Oxford: Oxford University Press, 1994), 200.

33. Consumers have come to expect constant innovation and are not satisfied with the status quo. One example of consumers speaking with their wallets in terms of new technology is the huge demand for new iPhone versions.

34. Maureen Dowd, "Elon Musk's Billion-Dollar Crusade to Stop the A.I. Apocalypse," *Vanity Fair*, April 2017, https://www.vanityfair.com/news/2017/03/elon-musk-billion-dollar-crusade-to-stop-ai-space-x

For a discussion of regrets expressed by inventors, see Rebecca J. Rosen, "'I've Created a Monster': On the Regrets of Inventors," *The Atlantic*, November 23, 2011, https://www.theatlantic.com/technology/archive/2011/11/ive-created-a-monster-on-the-regrets-of-inventors/249044/

35. Arend Hintze, "What an artificial intelligence researcher fears about AI," *Salon*, January 6, 2018, https://www.salon.com/2018/01/06/what-an-artificial-intelligence-researcher-fears-about-ai_partner/

In the article Hintze acknowledges, however, that she does contemplate the potential consequences resulting from her research: "Being a scientist doesn't absolve me of my humanity, though… As a moral and political being, I have to consider the potential implications of my work and its potential effects on society."

36. *Humans*. "Episode 8." Episode No. 8. Directed by China Moo-Young. Written by Sam Vincent and Jonathan Brackley. AMC, August 16, 2015.

37. Hintze expresses a growing fear that researchers may inadvertently "become 'the destroyer[s] of worlds," as Oppenheimer lamented after spearheading the construction of the nuclear bomb."

38. See Jena McGregor, "Some Swedish workers are getting microchips implanted in their hands," *The Washington Post*, April 4, 2017, www.washingtonpost.com/news/on-leadership/wp/2017/04/04/some-swedish-workers-are-getting-microchips-implanted-in-their-hands/?noredirect=on&utm_term=.7389c41ff39f

39. *Ibid*.

40. This portion of the episode is based on a short story written by illusionist Penn Jillette, who came up with the story after falling ill in a hospital in Spain. He was unable to communicate effectively with doctors and came up with the concept of a device that transfers sensations as a way to aid in the communication between doctor and patient. See Charlie Brooker, Annabel Jones and Jason Arnopp, *Inside Black Mirror* (New York: Crown Archetype, 2018), 296.

41. Originally this line appeared in a caption in the Amazing Fantasy #15 comic and had not been spoken by anyone, but it was spoken by Uncle Ben in the 2002 *Spiderman* film. See "Why does Uncle Ben always tell Peter Parker 'With Great Power Comes Great Responsibility'?," *Quora*, www.quora.com/why-does-uncle-ben-always-tell-peter-parker-with-great-power-comes-great-responsibility

Spiderman. Directed by Sam Raimi. Columbia Pictures, April 29, 2002.

42. *Metropolis*. Directed by Fritz Lang. Ufa, January 10, 1927.

43. *Ex Machina*. Directed by Alex Garland. A24, April 10, 2015.

44. "Privacy and Technology," *ACLU*, undated, www.aclu.org/issues/privacy-technology

45. *Ibid*.

46. See Sue Surkes, "As influence of AI, big data grows, cyber experts discuss tech safety and trust," *The Times of Israel*, November 15, 2018, https://www.timesofisrael.com/as-influence-of-ai-big-data-grows-cyber-experts-discuss-tech-safety-and-trust/

47. These issues are discussed as part of PLI's "Artificial intelligence Law—Judicial and Regulatory Trends." See *Practicing Law Institute*, May 2018, www.pli.edu/content/seminar/Artificial_Intelligence_Law_Judicial_and/_N-4KZ!z0zmxb?fromsearch=false&ID=341860

48. Jeffrey Datsin, "Amazon scraps secret AI recruiting tool that showed bias against women,"

Reuters, October 9, 2018, https://www.reuters.com/article/us-amazon-com-jobs-automation-insight/amazon-scraps-secret-ai-recruiting-tool-that-showed-bias-against-women-idUSKCN1MK08G

49. Jeffrey Neuburger, "YouTube Protected by CDA Immunity Over Claims that it Provided Material Support to Terrorists," *Proskauer Rose*, November 14, 2017, www.newmedialaw.proskauer.com/2017/11/14/youtube-protected-by-cda-immunity-over-claims-that-it-provided-material-support-to-terrorists/

50. See "47 U.S. Code Section 230—Protection for private blocking and screening of offensive material," https://www.law.cornell.edu/uscode/text/47/230

51. *Halt and Catch Fire*. AMC, June 1, 2014–October 14, 2017; *Silicon Valley*. HBO, April 6, 2014–present; *Steve Jobs*. Directed by Danny Boyle. Universal Pictures, October 9, 2015; *The Social Network*. Directed by David Fincher. Columbia Pictures, October 1, 2010.

52. Chris Li, "'Black Mirror' Isn't Just About Technology. It's About Us," *The Gospel Coalition*, December 29, 2017, https://www.thegospelcoalition.org/article/black-mirror-isnt-just-technology-us/

53. See "Black Mirror," *IMDb*, https://www.imdb.com/title/tt2085059/

54. See Debra Birnbaum, "Netflix Picks Up 'Black Mirror' for 12 New Episodes," *Variety*, September 25, 2015, http://variety.com/2015/digital/news/netflix-black-mirror-new-episodes-1201602037/

55. See Chris Li, "'Black Mirror' Isn't Just About Technology. It's About Us," *The Gospel Coalition*, December 29, 2017, https://www.thegospelcoalition.org/article/black-mirror-isnt-just-technology-us/

56. See *"Black Mirror: Awards," IMDb*, https://www.imdb.com/title/tt2085059/awards

57. Ibid.

58. Ibid.

59. See *"Electric Dreams*: Awards," *IMDb*, https://www.imdb.com/title/tt5711280/awards

60. Production designer Joel Collins explains these secret elements in detail during his discussion of this episode. See Charlie Brooker, Annabel Jones and Jason Arnopp, *Inside Black Mirror* (New York: Crown Archetype, 2018), 275.

61. Charlie Brooker, Annabel Jones and Jason Arnopp, *Inside Black Mirror* (New York: Crown Archetype, 2018), 261.

62. Belinda Carlisle, *Heaven Is a Place on Earth*, Ocean Way Studios, 1987.

63. Burt Bacharach and Hal David (*There's*) *Always Something There to Remind Me*, Lou Johnson, Reprise, 1964.

64. That is not to suggest that the shows do not depict some interesting characters. Rolo Haynes, the museum operator in "Black Museum" is an example of the type of character that might have a backstory that could be interesting to the audience.

65. David Sims, "Black Mirror: 'White Bear,'" *AV/TV Club*, December 10, 2013, www.tv.avclub.com/black-mirror-white-bear-1798178958

66. *Vulture* columnist Brian Tallerico observes that Brooker "has leaned into the idea that many of the show's stand-alone episodes exist in the same shared universe, dropping hidden Easter Eggs that connect one chapter to another." Brian Tallerico, "Every Major Easter Egg in Black Mirror Season Four," *Vulture*, January 4, 2018, http://www.vulture.com/2018/01/black-mirror-season-4-every-easter-egg.html One example: in "Black Museum," Nish refers to uploading "old people to the cloud," an oblique reference to the episode "San Junipero." "Black Museum" also shows a hospital named Saint Juniper's. The dresses worn by the women on "San Junipero" are on display at the museum.

67. *13 Reasons Why*. "The Chalk Machine." Episode No. 5. Directed by Eliza Hittman. Written by Nic Sheff. Netflix, May 18, 2018.

68. Jason Parham, "Why Black Mirror's Most Controversial New Episode Is Its Most Important," *Wired*, January 6, 2018, https://www.wired.com/story/black-mirror-black-museum/

69. See Emily Nussbaum, "Button-Pusher: The Seductive Dystopia of 'Black Mirror,'" *The New Yorker*, January 5, 2015, https://www.newyorker.com/magazine/2015/01/05/button-pusher

70. Charlie Brooker, Annabel Jones and Jason Arnopp, *Inside Black Mirror* (New York: Crown Archetype, 2018), 11.

71. Jason Parham, "Why Black Mirror's Most Controversial New Episode Is Its Most Important," *Wired*, January 6, 2018, https://www.wired.com/story/black-mirror-black-museum/

72. The original series aired during these years. Since then, there have been two revivals of the show (1985–1989; 2002–2003), and a movie (1983). Another reboot is currently planned and in production. See Dade Hayes and Patrick Hipes, "Twilight Zone Series Reboot in Works at CBS All Access," *Deadline*, November 1, 2017, http://deadline.com/2017/11/twilight-zone-reboot-cbs-all-access-1202200631/

73. *The Twilight Zone* episodes: "To Serve Man." Episode 89, Prod. 4807. Directed by Richard L. Bare. Written by Rod Serling. CBS, March 2, 1962; "Will the Real Martian

Please Stand Up?" Episode No. 64, Prod. 173–3660. Directed by Montgomery Pittman. Written by Rod Serling. CBS, May 26, 1961.

74. Steven Keslowitz, "*The Simpsons, 24*, and the Law: How Homer Simpson and Jack Bauer Influence Congressional Lawmaking and Judicial Reasoning," 29 *Cardozo Law Review* 2787 (May 2008): 2799.

75. *The Twilight Zone*, "A Thing About Machines." Episode No. 40, Prod. 173–3645. Directed by David Orrick McDearmon. Written by Rod Serling. CBS, October 28, 1960.

76. *The Twilight Zone* episodes: "You Drive." Episode No. 134, Prod. 2625. Directed by John Brahm. Written by Earl Hamner, Jr. CBS, January 3, 1964; "Nick of Time." Episode No. 43, Prod. 173–3643. Directed by Richard L. Bare. Written by Richard Matheson. CBS, November 8, 1960; The Fever." Episode No. 17, Prod. 173–3627. Directed by Robert Florey. Written by Rod Serling. CBS, January 29, 1960; "Long Distance Call." Episode No. 58, Prod. 173–3667. Directed by James Sheldon. Written by Charles Beaumont and William Idelson. CBS, March 31, 1961; "The Whole Truth." Episode 50, Prod. 173–3666. Directed by James Sheldon. Written by Rod Serling. CBS, March 31, 1961;"A Most Unusual Camera." Episode No. 46, Prod. 173–3606. Directed by John Rich. Written by Rod Serling. CBS, December 16, 1960; "Static." Episode No. 56, Prod. 173–3665. Directed by Buzz Kulik. Written by Charles Beaumont. CBS, March 10, 1961; "A Piano in the House." Episode No. 87, Prod. 4825. Directed by David Greene. Written by Earl Hamner, Jr. CBS, 1962; "Once Upon a Time." Episode No. 78, Prod. 4820. Directed by Norman Z. McLeod. Written by Ricahrd Matheson. CBS, Decmeber 15, 1961.

77. *The Twilight Zone* episodes: "The Lonely." Episode No. 7, Prod. 173–3602. Directed by Jack Smight. Written by Rod Serling. CBS, November 13, 1959; "I Sing the Body Electric." Episode No. 100, Prod. 4826. Directed by William Claxton and James Sheldon. Written by Ray Bradbury. CBS, May 18, 1962;"The Lateness of the Hour." Episode No. 44, Prod. 173–3652. Directed by Jack Smight. Written by Rod Serling. CBS, December 2, 1960.

78. *The Jetsons*. Hanna-Barbera Productions, September 23, 1962–March 17, 1963; *The Twilight Zone* episodes: "The Brain Center at Whipple's." Episode 153, Prod. 2632. Directed by Richard Donner. Written by Rod Serling. CBS, May 15, 1964; "The Lateness of the Hour." Episode No. 44, Prod. 173–3652. Directed by Jack Smight. Written by Rod Serling. CBS, December 2, 1960.

79. *The Twilight Zone*. "The Old Man in the Cave." Episode No. 127, Prod. 2603. Directed by Alan Crosland, Jr. Written by Rod Serling. CBS, November 8, 1963.

80. Adrienne LaFrance, "How *The Twilight Zone* Predicted Our Paranoid Present," *The Atlantic*, December 31, 2013, https://www.theatlantic.com/entertainment/archive/2013/12/how-em-the-twilight-zone-em-predicted-our-paranoid-present/282700/

81. *Ibid.*

82. Professor Hintze highlights some examples of potential workplace displacement caused by the introduction of artificial intelligence: "Instead of getting medical aid in an emergency room staffed by potentially overtired doctors, patients could get an examination and diagnosis from an expert system with instant access to all medical knowledge ever collected—and get surgery performed by a tireless robot with a perfectly steady 'hand.' Legal advice could come from an all-knowing legal database; investment advice could come from a market-prediction system." Arend Hintze, "What an artificial intelligence researcher fears about AI," *Salon*, January 6, 2018, https://www.salon.com/2018/01/06/what-an-artificial-intelligence-researcher-fears-about-ai_partner/

83. Hintze muses that "Perhaps one day, all human jobs will be done by machines. Even my own job could be done faster, by a large number of machines tirelessly researching how to make even smarter machines." See *The Twilight Zone*, "The Brain Center at Whipple's." Episode 153, Prod. 2632. Directed by Richard Donner. Written by Rod Serling. CBS, May 15, 1964; Adrienne LaFrance, "How *The Twilight Zone* Predicted Our Paranoid Present," *The Atlantic*, December 31, 2013, https://www.theatlantic.com/entertainment/archive/2013/12/how-em-the-twilight-zone-em-predicted-our-paranoid-present/282700/ (quoting a 1970 interview conducted by James Gunn, *Literature in Science Fiction series*, with Rod Serling, at https://www.youtube.com/watch?v=0wfazePQzj8).

84. Charlie Brooker, Annabel Jones and Jason Arnopp, *Inside Black Mirror* (New York: Crown Archetype, 2018), 239.

85. *Ibid.*

86. In addition to humanity's use of technology for destructive purposes, technology itself could possess dangerous agendas. We know that technology can and does outsmart us: highlights include computers defeating our top chess players. For example, IBM's computer program Deep Blue defeated chess grandmaster Gary Kasparov in 1996. See Steven Levy, "What Deep

Blue Tells Us About AI in 2017," *Wired*, Steven Levy, May 23, 2017, https://www.wired.com/2017/05/what-deep-blue-tells-us-about-ai-in-2017/

Popular culture has examined this phenomenon, too. In an episode of *The Office*, for example, salesman Dwight K. Schrute decides to compete in an intense sales competition with a website to see "who" could sell more paper within a designated period. He wants to win to maintain his dignity. *The Office*. "Launch Party." Episode No. 58 and 59, Prod. 405 and 406, respectively. Directed by Ken Whittingham. Written by Jennifer Celotta. NBC, October 11, 2007.

If we are indeed in competition with technology and lose the war, the consequences could be severe in terms of our survival as a species. Today, technology also competes with other technology. See Samuel Gibbs, "Alpha Zero AI Beats Champion Chess Program after teaching itself in four hours," *The Guardian*, December 7, 2017, https://www.theguardian.com/technology/2017/dec/07/alphazero-google-deepmind-ai-beats-champion-program-teaching-itself-to-play-four-hours

87. Jillian Eugenios, "Ray Kurzweil: Humans will be hybrids by 2030," *CNN Tech*, June 4, 2015, http://money.cnn.com/2015/06/03/technology/ray-kurzweil-predictions/index.html (quoting Kurzweill's talk at the 2015 Exponential Financial Conference in New York City).

88. See Kira Beilis, "How Your Technology Is Manipulating You," *The Cut*, October 24, 2014, https://www.thecut.com/2014/10/how-your-technology-is-manipulating-you.html

89. Shoshanna Solomon, "Late president Peres delivers hologram message at Israel Innovation Summit," *The Times of Israel*, October 25, 2018, www.timesofisrael.com/late-president-peres-delivers-hologram-message-at-israel-innovation-summit/

90. Douglas M. Hodge, interviewed by Steven Keslowitz via email, September 6, 2018.

91. For a further discussion of this point, see Chris Li, "'Black Mirror' Isn't Just About Technology. It's About Us," *The Gospel Coalition*, December 29, 2017, https://www.thegospelcoalition.org/article/black-mirror-isnt-just-technology-us/

92. See Sue Surkes, "As influence of AI, big data grows, cyber experts discuss tech safety and trust," *The Times of Israel*, November 15, 2018, https://www.timesofisrael.com/as-influence-of-ai-big-data-grows-cyber-experts-discuss-tech-safety-and-trust/

93. Benjamin Barber, *Jihad vs. McWorld: How Globalism and Tribalism are Reshaping the World* (New York: Ballantine Books, 1995).

94. *The Simpsons*. "Sideshow Bob's Last Gleaming." Episode No. 137, Prod. 3F08. Directed by Dominic Polcino. Written by Spike Feresten. FOX, November 26, 1995.

95. Certain groups (such as the Amish living in Pennsylvania) choose to live an existence where modern technology is nearly entirely absent.

96. *The Glass Castle*. Directed by Destin Daniel Cretton. Lionsgate, August 9, 2017.

97. Jillian Eugenios, "Ray Kurzweil: Humans will be hybrids by 2030," *CNN Tech*, June 4, 2015, http://money.cnn.com/2015/06/03/technology/ray-kurzweil-predictions/index.html

98. Maureen Dowd, "Elon Musk's Billion-Dollar Crusade to Stop the A.I. Apocalypse," *Vanity Fair*, April 2017, https://www.vanityfair.com/news/2017/03/elon-musk-billion-dollar-crusade-to-stop-ai-space-x (quoting Musk from a speech at the World Government Summit, Dubai, 2017).

99. Maureen Dowd, "Elon Musk's Billion-Dollar Crusade to Stop the A.I. Apocalypse," *Vanity Fair*, April 2017, https://www.vanityfair.com/news/2017/03/elon-musk-billion-dollar-crusade-to-stop-ai-space-x

100. See Dom Galeon and Christianna Reedy, "Kurzweil Claims that the Singularity Will Happen by 2045," *Futurism*, October 5, 2017, https://futurism.com/kurzweil-claims-that-the-singularity-will-happen-by-2045/ (quoting from Kurzweil's speech during the 2017 SXSW Conference in Austin, Texas, March 2017).

101. This concept is explored in *The Twilight Zone* episode "Steel," where a human boxer is bested by a machine during a fight. *The Twilight Zone*, "Steel." Episode No. 122, Prod. 2602. Directed by Don Weis. Written by Richard Matheson. CBS, October 4, 1963.

102. See Andzelika, "Japanese Café Found a Way to Employ Paralysed People as Waiters," *Bored Panda*, undated, https://www.boredpanda.com/disabled-people-robot-dawn-ver-beta-cafe-orby-lab-japan/?utm_source=google&utm_medium=organic&utm_campaign=organic

103. Alana Semuels, "I Delivered Packages for Amazon and It Was a Nightmare," *The Atlantic*, June 25, 2018, https://www.theatlantic.com/business/archive/2018/06/amazon-flex-workers/563444/

104. Ibid.

105. A similar concept is explored on *The Simpsons* episode "Them, Robot." In the episode, Mr. Burns seeks to replace the Springfield Nuclear Power Plant workers with robots. *The Simpsons*. "Them, Robot." Episode No. 503,

Prod. PABF10. Directed by Michael Polcino. Written by Michael Price. FOX, March 18, 2012.

106. See *The Twilight Zone*, "The Brain Center at Whipple's." Episode 153, Prod. 2632. Directed by Richard Donner. Written by Rod Serling. CBS, May 15, 1964.

A similar exchange regarding the role of work in an individual's life takes place during the series premiere of the TV series *Humans*. In the episode, commentators debate whether human beings have an inalienable "right" to work that should not be taken away by robots, or "synths." *Humans*. "Episode 1." Episode No. 1. Directed by Sam Donovan. Written by Jonathan Brackley and Sam Vincent. AMC, June 14, 2015.

A similar sentiment was also expressed by Louis Nizer who placed special emphasis on the emotional aspects of work, arguing that "He who works with his hands is a laborer. He who works with his hands and his head is a craftsman. He who works with his hands and his head and his heart is an artist." Louis Nizer, *Between You and Me* (Beechhurst Press, 1948).

107. *Humans*. "Episode 5." Episode No. 5. Directed by Lewis Arnold. Written by Emily Ballou. AMC, July 12, 2015.

108. See James Vincent, "Automation Threatens 800 Million Jobs, but Technology Could Still Save Us, says report," *The Verge*, November 30, 2017, https://www.theverge.com/2017/11/30/16719092/automation-robots-jobs-global-800-million-forecast. The article cites a study conducted by the McKinsey Global Institute. The study, as described in this article, predicts that "advances in AI and robotics will have a drastic effect on everyday working lives, comparable to the shift away from agricultural societies during the Industrial Revolution."

The report predicts that although income inequality is projected to increase due to automation, technology, as a general matter destroys jobs but not work itself. The transition to new lines of work could be challenging to manage. The 800 million number is viewed as a high estimate, with a more middle-ground number set at 400 million. Additionally, it is expected that technology will not just destroy jobs, it will also create new jobs and redefine existing ones.

Other experts have sought to define the types of new positions that may be produced as a result of automation and humanity's coexistence with artificially-intelligent machines. Accenture I.T. executives Paul R. Daughtery and H. James Wilson, for example, predict that human beings will qualify for new jobs such as "explainability strategist" and "data hygienist," as they employ skills such as "responsible normalizing" and "holistic meddling." They point out that customer-service robots "will need to be designed, updated and managed. Experts in unexpected disciplines such as human conversation, dialogue, humor, poetry, and empathy will need to lead the charge." Paul R. Daughtery and H. James Wilson, *Human + Machine: Reimagining Work in the Age Of AI* (Boston: Harvard Business Review Press, 2018), Introduction.

109. Workers have experienced significant changes in the workplace throughout history. As Warren Buffett pointedly observes, "If we were here in 1800 and conducting this, somebody would point out that eventually tractors would come along and better fertilizer and that 80 percent of the people are now employed on the farm and in couple hundred years it is going to be 2 or 3 percent, and what are we going to do with all these people? Well, the answer is we released them." Those workers were able to pursue other opportunities, ultimately strengthening the economy. See Catherine Clifford, "Warren Buffett and Bill Gates think it's crazy to view job-stealing robots as bad," *CNBC*, February 3, 2017, https://www.cnbc.com/2017/02/03/warren-buffett-and-bill-gates-think-its-crazy-to-view-robots-as-bad.html (quoting Buffett at a Facebook Live event from Columbia University, moderated by Charlie Rose).

110. Alana Semuels, "I Delivered Packages for Amazon and It Was a Nightmare," *The Atlantic*, June 25, 2018, https://www.theatlantic.com/business/archive/2018/06/amazon-flex-workers/563444/

111. See Catherine Clifford, "Warren Buffett and Bill Gates think it's crazy to view job-stealing robots as bad," *CNBC*, February 3, 2017, https://www.cnbc.com/2017/02/03/warren-buffett-and-bill-gates-think-its-crazy-to-view-robots-as-bad.html (quoting Buffett at a Facebook Live event from Columbia University, moderated by Charlie Rose). Buffett adds: "If one person could push a button and turn out everything we turn out now, is that good for the world or bad for the world? You would free up all kinds of possibilities for everything else."

112. For a discussion about the adverse psychological effects of industrialization on workers (including alienation from one's work), see Steven Keslowitz, *The World According to The Simpsons* (Naperville: Sourcebooks, 2006), 175–186. Mr. Burns' failure to remember Homer Simpson's name—even after many encounters with him—serves as satirical commentary of many employees' experiences of alienation in the workplace.

113. *The Simpsons*. "Treehouse of Horror II."

Episode No. 42, Prod. 8F02. Directed by Jim Reardon. Written by Sam Simon, et al. FOX, October 31, 1991.

114. John M. Cooper, ed. *Plato, Five Dialogues: Euthyphro, Apology, Crito, Meno, Phaedo* (Indianapolis: Haskett Classics 2nd edition, 2002), quoting from *Apology*.

115. Jason Parham, "Why Black Mirror's Most Controversial New Episode Is Its Most Important," *Wired*, January 6, 2018, https://www.wired.com/story/black-mirror-black-museum/

116. Chris Li, "'Black Mirror' Isn't Just About Technology. It's About Us," *The Gospel Coalition*, December 29, 2017, https://www.thegospelcoalition.org/article/black-mirror-isnt-just-technology-us/

117. Ibid., quoting Charlie Brooker. This sentiment is echoed by Jim Blascovich and Jeremy Bailenson, who observe that human beings are "driven by imaginations that have long sought to defy the sensory and physical constraints of physical reality." Jeremy Bailenson and Jim Blascovich, *Infinite Reality: Avatars, Eternal Life, New Worlds, and the Dawn of the Virtual Revolution* (New York: Harper Collins, 2011), 8.

118. Charlie Brooker, Annabel Jones and Jason Arnopp, *Inside Black Mirror* (New York: Crown Archetype, 2018), 222.

119. *Ibid; Psycho.* Directed by Alfred Hitchcok. Shamley Productions, June 16, 1960.

120. Charlie Brooker, Annabel Jones and Jason Arnopp, *Inside Black Mirror* (New York: Crown Archetype, 2018), 222.

121. "GOP Rep on Trump Jr.—Ocasio-Cortez Twitter Feud: 'Social Media is Making Us All Stupid,'" *FOX News Insider*, December 10, 2018, http://insider.foxnews.com/2018/12/10/donald-trump-jr-and-alexandria-ocasio-cortez-spar-social-media-outnumbered-reacts

122. *The Twilight Zone* episodes: "The Obsolete Man." Episode No. 65, Prod. 173–3661. Directed by Elliot Silverstein. Written by Rod Serling. CBS, June 2, 1961; "Deaths-Head Revisited." Episode No. 74, Prod. 4804. Directed by Don Medford. Written by Rod Serling. CBS, November 10, 1961.

123. *The Creepy Line*. Directed by M.A. Taylor. Wandering Foot Productions, October 2018.

124. *The Office*. "The List." Episode No. 153, Prod. 802. Directed by B.J. Novak. Written by B.J. Novak. NBC, September 22, 2011.

125. See Ryan Ellis, "The Scorpion and the Frog: A Tale of Modern Capitalism," *Forbes*, April 24, 2015, www.forbes.com/sites/ryanellis/2015/04/24/the-scorpion-and-the-frog-a-tale-of-modern-capitalism/#4da67cd76f7a

126. Sophocles, *Oedipus the King*, trans. F. Storr (Boston: Harvard University Press, 1912), 101.

127. *The Simpsons*. "Homer vs. the Eighteenth Amendment." Episode No. 171, Prod. 4F15. Directed by Bob Anderson. Written by John Swartzwelder. FOX, March 16, 1997.

128. *Rounders*. Directed by John Dahl. Miramax Films, September 4, 1998.

129. Jason Parham, "Why Black Mirror's Most Controversial New Episode Is Its Most Important," *Wired*, January 6, 2018, https://www.wired.com/story/black-mirror-black-museum/

130. See "Carl Jung: 'Who looks outside dreams; who looks inside awakes,' quoting from a letter addressed to Fanny Bowditch, October 22, 1916. See post on February 8, 2018, https://carljungdepthpsychologysite.blog/2018/02/08/carl-jung-i-am-afraid-that-the-mere-fact-of-my-presence-takes-you-away-from-yourself/#.W7ULiddKjHY

131. Douglas Hodge expressed a similar sentiment in our email exchange, observing that folks are "driven by the impulse to control or spy on each other rather than those impulses to heal or mend." Douglas M. Hodge, interviewed by Steven Keslowitz via email, September 6, 2018.

132. *The Office.* "Search Committee." Episode Nos. 151 and 152, Prod. 7025 and 7026. Directed by Jeffrey Blitz. Written by Paul Lieberstein. NBC, May 19, 2011.

133. *The Twilight Zone.* "Steel." Episode No. 122, Prod. 2602. Directed by Don Weis. Written by Richard Matheson. CBS, October 4, 1963.

Chapter 2

1. Emphasis added to quote. Edward Bernays, *Propaganda* (New York: H: Liveright, 1928), 37.

2. The program was an episode of the American radio anthology series *The Mercury Theatre on the Air* and was directed by Orson Welles. See "The Mercury Theatre on the Air," undated, www.mercurytheatre.info

3. Marshall McLuhan and Lewis H. Lapham, *Understanding Media: The Extensions of Man* (Cambridge: The MIT Press, reprint, 1994), 7.

4. *The Simpsons.* "They Saved Lisa's Brain." Episode 225, Prod. AABF18. Directed by Pete Michels. Written by Matt Selman. FOX, May 9, 1999.

5. Steven Keslowitz, "The Transformative Nature of Blogs and Their Effects on Legal Scholarship," 2009 *Cardozo Law Review de novo*

252 (July 2018): 253–254, cardozolawreview.com/wp-content/uploads/2018/07/Keslowitz_2009_252.pdf

6. Famed defense attorney and civil libertarian Alan Dershowitz has received criticism about his frequent appearances on FOX News to discuss the encroachment on civil liberties in connection with Special Counsel Robert Mueller's investigation of President Trump. Because the media outlet is known for its conservative political slant, his arguments are sometimes manipulated by partisans for the purposes of achieving political ends. His legal arguments are not viewed in a non-partisan vacuum, but rather create a politically-slanted symbiotic relationship with the audience because of the medium (FOX News) through which they are disseminated. As commentator Evan Mandes observes in describing the critique, "Dershowitz is retailing an argument in a place where it has an entirely different meaning." NYU Professor Burt Neuborne and former national legal director of the American Civil Liberties Union agrees, stating that he attempts to "separate the intrinsic merits of Alan's concerns from the propriety of the venue—whether we should be debating or expressing them on Fox News." See Evan Mandes, "What Happened to Alan Dershowitz: How a Liberal Harvard Professor Became Trump's Most Distinguished Defender on TV, Freaked Out His Friends and Got the Legal World Up in Arms," *Politico*, May 11, 2018, https://www.politico.com/magazine/story/2018/05/11/alan-dershowitz-donald-trump-what-happened-218359

7. *The Rachel Divide*. Directed by Laura Brownson. Netflix, April 23, 2018.

8. Based on interviews conducted for *The Rachel Divide*, it appears that many members of the African American community in Spokane may have welcomed Ms. Dolezal despite her lack of African American ancestry. The issue for those individuals was Ms. Dolezal's deception. She was a flawed messenger, and her messages would hold much less weight with others even if her deception was arguably unrelated to the substantive content of her advocacy messages.

Ms. Dolezal is not the only advocate whose voice is softened if not entirely muffled, irrespective of the substantive merit of the arguments and claims made by the individual. For example, FOX news political commentator Tucker Carlson questioned whether Michael Avenatti (attorney for porn star Stormy Daniels) is the best "standard bearer" for an anti-Trump message, given Avenatti's own checkered and questionable past. See "Tucker Carlson Tonight,"
FOX News Channel, May 11, 2018. Separating *ad hominem* attacks from the merits of an argument often proves difficult, especially in the context of our hyper-partisan society.

9. Jen Chaney, "From Veep to Scandal, How TV Foreshadowed the Presidential Election," *Vulture*, November 3, 2016, www.vulture.com/2016/11/tv-foreshadowed-the-presidential-election.html

Trump's status as a former reality-show host tends to further blend the line between politicians and entertainers.

10. See pinterest.com/pin/507006870540879597/?lp=true

11. Elie Wiesel, *The Elie Wiesel Foundation for Humanity*, www.eliewieselfoundation.org/about/

12. Martin Luther King, Jr., Address at the Fourth Annual Institute on Nonviolence and Social Change at Bethel Point Baptist Church, December 3, 1969, *The Martin Luther King, Jr. Research and Education Institute*, www.kings.institute.stanford.edu/king-papers/documents/address-fourth-annual-institute-nonviolence-and-social-change-bethel-baptist-0

13. Martin Luther King., Jr., *The King Center*, www.thekingcenter.org/blog/mlk-quote-week-sticking-love

14. See Steven Keslowitz, *The World According to The Simpsons*, 129–148, for a general discussion of the impact of television on political discourse and how debate in contemporary society differs in both form and content from a previous age (such as the Lincoln-Douglas debates).

15. *Black Mirror* creator Charlie Brooker noted that "When I wrote 'The Waldo Moment' script, at the time, I kind of felt like I'd not really nailed it." Rebecca Hawkes, "*Black Mirror*'s Charlie Brooker on predicting Trump, and the 'love' story that terrified him," *The Telegraph*, February 20, 2017, https://www.telegraph.co.uk/on-demand/0/black-mirrors-charlie-brooker-predicting-donald-trump-love-story/

The episode was widely panned by critics as well. See, for example, Morgan Jeffery, "'*Black Mirror*' series two 'The Waldo Moment' review," *Digital Spy*, February 25, 2013, http://www.digitalspy.com/tv/black-mirror/news/a461004/black-mirror-series-two-the-waldo-moment-review/

16. *The Wizard of Oz*. Directed by Victor Fleming, et al. Metro-Goldwyn-Mayer, 1939.

17. "Populism" is commonly defined as supporting the rights and power of the people in their struggle against a privileged elite. *American Heritage Dictionary*, Fifth Edition, s.v. "populism," accessed May 1, 2018.

18. Another parallel: violence at Waldo's and Trump's political rallies. As a response to Jamie's protests, Waldo (at this point, voiced by the producer) promises to pay money to the first person that physically hit Jamie. Similarly, there were many news reports about violence at Trump rallies. See, for example, Avi Selk, "The Violent Rally Trump Can't Move Past," *The Washington Post*, April 3, 2017, https://www.washingtonpost.com/news/the-fix/wp/2017/04/03/the-violent-rally-trump-cant-move-past/?noredirect=on&utm_term=.fe10e1fc880e

19. Rebecca Hawkes, "Black Mirror's Charlie Brooker on predicting Trump, and the 'love' story that terrified him," *The Telegraph*, February 20, 2017, https://www.telegraph.co.uk/on-demand/0/black-mirrors-charlie-brooker-predicting-donald-trump-love-story/

20. Christian Holub, "Black Mirror creator explains what a Trump episode would look like: Highlights from 5/21/17 Vulture Festival discussion with Andrew Sullivan," *Entertainment Weekly*, May 21, 2017, https://ew.com/tv/2017/05/21/black-mirror-vulture-fest-panel/

21. See Ryan Gaydos, "Filmmaker David Lynch believes Trump could be one of the greatest presidents in history," *FOX News*, June 25, 2018, http://www.foxnews.com/entertainment/2018/06/25/filmmaker-david-lynch-believes-trump-could-be-one-greatest-presidents-in-history.html

22. Stephen D. Reicher and S. Alexander Haslam, "Trump's Appeal: What Psychology Tells Us," *Scientific American*, March 1, 2017, https://www.scientificamerican.com/article/trump-rsquo-s-appeal-what-psychology-tells-us/

23. Jay Stanley, "New Technology Renews Old Fears of Manipulation and Control," *American Civil Liberties Union*, August 1, 2014, https://www.aclu.org/blog/national-security/new-technology-renews-old-fears-manipulation-and-control

24. *The Simpsons*. "New Kids on the Blecch." Episode No. 262, Prod. CABF12. Directed by Steven Dean Moore. Written by Tim Long. FOX, February 25, 2001.

25. *Saved by the Bell*. "The Zack Tapes." Episode No. 14. Directed by Don Barnhart. Written by Peter Engel and Tom Tenowich. NBC, December 2, 1989.

26. Footage of James Comey, aired during George Stephanopoulos' interview with James Comey. *20/20*, ABC, April 15, 2018.

27. See Leandra Bernstein, "Poll: Mainstream media continues to lose the public's trust," *WJLA*, http://wjla.com/news/nation-world/mainstream-media-continue-to-lose-the-publics-trust (citing a Gallup poll finding that Americans' confidence in the media "to report the news fully, accurately and fairly" reached its lowest level in the history of the poll with 32% declaring that they have "a great deal or fair amount" of trust in the media). The article also cites a 2016 Pew Research study, in which 22% of respondents indicated that they had "a lot" of trust in local news organizations, compared to only 18% with the same level of trust in national media outlets.

For a discussion of the public's mistrust of government, see Ronald Bailey, "Public Distrust of Government should worry us all, even conservatives and libertarians," *Los Angeles Daily News*, January 4, 2018, https://www.dailynews.com/2018/01/04/public-distrust-of-government-should-worry-us-all-even-conservatives-and-libertarians/, pointing out that general distrust in government is also a concern. The article cites a Pew Research Center poll that reports that "only 18% of Americans think they can trust the government to do what is right 'just about always' or 'most of the time.'"

28. See Eric Bradner, "Conway: Trump White House Offered 'Alternative Facts' on Crowd Size," CNNwww, January 23, 2017, https://www.cnn.com/2017/01/22/politics/kellyanne-conway-alternative-facts/index.html

Along similar lines, former New York City mayor Rudolph Giuliani stated in an interview that the "truth is relative," arguing (quiet ineffectively) that "They may have a different version of the truth than we do." See Josh Dawsey, "In reversal, Giuliani now says Trump should do interview with Mueller team," *The Washington Post*, May 23, 2018, https://www.washingtonpost.com/politics/in-reversal-giuliani-now-says-trump-should-do-interview-with-mueller-team/2018/05/23/82f8fa24-5eb8-11e8-9ee3-49d6d4814c4c_story.html?utm_term=.6d43b59cb1a7

29. See Joe Svetlik, "First look at 'Better Call Saul season 2,'" *uSwitch*, February 8, 2016, https://www.uswitch.com/tv/news/2016/02/first_look_at_better_call_saul_season_two/

30. Neil Postman, *Amusing Ourselves to Death: Public Discourse in the Age of Show Business* (New York: Penguin Books, 1986), 107.

31. This episode is a derivation of Philip K. Dick's short story "Foster, You're Dead." For a discussion of how these episodes were adapted from the original short stories, see Tobias Carroll, "How Electric Dreams Compares to Philip K. Dick's Short Stories," *Vulture*, February 5, 2018, http://www.vulture.com/2018/02/electric-

dreams-philip-k-dick-short-story-comparison.html. Film adaptations of Dick's stories include *Blade Runner* (1982) and *A Scanner Darkly* (2006). See *Blade Runner*. Directed by Ridley Scott. Warner Bros., June 25, 1982.
A Scanner Darkly. Directed by Richard Linklater. Warner Independent Pictures, May 25, 2006.

32. The failure of an Eastern citizen or visitor to obtain an electronic tracking device has consequences similar to those seen in the *Black Mirror* episode "Nosedive." In both situations, society limits, restricts or cuts off entirely certain benefits that more obedient (in the case of "Safe and Sound") or (in the case of "Nosedive") highly valued citizens receive.

33. Gloria Origgi, "Say Goodbye to the Information Age: It's All About Reputation Now," *Fast Company*, April 28, 2018, https://www.fastcompany.com/40565050/say-goodbye-to-the-information-age-its-all-about-reputation-now

34. See, for example, Katie Rogers and Engel Bromwich, "The Hoaxes, Fake News and Misinformation We Saw On Election Day," *New York Times*, November 8, 2016, www.nytimes.com/2016/11/09/us/politics/debunk-fake-news-election-day.html.

35. *The Simpsons*. "The Computer Wore Menace Shoes." Episode No. 254, Prod. CABF02. Directed by Mark Kirkland. Written by John Swartzwelder. FOX, December 3, 2000.

36. Big industries sometimes deploy disinformation to further commercial ends. For example, the documentary *That Sugar Film* (2014) alleges that the sugar industry pays scientists to conduct studies. The documentary alleges that when the science was unclear several decades ago, the sugar industry commissioned a report supportive of sugar to muddying the waters. The industry presents a low fat / low calorie / more sugar diet as a dietary solution. But modern science demonstrates that not all calories are created equal. *That Sugar Film*, Directed by Damon Gameau. Amsterdam International Documentary Film Festival, November 20, 2014.

37. For a discussion of the history of objectivity in journalism, see "The Lost Meaning of Objectivity," *The American Press Institute*, https://www.americanpressinstitute.org/journalism-essentials/bias-objectivity/lost-meaning-objectivity/ The authors observe that "Journalists who select sources to express what is really their own point of view, and then use the neutral voice to make it seem objective, are engaged in a form of deception. This damages the credibility of the craft by making it seem unprincipled, dishonest, and biased."

This article does suggest, however, that neutrality is not necessarily a fundamental tenet of reporting the news: "The impartial voice employed by many news organizations—that familiar, supposedly neutral style of newswriting—is not a fundamental principle of journalism."

38. See JPost staff, "Top 5 Most Egregious Anti-Israel Headlines in the International Media," *Jerusalem Post*, August 17, 2016, https://www.jpost.com/Arab-Israeli-Conflict/Top-5-most-egregious-anti-Israel-headlines-in-the-international-media-464351

39. See, for example, "'Jeff, Do You Even Care?': Hannity Blasts CNN President for Anti-Trump Bias," *Fox News Insider*, June 26, 2017, www.insider.foxnews.com/2017/06/26/sean-hannity-cnn-fake-news-jeff-zucker-destroy-donald-trump-administration-scaramucci

40. Norman Ornstein, foreword to *The Web of Politics: The Internet's Impact on the American Political System*, by Richard Davis (Oxford: Oxford University Press, March 4, 1999), xi-3.

41. See Coor Friedersdorf, "Tucker Carlson Is Hurting America Again," *The Atlantic*, June 20, 2018, https://www.theatlantic.com/politics/archive/2018/06/tucker-carlson-is-hurting-america-again/563138/ (quoting Carlson during an appearance on C-Span).

42. *Ibid*.

43. *The Simpsons*. "Holidays of Future Past." Episode No. 495, Prod. NABF18. Directed by Rob Oliver. Written by J. Stewart Burns. FOX, December 11, 2011.

44. *The Creepy Line*. Directed by M.A. Taylor. Wandering Foot Productions, October 2018.

45. See Avery Thompson, "Google Accidentally Broke Japan's Internet," *Popular Mechanics*, August 28, 2017, https://www.popularmechanics.com/technology/news/a27971/google-accident ally-broke-japans-internet/

46. For good measure, Google also owns the Android operating system.

47. *The Creepy Line*. Directed by M.A. Taylor. Wandering Foot Productions, October 2018.

48. *Ibid*.

49. *The Simpsons*. "Grift of the Magi." Episode No. 235, Prod. BABF07. Directed by Matthew Nastuk. Written by Tom Martin. FOX, December 19, 1999.

50. *The Creepy Line*. Directed by M.A. Taylor. Wandering Foot Productions, October 2018.

51. *Ibid*.

52. *Ibid*.

53. *Ibid*.

54. *Ibid*.; Dr. Epstein reported that his access to Google was similarly cut off on the day following the publication of an article in *The*

Washington Post discussing whether Google could turn a close election. Epstein notes that Google's Terms of Service permits it to cut an individual's access with or without cause.

55. Here, I am reminded of *The Office*'s Michael Scott's satirical commentary on the immense value of Wikipedia: "Wikipedia is the best thing ever. Anyone in the world can write anything they want about any subject. So you know you are getting the best possible information." *The Office*. "The Negotiation." Episode No. 47, Prod. 319. Directed by Jeffrey Blitz. Written by Michael Schur. NBC, April 5, 2007.

56. *The Simpsons*. "Fraudcast News." Directed by Bob Anderson. Written by Don Payne. Episode No. 335, Prod. FABF18. FOX, May 23, 2004.

57. Gloria Origgi, "Say Goodbye to the Information Age: It's All About Reputation Now," *Fast Company*, April 27, 2018, https://www.fastcompany.com/40565050/say-goodbye-to-the-information-age-its-all-about-reputation-now

58. Ibid.

59. Steven Keslowitz, "The Transformative Nature of Blogs," 256.

60. Ibid., 262.

61. *The Simpsons*. "Homer Badman." Episode No. 112, Prod. 2F06. Directed by Jeffrey Lynch. Written by Greg Daniels. FOX, November 27, 1994.

62. See "Adolf Hitler: Excerpts from Mein Kampf," *Jewish Virtual Library*, http://www.jewishvirtuallibrary.org/excerpts-from-mein-kampf

63. See "Joseph Goebbels on The Big Lie," *Jewish Virtual Library*, http://www.jewishvirtuallibrary.org/joseph-goebbels-on-the-quot-big-lie-quot

64. Phil Tinline, "The Art of the Big Lie: the history of fake news," *New Statesman*, March 17, 2018, https://www.newstatesman.com/world/2018/03/art-big-lie-history-fake-news

65. See "Joseph Goebbels on The Big Lie," *Jewish Virtual Library*, http://www.jewishvirtuallibrary.org/joseph-goebbels-on-the-quot-big-lie-quot

66. *The Twilight Zone*. "The Obsolete Man." Episode No. 65, Prod. 173–3661. Directed by Elliot Silverstein. Written by Rod Serling. CBS, June 2, 1961.

67. This episode also serves as an odd case study of a television series matching reality in an odd and unintentional manner. Unbeknownst to creator Charlie Brooker at the time that the episode was written, there happen to be unconfirmed, anecdotal reports that British Prime Minister David Cameron had placed his penis inside the mouth of a pig as part of a group initiation ritual while attending Oxford University. See Dan Stewart, "Why David Cameron's 'Pig-Gate' Scandal Isn't Going Away," *Time Magazine*, September 21, 2015, http://time.com/4043311/david-cameron-pig-gate-scandal/

Michael Hogan, writing for *The Daily Telegraph*, commented on the excellent satire presented in this episode, calling it "a shocking, but ballsy, blackly comic study of the modern media." Michael Hogan, "*Black Mirror*: The National Anthem, Channel 4, review," *The Telegraph*, December 4, 2011, https://www.telegraph.co.uk/culture/tvandradio/8932095/Black-Mirror-The-National-Anthem-Channel-4-review.html

68. A couple of examples from the series include terrorists forcing President Taylor to read a message onscreen, and planning to broadcast the decapitation of Secretary of Defense James Heller. See *24*, "Day 7: 8:00 p.m.–9:00 p.m. Directed by Brad Turner. Episode No. 157, Prod. 7AFF13. Written by Brannon Braga and Manny Coto. FOX, March 9, 2009, and "Day 4: 8:00 a.m.–9:00 a.m." Episode No. 74, Prod. 4AFF02. Directed by Jon Cassar. Written by Howard Gordon. FOX, January 9, 2005.

69. The attempted censorship in "The National Anthem" (as well as in *The Twilight Zone*'s "The Obsolete Man," where an authoritarian government bans books and religion) bears comparison to the actions of technology titans (such as Facebook, Twitter and YouTube) who have engaged in the controversial practice of removing certain content that they (and many others) deem objectionable from their websites. One main difference between this practice and the censorship in "The National Anthem" and "The Obsolete Man" is that these technology companies have removed such content not at the request of the government but rather due to their own political positions and, presumably, economic rationales. See, e.g., Charles Riley, "YouTube, Apple and Facebook remove content from InfoWars and Alex Jones," *CNN*, August 6, 2018, https://money.cnn.com/2018/08/06/technology/facebook-infowars-alex-jones/index.html

70. Controlling the press and exerting pressure over what and how it reports is often a first step toward authoritarianism. When journalists fear for their lives and publications are intimidated by powerful government forces, the public's ability to hold elected officials accountable via accurate and actionable information is threatened. This issue is examined in the film *Kill the Messenger* (2014), where a journalist

writes a truthful account of the government's role in the drug epidemic in the United States. The film—which was based on actual events—demonstrates the power and will of the CIA to effectively cover up and kill a story, destroy folks' careers and, most alarmingly, control the nature of flow of information in the mainstream media. Democracy cannot survive when government forces manipulate us and undermine the freedom of the press. This is why we must remain vigilant and condemn rhetoric from elected officials that questions the value of an independent free press—flawed though such press may be. See *Kill the Messenger*, Directed by Michael Cuesta. Bluegrass Films, October 10, 2014; *Network*, Directed by Sidney Lumet. Metro-Goldwyn-Mayer, November 27, 1976; *The Show*. Directed by Giancarlo Esposito. Grindstone Entertainment Group, March 11, 2017.

71. Hunt Alcott and Matthew Gentzkow, "Social Media and Fake News in the 2016 Election," *Journal of Economic Perspectives*, Volume 31, No. 2 (2017): 214; The authors state that "... [O]n social media, the fixed costs of entering the market and producing content are vanishingly small. This increases the relative profitability of the small-scale, short-term strategies often adopted by fake news producers, and reduces the relative importance of building a long-term reputation for quality." Alcott and Gentzkow, 221.

72. Ibid., 215.

73. In *The Office* episode "Customer Loyalty," Erin and Pete create a fake social media profile of an individual who likes Dunder Mifflin to make their company seem popular with millennials. *The Office*. "Customer Loyalty." Episode No. 188, Prod. 9013. Directed by Kelly Kantley. Written by Jonathan Green and Gabe Miller. NBC, January 24, 2013.

During and after the 2016 United States presidential election, the Internet Research Agency (which is backed by the Russian government) made use of fake social media profiles. See Swapna Krishna, "Russians used fake social accounts to gather Americans' personal data," *Engadget*, March 7, 2018, www.engadget.com/2018/03/07/russians-faken-social-media-accounts-steal-personal-data/

74. Hunt Alcott and Matthew Gentzkow, "Social Media and Fake News in the 2016 Election," *Journal of Economic Perspectives*, Volume 31, No. 2 (2017), citing a 2016 study by Jeffrey Gottfried and Elisa Shearer, "News Use Across Social Media Platforms," *Pew Research Center*, May 26, 2016, www.journalism.org/2016/05/26/news-use-across-social-media-platforms-2016. A survey conducted by Alcott and Gentzkow shows that only 14% of adults say that social media is their primary source of news.

75. *The Creepy Line*. Directed by M.A. Taylor. Wandering Foot Productions, October 2018.

76. *Nerve*. Directed by Henry Joost and Ariel Schulman. Lionsgate, July 12, 2016. The data gathering featured in this film is reminiscent of the collection of real-time data to determine folks' fears in "Playtest."

77. See James Vincent, "Tim Cook Warns of 'Data-Industrial Complex' in Call for Comprehensive U.S. privacy laws," *The Verge*, October 24, 2018, https://www.theverge.com/2018/10/24/18017842/tim-cook-data-privacy-laws-us-speech-brussels

78. See Coor Friedersdorf, "Tucker Carlson Is Hurting America Again," *The Atlantic*, June 20, 2018, https://www.theatlantic.com/politics/archive/2018/06/tucker-carlson-is-hurting-america-again/563138/ (quoting Carlson during an appearance on C-Span).

79. For further discussion, see Michael Nunez, "Former Facebook Workers: We Routinely Suppressed Conservative News," *Gizmodo*, May 9, 2016, www.gizmodo.com/former-facebook-workers-we-routinely-suppressed-conser-1775461006

80. For further discussion of this issue, see Will Knight, "Biased Algorithms are Everywhere, and No One Seems to Care," *MIT Technology Review*, July 12, 2017, https://www.technologyreview.com/s/608248/biased-algorithms-are-everywhere-and-no-one-seems-to-care/

81. Andra Brichacek, "Six Ways the Media Influences Elections," *University of Oregon School of Journalism and Communication*, November 8, 2016, http://journalism.uoregon.edu/news/six-ways-media-influences-elections/

82. Acclaimed journalist and author Malcolm Gladwell advocates for the free expression of ideas in an open marketplace, as opposed to a closed echo chamber, arguing that "the point of a festival of ideas [is] to expose the audience to ideas. If you only invite your friends over, it's called a dinner party." See Kristy Puchko, "The New Yorker, Steve Bannon and Why We're Mad at Malcolm Gladwell," *Pajiba*, September 4, 2018, http://www.pajiba.com/politics/the-new-yorker-steve-bannon-and-why-were-mad-at-malcolm-gladwell.php (quoting from Gladwell's Twitter post, September 3, 2018).

See Vyacheslav Polonski, "How artificial intelligence conquered democracy," *The Conversation*, August 8, 2017, https://theconversation.

com/how-artificial-intelligence-conquered-democracy-77675

83. See Vyacheslav Polonski, "How artificial intelligence conquered democracy," *The Conversation*, August 8, 2017, https://theconversation.com/how-artificial-intelligence-conquered-democracy-77675

84. *Ibid.*

85. *Ibid.*

86. See "47 U.S. Code Section 230—Protection for private blocking and screening of offensive material," https://www.law.cornell.edu/uscode/text/47/230

87. See Alina Selyukh, "Section 230: A Key Legal Shield for Facebook, Google Is About to Change," *NPR*, March 21, 2018, https://www.npr.org/sections/alltechconsidered/2018/03/21/591622450/section-230-a-key-legal-shield-for-facebook-google-is-about-to-change

88. *Ibid.*

89. *The Creepy Line.* Directed by M.A. Taylor. Wandering Foot Productions, October 2018.

90. *Ibid.*

91. See "Facebook Community Standards Policy," https://www.facebook.com/communitystandards/

92. See Elliot Harmon, "No, Section 230 Does Not Require Platforms to be 'Neutral,'" *Electronic Frontier Foundation*, April 12, 2018, https://www.eff.org/deeplinks/2018/04/no-section-230-does-not-require-platforms-be-neutral

The law was amended on April 11, 2018 to "limit the immunity of platform providers ... for online services that knowingly host third-party content that promotes or facilitates sex trafficking." See Jeffrey Neuburger, "FOSTA Signed into Law, Amends CDA Section 230 to Allow Enforcement against Online Providers for Knowingly Facilitating Sex Trafficking," *Proskauer Rose*, April 11, 2018, https://newmedialaw.proskauer.com/2018/04/11/fosta-signed-into-law-amends-cda-section-230-to-allow-enforcement-against-online-providers-for-knowingly-facilitating-sex-trafficking/

93. *Facebook: Cracking the Code.* Directed by Peter Greste. ABC Australia, April 11, 2017.

94. Human beings are naturally inclined to maintain their own perspectives and seek out affirmations of closely-held beliefs, as opposed to exploring alternative viewpoints—especially on social media. Case in point: How often has anyone been convinced of the validity of a different political perspective in a Facebook comment debate?

95. See Michael M. Grynbaum, "The New Yorker Festival Boots Bannon, and Liberals are Torn," *The New York Times*, September 4, 2018, https://www.nytimes.com/2018/09/04/business/media/bannon-new-yorker-festival-liberals.html

96. Note that some restrictive nations close off or prevent access to the Internet and/or certain websites. But given the agendas, are societies with a free and open Internet necessarily better informed? Or is the information received by both open and closed societies dis-informative in nature? Query whether being subjected to a greater number of distorted agendas as opposed to just one (the State's) political agenda makes for a better-informed society.

97. Homer Simpson would agree with this assessment, memorably becoming confused when confronted with evidence provided on television against his position on gun control. *The Simpsons.* "The Cartridge Family." Episode 183, Prod. 5F01. Directed by Pete Michels. Written by John Schwartzwelder. FOX, November 2, 1997.

98. This exertion of control has deadly consequences in "Hated in the Nation," where a hacker takes control of "honeybee-mimicking drones," or ADIs.

"White Bear" is particularly interesting in this context because the community falsely blames a technological malfunction (a weird, powerful signal appearing on digital devices) when the ruse / torture / punishment is entirely designed by the community—with the aid of mind-erasing technology.

99. "12 Alarming Cyber Security Facts and Stats," *Cybint: Barbri Cyber Solutions*, March 16, 2018, https://www.cybintsolutions.com/cyber-security-facts-stats/

100. *Ibid.*

101. *Ibid.*

102. Bruce Schneier, *Click Here to Kill Everybody: Security and Survival in a Hyper-Connected World* (New York; W.W. Norton & Company, 2018), 136.

See Henry Farrell, "Hackers used a fish tank to break into a Vegas casino. We're all in trouble," *The Washington Post*, September 4, 2018, https://www.washingtonpost.com/news/monkey-cage/wp/2018/09/04/hackers-used-a-fishtank-to-break-into-a-vegas-casino-were-all-in-trouble/?utm_term=.7dccf8071984

103. Laura Kelly, "Teen suicide rate suddenly rises with heavy use of smartphones, social media," *The Washington Times*, November 14, 2017, www.washingtontimes.com/news/2017/nov/14/teen-suicidies-rise-with-smartphone-social-media-us/

104. See, for example, Nina Golgowski, "Washington teen jumps to death after being

shamed in online video taken by dad," *NY Daily News*, June 5, 2015, www.nydailynews.com/news/national/teen-kills-public-shaming-allegedly-dad-article-1.2247168

105. Recent developments in artificial intelligence often track the technology shown on *Black Mirror* and *Electric Dreams* episodes. For example, researchers have developed "an insect-sized drone capable of artificial pollination"—in other words, robotic bees similar to those featured on "Hated in the Nation." Crystal Ponti, "Rise of the Robot Bees: Tiny Drones Turned into Artificial Pollinators," *NPR*, March 3, 2017, www.npr.org/sections/thesalt/2017/03/03/517785082/rise-of-the-robot-bees-tiny-drones-turned-into-artificial-pollinators

Black Mirror is not the first television series to address potential fears about killer bees. In *The Simpsons* episode "Burns' Heir," Homer predicts that Mr. Burns will release dogs that shoot bees out of their mouths when the dogs bark. And in the episode "The Burns and the Bees," a swarm of killer bees attacks fans and players at a basketball arena. See *The Simpsons*, "Burns' Heir." Episode No. 99, Prod. 1F16. Directed by Mark Kirkland. Written by Jace Richdale. FOX, April 14, 1994; "The Burns and the Bees." Episode No. 428, Prod. KABF21. Directed by Mark Kirkland. Written by Stephanie Gillis. FOX, December 7, 2008.

An invasion by killer bees is also the focus of the horror flick *The Swarm*. See *The Swarm*, Directed by Irwin Allen. Warner Bros., July 14, 1978.

106. See, for example, Sue Scheff, "Was 2017 the Rise of Online Shaming?," *Huffpost*, December 2017, https://www.huffingtonpost.com/entry/was-2017-the-rise-of-online-shaming_us_5a43fa33e4b0d86c803c748f

107. Vigilantism is explored in the *Black Mirror* episode "Hated in the Nation," too. In that episode, a hacker seeks to teach the world a "moral lesson" by holding individuals accountable for their online behavior.

108. One of the hacker's victims is a married man who hires a prostitute. While the man's actions are immoral and, in most locations, illegal, the consensual actions are different—in both nature and degree—from crimes involving possession of child pornography.

109. These issues are explored in "White Christmas," too, as due process is ignored and technology is used to alter a digital cookie's sense of space and time.

110. Zack Handlen, "No one's watching the watchmen on a so-so *Black Mirror*," *The A.V. Club*, October 23, 2016, https://tv.avclub.com/no-one-s-watching-the-watchmen-on-a-so-so-black-mirror-1798189235

It is also noteworthy that the blackmailer in "Shut Up and Dance" acts recklessly and causes significant harm to others in the community. By forcing Kenny to rob a bank and fight another individual to the death, the blackmailer turns Kenny from a sick, twisted and troubled pedophile into a thief and killer. The horrific results of the blackmailer's demands are a direct consequence of the blackmailer's perverted scheme.

111. Matt Donnelly and Tim Molloy, "All 13 Black Mirror Episodes Ranked, from Good to Mind-Blowing," *The Wrap*, August 12, 2007, https://www.thewrap.com/all-19-black-mirror-episodes-ranked-from-good-to-mind-blowing-photos/ Television columnist Robbie Collin makes a similar observation, stating that the episode is "the most nihilistic episode of *Black Mirror* so far." Robbie Collin, "Black Mirror Season 3, Shut Up and Dance review: 'soul-scorching, dark and riveting'," *The Daily Telegraph*, October 2016, https://www.telegraph.co.uk/on-demand/0/black-mirror-season-3-shut-up-and-dance-review-soul-scorching-da/

112. Zack Handlen, "No one's watching the watchmen on a so-so *Black Mirror*," *The A.V. Club*, October 23, 2016, https://tv.avclub.com/no-one-s-watching-the-watchmen-on-a-so-so-black-mirror-1798189235

Chapter 3

1. Marilyn Butler and Mary W. Shelley, *Frankenstein, Or the Modern Prometheus: The 1818 Text* (Oxford: Oxford University Press, 1994), 120.

2. David Brooks, *On Paradise Drive: How We Live Now (And Always Have) in the Future Tense* (New York: Simon & Schuster, 2004), 86–88.

3. Ibid.

4. Most individuals in Lacie's world appear to be similarly obsessed with their rankings. The typical encounter between like-minded people consists of a brief, meaningless, phony interaction followed by pointing their phones at each other to click to record the ranking. The ranking system establishes a hierarchy in society where low-ranking individuals are ignored, while high-ranking folks are respected and treated to special social and economic benefits (such as joining the "Prime Influencers Programme)."

The influence of technology on an individual's daily actions is also explored on *Black Mirror*'s

"Fifteen Million Merits." In that episode, folks pedal a bicycle to collect points and then use those points to access technology.

As she moves up the ladder, Lacie would be wise to heed the advice of playwright Wilson Mizner: "Be nice to people on your way up because you'll meet them on the way down." See https://www.passiton.com/inspirational-quotes/7153-be-nice-to-people-on-your-way-up-because-youll

5. Warren Buffett, quoted in "Warren Buffett: The Inner Scorecard," Farnam Street, https://www.fs.blog/2016/08/the-inner-scorecard/

6. *God Friended Me.* CBS, September 30, 2018–present.

7. Quoted in Joseph Rago, "Status Reporter," *The Wall Street Journal*, March 11, 2006, https://www.wsj.com/articles/SB114204279173895576

8. See Kira Beilis, "How Your Technology Is Manipulating You," *The Cut*, October 24, 2014, https://www.thecut.com/2014/10/how-your-technology-is-manipulating-you.html

9. Nellie Bowles, "The Digital Gap Between Rich and Poor Kids Is Not What We Expect," *The New York Times*, October 26, 2018, https://www.nytimes.com/2018/10/26/style/digital-divide-screens-schools.html

10. M. Ryan Calo, "People Can Be So Fake: A New Dimension to Privacy and Technology Scholarship," 114 *Penn St. L. Rev.* 809 (2009–2010): 841.

11. *You.* Lifetime, September 9, 2018–present.

12. See Jessica Rawden, "Bryce Dallas Howard Reveals Why She Gained 30 Pounds for Black Mirror," *Cinema Blend*, August 2018, https://www.cinemablend.com/television/2455424/bryce-dallas-howard-reveals-why-she-gained-30-pounds-for-black-mirror

13. See Scott A. Rosenberg, "The Sneeze and the fury of 'Snotgirl,'" *amNY*, May 30, 2018.

14. *The American Meme.* Directed by Bert Marcus. Netflix, December 7, 2018.

15. There is some evidence to suggest that social media usage among select demographics is, surprisingly, ebbing. According to research by Bloomberg and Pew, 51% of 13–17-year old teenagers use Facebook in 2018. In 2015, the figure was 71%. See Sarah Frier, "America's Teens are Choosing YouTube over Facebook," *Bloomberg*, May 31, 2018, https://www.bloomberg.com/news/articles/2018-05-31/america-s-teens-are-choosing-youtube-over-facebook

The power of social media to ruin lives is enormous. Solely looking at the final week of May 2018 as an example, both actress Roseanne Barr and Philadelphia 76ers' President of Basketball Operations Bryan Colangelo pu their careers in jeopardy by posting irresponsible—and in the case of Barr, abhorrent—tweets. (Colangelo denies sending the controversial tweets, and reports suggest that they may have been written and sent by his wife). See John Koblin, "After Racist Tweet, Roseanne Barr's Show Is Canceled by ABC," *The New York Times*, May 29, 2018, https://www.nytimes.com/2018/05/29/business/media/roseanne-barr-offensive-tweets.html; and Des Bieler, "Bryan Colangelo takes heat for throwing his wife under the bus in resignation," *The Washington Post*, June 7, 2018, https://www.washingtonpost.com/news/early-lead/wp/2018/06/07/bryan-colangelo-takes-heat-for-throwing-his-wife-under-the-bus-in-resignation/?noredirect=on&utm_term=.d10bd88c9638

16. "Number of monthly active Facebook users worldwide as of 4th quarter 2017," www.statista.com/statistics/264810/number-of-monthly-active-facebook-users-worldwide/

17. "Daily time spent on social networking by internet users worldwide from 2012 to 2017 (in minutes)," *The Statistics Portal*, Statista, https://www.statista.com/statistics/433871/daily-social-media-usage-worldwide/

18. David Cohen, "How Much Time Will the Average Person Spend on Social Media During Their Life?," *Adweek*, March 22, 2017, http://www.adweek.com/digital/mediakix-time-spent-social-media-infographic/

19. Social media platforms typically consider it their mission, at least in part, to connect individuals. Facebook, for example, has used various taglines and slogans intended to convey this intention. The success of these companies in achieving this stated goal is debatable.

For further discussion, see Josh Constine, "Facebook changes mission statement to 'bring the world closer together,'" *TechCrunch*, June 22, 2017, https://techcrunch.com/2017/06/22/bring-the-world-closer-together/

20. Monica Kim, "The Good and the Bad of Escaping to Virtual Reality," *The Atlantic*, February 8, 2015, www.theatlantic/com/health/archive/2015/02/the-good-and-the-bad-of-escaping-to-virtual-reality/385134

21. Alice G. Watson, "6 Ways Social Media Affects Our Mental Health," *Forbes*, June 30, 2017, https://www.forbes.com/sites/alicegwalton/2017/06/30/a-run-down-of-social-medias-effects-on-our-mental-health/#188a61592e5a (citing R.I.M. Dunbar, "Do online social media cut through the constraints that limit the size of offline social networks?," *The Royal Society Publishing*, January 20, 2016, www.rsos.royalsocietypublishing.org/content/3/1/150292)

22. *Ibid.*

As rapper Tupac Shakur observes, "The realest people don't have a lot of friends. You know why? Cause they don't tolerate phony shit. There's a lot of phony people out there who would do anything for attention and money. That's why real people keep their circle small." See *Ball Memes*, https://ballmemes.com/i/the-realest-people-dont-have-a-lot-of-friends-you-7bf1282f09f142ed96cae6c3b3908e95

23. See Honors Whiteman, "Loneliness a bigger killer than obesity, say researchers," *Medical News Today*, August 6, 2017, www.medicalnewstoday.com/articles/318723.php (citing two analyses from Brigham Young University finding that loneliness and social isolation may increase the risk of premature death by up to 50%. This finding was presented by Dr. Julianne Holt-Lunstad at the 125th Annual Convention of the American Psychological Association on August 5, 2018.

24. *Catfish: The TV Show*. Viacom Media Networks, 2012–present.

25. Bill Murray, Twitter Post. Murray expresses disappointment that many social media users "feel they should document their life rather than live it." Dailymail.com Reporter, "Bill Murray laments the rise of social media: 'People document their life rather than live it,'" *Daily Mail*, June 1, 2018, http://www.dailymail.co.uk/tvshowbiz/article-5795959/Bill-Murray-laments-rise-social-media-People-document-life-live-it.html

26. Seth Rogen, Twitter Post. September 16, 2018.

27. Alice G. Watson, "6 Ways Social Media Affects Our Mental Health," *Forbes*, June 30, 2017, https://www.forbes.com/sites/alicegwalton/2017/06/30/a-run-down-of-social-medias-effects-on-our-mental-health/#188a61592e5a (citing Gwenn Schurgin O' Keefe, Kathleen Clarke-Pearson. "The Impact of Social Media on Children, Adolescents, and Families," *Pediatrics Council on Communications and Media*, Volume 127, Issue 4 (2011), pediatrics.aapublications.org/content/127/4/800.short).

28. Alice G. Watson, "6 Ways Social Media Affects Our Mental Health," *Forbes*, June 30, 2017, https://www.forbes.com/sites/alicegwalton/2017/06/30/a-run-down-of-social-medias-effects-on-our-mental-health/#188a61592e5a (citing Ethan Kross et al., "Facebook Use Predicts Declines in Subjective Well-Being in Young Adults," *PLOS One*, August 14, 2013, www.journals.plos.org/plosone/article?id=10.1371/journal.pone.0069841&mbid=synd_msnhealth

29. Alice G. Watson, "6 Ways Social Media Affects Our Mental Health," *Forbes*, June 30, 2017, https://www.forbes.com/sites/alicegwalton/2017/06/30/a-run-down-of-social-medias-effects-on-our-mental-health/#188a61592e5a (citing Brian A. Primack et al., "Social Media Use and Perceived Social Isolation Among Young Adults in the U.S.," *American Journal of Preventive Medicine*, Volume 53, Issue 1 (2017): 1–8, www.ajpmonline.org/article/S0749-3797(17)30016-8/fulltext

30. See Michele W. Berger, "Social media use increases depression and loneliness," *Penn Today*, November 9, 2018, https://penntoday.upenn.edu/news/social-media-use-increases-depression-and-loneliness (citing Melissa G. Hunt et al., "No More FOMO: Limiting Social media Decreases Loneliness and Depression," *Journal of Social and Clinical Psychology*, Vol. 37, No. 10 (2018): 751–768, https://guilfordjournals.com/doi/pdf/10.1521/jscp.2018.37.10.751

31. See Rebecca Joseph, "Frequent social media users nearly 3 times more likely to have depression: study," *Global News*, March 26, 2016, https://globalnews.ca/news/2601572/frequent-social-media-users-nearly-3-times-more-likely-to-have-depression-study/

32. Alice G. Watson, "6 Ways Social Media Affects Our Mental Health," *Forbes*, June 30, 2017, https://www.forbes.com/sites/alicegwalton/2017/06/30/a-run-down-of-social-medias-effects-on-our-mental-health/#188a61592e5a

33. *Ibid.*

34. *Ibid.*

35. *Ibid.*, citing Christina Sagioglou and Tobias Greitemeyer, "Facebook's emotional consequences: Why Facebook causes a decrease in mood and why people still use it," *ScienceDirect*, Volume 35 (June 2014): 359–363, www.sciencedirect.com/science/article/pii/S0747563214001241)

36. See Erin Fuchs, "The tech execs who have called out Facebook's trust problem," *Yahoo Finance*, May 16, 2018, https://finance.yahoo.com/news/tech-execs-called-facebooks-trust-problem-152935213.html (quoting Marc Benioff during his appearance on *CBS This Morning*, May 16, 2018, https://www.cbsnews.com/video/salesforce-ceo-marc-benioff-calls-for-national-privacy-law/)

37. Another episode in this category is "Shut Up and Dance," which reflects and examines contemporary fears related to hacking. Creator Charlie Brooker points out the lack of science fiction elements in "Shut Up and Dance," and observes that "The National Anthem" and "The Waldo Moment" similarly "touch base with the real world." See James Hibberd, "Black Mirror postmortem: Showrunner talks Season 3 twists,"

Entertainment Weekly, October 21, 2016, http://ew.com/article/2016/10/23/black-mirror-postmortem-interview-season-3/

38. *The Circle*. All3Media, September 2018–present.

39. *The Office*. "A.A.R.M." Episode Nos. 198 and 199, Prod. 9022 and 9023, respectively. Directed by David Rogers. Written by Brent Forrester. NBC, May 9, 2013.

40. *The Office*. "Promos." Episode No. 193, Prod. 9018. Directed by Jennifer Celotta. Written by Tim McAuliffe. NBC, April 4, 2013.

41. *Brockmire*. IFC, April 5, 2017–present.

42. China uses apps such as WeChat Pay and Alipay to collect data on citizens. Alipay, which is owned by Ant Financial (an affiliate of Alibaba corporation) created a private version (Sesame Credit) of a future government social credit system. See The Week Staff, "China's Black Mirror moment," *The Week*, February 3, 2018, www.theweek.com/articles/752442/chinas-black-mirror-moment

43. See The Week Staff, "China's Black Mirror moment," *The Week*, February 3, 2018, www.theweek.com/articles/752442/chinas-black-mirror-moment

44. Ibid.

45. Ibid.

46. Ibid.

47. See Harry Cockburn, "China blacklists millions of people from booking flights as 'social credit' system introduced," *The Independent*, November 22, 2018, https://www.independent.co.uk/news/world/asia/china-social-credit-system-flight-booking-blacklisted-beijing-points-a8646316.html

48. See Mara Hvistendahl, "Inside China's Vast New Experiment In Social Ranking," *Wired*, December 14, 2017, www.wired.com/story/age-of-social-credit

49. Ibid.

50. Ibid.

51. Ibid. In "Nosedive," Lacie is forced to use an outdated car during her freefall.

52. Ibid.

53. The Week Staff, "China's Black Mirror moment," *The Week*, February 3, 2018, www.theweek.com/articles/752442/chinas-black-mirror-moment

54. Ibid.

55. See George Martin, "China 'launches an app that tells you if you are within 500 yards of someone in debt—and encourages you to report them if they seem capable of paying up,'" *Daily Mail*, January 22, 2019, https://www.dailymail.co.uk/news/article-6620879/China-launches-app-tells-500-yards-debt.html

56. Quoted in *Ibid*.

57. Preeminent criminal defense attorney and civil libertarian Alan Dershowitz states that the "essence of criminal law is to separate criminal conduct from just bad conduct." See Josh Feldman, "Alan Dershowitz and Richard Painter Get in Tense Clash: Mueller May Be a Good American But 'You're Not,'" *Mediaite*, May 5, 2018, https://www.mediaite.com/tv/alan-dershowitz-and-richard-painter-get-in-tense-clash-mueller-may-be-a-good-american-but-youre-not/ (includes link to MSNBC debate, May 4, 2018).

A social credit system would tear away at the fabric of societies with narrowly defined criminal codes and could lead to significant government oversight and control over the lives of individuals.

58. *The Good Place*. NBC, 2016–present.

59. *Nerve*. Directed by Henry Joost and Ariel Schulman. Lionsgate, July 12, 2016.

60. *Cam*. Directed by Daniel Goldhaber. Netflix, November 16, 2018.

61. See Caitlin Dewey, "Everyone you know will be able to rate you on the terrifying 'Yelp for people'—whether you want them to or not," *The Washington Post*, September 30, 2015, https://www.washingtonpost.com/news/the-intersect/wp/2015/10/05/after-internet-backlash-peeple-co-founder-will-revise-her-app-to-make-it-positive/?utm_term=.385382e0c425

Plans for the original version of the app were announced in 2015, but the app officially launched in 2016. A more recent article in *The Washington Post* states that, due to backlash against the original version, the app has been revamped to require folks to "opt in" if they wish to be reviewed. The launched version also includes a veto right, whereby the subject of a review could object to public disclosure of the review. See Caitlin Dewey, "Peeple, the terrifying 'Yelp for people' is (sort of) launching on March 7," *The Washington Post*, March 4, 2016, https://www.washingtonpost.com/news/the-intersect/wp/2015/10/05/after-internet-backlash-peeple-co-founder-will-revise-her-app-to-make-it-positive/?utm_term=.3766b90cd652

62. Sherrise Pham, "You can now get kicked off Uber in Australia for being rude to drivers," *CNN Tech*, September 5, 2018, money.cnn.com/2018/09/05/technology/uber-australia-new-zealand-riders/index.html

63. Angus Berwick, "How ZTE helps Venezuela create China-style social control," *Reuters*, November 14, 2018, https://www.reuters.com/investigates/special-report/venezuela-zte/

64. Ibid.

65. Alice G. Watson, "6 Ways Social Media

Affects Our Mental Health," *Forbes*, June 30, 2017, https://www.forbes.com/sites/alicegwalton/2017/06/30/a-run-down-of-social-medias-effects-on-our-mental-health/#188a61592e5a (citing Daria J. Kuss and Mark D. Griffiths, "Online Social Networking and Addiction—A Review of the Psychological Literature," *International Gaming Research Unit, Psychology Division*, Nottingham Trent University, August 29, 2011, www.mdpi.com/1660-4601/8/9/3528/htm?hc_location=ufi)

66. Richard Raysman, "Ethics in Social Media," *Practicing Law Institute*, March 15, 2018.

67. Lacie's explosion of emotion later in the episode was a key turning point in her life. Like the other brunettes, there is no reason for her to constrain her emotions for fear of social media reprisals; she has dropped so far that any further freefall would be meaningless.

68. In the world in which Lacie lives, nostalgia has no true place. When she posts a photo of a doll from her and the bride's childhood to get the attention of the bride, she does so only to obtain an invite to the wedding and achieve a higher social status. Neither she nor the bride value the memories of their teenage years together; rather, each uses the doll as an excuse for connecting with each other.

69. Note that the social media consultant engaged by Lacie advises her to get a "boost" from "high-range," "quality" individuals. Folks with low rankings desperately try to boost their ranking by doing special things for others (such as Chester, with a 3.1 ranking, who buys his coworkers smoothies).

70. Lois Lowry, *The Giver* (Boston: Houghton Mifflin, 1993).

71. George Orwell, *1984* (London: Secker and Warburg, 1949).

72. *Pleasantville*. Directed by Gary Ross. New Line Cinema, 1998.

73. *The Stepford Wives*. Directed by Bryan Forbes. Palomar Pictures, 1975.

74. *The Twilight Zone*. "Number 12 Looks Just Like You." Episode No. 137, Prod. 2618. Directed by Abner Biberman. Written by John Tomerlin. CBS, January 24, 1964.

75. See Daniel Jones, "Alexa, will we divorce?," *The Sun*, November 29, 2018, www.thesun.co.uk/tech/7854556/virtual-assistants-amazon-alexa-relationship-break-up/

76. Ibid.

77. Hayley Matthews, "Online Dating Statistics: Dating Stats from 2017," *Zoosk*, December 3, 2017, www.zoosk.com/date-mix/online-dating-advice/online-dating-statistics-dating-stats-2017/

78. "Only 1 in 3 U.S. Marriage Proposals Are a Surprise; Engagement Ring Spend Rise, According to The Knot 2017 Jewelry and Engagement Study," *The Knot*, November 9, 2017, https://www.prnewswire.com/news-releases/only-1-in-3-us-marriage-proposals-are-a-surprise-engagement-ring-spend-rises-according-to-the-knot-2017-jewelry—engagement-study-300552669.html

79. Hayley Matthews, "Online Dating Statistics: Dating Stats from 2017," *Zoosk*, December 3, 2017, www.zoosk.com/date-mix/online-dating-advice/online-dating-statistics-dating-stats-2017/

80. Ibid.

81. Ibid., referencing Janet Burns, "There's Now Evidence That Online Dating Causes Stronger, More Diverse Marriages," *Forbes*, October 25, 2017, www.forbes.com/sites/janetwburns/2017/10/25/theres-now-evidence-that-online-dating-causes-stronger-more-diverse-relationships/#760adde58bdf

82. "Online Dating—Statistics & Facts," www.statistica.com/topics/2158/online-dating/

83. Telegraph Reporters, "Online dating ad banned after scientific claims were dismissed as 'fake news,'" *The Telegraph*, January 3, 2018, www.telegraph.co.uk/news/2018/01/03/online-dating-ad-banned-scientific-claims-dismissed-fake-news/

eHarmony touts itself as the "#1 Trusted Dating Site for Like-Minded Singles."

84. Algorithms are frequently employed in the context of sports predictions. For example, a "proven" computer model runs through 10,000 simulations for NFL games and "has been very accurate" in terms of its game predictions. See CBS Sports Staff, "Cowboys vs. Giants Odds: Sunday Night Football Picks, Predictions from Proven Model on 51–35 Run," *CBS Sports*, September 16, 2018, https://www.cbssports.com/nfl/news/cowboys-vs-giants-odds-sunday-night-football-picks-predictions-from-proven-model-on-51-35-run/

85. See Jess Commons, "*Black Mirror*'s Charlie Brooker: 'I Feel Sorry for Millennials. You get a Bad Rep!,'" *Grazia*, October 22, 2016, https://graziadaily.co.uk/life/tv-and-film/black-mirror-season-3-charlie-brooker-san-junipero/

86. See "Actus Reus," *Legal Information Institute, Cornell University*, https://www.law.cornell.edu/wex/actus_reus

See "Mens Rea," *Legal Information Institute, Cornell University*, https://www.law.cornell.edu/wex/mens_rea

87. See Brandenburg v. Ohio, 395 U.S. 444 (1969) (holding that inflammatory speech cannot be prohibited by the government unless

such speech is "directed to inciting or producing imminent lawless action and is likely to incite or produce such action."

88. While the elements of murder crimes differ by jurisdiction, first degree murder typically requires willfulness, premeditation and malice aforethought. See "First-Degree Murder," *Justia*, https://www.justia.com/criminal/offenses/homicide/first-degree-murder/ Second degree murder, by contrast, requires intentionality and malice aforethought, but is not premeditated or planned. See "Second-Degree Murder," *Justia*, https://www.justia.com/criminal/offenses/homicide/second-degree-murder/

89. See www.criminal-law.freeadvice.com

90. Under U.S. criminal law, this is the standard for determining whether behavior is negligent. See "Standards of Care and the 'Reasonable Person,'" *FindLaw*, www.injury.findlaw.com/accident-injury-law/standards-of-care-and-the-reasonable-person.html

91. The "but-for" causation tests asks "'but for the existence of X, would Y have occurred?' If the answer is yes, then factor X is an actual cause of result Y." "But-for test," *Legal Information Institute, Cornell Law School*, www.law.cornell.edu/wex/but-for_test

Proximate cause is defined as "an actual cause that is also legally sufficient to support liability.... The likelihood of calling something a proximate cause increases as the cause becomes more direct and more necessary for the injury to occur." "Proximate cause," *Legal Information Institute, Cornell Law School*, www.law.cornell.edu/wex/proximate_cause

As an aside, subject to certain limited exceptions, Internet users have no legal duty to warn a target about a threat.

92. Conspiracy requires the following elements: (1) a demonstration that two or more individuals agreed to commit a crime; (2) the conspirators all must possess the specific intent to commit the objective of the conspiracy; and (3) in most states, an "overt act" taken in furtherance of the crime. See "Conspiracy," *Justia*, www.justia.com/criminal/offenses/inchoate-crimes/conspiracy/

93. See Jess Commons, "*Black Mirror*'s Charlie Brooker: 'I Feel Sorry for Millennials. You get a Bad Rep!,'" *Grazia*, October 22, 2016, https://graziadaily.co.uk/life/tv-and-film/black-mirror-season-3-charlie-brooker-sanjunipero/

94. Alex Mulane, "*Black Mirror* Season 3: 'Hated in the Nation' review: a blockbuster with a sting in its tail," *Digital Spy*, October 23, 2016, http://www.digitalspy.com/tv/black-mirror/news/a811894/black-mirror-season-3-hated-in-the-nation-review/

95. See Maureen Dowd, "Elon Musk's Billion-Dollar Crusade to Stop the A.I. Apocalypse," *Vanity Fair*, April 2017, https://www.vanityfair.com/news/2017/03/elon-musk-billion-dollar-crusade-to-stop-ai-space-x

Popular culture has explored the potential utilization of powerful software to predict the future, allowing others to know what actions folks will take before they happen. The film *Minority Report* (2002), for example, envisions a futuristic world where psychic technology is employed (in a special "pre-crime division") to arrest and convict would-be murderers before the crime is committed. The film explores issues such as the relationship between free will and determinism. Note that like the *Electric Dreams* series, *Minority Report* was based on a short story penned by Philip K. Dick. See *Minority Report*. Directed by Steven Spielberg. 20th Century FOX / DreamWorks Pictures, 2002. Films focused on time-travel frequently touch on these issues as well. If a third-party can go back in time and effectively change the course of history by altering certain events, is it accurate to suggest that folks have free will at all? See, for example, *Déjà Vu*. Directed by Tony Scott. Buena Vista Pictures, November 22, 2006.

96. *Nerve*. Directed by Henry Joost and Ariel Schulman. Lionsgate, July 12, 2016. The data gathering featured in this film is reminiscent of the collection of real-time data to determine folks' fears in "Playtest."

Chapter 4

1. C.S. Lewis, *The Weight of Glory* (New York: HarperOne, 1949), 161.

2. It is ironic that Ron Swanson is part of a mockumentary where his daily actions are filmed!

3. Hannah Arendt, *The Human Condition* (Chicago: University of Chicago Press, 1958), 71 (cited in Calo, "People Can Be So Fake," 842.

4. Ayn Rand, *The Fountainhead* (New York: Bobbs Merrill, 1943), 669.

5. Alan Westin, *Privacy and Freedom* (New York: Atheneum, 1967), 35 (cited in Calo, "People Can Be So Fake, 813).

6. Director Euros Lyn observes that protagonist in the episode (Bing) expresses his "existential rage at this meaningless world and the way it's [sic] imprisoned its citizens." Charlie Brooker, Annabel Jones and Jason Arnopp, *Inside Black Mirror* (New York: Crown Archetype, 2018), 43.

Notes—Chapter 4

7. *The Show*. Directed by Giancarlo Esposito. Grindstone Entertainment Group, March 11, 2017.

8. *Curb Your Enthusiasm*. "The Doll." Episode No. 17. Directed by Robert Weide. Written by Larry David. HBO, November 4, 2001.

9. *The Simpsons*. "When You Dish Upon A Star." Episode No. 208, Prod. 5F19. Directed by Pete Michels. Written by Richard Appel. FOX, November 8, 1998.

10. *The Office*. "Promos." Episode No. 193, Prod. 9018. Directed by Jennifer Celotta. Written by Tim McAuliffe. NBC, April 4, 2013.

11. Calo, "People Can Be So Fake," 847, citing "Editorial, Enter Search Term Here, Forever," *The New York Times*, August 21, 2006, A16.

12. Jeffrey Dastin, "'Kill your foster parents': Amazon's Alexa talks murder, sex in AI experiment," *Reuters*, December 21, 2018, www.reuters.com/article/us-amazon-com-alexa-insight/kill-your-foster-parents-amazons-alexa-talks-murder-sx-in-ai-experiment-idUSKCN1)K1AJ

13. Olivia Solon, "Amazon patents wristband that tracks warehouse workers' movements," *The Guardian*, January 31, 2018, www.theguardian.com/technology/2018/jan/31/amazon-warehouse-wristband-tracking

14. In this segment of "White Christmas," the man appears to have consented to his privacy being invaded but the woman has not done so.

15. *Inception*. Directed by Christopher Nolan. Warner Bros. Pictures, July 8, 2010.

16. In "Kill All Others," Philbert's wife even has a sexual relationship with a digital image from one of the advertisements.

See Daniel Jones, "Alexa, will we divorce?," *The Sun*, November 29, 2018, www.thesun.co.uk/tech/7854556/virtual-assistants-amazon-alexa-relationship-break-up/

17. Calo, "People Can Be So Fake," 815.

18. See generally, Calo, "People Can Be So Fake."

19. Clara Shih, "Hearsay Social CEO Clara Shih: 5 tech trends to watch in 2015," *Fortune*, January 28, 2015, www.fortune.com/2015/01/28/hearsay-social-ceo-clara-shih-5-tech-trends-to-watch-in-2015/

20. See "Meme," me.me/i/1998-don't-get-in-a-car-with-strangers-2008-don't-e17714799d0e4cb6a9823247ef06df90

21. *The Twilight Zone*. "A Penny For Your Thoughts." Episode No. 52, Prod. 173–3650. Directed by James Sheldon. Written by George Clayton Johnson. CBS, February 13, 1961.

22. "The Hood Maker" muddies the water with respect to this point. In reading thoughts, it seems as if Teeps may have the ability to learn (and even experience, accompanied by physical manifestations) folks' feelings and emotions. But their ability in this regard is questionable.

23. *The Twilight Zone*. "People Are Alike All Over." Episode No. 25, Prod. 173–3613. Directed by Mitchell Leisen. Written by Rod Serling. CBS, March 25, 1960.

24. *The Twilight Zone*. "Where Is Everybody?" Episode No. 1, Prod. 173–3601. Directed by Robert Stevens. Written by Rod Serling. CBS, October 2, 1959.

25. *The Twilight Zone*. "Time Enough at Last." Episode No. 8, Prod. 173–3614. Directed by John Brahm. Written by Rod Serling. CBS, November 20, 1959.

26. The messaging in "Time Enough at Last" is a bit more nuanced. On the one hand, the episode explores the value of serenity, but on the other hand pushes back against the idea that there may be any inherent value in an isolated existence.

27. *Futurama*. "A Fishful of Dollars." Episode No. 6, Prod. 1ACV06. Directed by Ron Hughart and Gregg Vanzo. Written by Patric M. Verrone. FOX, April 27, 1999.

28. *The Simpsons*. "New Kids on the Blecch." Episode No. 262, Prod. CABF12. Directed by Steven Dean Moore. Written by Tim Long. FOX, February 25, 2001; *Saved by the Bell*. "The Zack Tapes." Episode No. 14. Directed by Don Barnhart. Written by Peter Engel and Tom Tenowich. NBC, December 2, 1989.

29. George Orwell, *1984* (London: Secker and Warburg, 1949).

30. See www.brainyquote.com/quotes/anselm_kiefer_334618

31. See www.brainyquote.com/quotes/arthur_m_schlesinger_109503

32. See www.quotes.net/quote/52460

33. Maya Kosoff, "Apple Predicts *Black Mirror* Memory Implants Could Soon Be a Reality," *Vanity Fair*, April 25, 2017, https://www.vanityfair.com/news/2017/04/apple-exec-predicts-black-mirror-tech-could-soon-be-a-reality

34. Ibid.

35. *Homecoming*. Amazon Video, November 2, 2018–present.

36. See generally, Calo, "People Can Be So Fake."

37. *Altered Carbon*. Netflix, February 2, 2018–present.

38. *Eternal Sunshine of the Spotless Mind*. Directed by Michael Gondry. Focus Features, March 19, 2004; *Homecoming*. Amazon Video, November 2, 2018–present; *Westworld*. HBO Entertainment, October 2, 2016–present.

Notes—Chapter 4

39. Thomas Fuller, *The Holy State and the Profane State* (California: University of California Libraries, 1841), 174.

40. Elie Wiesel, "A God Who Remembers," *NPR*, April 7, 2008, www.npr.org/2008/04/07/89357808/a-god-who-remembers

41. Brooker raises other potential concerns with "the grain," pointing out that it could be used to violate copyright laws. Folks could, for example, watch a movie at a theater and record and store it in their grain and could then decide to share it with others. See Charlie Brooker, Annabel Jones and Jason Arnopp, *Inside Black Mirror* (New York: Crown Archetype, 2018), 52.

42. *Eternal Sunshine of the Spotless Mind*. Directed by Michael Gondry. Focus Features, March 19, 2004.

43. *The Twilight Zone*. "The Lateness of the Hour." Episode No. 44, Prod. 173–3652. Directed by Jack Smight. Written by Rod Serling. CBS, December 2, 1960.

44. Regarding the unreliability of memories, Canadian psychologist Steven Pinker observes that "Cognitive psychology tells us that the unaided human mind is vulnerable to many fallacies and illusions because of its reliance on its memory for vivid anecdotes rather than systematic statistics." See John Naughton, "Steven Pinker: Fighting Talk from the Prophet of Peace," *The Guardian*, October 15, 2011, www.theguardian.com/science/2011/oct/15/steven-pinker-better-angels-violence-interview

45. See brainyquote.com/quotes/Aeschylus_383359

46. *Eternal Sunshine of the Spotless Mind*. Directed by Michael Gondry. Focus Features, March 19, 2004.

47. *Homecoming*. Amazon Video, November 2, 2018–present.

48. Ibid.

49. Charlie Brooker, Annabel Jones and Jason Arnopp, *Inside Black Mirror* (New York: Crown Archetype, 2018), 56.

50. Ibid.

51. See brainyquote.com/quotes/susumu_tonegawa_731820

52. See brainyquote.com/quotes/Michael_de_montaigne_138368

53. See brainyquote.com/quotes/john_dewey_163896

54. Travis Clark, "All 19 Episodes of '*Black Mirror*' Ranked from Worst to Best," *Business Insider*, September 10, 2018, https://www.businessinsider.com/every-black-mirror-episode-on-netflix-ranked-from-worst-to-best-2018-5

55. See brainyquote.com/quotes/barbara_kingsolver_161793

56. Alexa Lardieri, "Amazon Employees Protesting Sale of Facial Recognition Software," *U.S. News & World Report*, October 18, 2018, www.usnews.com/news/politics/articles/2018-10-18/amazon-employees-protesting-sale-of-facial-recognition-software

If successful, this approach could usher in a new paradigm: instead of relying on laws or regulations, could corporations effectively self-police themselves by giving employees an active voice in terms of what technology the company should produce and sell?

57. *The Twilight Zone*. "Uncle Simon." Episode No. 128, Prod. 2604. Directed by Don Siegel. Written by Rod Serling. CBS, November 15, 1963.

58. Harvey Solomon-Brady, "Sex doll rental company will make a replica of your dead lover," *New York Post*, October 16, 2018, www.nypost.com/2018/10/16/sex-doll-rental-company-will-make-a-replica-of-your-dead-lover/

Not surprisingly, there is some resistance from various corners to the use of robots to fulfill sexual desires. And politicians have expressed their discomfort with the idea of robot sex brothels opening in their communities. See, for example, Benjamin Brown, "'Robot sex brothel' slated to open is not wanted, Houston's mayor says," *FOX News*, September 26, 2018, www.foxnews.com/tech/robot-sex-brothel-slated-to-open-is-not-wanted-houstons-mayor-says

59. See Bobby Hellard, "How an episode of *Black Mirror* became a creepy reality," *i-D vice*, November 13, 2018, https://i-d.vice.com/en_uk/article/nepbdg/black-mirror-artificial-intelligence-roman-mazurenko

Charlotte Runius, the CEO and founder of Fenix, the company planning to produce this technology: "We have this vision, that when you are old and lonely because your spouse has passed away, you can put on your virtual reality goggles and go have breakfast with them. Of course, you know it's not for real, but we see it more like a computer game really."

60. See Bobby Hellard, "How an episode of *Black Mirror* became a creepy reality," *i-D vice*, November 13, 2018, https://i-d.vice.com/en_uk/article/nepbdg/black-mirror-artificial-intelligence-roman-mazurenko

61. Marshall McLuhan and Lewis H. Lapham, *Understanding Media: The Extensions of Man* (Cambridge: The MIT Press, reprint, 1994), 7.

62. *The Office*. "The Lover." Episode No. 107, Prod. 607. Directed by Lee Eisenberg. Written by Lee Eisenberg and Gene Stupnitsky. NBC, October 22, 2009.

63. Calo, "People Can Be So Fake," 842 (quoting Julie E. Cohen, "Examined Lives: Informational Privacy and the Subject as Object," 52 Stanford Law Review 1373 (2000): 1426).

64. *Calo, "People Can Be So Fake," 854.*

65. *Ibid.*, 843 (quoting Charles Fried, "Privacy," 77 Yale Law Journal 475 (1968): 483–484).

66. Riley V. California, 573 U.S. _ (2014).

67. Suzanne Barlyn, "John Hancock will only sell interactive life insurance with fitness data tracking," *Insurance Journal,* September 19, 2018, https://www.insurancejournal.com/news/national/2018/09/19/501747.htm

68. Charlie Brooker, Annabel Jones and Jason Arnopp, *Inside Black Mirror* (New York: Crown Archetype, 2018), 255.

69. Alan Westin, *Privacy and Freedom* (New York: Atheneum, 1968), 7.

70. John Twelve Hawks, "New surveillance states have placed us in an invisible prison," *Salon,* September 15, 2014, www.salon.com/2014/09/14/john_twelve_hawks_new_surveillance_states_have_placed_us_in_an_invisible_prison/

71. Amit Regev, "Drone Deliveries are No Longer Pie in the Sky," *Forbes,* April 10, 2018, www.forbes.com/sites/startupnationcentral/2018/04/10/drone-deliveries-are-no-longer-pie-in-the-sky/#30ac02cc4188

72. See "A Selection of Supreme Court Cases Involving the Fourth Amendment & the Body," *American Bar Association,* undated, www.americanbar.org/content/dam/aba/images-.../BodySearchCases_list.docx

See also "Your Fourth Amendment Rights: Landmark Cases," *Judicial Learning Center,* undated, www.judiciallearningcenter.org/your-4th-amendment-rights/

Veronia School District 47J v. Acton, 515 U.S. 646 (1995); New Jersey v. T.L.O., 469 U.S. 325 (1985); Terry v. Ohio, 392 U.S. 1 (1968); United States v. Dionisio, 410 U.S. 1 (1973); United States v. Mara, 410 U.S. 19 (1973); United States v. Jones, 565 U.S. 400 (2012); Maryland v. King, 569 U.S. 435 (2013); Florida v. Jardines, 569 U.S. 1 (2013); Riley v. California, 573 U.S. _ (2014).

73. See Calo, 818 (quoting Will Thomas Devries, "Protecting Privacy in the Digital Age," 18 Berkeley Technology Law Journal 283 (2003): 285).

74. Curt Levey, "Supreme Court Ruling in cell phone case is a victory for our privacy rights," Foxnewswww, June 22, 2018, https://www.foxnews.com/opinion/supreme-court-ruling-in-cell-phone-case-is-a-victory-for-our-privacy-rights

75. See Calo, "People Can Be So Fake," 818 (quoting Orin Kerr, "Applying the Fourth Amendment to the Internet: A General Approach," Stanford Law Review (2009): 7.

76. Calo, "People Can Be So Fake," 814.

77. Carpenter v. United States, 484 U.S. _ (2018).

78. See Nina Totenberg, "In Major Privacy Win, Supreme Court Rules Police Need Warrant to Track Your Cellphone," *NPR,* June 22, 2018, https://www.npr.org/2018/06/22/605007387/supreme-court-rules-police-need-warrant-to-get-location-information-from-cell-to

79. *Ibid.*

80. *Ibid.*

81. *Ibid.*

82. *Ibid.*

83. Judge Learned Hand, "The Spirit of Liberty" speech, 1944, https://www.btboces.org/Downloads/1_The%20Spirit%20of%20Liberty%20by%20Learned%20Hand.pdf

84. See Minda Zetlin, "The 9 Most Weird and Hilarious Questions Congress Asked Mark Zuckerberg," Incwww, April 12, 2018, https://www.inc.com/minda-zetlin/mark-zuckerberg-congress-hearings-funny-stupid-questions.html

85. Justin Keslowitz, interviewed by Steven Keslowitz via email, November 29, 2018.

86. See Steven Levy, "Bill Gates and President Bill Clinton on the NSA, Safe Sex, and American Exceptionalism," *Wired,* November 12, 2013, www.wired.com/2013/11/bill-gates-bill-clinton-wired/

87. See Editorial, "The Guardian view on Internet privacy: it's the psychology, stupid," *The Guardian,* February 8, 2018, www.theguardian.com/global/commentisfree/2018/feb/08/the-guardian-view-on-internet-privacy-its-the-psychology-stupid

88. "Privacy and Technology," *ACLU,* undated, www.aclu.org/issues/privacy-technology

89. *Ibid.*

90. *The Twilight Zone.* "The Obsolete Man." Episode No. 65, Prod. 173-3661. Directed by Elliot Silverstein. Written by Rod Serling. CBS, June 2, 1961.

91. See generally Giorgio Agamben, *State of Exception,* trans. Kevin Attell (Chicago: University of Chicago Press, 2015).

92. *24.* "Day 7: 3:00 pm–4:00 pm." Episode No. 152, Prod. 7AFF08. Directed by Milan Cheylov. Written by Robert Cochran and Evan Katz. FOX, February 9, 2009.

93. Amitai Etzioni, *How Patriotic Is the Patriot Act: Freedom versus Security in the Age of Terrorism* (New York: Routledge, 2005), 11.

94. George Orwell, *1984* (London: Secker and Warburg, 1949); *The Twilight Zone.* "The Jeopardy Room." Episode No. 149, Prod. 2639.

Directed by Richard Donner. Written by Rod Serling. CBS, April 17, 1964.

95. Calo, "People Can Be So Fake," 824–825.

96. The strategies used by the elites in "Kill All Others" and "1984" bear striking resemblances to each other. In "1984," the government shows the hanging of free thinkers; in "Kill All Others," hanging folks next to a billboard displaying the words 'Kill All Others' is intended for public consumption.

97. Alan Dershowitz, "Should we fight terror with torture?," *Independent*, July 3, 2006, www.independent.co.uk/news/world/americas/alan-dershowitz-should-we-fight-terror-with-torture-6096463.html

98. Alan Dershowitz, "An op-ed by Professor Alan Dershowitz: warming up to torture?," *Harvard Law Today*, October 7, 2006, www.today.law.harvard.edu/an-op-ed-by-professor-alan-dershowitz-warming-up-to-torture/

99. Ibid.

100. *Google Dictionary*, s.v. "categorical imperative," accessed December 1, 2018.

101. Alan Dershowitz, "An op-ed by Professor Alan Dershowitz: warming up to torture?," *Harvard Law Today*, October 7, 2006, www.today.law.harvard.edu/an-op-ed-by-professor-alan-dershowitz-warming-up-to-torture/

102. Ibid.

103. Bright line rules in other contexts are frequently unworkable. For example, while the unfettered right to enter into contracts is considered by many to be of paramount importance in a robust democracy, courts and legislators have taken a practical approach to the issue, softening the concept by adding exceptions such as unconscionability, detrimental reliance and duress to address potential unfavorable and inequitable results for consumers and others. Liability waivers, discussed herein, are a prime example on the rules regarding the enforceability (or lack thereof) of certain contracts on public policy grounds.

104. See "Google Terms of Service—Privacy & Terms," last modified October 25, 2017, https://policies.google.com/terms?hl=en.

105. See Rainbow Country Rentals and Retail, Inc. v. Ameritech Publishing, Inc., 205 Wis. 153 (2005), para. 35.

Chapter 5

1. See "Holy Hill Hermitage," www.holyhill.ie/hafiz-of-shiraz/

2. Plato, *The Allegory of the Cave*, trans. Benjamin Jowett (Los Angeles: Enhanced Media, 2017), from Book VII of Plato, *The Republic*, trans. Jowett, first published in 1888.

3. We often have difficulty understanding and articulating differences of experiences in our existing world. Michael Peterson—the man accused of murdering his wife and subject of the Nexflix documentary *The Staircase* (2018)—struggles to explain the differences between life in prison and life on the outside to those who never experienced life in prison. *The Staircase*. "The Last Chance." Episode No. 10. Directed by Jean-Xavier de Lestrade. Maha Productions, November 21, 2013.

4. *The Twilight Zone* episodes:
"Walking Distance." Episode No. 5, Prod. 173-3605. Directed by Robert Stevens. Written by Rod Serling. CBS, October 30, 1959; "Person or Persons Unknown." Episode No. 92, Prod. 4829. Directed by John Brahm. Written by Charles Beaumont. CBS, March 23, 1962;"The Mind and the Matter." Episode No. 63, Prod. 173–3659. Directed by Buzz Kulik. Written by Rod Serling. CBS, May 12, 1961;"Valley of the Shadow." Episode No. 105, Prod. 3861. Directed by Perry Lafferty. Written by Charles Beaumont. CBS, January 17, 1963;"Five Characters in Search of An Exit." Episode No. 79, Prod. 4805. Directed by Lamont Johnson. Written by Rod Serling. CBS, December 22, 1961; "A Quality of Mercy." Episode No. 80, Prod. 4809. Directed by Buzz Kulik. Written by Rod Serling. CBS, December 29, 1961; "The Hunt." Episode No. 84, Prod. 4810. Directed by Harold Schuster. Written by Earl Hamner, Jr. CBS, January 26, 1962.

5. *The Twilight Zone*. "One More Pallbearer." Episode No. 82, Prod. 4823. Directed by Lamont Johnson. Written by Rod Serling. CBS, January 12, 1962.

6. The episode shows a post-wartime application of sensory-altering technology. This technology is also used by the government to control and formulate dreams. Once an individual gives consent to have the MASS implant, the way in which they view the world is at the sole discretion of those in power. The government retains the ability to remove one's eyesight or force the soldier to watch unadulterated recordings of the soldier's real actions—the brutal killing of poor people. Removal of the implant after the initial consent is not an option. Imprisonment or resettling of the MASS implant system are the soldier's only options. A person's reality is effectively controlled by the government.

7. *The Matrix*. Directed by Lana Wachowski and Lilly Wachowski. Warner Bros., March 31, 1999.

8. *The Twilight Zone.* "Shadow Play." Episode No. 62, Prod. 173–3657. John Brahm. Written by Charles Beaumont. CBS, May 5, 1961.

9. *The Twilight Zone.* "Stopover in a Quiet Town." Episode No. 150, Prod. 2611. Directed by Ron Winston. Written by Earl Hamner, Jr. CBS, April 24, 1964.

10. *Groundhog Day.* Directed by Harold Ramis. Columbia Pictures, February 12, 1993.

11. *50 First Dates.* Directed by Peter Segal. Columbia Pictures, February 13, 2004.

12. *The Wolfpack.* Directed by Crystal Moselle. Kotva Films, January 25, 2015.

13. Sara Stewart, "Locked up for 14 years, these brothers learned everything they know from 5,000 movies," *New York Post*, June 9, 2015, www.nypost.com/2015/06/09/how-6-brothers-learned-about-the-world-by-watching-5000-movies/

14. *Blast from the Past.* Directed by Hugh Wilson. New Line Cinema, February 12, 1999.

15. *The Game.* Directed by David Fincher. Propaganda Films, September 12, 1997.

16. *Wayward Pines.* 20th Century FOX Television, May 14, 2015–July 27, 2016.

17. *Total Recall.* Directed by Paul Verhoeven. TriStar Pictures, June 1, 1990.

18. *Maniac.* Netflix, September 21, 2018.

19. *Homecoming.* Amazon Video, November 2, 2018–present.

20. *The Twilight Zone.* "The Monsters are Due on Maple Street." Episode No. 22, Prod. 173–3620. Directed by Ronald Winston. Written by Rod Serling. CBS, March 4, 1960.

21. *The Twilight Zone.* "The Shelter." Episode No. 68, Prod. 4803. Directed by Lamont Johnson. Written by Rod Serling. CBS, September 29, 1961.

22. *The Simpsons.* "Bart's Comet." Episode No. 117, Prod. 2F11. Directed by Bob Anderson. Written by John Swartzwelder. FOX, February 5, 1995.

23. *The Truman Show.* Directed by Peter Weir. Paramount Pictures, June 1, 1998.

24. Jon Austin, "Is this the true meaning of life? Shock theory could change how we view the world forever," *Daily Express*, May 20, 2017, www.express.co.uk/news/weird/807193/meaning-of-life-scientists-virtual-world-theory-Elon-Musk-Rich-Terrile-Neil-deGrasse-Tyson

25. Ibid.
26. Ibid.
27. Ibid.
28. Ibid.
29. Ibid.

30. *The Twilight Zone.* "In His Image." Episode No. 103, Prod. 4851. Directed by Perry Lafferty. Written by Charles Beaumont. CBS, January 3, 1963.

31. "San Junipero" has been widely praised, earning five stars out of five in publications such as *Irish Independent* and an "A" from *The A.V. Club*. Zack Handlen stated that the episode is "one of the best hours of television" in 2016. Zack Handlen, "*Black Mirror* finds love (and a great episode) in a hopeful place," *The A.V. Club*, October 24, 2016, www.tv.avclub.com/black-mirror-finds-love-and-a-great-episode-in-a-hope-1798189275

32. The show won, among other accolades, two Primetime Emmy Awards, including the Primetime Emmy Award for Outstanding Television Movie. See Jacob Stolworthy, "Emmys 2017: *Black Mirror* Episode 'San Junipero' wins two awards," *The Independent*, September 18, 2017, https://www.independent.co.uk/arts-entertainment/tv/news/emmys-2017-winners-black-mirror-san-junipero-charlie-brooker-outstanding-writing-tv-movie-a7952266.html

33. Television critics cheered the show's messages and tone. For example, *Guardian* critic Benjamin Lee praised its "surprising and ultimately poignant" nature, while *GQ*'s Scott Meslow called it "breathtakingly and tear-jerkingly human." And *Esquire*'s Corey Atad predicted that viewers would cry while watching the episode. See Benjamin Lee, "*Black Mirror* Review—Charlie Brooker's splashy new series is still a sinister marvel," *The Guardian*, September 16, 2016, www.theguardian.com/tv-and-radio/2016/sep/16/black-mirror-first-look-review-charlie-brooker; Scott Meslow, "The Best TV Episodes of 2016," *GQ*, December 15, 2016, www.gq.com/story/best-tv-2016; Corey Atad, "Every Episode of *Black Mirror*, Ranked," *Esquire*, December 29, 2017, www.esquire.com/entertainment/tv/a49919/black-mirror-episodes-ranked/

34. Age and physical disability in the real world are irrelevant and disregarded in San Junipero. In the real world, one of the women (Yorkie) was paralyzed at age 21 after crashing her car. This occurred as a direct result of her parents' negative reaction to her coming out as a lesbian.

35. Yorkie's parents strongly disapproved of her sexual orientation.

36. For further discussion of this technology, see Joshua Rothman, "Are We Already Living in Virtual Reality?," *The New Yorker*, April 2, 2018, www.newyorker.com/magazine/2018/04/02/are-we-already-living-in-virtual-reality Rothman discusses virtual embodiment research conducted by virtual reality researchers Mel Slater and Mavi Sanchez-Vives, among others, in con-

nection with the Virtual Embodiment and Robotic Re-Embodiment project. He describes the goal of virtual embodiment as "convincing you that you are someone else."

37. Joshua Rothman, "Are We Already Living in Virtual Reality?," *The New Yorker*, April 2, 2018, www.newyorker.com/magazine/2018/04/02/are-we-already-living-in-virtual-reality; Per Mel Slater: "On some level, the brain doesn't know the difference between real reality and virtual reality".

38. *Altered Carbon*. Netflix, February 2, 2018–present.

39. See Dom Galeon and Christianna Reedy, "Kurzweil Claims that the Singularity Will Happen by 2045," *Futurism*, October 5, 2017, https://futurism.com/kurzweil-claims-that-the-singularity-will-happen-by-2045/ (quoting from Kurzweil's speech during the 2017 SXSW Conference in Austin, Texas, March 2017).

40. Quoted in Marlow Stern, "Inside 'San Junipero': The Magical '*Black Mirror*' Episode That Will Help Take Your Mind Off Trump," *The Daily Beast*, November 27, 2016, www.thedailybeast.com/inside-san-junipero-the-magical-black-mirror-episode-that-will-help-take-your-mind-off-trump

41. Elizabeth Howell, "Parallel Universes: Theories and Evidence," Spacewww, May 9, 2018, www.space.com/32728-parallel-universes.html

42. Ethan Siegel, "Is There Another 'You' Out There in a Parallel Universe," *Forbes*, November 18, 2016, https://www.forbes.com/sites/startswithabang/2016/11/18/is-there-another-you-out-there-in-a-parallel-universe/#79f5b11a634f

43. Ibid.

44. Elizabeth Howell, "Parallel Universes: Theories and Evidence," Spacewww, May 9, 2018, www.space.com/32728-parallel-universes.html

45. Ibid.

46. Ethan Siegel, "Is There Another 'You' Out There in a Parallel Universe," *Forbes*, November 18, 2016, https://www.forbes.com/sites/startswithabang/2016/11/18/is-there-another-you-out-there-in-a-parallel-universe/#79f5b11a634f

47. Ibid.

48. *The Simpsons*. "Treehouse of Horror V." Episode No. 109, Prod. 2F03. Directed by Jim Reardon. Written by Greg Daniels et al. FOX, October 30, 1994.

49. *Back to the Future*. Directed by Robert Zemeckis. Universal Pictures, July 3, 1985.

50. See Elizabeth Howell, "Parallel Universes: Theories and Evidence," Spacewww, May 9, 2018, www.space.com/32728-parallel-universes.html for a list of other examples throughout pop culture where parallel universes have been examined.

51. The original *Choose Your Own Adventure* book series was published Bantam Books from 1979–1998 and consists of 184 titles.

52. See Jesse Damiani, "*Black Mirror*: Bandersnatch Could Become Netflix's Secret Marketing Weapon," *The Verge*, January 2, 2019, https://www.theverge.com/2019/1/2/18165182/black-mirror-bandersnatch-netflix-interactive-strategy-marketing

53. Maureen Ryan et al., "Bandersnatch Has Many Paths But Do Any of Them Add Up to Anything?," *The New York Times*, January 4, 2019, https://www.nytimes.com/2019/01/04/arts/television/bandersnatch-black-mirror-netflix.html

54. See Jesse Damiani, "*Black Mirror*: Bandersnatch Could Become Netflix's Secret Marketing Weapon," *The Verge*, January 2, 2019, https://www.theverge.com/2019/1/2/18165182/black-mirror-bandersnatch-netflix-interactive-strategy-marketing

55. "The Ultimate Quotation Repository," www.quodIbid.com/quotes/1400/max-frisch/technology-is-a-way-of-organizing-the-universe

56. *The Flintstones*. ABC, September 30, 1960–April 1, 1966.

57. Anthony Scibelli, "Why *The Flintstones* Takes Place in a Post-Apocalyptic Future," *Cracked*, June 20, 2012, www.cracked.com/quick-fixes/why-flintstones-takes-place-in-post-apocalyptic-future/

58. Jordan Minor, "*The Flintstones* Internet of Living Things," Geekwww, January 30, 2017, www.geek.com/tech/the-flintstones-internet-of-living-things-1686807/

59. Monica Kim, "The Good and the Bad of Escaping to Virtual Reality," *The Atlantic*, February 8, 2015, www.theatlantic/com/health/archive/2015/02/the-good-and-the-bad-of-escaping-to-virtual-reality/385134

Popular movies have explored the potentiality of the occurrence of this phenomenon. In the film *Lawnmower Man* (1992), for example, a man enters a mainframe computer, abandoning his physical body and transforming into a virtual being.

60. "Virtual Reality vs. Augmented Reality," *Augment*, October 6, 2015, www.augment.com/blog/virtual-reality-vs-augmented-reality/

61. Ibid.

62. Ken Hillis, *Digital Sensations: Space, Identity, and Embodiment in Virtual Reality* (Minneapolis: University of Minnesota Press, 1999), vii.

63. "Virtual Reality vs. Augmented Reality," *Augment*, October 6, 2015, www.augment.com/blog/virtual-reality-vs-augmented-reality/
64. *Ibid.*
65. See, e.g., Dave Lee, "Pokemon Go: Hiding Pikachu may hold key to AR's future," *BBC News*, June 28, 2018, www.bbc.com/news/technology-44638604
66. See "The Ultimate Guide to Mixed Reality (MR) Technology," www.realitytechnologies.com/mixed-reality
67. Reenita Das, "Virtual Reality: The Alternative to Marijuana and Opioids for Pain Management," *Forbes*, May 31, 2018, www.forbes.com/sites/reenitadas/2018/05/31/virtual-reality-the-alternative-to-marijuana-and-opioids-for-pain-management/#1af0f7d151d6
68. *Ibid.*
69. *Ibid.*
70. David Evans Bailey, "Ten Cool Applications for virtual reality that aren't just games," *The Conversation*, March 22, 2016, www.theconversation.com/ten-cool-applications-for-virtual-reality-that-arent-just-games-56365
71. *Ibid.*
72. *Ibid.*
73. *Other Life*. Directed by Ben C. Lucas. See Pictures, June 16, 2017.
74. *The Matrix*. Directed by Lana Wachowski and Lilly Wachowski. Warner Bros., March 31, 1999.
75. *Ready Player One*. Directed by Steven Spielberg. Warner Bros. Pictures, March 11, 2018.
76. *Lawnmower Man*. Directed by Brett Leonard. New Line Cinema, March 6, 1992.
77. Billy Joel, *Sometimes a Fantasy*, Columbia Records, 1980.
78. The theme of powerful dreams as a source of conflating fiction with reality has been examined throughout popular culture, perhaps most famously in the film *The Wizard of Oz*, where Dorothy dreams that she leaves Kansas and enters Munchkinland. Dorothy's dream is an essential part of the narrative technique used in the film, as the audience only learns that her experience is a dream as a surprise twist at the end. See *The Wizard of Oz*. Directed by Victor Fleming, et al. Metro-Goldwyn-Mayer, 1939. Harold Arlen and Yip Harburg, *Over the Rainbow*, Judy Garland, The Wizard of Oz, 1939.
79. *The Twilight Zone*. "Walking Distance." Episode No. 5, Prod. 173-3605. Directed by Robert Stevens. Written by Rod Serling. CBS, October 30, 1959.
80. *The Twilight Zone* episodes:
"A Short Drink From a Certain Fountain." Episode No. 131, Prod. 2614. Directed by Bernard Girard. Written by Rod Serling. CBS, December 13, 1963; "The Bewitchin' Pool." Episode No. 156, Prod. 2619. Directed by Joseph M. Newman. Written by Earl Hamner, Jr. CBS, June 19, 1964; "The Mind and the Matter." Episode No. 63, Prod. 173-3659. Directed by Buzz Kulik. Written by Rod Serling. CBS, May 12, 1961; "Back There." Episode No. 49, Prod. 173-3648. Directed by David Orrick McDearon. Written by Rod Serling. CBS, January 13, 1961; "The Trouble with Templeton." Episode No. 45, Prod. 173-3649. Directed by Buzz Kulik. Written by E. Jack Newman. CBS, December 9, 1960; "A Stop at Willoughby." Episode No. 30, Prod. 173-3629. Directed by Robert Parrish. Written by Rod Serling. CBS, May 6, 1990; "Static." Episode No. 56, Prod. 173-3665. Directed by Buzz Kulik. Written by Charles Beaumont. CBS, March 10, 1961; "Miniature." Episode No. 110, Prod. 3862. Directed by Walter Grauman. Written by Charles Beaumont. CBS, February 21, 1963.
81. Bryan Cranston, *A Life In Parts* (New York: Scribner, reprint edition, 2017), 1-3.
82. *Ibid.*
83. *The Twilight Zone*. "A World of Difference." Episode No. 23, Prod. 173-3624. Directed by Ted Post. Written by Richard Matheson. CBS, March 11, 1960.
84. This idea is satirized in "The Theatre" portion of *The Twilight Zone: Rod Serling's Lost Classics* (1994), where a woman fails to escape her own reality while attempting to watch a fictional movie. Instead of seeing the movie, she sees past and future events from her own life appear onscreen. See *The Twilight Zone: Rod Serling's Lost Classics*. "The Theatre." Directed by Robert Markowitz. Written by Rod Serling et al. O'Hara—Horowitz Productions, May 19, 1994.
85. *The Office*. "Murder." Episode No. 110, Prod. 6010. Directed by Greg Daniels. Written by Daniel Chun. NBC, November 12, 2009.
86. *Kiss Me First*. Directed by Misha Manson-Smith. Kindle Entertainment, April 2, 2018-present.
87. Billy Joel, *Piano Man*, Columbia Records, 1973.
88. *The Twilight Zone*. "16 Millimeter Shrine." Episode No. 4, Prod. 173-3610. Directed by Mitchell Leisen. Written by Rod Serling. CBS, October 23, 1959.
89. Monica Kim, "The Good and the Bad of Escaping to Virtual Reality," *The Atlantic*, February 8, 2015, www.theatlantic/com/health/archive/2015/02/the-good-and-the-bad-of-escaping-to-virtual-reality/385134

90. Bailenson and Blascovich, *Infinite Reality*, 7.

91. Matt Burgess, "Digital Escapism: VR will allow us to live in the world we want to," *Factor*, October 14, 2014, www.factor-tech.com/connected-world/8747-digital-escapism-vr-will-allow-us-to-live-in-the-world-we-want-to/

92. Ibid.

93. Monica Kim, "The Good and the Bad of Escaping to Virtual Reality," *The Atlantic*, February 8, 2015, www.theatlantic/com/health/archive/2015/02/the-good-and-the-bad-of-escaping-to-virtual-reality/385134

94. Monica Kim, "The Good and the Bad of Escaping to Virtual Reality," *The Atlantic*, February 8, 2015, www.theatlantic.com/health/archive/2015/02/the-good-and-the-bad-of-escaping-to-virtual-reality/385134 (quoting "Parents sue game distributor over son's suicide," *China Daily*, May 12, 2006, www.chinadaily.com.cn/china/2006-05/12/content_588456.htm).

95. Ibid.

96. Consider, for example, the fact that some folks are color blind. Does this mean that "reality" as it exists for such individuals is less objectively "real" than the reality of those who see colors?

97. *The Office*. "Local Ad." Episode No. 62, Prod. 409. Directed by Jason Reitman. Written by B.J. Novak. NBC, October 25, 2007.

98. Dwight's colleague, Jim Halpert, creates an avatar to spy on Dwight—highlighting a lack of privacy even in virtual game universes.

99. The purpose of entering the altered state of reality is to take a "vacation" from her life. She needs a vacation because her fellow cops were killed, and she replays the event over in her mind. She needs a way to escape this trauma. In both dreams and virtual reality experiences, an individual could lose track of what constitutes reality. For example, future punishments for criminals may involve using a pill to cause a convicted criminal into believing they have served a 1,000 year sentence when only 8 actual hours have passed. See Rhiannon Williams, "Prisoners 'could serve 1,000 year sentence in eight hours,'" *The Telegraph*, March 14, 2014, www.telegraph.co.uk/technology/news/10697529/Prisoners-could-serve-1000-year-sentence-in-eight-hours.html

100. Bailenson and Blascovich, *Infinite Reality*, 1.

101. Ibid., 3.

102. *Kiss Me First*. Directed by Misha Manson-Smith. Kindle Entertainment, April 2, 2018–present.

103. Monica Kim, "The Good and the Bad of Escaping to Virtual Reality," *The Atlantic*, February 8, 2015, www.theatlantic/com/health/archive/2015/02/the-good-and-the-bad-of-escaping-to-virtual-reality/385134

104. Ibid.; Dr. Aboujaoude also observes that folks have already developed a form of a second life online via use of social media platforms.

105. Andrew Evans, *The Virtual Life: Escapism and Simulation in Our Media World* (London: Fusion Press, 2001), quoted in Monica Kim, "The Good and the Bad of Escaping to Virtual Reality," *The Atlantic*, February 8, 2015, www.theatlantic/com/health/archive/2015/02/the-good-and-the-bad-of-escaping-to-virtual-reality/385134

106. *Dexter*. CBS Television Distribution, October 1, 2006–September 22, 2013.

107. *Bates Motel*. A&E Networks, March 18, 2013–April 24, 2017.

108. *Bates Motel*. "Hidden." Episode No. 44. Directed by Max Theriot. Written by Torrey Speer. AMC, March 13, 2017.

109. Evans, *The Virtual Life*, quoted in Monica Kim, "The Good and the Bad of Escaping to Virtual Reality," *The Atlantic*, February 8, 2015, www.theatlantic/com/health/archive/2015/02/the-good-and-the-bad-of-escaping-to-virtual-reality/385134

110. The fear that entering alternate realities could impact existing realities was examined on *The Simpsons* episode "Treehouse of Horror V." In the episode, Homer accidentally turns a broken toaster into a time machine. When briefly exploring past worlds, even the slightest change that Homer makes affects his reality back home, causing a variety of oddities: his family has long tongues, and rain is comprised of donuts instead of water. *The Simpsons*. "Treehouse of Horror V." Episode No. 109, Prod. 2F03. Directed by Jim Reardon. Written by Greg Daniels et al. FOX, October 30, 1994.

"The Commuter" is reminiscent of *The Twilight Zone*'s "The Man in the Bottle." See *The Twilight Zone*. "The Man in the Bottle." Episode No. 38, Prod. 173–3638. Directed by Don Medford. Written by Rod Serling. CBS, October 7, 1960. The episode also sparks comparisons to the Simpson family's exploration of a "lucky" monkey paw in "Treehouse of Horror II." See *The Simpsons*. "Treehouse of Horror II." Episode No. 42, Prod. 8F02. Directed by Jim Reardon. Written by Al Jean et al. FOX, October 31, 1991. In all these episodes, we learn that wishes coming true can have unintended and unexpected adverse consequences. The grass is not always greener on the other side, and hidden dangers and sadness may be lurking.

111. Ed's perspective is reminiscent of the song *I'd Rather*, where the singer states that he would rather spend bad times with the woman he loves rather than good times with someone else. See Shep Crawford, *I'd Rather*, Luther Vandross, J Records, 2002.

112. See the "Homer" portion of *The Simpsons*. "Treehouse of Horror VI." Episode No. 134, Prod. 3F04. Directed by Bob Anderson. Written by John Swartzwelder et al. FOX, October 29, 1995. The phenomenon of entering into alternate dimensions was also examined on *The Twilight Zone*. See *The Twilight Zone*. "Little Girl Lost." Episode No. 91, Prod. 4828. Directed by Paul Stewart. Written by Richard Matheson. CBS, March 16, 1962. Entrance into alternate time periods and realities is a theme common to a host of other episodes of *The Twilight Zone* as well. See, for example, *The Twilight Zone*. "100 Yards Over the Rim." Episode No. 59, Prod. 173–3654. Directed by Buzz Kulik. Written by Rod Serling. CBS, April 17, 1961.

113. Robert turns disobedient copies into monsters and threatens to torture and harm other copies into submission and subservience.

114. Some commentators have compared Robert's poor treatment of women to the allegations made against Harvey Weinstein. See, e.g., Sara M. Moniuszko, "'Black Mirror' Season 4 includes a timely episode on power dynamics and sexual harassment," *USA Today*, December 29, 2017, www.usatoday.com/story/life/entertainthis/2017/12/29/black-mirrors-u-s-s-callister-freakishly-similar-highlights-societys-problem-power-today/974052001/ His actions have also been compared to someone who becomes a bully after being bullied. See Charles Bramesco, "*Black Mirror* Recap: The Dark Side of Fan Fiction," *Vulture*, December 29, 2017, www.vulture.com/2017/12/black-mirror-recap-season-4-uss-callister.html Robert is a quintessential coward in that he does not confront his perceived abusers at the office and instead deals with "them" when they have no power to respond.

In a not-so-subtle nod to President Donald Trump, Brooker joked that "it's quite odd" that the episode was nominated for an Emmy award in the fictional programming category, since it features "a misogynist bully with a bizarre haircut, put into a position of authority he should never be in." See Lisa de Moraes, "Sci-Fi Anthology *Black Mirror* Repeats TV Movie Win with Donald Trump-ian 'USS Callister—Emmys," *Deadline Hollywood*, September 8, 2018, https://deadline.com/2018/09/uss-callister-black-mirror-wins-best-tv-movie-emmy-1202460277/

115. Robert's desire to exercise complete control over others is reminiscent of Anthony Fremont's use of mind-reading abilities to demand obedience in *The Twilight Zone*'s "The Good Life." See *The Twilight Zone*. "The Good Life." Episode No. 73, Prod. 4801. Directed by James Sheldon. Written by Rod Serling. CBS, November 3, 1961.

116. In our email exchange, actor Douglas Hodge described Haynes as "clever," manipulative, lacking a moral compass and, most significantly, devoid of empathy: "He doesn't empathize. He pretends to. He outwardly affects to. But he doesn't feel any pang of guilt or compassion or remorse for his victims." Douglas M. Hodge, interviewed by Steven Keslowitz via email, September 6, 2018.

The events depicted in this episode showcase the dangers of powerful technologies falling into the hands of irresponsible folks like Mr. Haynes.

117. The monkey only spoke two recorded phrases. Haynes reports that a new law provides that the transfer of consciousness must be made to a host with at least five sayings for the result to be considered "humane."

118. Charlie Brooker describes this segment as a "story about someone with literal voices in their head encountering someone with delusional voices in their head." Charlie Brooker, Annabel Jones and Jason Arnopp, *Inside Black Mirror* (New York: Crown Archetype, 2018), 115.

119. The extraction of the cookie seems like an out of body experience, but it turns out that the cookie was alert and protesting the extraction. The physical person felt nothing during this process.

120. If they do snap, he explains, the cookie would be sold as "fodder" for use in a video game.

121. See *Groupthink* definition, https://www.google.com/search?q=groupthink&rlz=1C1GGRV_enUS752US752&oq=groupthink&aqs=chrome..69i57j0l5.1743j0j4&sourceid=chrome&ie=UTF-8

122. After being arrested for approaching his estranged wife on the street, the block gains "legal backing" and the block covers the woman's offspring as well.

123. Both are simulations, but only the informant is cognizant of this fact.

124. The informant is the individual at the center of the stories in parts 1 and 2 of the episode.

125. The informant tells the "cookie" that their conversation is "not an interrogation."

126. As noted earlier, research is underway to develop a pill to alter prisoners' sense of space and time as part of their punishment. See Jena

McGregor, "Some Swedish workers are getting microchips implanted in their hands," *The Washington Post*, April 4, 2017, www.washingtonpost.com/news/on-leadership/wp/2017/04/04/some-swedish-workers-are-getting-microchips-implanted-in-their-hands/?noredirect=on&utm_term=.7389c41ff39f

127. Charlie Brooker asks the number of simulations and change of scenery questions in his discussion of the episode. See Charlie Brooker, Annabel Jones and Jason Arnopp, *Inside Black Mirror* (New York: Crown Archetype, 2018), 278.

128. Note that the torture of the hologram in part 3 of "Black Museum" would definitely violate this standard, if the hologram is afforded Constitutional rights and protections.

129. Furman v. Georgia, 408 U.S. 238 (1972).

130. Ibid.

131. *The Twilight Zone.* "Number 12 Looks Just Like You." Episode No. 137, Prod. 2618. Directed by Abner Biberman. Written by John Tomerlin. CBS, January 24, 1964.

132. *The Twilight Zone.* "The Trade-Ins." Episode No. 96, Prod. 4831. Directed by Elliot Silverstein. Written by Rod Serling. CBS, April 13, 1962.

133. *The Twilight Zone.* "Mirror Image." Episode No. 21, Prod. 173–3623. Directed by John Brahm. Written by Rod Serling. CBS, February 26, 1960.

134. *The Twilight Zone.* "The Fugitive." Episode No. 90, Prod. 4816. Directed by Richard L. Bare. Written by Charles Beaumont. CBS, March 9, 1962.

135. *The Twilight Zone.* "In His Image." Episode No. 103, Prod. 4851. Directed by Perry Lafferty. Written by Charles Beaumont. CBS, January 3, 1963.

136. *Family Matters.* Warner Bros. Domestic Television Distribution, September 22, 1989–July 17, 1998.

137. Films in which folks transform their identities, by technology or magic, are quite commonplace. Examples include: *Wish Upon a Star, Seventeen Again, Sister Switch, The Change-Up, 18 Again!, All of Me, All Screwed Up, Dating the Enemy,* and *Dream a Little Dream,* among others. *Wish Upon a Star.* Directed by Blair Treu. Leucadia Film Corporation, October 12, 1996; *Seventeen Again.* Directed by Jeffrey W. Byrd. Tri-Ess Productions, November 12, 2000; *Sister Switch.* Directed by Torry Colvin. 24K Black Films, February 24, 2015; *The Change-Up.* Directed by David Dobkin. Universal Pictures, August 5, 2011; *18 Again!* Directed by Paul Flaherty. New World Pictures, April 8, 1988; *All of Me.* Directed by Carl Reiner. Universal Pictures, September 21, 1984; *All Screwed Up.* Directed by Neil Stephens. Red Line Studios, September 4, 2012; *Dating the Enemy.* Directed by Megan Simpson Huberman. Pandora Film, September 19, 1996; *Dream a Little Dream.* Directed by Marc Rocco. Vestron Pictures, March 3, 1989.

Popular culture has also explored the ways in which "switching" identities (while retaining one's physical characteristics) can also be accomplished through subterfuge. See, for example, the antics of Tia and Tamera—identical twins who change places to take tests and fool adults—in the television series *Sister, Sister* (1994–1999). See *Sister, Sister.* ABC, April 1, 1994–May 23, 1999.

138. *The Twilight Zone.* "The Masks." Episode No. 145, Prod. 2601. Directed by Ida Lupino. Written by Rod Serling. CBS, March 20, 1964.

139. *The Twilight Zone.* "Eye of the Beholder." Episode No. 42, Prod. 173–3640. Directed by Douglas Heyes. Written by Rod Serling. CBS, November 11, 1960.

140. *Altered Carbon.* Netflix, February 2, 2018–present.

141. Virgil, *The Aeneid of Virgil,* trans. Allen Mandelbaum (New York: Bantam Classics, 2004), 226.

142. Charlie Brooker, Annabel Jones and Jason Arnopp, *Inside Black Mirror* (New York: Crown Archetype, 2018), 64.

143. Ibid.

144. See *Transcendence.* Directed by Wally Pfister. Warner Bros. Pictures, April 10, 2014.

145. Calo, "People Can Be So Fake," generally.

146. Ibid.

147. Calo, "People Can Be So Fake," 835 (citing M. Slater et al., "Analysis of Physical Responses to Social Situations in an Immersive Virtual Environment," 15 Presence: Teleoperators & Virtual Environment 553 [2006]).

148. See Benjamin Haas, "Chinese man 'marries' robot he built himself," *The Guardian,* April 4, 2017, https://www.theguardian.com/world/2017/apr/04/chinese-man-marries-robot-built-himself

149. Calo, "People Can Be So Fake," 836 (quoting Byron Reeves and Cliff Nass, *The Media Equation: How People Treat Computers, Television, and New Media Like Real People and Places* (Connecticut: Center for the Study of Language and Information, 2003), 12.

150. *The Twilight Zone.* "Uncle Simon." Episode No. 128, Prod. 2604. Directed by Don Siegel. Written by Rod Serling. CBS, November 15, 1963.

Notes—Chapter 5

151. Calo, "People Can Be So Fake," 839.

152. Joshua Rothman, "Are We Already Living in Virtual Reality?," *The New Yorker*, April 2, 2018, www.newyorker.com/magazine/2018/04/02/are-we-already-living-in-virtual-reality See also Bailenson and Blascovich, *Infinite Reality*, 1.

153. See https://www.brainyquote.com/quotes/soren_kierkegaard_105030

154. *Humans*. "Episode 8." Episode No. 8. Directed by China Moo-Young. Written by Jonathan Brackley and Sam Vincent. AMC, August 2, 2015.

155. *1984*. Directed by Michael Radford. 20th Century FOX, October 10, 1984.

156. Jillian Eugenios, "Ray Kurzweil: Humans will be hybrids by 2030," *CNN Tech*, June 4, 2015, http://money.cnn.com/2015/06/03/technology/ray-kurzweil-predictions/index.html (quoting Kurzweill's talk at the 2015 Exponential Financial Conference in New York City).

157. See Chris Matyszczyk, "The 1 Reason Why You Should Worry About Google Most of All (It Involves a Word that Might be New to You)," *Inc.com*, May 6, 2018, https://www.inc.com/chris-matyszczyk/the-1-reason-why-you-should-fear-google-most-of-all-it-involves-a-word-that-might-be-new-to-you.html

158. Ibid.

159. Ibid.

160. Ibid.

161. *Avatar*. Directed by James Cameron. 20th Century FOX, December 10, 2009.

162. We can apply such an analysis to the abuse of android "hosts" in the HBO television series *Westworld* (2016–present), where folks are free to have sex with and kill the hosts in a wild west amusement park setting. *Westworld*. HBO Entertainment, October 2, 2016–present.

163. *AI Artificial Intelligence*. Directed by Steven Spielberg. Warner Bros. Pictures, June 29, 2001.

The New Yorker's Tad Friend observes that "Love is also how we imagine that Pinocchio becomes a real live boy and the Velveteen Rabbit a real live bunny." See Tad Friend, "How Frightened Should We Be of A.I.?," *The New Yorker*, May 7, 2018, https://www.newyorker.com/magazine/2018/05/14/how-frightened-should-we-be-of-ai

164. *Blade Runner*. Directed by Ridley Scott. Warner Bros., June 25, 1982.

165. *Terminator 2: Judgment Day*. Directed by James Cameron. Carolco Pictures, July 3, 1991.

166. See "The Ultimate Guide to Mixed Reality (MR) Technology," www.realitytechnologies.com/mixed-reality

167. Ibid.

168. See Dr. Juan Carlos Marvizon, "Not Just Intelligence: why humans deserve to be treated better than animals," December 6, 2016, https://speakingofresearch.com/2016/12/06/not-just-intelligence-why-humans-deserve-to-be-treated-better-than-animals/

169. Ibid., citing James Rachels, *Created from Animals: The Moral Implications of Darwinism* (Oxford: Oxford University Press, 1990).

170. *Humans*. "Episode 5." Episode No. 5. Directed by Lewis Arnold. Written by Emily Ballou. AMC, July 12, 2015.

171. See Dr. Zuleyka Zevallos, "What Is Otherness," www.othersociologist.com/otherness-resources (citing Zygmunt Bauman, *Modernity and Ambivalence* (Oxford: Polity Press, 1993), 8.

172. Ibid.

173. *The Simpsons*. "A Tale of Two Springfields." Episode No. 250, Prod. BABF20. Directed by Shaun Cashman. Written by John Swartzwelder. FOX, November 5, 2000.

174. We see this cross-border social warfare in episodes such as "Lemon of Troy." *The Simpsons*. "Lemon of Troy." Episode No. 127, Prod. 2F22. Directed by Jim Reardon. Written by Brent Forrester. FOX, May 14, 1995. In one episode, guest star Kiefer Sutherland (playing his iconic role of Jack Bauer) picks up on the disdain that Springfield residents have for those of Shelbyville. Springfield residents are alarmed when they hear a loud explosion from a bomb, but Bauer reassures them that it exploded in Shelbyville. The Springfield residents quickly express their relief and show no care or worry for the impact to Shelbyville or its residents. *The Simpsons*. "24 Minutes." Episode No. 399, Prod. JABF14. Directed by Raymond Persi. Written by Ian Maxtone-Graham et al. FOX, May 20, 2007.

175. For a thorough examination of *The Simpsons* and the concept of American Exceptionalism, please see Steven Keslowitz, *The World According to The Simpsons*, 149–174.

176. *Parks and Recreation*. "Eagleton." Episode No. 42. Directed by Nicole Holofcener. Written by Emily Spivey. NBC, May 5, 2011.

177. *Gilligan's Island*. Warner Bros. Television, 1964–1967.

178. *Perfect Strangers*. Warner Bros. Television, 1986–1993.

179. *The Twilight Zone*. "People Are Alike All Over." Episode No. 25, Prod. 173-3613. Directed by Mitchell Leisen. Written by Rod Serling. CBS, March 25, 1960.

180. *The Twilight Zone*. "Eye of the Beholder." Episode No. 42, Prod. 173-3640. Directed by

Douglas Heyes. Written by Rod Serling. CBS, November 11, 1960.

181. While it is not entirely clear why these folks have been so isolated, there is mention of a war. The audience may reasonably surmise that the "roaches" are a group of conquered people that are viewed as a threat to the ruling class.

182. Much like in *The Twilight Zone*'s "Eye of the Beholder," the television audience does not know that the oppressed, dehumanized class is comprised of human beings.

183. Charlie Brooker, Annabel Jones and Jason Arnopp, *Inside Black Mirror* (New York: Crown Archetype, 2018), 194.

184. The roaches develop a device to reverse engineer the government's MASS implant system. This allows one soldier (Stripe) to see the roaches as they exist naturally. He exhibits empathy toward them.

185. S.L.A. Marshall, *Men Against Fire: The Problem of Battle Command* (Washington, D.C.: Combat Forces Press, 1947); Charlie Brooker, Annabel Jones and Jason Arnopp, *Inside Black Mirror* (New York: Crown Archetype, 2018), 201.

186. Charlie Brooker, Annabel Jones and Jason Arnopp, *Inside Black Mirror* (New York: Crown Archetype, 2018), 194.

187. Dave Grossman, *On Killing: The Psychological Cost of Learning to Kill in War and Society* (Boston: Little, Brown, 1995).

188. This quotation is often falsely attributed to Edmund Burke. See John Rentoul, *The Top 10: Misattributed Quotations*, The Independent, August 25, 2017, https://www.independent.co.uk/voices/the-top-10-misattributed-quotations-a7910361.html

189. Rod Serling (1967). See Anne Serling. Twitter Post. March 7, 2018.

190. For an account of my grandparents' experiences during the Holocaust, including the couple who saved my grandmother from the Nazis in Poland, see Steven Keslowitz, *From Poland to Brooklyn* (Bloomington: iUniverse, 2008). A magnanimous couple (the Shuydkos) provided my grandmother Cecilie Matzner with safe harbor during a portion of the Holocaust. See Ibid., 30–35.

191. Simone de Beauvoir, *The Second Sex*, trans. H.M. Pashley (London: Pan Books, 1988), 16.

192. Isobel Asher Hamilton, "People kicking these food delivery robots is an early insight into how cruel humans could be to robots," *Business Insider*, June 9, 2018, https://www.businessinsider.com/people-are-kicking-starship-technologies-food-delivery-robots-2018-6

193. *Ibid.*

194. See Max Tegmark, *Life 3.0: Being Human in the Age of Artificial Intelligence* (New York: Knopf, 2017), 32. (quoted in Chris Matyszczyk, "The 1 Reason Why You Should Worry About Google Most of All (It Involves a Word that Might be New to You)," Incwww, May 6, 2018, https://www.inc.com/chris-matyszczyk/the-1-reason-why-you-should-fear-google-most-of-all-it-involves-a-word-that-might-be-new-to-you.html

195. See Zach Vasquez, "The Truth About Killer Robots: the year's most terrifying documentary," *The Guardian,* November 26, 2018, https://www.theguardian.com/film/2018/nov/26/the-truth-about-killer-robots-the-years-most-terrifying-documentary See also *The Truth About Killer Robots.* Directed by Maxim Pozdorovkin. Joe Bender, Maxim Pozdorovkin, September 10, 2018.

196. See *The Wizard of Oz.* Directed by Victor Fleming, et al. Metro-Goldwyn-Mayer, 1939. Harold Arlen and Yip Harburg, *If I Only Had a Heart*, Jack Haley, The Wizard of Oz, 1939.

197. *The Twilight Zone.* "The Mighty Casey." Episode No. 35, Prod. 173–3617. Directed by Robert Parrish. Written by Rod Serling. CBS, June 17, 1960.

198. Alan Dershowitz, *Shouting Fire* (Boston: Little, Brown and Company, 2002), 44.

199. *Ibid.*

200. The digital simulations of Frank and Amy in "Hang the DJ" are a unique case study in that they believe they have chosen to use the dating technology and seek to break free of its consequences by escaping together. The simulated beings believe that they have free will and seek to further their own interests, but the only interests that they ultimately serve are those of the natural Frank and Amy. The digital copies in "U.S.S. Callister" face a similar dilemma. They seek to advance their own interests but are constrained by Robert's totalitarian control over them.

201. *Humans.* AMC, June 14, 2015–present.

202. *Bicentennial Man.* Directed by Chris Columbus. Buena Vista Pictures, December 17, 1999.

203. *The Twilight Zone.* "The Lonely." Episode No. 7, Prod. 173–3602. Directed by Jack Smight. Written by Rod Serling. CBS, November 13, 1959.

204. *The Twilight Zone* also examined the consequences of the converse scenario, namely a machine falling in love with a human being and sabotaging his love life with women. See *The Twilight Zone.* "From Agnes—With Love." Episode No. 140, Prod. 2629. Directed by Richard Donner. Written by Bernard C. Schoenfeld. CBS, February 14, 1964. The episode en-

courages us to consider whether the ability to feel and experience love is a defining human characteristic. Other potentially defining characteristics include "doubt, fear, and shame, all the allotropes of untrustworthiness." Tad Friend, "How Frightened Should We Be of A.I.?," *The New Yorker*, May 7, 2018, https://www.newyorker.com/magazine/2018/05/14/how-frightened-should-we-be-of-ai

205. Calo, "People Can Be So Fake," 811.
206. *The Twilight Zone*. "The Lonely." Episode No. 7, Prod. 173–3602. Directed by Jack Smight. Written by Rod Serling. CBS, November 13, 1959.
207. *Ex Machina*. Directed by Alex Garland. A24, April 10, 2015.
208. *The Big Bang Theory*. "The Beta Test Initiation." Episode No. 101, Prod. 3X6864. Directed by Mark Cendrowski. Written by Bill Prady et al. CBS, January 26, 2012.
209. *Cherry 2000*. Directed by Steve De Jarnatt. Orion Pictures, November 17, 1988.
210. *Her*. Directed by Spike Jonze. Warner Bros. Pictures, October 13, 2013.
211. Calo, "People Can Be So Fake," 811.
212. *Ibid*.
213. *Ibid*.
214. *The Big Bang Theory*. "The Beta Test Initiation." Episode No. 101, Prod. 3X6864. Directed by Mark Cendrowski. Written by Bill Prady et al. CBS, January 26, 2012.
215. Joe's wife Laura also points out that Anita had saved their child's life and has become an indispensable part of the family.
216. "The Lonely." Episode No. 7, Prod. 173–3602. Directed by Jack Smight. Written by Rod Serling. CBS, November 13, 1959.
217. Calo, "People Can Be So Fake," 841.
218. *The Twilight Zone*. "The Lateness of the Hour." Episode No. 44, Prod. 173–3652. Directed by Jack Smight. Written by Rod Serling. CBS, December 2, 1960.
219. *Extant*. CBS Television Distribution, July 9, 2014–September 9, 2015.
220. *The Twilight Zone*. "In His Image." Episode No. 103, Prod. 4851. Directed by Peter Lafferty. Written by Charles Beaumont. CBS, January 3, 1963.
221. See Dr. Juan Carols Marvizon, "Not Just Intelligence: why humans deserve to be treated better than animals," December 6, 2016, https://speakingofresearch.com/2016/12/06/not-just-intelligence-why-humans-deserve-to-be-treated-better-than-animals/
222. *Ibid*.
223. *Ibid*.
224. See Dr. Juan Carols Marvizon, "Not Just Intelligence: why humans deserve to be treated better than animals," December 6, 2016, https://speakingofresearch.com/2016/12/06/not-just-intelligence-why-humans-deserve-to-be-treated-better-than-animals/ (citing Michael S. Gazzaniga, *Human: The Science Behind What Makes Us Unique* (New York: HarperCollins Publishers, 2008), 279.

225. See Dr. Juan Carols Marvizon, "Not Just Intelligence: why humans deserve to be treated better than animals," December 6, 2016, https://speakingofresearch.com/2016/12/06/not-just-intelligence-why-humans-deserve-to-be-treated-better-than-animals/ (citing Antonio Damasio, *The Feeling of What Happens: Body and Emotion in the Making of Consciousness* (Wilmington: Mariner Books, 2000), 122.
226. See *The Twilight Zone*. "From Agnes—With Love." Episode No. 140, Prod. 2629. Directed by Richard Donner. Written by Bernard C. Schoenfeld. CBS, February 14, 1964.
227. *Futurama*. FOX / Comedy Central, 1999–2003 / 2008–2013, respectively.
228. *Bicentennial Man*. Directed by Chris Columbus. Buena Vista Pictures Distribution, December 17, 1999.
229. Hybrid beings may remain recognizable to us if they share the characteristics, traits and other attributes of natural humans. A 2018 commercial for *The Simpsons* provides satirical commentary on this point: "Robot Homer" is depicted as being fueled by donuts and Duff beer, much like the natural version of Homer.

Chapter 6

1. See Maureen Dowd, "Elon Musk's Billion-Dollar Crusade to Stop the A.I. Apocalypse," *Vanity Fair*, April 2017, https://www.vanityfair.com/news/2017/03/elon-musk-billion-dollar-crusade-to-stop-ai-space-x
2. See http://quotespictures.com/a-photographer-went-to-a-socialite-party-in-new-york-as-he-entered-the-front-door-the-host-said-i-love-your-pictures-clever-quotes/
3. *Mister Rogers' Neighborhood*. "The Pie Restaurant: Part 1." Episode No. 201. NET, February 9, 1970.
4. "Blood Drive." Episode No. 90, Prod. 518. Directed by Randall Einhorn. Written by Brett Forrester. NBC, March 5, 2009.
5. Tad Friend, "How Frightened Should We Be of A.I.?," *The New Yorker*, May 7, 2018, https://www.newyorker.com/magazine/2018/05/14/how-frightened-should-we-be-of-ai
6. *Ibid*.
7. See Ivan Mehta, "Amazon's new patent

will allow Alexa to detect a cough or a cold," *The Next Web*, October 15, 2018, https://thenextweb.com/artificial-intelligence/2018/10/15/amazons-new-patent-will-allow-alexa-to-detect-your-illness/

8. See Keith Noonan, "Why Is Everyone Talking About iQiyi stock?," *The Motley Fool*, June 25, 2018, https://www.fool.com/investing/2018/06/25/why-is-everyone-talking-about-iqiyi-stock.aspx (discussing the Chinese company iQiyi's use of artificial intelligence in connection with its content production and development strategies).

9. See "AIEQ," http://www.equbotetf.com/about-aieq/ The AIEQ investor website states that "Watson represents a new era in computing called cognitive computing, where systems understand the world the way humans do: through senses, learning, and experience. Watson continuously learns, gaining in value and knowledge over time, from previous interactions." The use of artificial intelligence in the context of investing is particularly interesting, given the natural human tendency to react to stock market volatility with an emotional response. Superintelligence would presumably not experience such emotions, and its reactions may vary from those of humans. Query whether artificial intelligence has an advantage over humans for this reason in the context of investing.

10. See Zach Vasquez, "The Truth About Killer Robots: the year's most terrifying documentary," *The Guardian*, November 26, 2018, https://www.theguardian.com/film/2018/nov/26/the-truth-about-killer-robots-the-years-most-terrifying-documentary

11. *Ibid.*

12. *Ibid.*

13. *The Creepy Line*. Directed by M.A. Taylor. Wandering Foot Productions, October 2018.

14. See Jonathan Vanian, "The Multi-Billion Dollar Robotics Market Is About to Boom," *Fortune*, February 24, 2016, http://fortune.com/2016/02/24/robotics-market-multi-billion-boom/

15. See Lilly Maier, "Mark Cuban Advises Trump to Invest $100 Billion in Robotics," *Forward*, December 19, 2016, https://forward.com/fast-forward/357571/mark-cuban-advises-trump-to-invest-100-billion-in-robotics/ Cuban added that "We have to win the robotics race. We are not even close right now." *Ibid.*

16. *Ibid.*

17. See James Barrat, *Our Final Invention*, www.jamesbarrat.com

18. *Ibid.*

19. See Dom Galeon and Christianna Reedy,

"Kurzweil Claims that the Singularity Will Happen by 2045," *Futurism*, October 5, 2017, https://futurism.com/kurzweil-claims-that-the-singularity-will-happen-by-2045/ (quoting from Kurzweil's speech during the 2017 SXSW Conference in Austin, Texas, March 2017).

20. *Ibid.*

21. I.J. Good, "Speculations Concerning the First Ultraintelligent Machine," *Advances in Computers*, vol. 6 (1965).

22. See James Barrat, "Why Stephen Hawking and Bill Gates are Terrified of Artificial Intelligence," *HuffPost*, April 9, 2015, https://www.huffingtonpost.com/james-barrat/hawking-gates-artificial-intelligence_b_7008706.html

23. Anonymous Editorial, "Anticipating Artificial Intelligence," *Nature*, April 26, 2016, www.nature.com/news/anticipating-artificial-intelligence-1.19825

24. Natalie Wolchover, "Concerns of an Artificial Intelligence Pioneer," *Quanta Magazine*, April 21, 2015, www.quantamagazine.org/artificial-intelligence-aligned-with-human-values-qa-with-stuart-russell-20150421/

25. Arend Hintze, "What an artificial intelligence researcher fears about AI," *Salon*, January 6, 2018, https://www.salon.com/2018/01/06/what-an-artificial-intelligence-researcher-fears-about-ai_partner/

Hintze wonders whether "a superintelligence system" will "find it no longer needs humans," and asks "How will we justify our existence in the face of a superintelligence that can do things humans could never do? Can we avoid being wiped off the face of the Earth by machines we helped create?" Arend Hintze, "What an artificial intelligence researcher fears about AI," *Salon*, January 6, 2018, https://www.salon.com/2018/01/06/what-an-artificial-intelligence-researcher-fears-about-ai_partner/

26. See Sue Surkes, "As influence of AI, big data grows, cyber experts discuss tech safety and trust," *The Times of Israel*, November 15, 2018, https://www.timesofisrael.com/as-influence-of-ai-big-data-grows-cyber-experts-discuss-tech-safety-and-trust/

27. Some critics, however, believe that the regulation of research into artificial intelligence would be futile. See, for example, Brad Allenby, "The Wrong Cognitive Measuring Stick," *Slate*, April 11, 2016, http://www.slate.com/articles/technology/future_tense/2016/04/why_it_s_a_mistake_to_compare_a_i_with_human_intelligence.html ("It is fantasy to suggest that the accelerating development and deployment of technologies that taken together are considered to be A.I. will be

stopped or limited, either by regulation or even by national legislation.").

28. See, e.g., Rebecca J. Rosen, "'I've Created a Monster': On the Regrets of Inventors," *The Atlantic*, November 23, 2011, https://www.theatlantic.com/technology/archive/2011/11/ive-created-a-monster-on-the-regrets-of-inventors/249044/

29. See Catherine Clifford, "Elon Musk: 'Mark my words—A.I. is far more dangerous than nukes,'" *CNBC*, March 13, 2018, https://www.cnbc.com/2018/03/13/elon-musk-at-sxsw-a-i-is-more-dangerous-than-nuclear-weapons.html

30. See Peter Holley, "Bill Gates on dangers of artificial intelligence: 'I don't understand why some people are not concerned,'" *The Washington Post*, January 29, 2015, https://www.washingtonpost.com/news/the-switch/wp/2015/01/28/bill-gates-on-dangers-of-artificial-intelligence-dont-understand-why-some-people-are-not-concerned/?utm_term=.037f1f650fe4&noredirect=on

31. Arjun Kharpal, "Stephen Hawking says A.I. could be 'worst event in the history of our civilization,'" *CNBC*, November 6, 2017, https://www.cnbc.com/2017/11/06/stephen-hawking-ai-could-be-worst-event-in-civilization.html

32. Ibid.

33. James Barrat, *Our Final Invention: Artificial Intelligence and the End of the Human Era* (New York: Thomas Dunne Books, 2013).

34. Richard Patrick William Loosemore, "The Maverick Nanny with a Dopamine Drip: Debunking Fallacies," 2014 AAAI Spring Symposium Series, http://www.aaai.org/ocs/index.php/SSS/SSS14/paper/viewPaper/7752

35. Arend Hintze, "What an artificial intelligence researcher fears about AI," *Salon*, January 6, 2018, https://www.salon.com/2018/01/06/what-an-artificial-intelligence-researcher-fears-about-ai_partner/

36. Ibid.

37. Ibid.

38. See generally Paul R. Daughtery and H. James Wilson, *Human + Machine: Reimagining Work in the Age Of AI* (Boston: Harvard Business Review Press, 2018).

39. See Chris Matyszczyk, "The 1 Reason Why You Should Worry About Google Most of All (It Involves a Word that Might be New to You)," Incwww, May 6, 2018, https://www.inc.com/chris-matyszczyk/the-1-reason-why-you-should-fear-google-most-of-all-it-involves-a-word-that-might-be-new-to-you.html

40. See Catherine Clifford, "Facebook CEO Mark Zuckerberg: Elon Musk's doomsday AI predictions are 'pretty irresponsible,'" *CNBC*, July 24, 2017, https://www.cnbc.com/2017/07/24/mark-zuckerberg-elon-musks-doomsday-ai-predictions-are-irresponsible.html

41. Nick Bostrom, *Superintelligence: Paths, Dangers, Strategies* (Oxford, United Kingdom: Oxford University Press, 2014), 116.

42. Ibid.

43. Nick Bostrom, "The Superintelligent Will: Motivation and Instrumental Rationality in Advanced Artificial Agents," 2012, www.nickbostrom.com/superintelligentwill.pdf

44. Ibid.

45. Nick Bostrom, "Ethical Issues in Advanced Artificial Intelligence," 2003, www.nickbostrom.com/ethics/ai.html

46. *Singularity*. Directed by Robert Kouba. Vertical Entertainment, November 3, 2017.

47. *The Matrix*. Directed by Lana Wachowski and Lilly Wachowski. Warner Bros., March 31, 1999.

48. *2001: A Space Odyssey*. Directed by Stanley Kubrick. Metro-Goldwyn-Mayer, April 2, 1968.

49. See generally, James Barrat, *Our Final Invention*.

50. Tad Friend, "How Frightened Should We Be of A.I.?," *The New Yorker*, May 7, 2018, https://www.newyorker.com/magazine/2018/05/14/how-frightened-should-we-be-of-ai

51. Artificial intelligence could advance to such a state that it generates its own goals as well.

52. Maureen Dowd, "Elon Musk's Billion-Dollar Crusade to Stop the A.I. Apocalypse," *Vanity Fair*, April 2017, https://www.vanityfair.com/news/2017/03/elon-musk-billion-dollar-crusade-to-stop-ai-space-x

53. *The Twilight Zone*. "The Howling Man." Episode No. 41, Prod. 173–3642. Directed by Douglas Heyes. Written by Charles Beaumont. CBS, November 4, 1960.

54. Arend Hintze, "What an artificial intelligence researcher fears about AI," *Salon*, January 6, 2018, https://www.salon.com/2018/01/06/what-an-artificial-intelligence-researcher-fears-about-ai_partner/

55. Ibid.

56. Ibid.

57. Nick Bostrom, *Superintelligence: Paths, Dangers, Strategies* (Oxford, United Kingdom: Oxford University Press, 2014), 259.

58. Steven Keslowitz, "*The Simpsons*, 24, and the Law: How Homer Simpson and Jack Bauer Influence Congressional Lawmaking and Judicial Reasoning," 29 *Cardozo Law Review* 2787 (May 2008): 2799.

59. *Ibid.*, 2799.
60. *Humans.* "Episode 4." Episode No. 12, Directed by Carl Tibbetts. AMC, November 20, 2016.
61. *DriverX.* Directed by Henry Barrial. Sundance Selects, November 30, 2018.
62. Marilyn Butler and Mary W. Shelley, *Frankenstein, Or the Modern Prometheus: The 1818 Text* (Oxford: Oxford University Press, 1994); *Pinnochio.* Walt Disney Productions, February 7, 1940; *Weird Science.* Directed by John Hughes. Universal Pictures, August 2, 1985.
63. *Wall-E.* Directed by Andrew Stanton. Walt Disney Pictures, June 23, 2008; *Robot & Frank.* Directed by Jake Schreier. Samuel Goldwyn Films, January 20, 2012; *A.I. Artificial Intelligence.* Directed by Steven Spielberg. Warner Bros. Pictures, June 29, 2001.
64. *The Terminator.* Directed by James Cameron. Orion Pictures, October 26, 1984; *9.* Directed by Shane Acker. Focus Features, September 9, 2009.
65. *The Machine.* Directed by Caradog w. James. Content Media, April 20, 2013; *Kill Command.* Directed by Steven Gomez. Vertigo Films, May 13, 2016; *American Cyborg: Steel Warrior.* Directed by Boaz Davidson. Global Pictures, January 7, 1994.
66. Karel Čapek, *R.U.R. (Rossum's Universal Robots)* trans. Claudia Novack-Jones (London: Penguin Classics, 2004).
67. Eileen Hunt Botting, "Godmother of intelligences," *Aeon*, October 3, 2018, www.aeon.co/essays/what-frankensteins-creature-can-really-tell-us-about-ai
68. Eileen Hunt Botting, "Godmother of intelligences," *Aeon*, October 3, 2018, www.aeon.co/essays/what-frankensteins-creature-can-really-tell-us-about-ai (quoting Čapek, *R.U.R.*, 56).
69. *Ibid.*
70. Eileen Hunt Botting, "Godmother of intelligences," *Aeon*, October 3, 2018, www.aeon.co/essays/what-frankensteins-creature-can-really-tell-us-about-ai
71. *Ibid.*
72. *The Simpsons.* "Girly Edition." Episode No. 199, Prod. 5F15. Directed by Mark Kirkland. Written by Larry Doyle. FOX, April 19, 1998.
73. *Frankenstein AI—A Monster Made by Many.* Directed by Lance Weiler. Columbia University School of the Arts' Digital Storytelling Lab, January 2018.
74. *Ex Machina.* Directed by Alex Garland. A24, April 10, 2015; *Chappie.* Directed by Neill Blomkamp. Columbia Pictures, March 4, 2015; *Tau.* Directed by Federico D'Alessandro. Netflix, June 29, 2018.

Observers predict that within 5 years, autonomous weapons systems and "drone swarms" could use facial recognition software to target / attack humans.

For further reading, see Miles Brundage et al., "The Malicious Use of Artificial Intelligence: Forecasting, Prevention, and Mitigation" (February 2018), www.arxiv.org/ftp/arxiv/papers/1802/1802.07228.pdf

75. Application of these laws is explored in the film *I, Robot.* See *I, Robot.* Directed by Alex Proyas. Davis Entertainment, July 16, 2004. Isaac Asimov introduced his Laws of Robotics in the short story *Runaround.* See Isaac Asimov, *Runaround, Astounding Science Fiction* (1942): 94–103. Asimov's Laws of Robotics were satirized on the "I (Annoyed Grunt)-Bot" episode of *The Simpsons*, as a robot who is in a boxing match with Homer declines to harm Homer and instead serves him a martini. *The Simpsons.* "I (Annoyed Grunt)-Bot." Episode No. 322, Prod. FABF04. Directed by Lauren MacMullan. Written by Dan Greaney and Allen Glazier. FOX, January 11, 2004.

76. *RoboCop.* Directed by Paul Verhoeven. Orion Pictures, July 17, 1987.

77. United States law continues to evolve with respect to the legality of commercial drones. In June 2014, the Federal Aviation Administration (FAA) banned the commercial use of UAVs. In August 2016, the FAA updated its rules to allow small UAVs to be used for commercial purposes. In June 2017, the United States Senate proposed legislation to allow package deliveries to be made by drones. In October 2017, the Trump administration issued a presidential directive calling upon the FAA and the Transportation Department to work with local officials to create initiatives to enable the use of drones for delivery purposes. See Abby Speicher, "Drone Laws: The History of Drone Regulations and Laws," *Dart Drones*, November 9, 2016, www.dartdrones.com/blog/drone-laws/

See also Jonathan Vanian, "Everything to Know About President Donald Trump's New Drone Program," *Fortune*, October 25, 2017, www.fortune.com/2017/10/25/donald-trump-drone-program/

78. See Gina Hall, "Amazon's latest drone prototypes can carry packages up to 5 pounds," *Silicon Valley Business Journal*, November 30, 2015, www.bizjournals.com/sanjose/news/2015/11/30/amazons-latest-drone-prototypes-can-carry-packages.html

79. See Amit Regev, "Drone Deliveries are

no Longer Pie in the Sky," *Forbes,* April 10, 2018, https://www.forbes.com/sites/startupnationcentral/2018/04/10/drone-deliveries-are-no-longer-pie-in-the-sky/#49185fd24188

80. *The Twilight Zone.* "The Brain Center at Whipple's." Episode 153, Prod. 2632. Directed by Richard Donner. Written by Rod Serling. CBS, May 15, 1964.

81. *Cam.* Directed by Daniel Goldhaber. Netflix, November 16, 2018.

82. *Humans.* AMC, June 14, 2015–present.

83. *The Twilight Zone* episodes: "The Trade-Ins." Episode No. 96, Prod. 4831. Directed by Elliot Silverstein. Written by Rod Serling. CBS, April 13, 1962; "The Four of Us Are Dying." Episode No. 13, Prod. 173-3618. Directed by John Brahm. Written by Rod Serling. CBS, January 1, 1960; "The Self-Improvement of Salvadore Ross." Episode No. 136, Prod. 2612. Directed by Don Siegel. Written by Jerry McNeely.

84. *The Twilight Zone.* "Young Man's Fancy." Episode No. 99, Prod. 4813. Directed by John Brahm. Written by Richard Matheson. CBS, May 11, 1962.

85. *Parks and Recreation.* "Leslie and Ron." Episode No. 116. Directed by Beth McCarthy-Miller. Written by Michael Schur. NBC, January 20, 2015.

86. *Halt and Catch Fire.* AMC, June 1, 2014–October 14, 2017.

87. *The Wonder Years.* ABC, January 31, 1988–May 12, 1993.

88. *The Twilight Zone* episodes: "Kick the Can." Episode No. 86, Prod. 4821. Directed by Lamont Johnson. Written by George Clayton Johnson. CBS, February 9, 1962; "The Incredible World of Horace Ford." Episode, 117, Prod. 4854. Directed by Abner Biberman. Written by Reginald Rose. CBS, April 18, 1963; "Walking Distance." Episode No. 5, Prod. 173-3605. Directed by Robert Stevens. Written by Rod Serling. CBS, October 30, 1959.

89. Billy Joel, *Souvenir,* Columbia Records, 1974.

90. *The Twilight Zone.* "The Lateness of the Hour." Episode No. 44, Prod. 173-3652. Directed by Jack Smight. Written by Rod Serling. CBS, December 2, 1960.

91. Billy Joel, *This Is the Time,* Columbia Records, 1986. We also use music as a way to connect to the past. See, for example, *The Twilight Zone's* "Static" episode.

92. *Homecoming.* "Helping." Episode No. 5. Directed by Sam Esmail. Written by Cami Delavigne. Amazon Video, November 2, 2018.

93. *The Simpsons.* "Rosebud." Episode No.

85, Prod. 1F01. Directed by Wes Archer. Written by John Swartzwelder. FOX, October 21, 1993.

94. *Citizen Kane.* Directed by Orson Welles. RKO Radio Pictures, May 1, 1941.

95. Uri Berliner, "A Toy Monkey that Escaped Nazi Germany and Reunited a Family," *NPR,* November 14, 2018, https://www.npr.org/2018/11/14/663059048/a-toy-monkey-that-escaped-nazi-germany-and-reunited-a-family

96. Ibid.

97. Ibid.

98. Ibid.

99. See Simon Worrall, "Yes, Animals Think and Feel. Here's How We Know," *National Geographic,* July 15, 2015, www.news.nationalgeographic.com/2015/07/150714-animal-dog-thinking-feelings-brain-science/

100. See Charlie Brooker, Annabel Jones and Jason Arnopp, *Inside Black Mirror* (New York: Crown Archetype, 2018), 64.

101. One point of contrast here is the poor way that society treats the elderly. These folks represent a bridge from the past to the present yet are often not treated with the respect of dignity that they deserve. They are, unfortunately, deemed "replaceable" by younger generations of folks.

102. See "Walt Disney's Carousel of Progress," November 23, 2017, www.travelwiththemagic.com/walt-disney's-carousel-progress/

103. *Back to the Future.* Directed by Robert Zemeckis. Universal Pictures, July 3, 1985; *Futurama.* FOX / Comedy Central, 1999–2003 / 2008–2013, respectively; *The Jetsons.* Hanna-Barbera Productions, September 23, 1962–March 17, 1963.

104. *DriverX.* Directed by Henry Barrial. Sundance Selects, November 30, 2018.

105. *The Office.* "Dunder Mifflin Infinity." Episode Nos. 56 and 57, Prods. 403 and 404. Directed by Craig Zisk. Written by Michael Schur. NBC, October 4, 2007.

106. *DriverX.* Directed by Henry Barrial. Sundance Selects, November 30, 2018.

107. See Soo Youn, "24 Amazon workers sent to hospital after robot accidentally unleashes bear spray," *ABC News,* December 6, 2018, https://abcnews.go.com/U.S./24-amazon-workers-hospital-bear-repellent-accident/story?id=59625712

108. See Aimee Picchi, "Amazon's Patent for Caging Workers was 'Bad' Idea, Exec Admits," *CBS News Money Watch,* September 11, 2018, https://www.cbsnews.com/news/amazons-patent-for-caging-workers-was-a-bad-idea-exec-admits/

109. See Aimee Picchi, "Amazon's Patent for

Caging Workers was 'Bad' Idea, Exec Admits," *CBS News Money Watch*, September 11, 2018, https://www.cbsnews.com/news/amazons-patent-for-caging-workers-was-a-bad-idea-exec-admits/ (quoting Kate Crawford and Vladan Joler, "Anatomy of an AI System, The Amazon Echo As An Anatomical Map of Human Labor, Data and Planetary Resources," *AI Now Institute and Share Lab*, September 7, 2018, https://anatomyof.ai).

110. Aimee Picchi, "Amazon's Patent for Caging Workers was 'Bad' Idea, Exec Admits," *CBS News Money Watch*, September 11, 2018, https://www.cbsnews.com/news/amazons-patent-for-caging-workers-was-a-bad-idea-exec-admits/ (quoting from the Twitter account of Dave Clark, September 7, 2018).

111. *The Twilight Zone*. "People Are Alike All Over." Episode No. 25, Prod. 173–3613. Directed by Mitchell Leisen. Written by Rod Serling. CBS, March 25, 1960.

112. The backstory leading up to the events depicted on "Metalhead" is not clear. It is possible, for example, that humans are in fact controlling the robots, directing them to kill other humans. Brooker had, in fact, laid out this scenario in the original version of the script. In deciding to revise the script to remove these background elements, the team felt that it would be scarier to imagine the robots running completely wild, without any human control or oversight whatsoever. See Charlie Brooker, Annabel Jones and Jason Arnopp, *Inside Black Mirror* (New York: Crown Archetype, 2018), 284.

113. See Aimee Ortiz, "Terrifying Boston Dynamics robots, '*Black Mirror*,' and the end of the world," *Boston Globe*, January 5, 2018, https://www.bostonglobe.com/arts/2018/01/05/boston-dynamics-black-mirror-and-end-world/cL9RYkg6O6MqyPuhmgxVjP/story.html

As artificial intelligence expands, Stanford researchers are busy developing a robotic nerve system to deal with certain physical limitations inherent in lack of robotic sensory capabilities. See Tom Abate, "An artificial nerve system developed at Stanford gives prosthetic devices and robots a sense of touch," *Stanford News*, May 31, 2018, https://news.stanford.edu/2018/05/31/artificial-nerve-system-gives-prosthetic-devices-robots-sense-touch/

Superintelligence combined with the ability to feel sensations could have significant consequences for humanity.

114. *Android*. Directed by Aaron Lipstadt. New World Pictures, October 1982; *Electric Dreams*. Directed by Steve Barron. MGM / UA Entertainment Co., July 20, 1984; *The Simpsons*.

"The Simpsons Spin-Off Showcase." Episode No. 177, Prod. 4F20. Directed by Neil Affleck. Written by David S. Cohen et al. FOX, May 11, 1997.

115. See Aatif Sulleyman, "Elon Musk Slams Proposal to Create an Artificial Intelligence 'God' that People Will Worship," *The Independent*, October 24, 2017, https://www.independent.co.uk/life-style/gadgets-and-tech/news/ai-god-elon-musk-artificial-intelligence-religion-anthony-levandowski-way-of-the-future-a8017296.html

116. *Ibid.*

117. See John Brandon, "An AI god will emerge by 2042 and write its own bible. Will you worship it?," *VentureBeat*, October 2, 2017, https://venturebeat.com/2017/10/02/an-ai-god-will-emerge-by-2042-and-write-its-own-bible-will-you-worship-it/

118. *Ibid.*

119. *The Twilight Zone*. "The Old Man in the Cave." Episode No. 127, Prod. 2603. Directed by Alan Crosland, Jr. Written by Rod Serling. CBS, November 8, 1963.

120. *The Office*. "Dunder Mifflin Infinity." Episode Nos. 56 and 57, Prods. 403 and 404. Directed by Craig Zisk. Written by Michael Schur. NBC, October 4, 2007.

121. See John Brandon, "An AI god will emerge by 2042 and write its own bible. Will you worship it?," *VentureBeat*, October 2, 2017, https://venturebeat.com/2017/10/02/an-ai-god-will-emerge-by-2042-and-write-its-own-bible-will-you-worship-it/

122. Jeffrey Dastin, "'Kill your foster parents': Amazon's Alexa talks murder, sex in AI experiment," *Reuters*, December 21, 2018, www.reuters.com/article/us-amazon-com-alexa-insight/kill-your-foster-parents-amazons-alexa-talks-murder-sx-in-ai-experiment-idUSKCN1)K1AJ

123. *Ibid.*

Conclusion

1. See www.brainyquote.com/quotes/tupac_shakur_100941

2. *Parks and Recreation*. "The Trial of Leslie Knope." Episode No. 55. Directed by Dean Holland. Written by Dan Goor and Michael Schur. NBC, December 1, 2011. The scene bears similarity to another one in a different episode. In the episode "Correspondents' Lunch," Leslie Knope smashes a smartphone to prevent further hacking. But we know that it is not destruction of the physical device that will create a safe environment. Ron's response—namely that a type-

writer is superior because it cannot be hacked—belies a certain level of ignorance regarding, or unwillingness to acknowledge, the significant benefits of accessing and using modern technology. See *Parks and Recreation*. "Correspondents' Lunch." Episode No. 83. Directed by Nick Offerman. Written by Alexandra Rushfield. NBC, February 21, 2013.

3. *The Twilight Zone*. "The Howling Man." Episode No. 41, Prod. 173–3642. Directed by Douglas Heyes. Written by Charles Beaumont. CBS, November 4, 1960.

4. Philip Ball, "We can't ban robots—it's already too late," *The Guardian*, August 22, 2017, https://www.theguardian.com/commentisfree/2017/aug/22/killer-robots-international-arms-traders

5. *Ibid*.

6. Billy Joel, *All You Want to Do Is Dance*, Columbia Records, 1976.

7. *Ferris Bueller's Day Off*. Paramount Pictures, June 11, 1986.

8. See James Vincent, "Automation Threatens 800 Million Jobs, but Technology Could Still Save Us, says report," *The Verge*, November 30, 2017, https://www.theverge.com/2017/11/30/16719092/automation-robots-jobs-global-800-million-forecast. Given the potential magnitude of the impact of automation, many observers have argued that government should pursue an active role in dealing with it to mitigate its adverse effects.

9. See Sue Surkes, "As influence of AI, big data grows, cyber experts discuss tech safety and trust," *The Times of Israel*, November 15, 2018, https://www.timesofisrael.com/as-influence-of-ai-big-data-grows-cyber-experts-discuss-tech-safety-and-trust/ Researcher Roey Tzezana discusses this potentiality in the article.

10. Jim Croce, *Time in A Bottle*, ABC, 1972.

11. See the opening sequence to the "Mabel" episode of *Better Call Saul*. See *Better Call Saul*. "Mabel." Episode No. 21. Directed by Vince Gilligan. Written by Peter Gould and Vince Gilligan. AMC, April 10, 2017.

12. Federal Agent Jack Bauer (from the television series *24*) is another prime example. Despite attempts to retire from the Counter Terrorist Unit, Bauer frequently finds himself back in the terrorist-hunting game either by circumstances hoisted upon him or voluntarily choice. In any event, Bauer seems to thrive best when he is actively hunting terrorists as opposed to sitting back and letting others handle this work.

13. See www.quoteinvestigator.com/2017/03/19/candle/

14. Elie Wiesel, Nobel lecture, December 11, 1986, www.nobelprize.org/prizes/peace/1986/wiesel/lecture/

15. See "Reflection of Light," *Science Learning Hub*, undated, www.sciencelearn.org.nz/resources/48-reflection-of-light

16. *Ibid*.

17. *The Twilight Zone*. "The Mirror." Episode No. 71, Prod. 4819. Directed by Don Medford. Written by Rod Serling. CBS, October 20, 1961.

18. See "Clarke as ICT Promoter," undated, www.arthurcclarke.org/site/sri-lanka/clarke-and-sri-lanka/communications/

19. See Mary Bowerman and Ashley May, "Martin Luther King, Jr., quotes: 10 most popular from the civil rights leader," *USA Today*, January 21, 2019, https://www.usatoday.com/story/news/nation/2019/01/21/martin-luther-king-jr-quotes-10-most-popular/2636024002/

20. *The Twilight Zone*. "Steel." Episode No. 122, Prod. 2602. Directed by Don Weis. Written by Richard Matheson. CBS, October 4, 1963.

21. See Lester J. Cappon, *Adams-Jefferson Letters*—Thomas Jefferson Letter to John Adams, August 1, 1816 (Chapel Hill: University of North Carolina Press, 1959), 483–485.

22. *Breaking Bad*. "Better Call Saul." Episode No. 15. Directed by Terry McDonough. Written by Peter Gould. AMC, April 26, 2009.

23. Walt Whitman, *Leaves of Grass: The Original 1855 Edition* (Nashville: American Renaissance, 1855).

Bibliography

Books

Agamben, Giorgio. *State of Exception.* Translated by Kevin Attell. Chicago: University of Chicago Press, 2015.

Arendt, Hannah. *The Human Condition.* Chicago: University of Chicago Press, 1958.

Bailenson, Jeremy, and Jim Blascovich. *Infinite Reality: Avatars, Eternal Life, New Worlds, and the Dawn of the Virtual Revolution.* New York: HarperCollins, 2011.

Barber, Benjamin. *Jihad vs. McWorld: How Globalism and Tribalism Are Reshaping the World.* New York: Ballantine Books, 1995.

Barrat, James. *Our Final Invention: Artificial Intelligence and the End of the Human Era.* New York: Thomas Dunne Books, 2013.

Bauman, Zygmunt. *Modernity and Ambivalence.* Oxford: Polity Press, 1993.

Beauvoir, Simone de. *The Second Sex.* Translated by H.M. Pashley. London: Pan Books, 1988.

Bernays, Edward. *Propaganda.* New York: H: Liveright, 1928.

Bostrom, Nick. *Superintelligence: Paths, Dangers, Strategies.* Oxford, United Kingdom: Oxford University Press, 2014.

Brooker, Charlie, Annabel Jones and Jason Arnopp. *Inside Black Mirror.* New York: Crown Archetype, 2018.

Brooks, David. *On Paradise Drive: How We Live Now (And Always Have) in the Future Tense.* New York: Simon & Schuster, 2004.

Butler, Marilyn, and Mary W. Shelley. *Frankenstein, Or the Modern Prometheus: The 1818 Text.* Oxford: Oxford University Press, 1994.

Čapek, Karel. *R.U.R. (Rossum's Universal Robots).* Translated by Claudia Novack-Jones. London: Penguin Classics, 2004.

Cappon, Lester J. *Adams-Jefferson Letters—* Thomas Jefferson Letter to John Adams, August 1, 1816. Chapel Hill: University of North Carolina Press, 1959.

Clement, Joe, and Matt Miles. *Screen Schooled: Two Veteran Teachers Expose How Technology Use Is Making Our Kids Dumber.* Illinois: Chicago Review Press, 2017.

Cooper, John M. ed. *Plato, Five Dialogues: Euthyphro, Apology, Crito, Meno, Phaedo.* Indianapolis: Haskett Classics 2nd edition, 2002.

Cranston, Bryan. *A Life In Parts.* New York: Scribner's, reprint edition, 2017.

Damasio, Antonio. *The Feeling of What Happens: Body and Emotion in the Making of Consciousness.* Wilmington: Mariner Books, 2000.

Daughtery, Paul R., and H. James Wilson. *Human + Machine: Reimagining Work in the Age Of AI.* Boston: Harvard Business Review Press, 2018.

Dershowitz, Alan. *Shouting Fire.* Boston: Little, Brown and Company, 2002.

Etzioni, Amitai. *How Patriotic Is the Patriot Act: Freedom versus Security in the Age of Terrorism.* New York: Routledge, 2005.

Evans, Andrew. *The Virtual Life: Escapism and Simulation in Our Media World.* London: Fusion Press, 2001.

Fuller, Thomas. *The Holy State and the Profane State.* California: University of California Libraries, 1841.

Gazzaniga, Michael S. *Human: The Science Behind What Makes Us Unique.* New York: HarperCollins Publishers, 2008.

Grossman, Dave. *On Killing: The Psychological Cost of Learning to Kill in War and Society.* Boston: Little, Brown, 1995.

Hillis, Ken. *Digital Sensations: Space, Identity, and Embodiment in Virtual Reality.* Minneapolis: University of Minnesota Press, 1999.

Keslowitz, Steven. *From Poland to Brooklyn.* Bloomington: iUniverse, 2008.

Keslowitz, Steven. *The World According to The Simpsons.* Naperville: Sourcebooks, 2006.

Lewis, C.S. *The Weight of Glory.* New York: HarperOne, 1949.

Lowry, Lois. *The Giver*. Boston: Houghton Mifflin, 1993.

Marshall, S.L.A. *Men Against Fire: The Problem of Battle Command*. Washington, D.C.: Combat Forces Press, 1947.

McLuhan, Marshall, and Lewis H. Lapham. *Understanding Media: The Extensions of Man*. Cambridge: The MIT Press, reprint, 1994.

Nizer, Louis. *Between You and Me*. Beechhurst Press, 1948.

Ornstein, Norman. Foreword to *The Web of Politics: The Internet's Impact on the American Political System*, by Richard Davis, xi-3. Oxford: Oxford University Press, March 4, 1999.

Orwell, George. *1984*. London: Secker and Warburg, 1949.

Plato. *The Allegory of the Cave*. Translated by Benjamin Jowett. Los Angeles: Enhanced Media, 2017).

Postman, Neil. *Amusing Ourselves to Death: Public Discourse in the Age of Show Business*. New York: Penguin Books, 1986.

Rachels, James. *Created from Animals: The Moral Implications of Darwinism*. Oxford: Oxford University Press, 1990.

Rand, Ayn. *The Fountainhead*. New York: Bobbs Merrill, 1943.

Reeves, Byron, and Cliff Nass. *The Media Equation: How People Treat Computers, Television, and New Media Like Real People and Places*. Connecticut: Center for the Study of Language and Information, 2003.

Richtel, Matt. *A Deadly Wandering: A Tale of Tragedy and Redemption in the Age of Attention*. New York: William Morrow, 2014.

Schneier, Bruce. *Click Here to Kill Everybody: Security and Survival in a Hyper-Connected World*. New York; W.W. Norton & Company, 2018.

Sophocles. *Oedipus the King*. Translated by F. Storr. Boston: Harvard University Press, 1912.

Tegmark, Max. *Life 3.0: Being Human in the Age of Artificial Intelligence*. New York: Knopf, 2017).

Virgil. *The Aeneid of Virgil*. Translated by Allen Mandelbaum. New York: Bantam Classics, 2004.

Westin, Alan. *Privacy and Freedom*. New York: Atheneum, 1967.

Whitman, Walt. *Leaves of Grass: The Original 1855 Edition*. Nashville: American Renaissance, 1855.

Journal Articles

Alcott, Hunt, and Matthew Gentzkow. "Social Media and Fake News in the 2016 Election," *Journal of Economic Perspectives*, Volume 31, No. 2 (2017): 214.

Asimov, Isaac. "Runaround," *Astounding Science Fiction* (1942): 94–103.

Brundage, Miles, et al. "The Malicious Use of Artificial Intelligence: Forecasting, Prevention, and Mitigation" (February 2018), www.arxiv.org/ftp/arxiv/papers/1802/1802.07228.pdf

Calo, M. Ryan. "People Can Be So Fake: A New Dimension to Privacy and Technology Scholarship," 114 *Penn St. L. Rev.* 809 (2009–2010): 841.

Cohen, Julie E. "Examined Lives: Informational Privacy and the Subject as Object," 52 Stanford Law Review 1373 (2000): 1426.

Devries, Will Thomas. "Protecting Privacy in the Digital Age," 18 Berkeley Technology Law Journal 283 (2003): 285.

Fried, Charles. "Privacy," 77 Yale Law Journal 475 (1968): 483–484.

Good, I.J. "Speculations Concerning the First Ultraintelligent Machine," *Advances in Computers*, vol. 6 (1965).

Hunt, Melissa G. et al. "No More FOMO: Limiting Social media Decreases Loneliness and Depression," *Journal of Social and Clinical Psychology*, Vol. 37, No. 10 (2018): 751–768, https://guilfordjournals.com/doi/pdf/10.1521/jscp.2018.37.10.751.

Keslowitz, Steven. "*The Simpsons, 24*, and the Law: How Homer Simpson and Jack Bauer Influence Congressional Lawmaking and Judicial Reasoning," 29 *Cardozo Law Review* 2787 (May 2008): 2799.

Keslowitz, Steven. "The Transformative Nature of Blogs and Their Effects on Legal Scholarship," 2009 *Cardozo Law Review de novo* 252 (July 2018): 253–254, cardozolawreview.com/wp-content/uploads/2018/07/Keslowitz_2009_252.pdf

Kross, Ethan, et al. "Facebook Use Predicts Declines in Subjective Well-Being in Young Adults," *PLOS One*, August 14, 2013, www.journals.plos.org/plosone/article?id=10.1371/journal.pone.0069841&mbid=synd_msnhealth.

Loosemore, Richard Patrick William. "The Maverick Nanny with a Dopamine Drip: Debunking Fallacies," 2014 AAAI Spring Symposium Series, http://www.aaai.org/ocs/index.php/SSS/SSS14/paper/viewPaper/7752

Primack, Brian A., et al. "Social Media Use and Perceived Social Isolation Among Young Adults in the U.S.," *American Journal of Preventive Medicine*, Volume 53, Issue 1 (2017): 1–8, www.ajpmonline.org/article/S0749-3797(17)30016-8/fulltext.

Sagioglou, Christina, and Tobias Greitemeyer. "Facebook's emotional consequences: Why Facebook causes a decrease in mood and why people still use it," *ScienceDirect*, Volume 35 (June 2014): 359–363, www.sciencedirect.com/science/article/pii/S0747563214001241.

Schurgin O' Keefe, Gwenn, and Kathleen Clarke-Pearson. "The Impact of Social Media on Children, Adolescents, and Families," *Pediatrics Council on Communications and Media*, Volume 127, Issue 4 (2011), pediatrics.aapublications.org/content/127/4/800.short.

Slater, M., et al. "Analysis of Physical Responses to Social Situations in an Immersive Virtual Environment," 15 Presence: Teleoperators & Virtual Environment 553 (2006).

Newspaper and Magazine Articles

Abate, Tom. "An artificial nerve system developed at Stanford gives prosthetic devices and robots a sense of touch." *Stanford News*, May 31, 2018. https://news.stanford.edu/2018/05/31/artificial-nerve-system-gives-prosthetic-devices-robots-sense-touch/

"Adolf Hitler: Excerpts from Mein Kampf." *Jewish Virtual Library*, http://www.jewishvirtuallibrary.org/excerpts-from-mein-kampf

Allenby, Brad. "The Wrong Cognitive Measuring Stick." *Slate*, April 11, 2016. http://www.slate.com/articles/technology/future_tense/2016/04/why_it_s_a_mistake_to_compare_a_i_with_human_intelligence.html

Andrews, Evan. "Who Were the Luddites?" *History Channel*, August 7, 2015. www.history.com/news/who-were-the-luddites

Andzelika. "Japanese Café Found a Way to Employ Paralysed People as Waiters." *Bored Panda*. Accessed November 25, 2018. https://www.boredpanda.com/disabled-people-robot-dawn-ver-beta-cafe-orby-lab-japan/?utm_source=google&utm_medium=organic&utm_campaign=organic

"Anticipating Artificial Intelligence." *Nature*, April 26, 2016. www.nature.com/news/anticipating-artificial-intelligence-1.19825

"Artificial intelligence Law—Judicial and Regulatory Trends." *Practicing Law Institute*, May 2018. www.pli.edu/content/seminar/Artificial_Intelligence_Law_Judicial_and_/_N-4KZ!z0zmxb?fromsearch=false&ID=341860

Atad, Corey. "Every Episode of *Black Mirror*, Ranked." *Esquire*, December 29, 2017. www.esquire.com/entertainment/tv/a49919/black-mirror-episodes-ranked/

Austin, Jon. "Is this the true meaning of life? Shock theory could change how we view the world forever." *Daily Express*, May 20, 2017. www.express.co.uk/news/weird/807193/meaning-of-life-scientists-virtual-world-theory-Elon-Musk-Rich-Terrile-Neil-deGrasse-Tyson

Bailey, David Evans. "Ten Cool Applications for virtual reality that aren't just games." *The Conversation*, March 22, 2016. www.theconversation.com/ten-cool-applications-for-virtual-reality-that-arent-just-games-56365

Bailey, Ronald. "Public Distrust of Government should worry us all, even conservatives and libertarians." *Los Angeles Daily News*, January 4, 2018. https://www.dailynews.com/2018/01/04/public-distrust-of-government-should-worry-us-all-even-conservatives-and-libertarians/

Ball, Philip. "We can't ban robots—it's already too late." *The Guardian*, August 22, 2017. https://www.theguardian.com/commentisfree/2017/aug/22/killer-robots-international-arms-traders

Barlyn, Suzanne. "John Hancock will only sell interactive life insurance with fitness data tracking." *Insurance Journal*, September 19, 2018. https://www.insurancejournal.com/news/national/2018/09/19/501747.htm

Barrat, James. "Why Stephen Hawking and Bill Gates are Terrified of Artificial Intelligence." *HuffPost*, April 9, 2015. https://www.huffingtonpost.com/james-barrat/hawking-gates-artificial-intelligence_b_7008706.html

Bary, Emily. "Apple never meant for you to spend so much time on your phone, Tim Cook says." *MarketWatch*, June 27, 2018. https://www.marketwatch.com/story/apple-never-meant-for-you-to-spend-so-much-time-on-your-phone-tim-cook-says-2018-06-26

Beilis, Kira. "How Your Technology Is Manipulating You." *The Cut*, October 24, 2014. https://www.thecut.com/2014/10/how-your-technology-is-manipulating-you.html

Berger, Michele W. "Social media use increases depression and loneliness." *Penn Today*, November 9, 2018. https://penntoday.upenn.edu/news/social-media-use-increases-depression-and-loneliness

Berliner, Uri. "A Toy Monkey that Escaped Nazi Germany and Reunited a Family." *NPR*, November 14, 2018. https://www.npr.org/2018/11/14/663059048/a-toy-monkey-that-escaped-nazi-germany-and-reunited-a-family

Bernstein, Leandra. "Poll: Mainstream media continues to lose the public's trust." *WJLA*. Accessed September 5, 2018. http://wjla.com/news/nation-world/main-stream-media-continue-to-lose-the-publics-trust

Berwick, Angus. "How ZTE helps Venezuela create China-style social control." *Reuters*, November 14, 2018. https://www.reuters.com/investigates/special-report/venezuela-zte/

Bieler, Des. "Bryan Colangelo takes heat for throwing his wife under the bus in resignation." *The Washington Post*, June 7, 2018. https://www.washingtonpost.com/news/early-lead/wp/2018/06/07/bryan-colangelo-takes-heat-for-throwing-his-wife-under-the-bus-in-resignation/?noredirect=on&utm_term=.d10bd88c9638

Birnbaum, Debra. "Netflix Picks Up 'Black Mirror' for 12 New Episodes." *Variety*, September 25, 2015. http://variety.com/2015/digital/news/netflix-black-mirror-new-episodes-1201602037/

Bostrom, Nick. "Ethical Issues in Advanced Artificial Intelligence." 2003. www.nickbostrom.com/ethics/ai.html

Bostrom, Nick. "The Superintelligent Will: Motivation and Instrumental Rationality in Advanced Artificial Agents." 2012. www.nickbostrom.com/superintelligentwill.pdf

Botting, Eileen Hunt. "Godmother of intelligences." *Aeon*, October 3, 2018. www.aeon.co/essays/what-frankensteins-creature-can-really-tell-us-about-ai

Bowerman, Mary, and Ashley May. "Martin Luther King, Jr., quotes: 10 most popular from the civil rights leader." *USA Today*, January 21, 2019. https://www.usatoday.com/story/news/nation/2019/01/21/martin-luther-king-jr-quotes-10-most-popular/2636024002/

Bowles, Nellie. "The Digital Gap Between Rich and Poor Kids Is Not What We Expect." *The New York Times*, October 26, 2018. https://www.nytimes.com/2018/10/26/style/digital-divide-screens-schools.html

Bradner, Eric. "Conway: Trump White House Offered 'Alternative Facts' on Crowd Size." CNNwww, January 23, 2017. https://www.cnn.com/2017/01/22/politics/kellyanne-conway-alternative-facts/index.html

Bramesco, Charles. "*Black Mirror* Recap: The Dark Side of Fan Fiction." *Vulture*, December 29, 2017. www.vulture.com/2017/12/black-mirror-recap-season-4-uss-callister.html

Brandon, John. "An AI god will emerge by 2042 and write its own bible. Will you worship it?" *VentureBeat*, October 2, 2017. https://venturebeat.com/2017/10/02/an-ai-god-will-emerge-by-2042-and-write-its-own-bible-will-you-worship-it/

Brichacek, Andra. "Six Ways the Media Influences Elections." *University of Oregon School of Journalism and Communication*, November 8, 2016. http://journalism.uoregon.edu/news/six-ways-media-influences-elections/

Brown, Benjamin. "'Robot sex brothel' slated to open is not wanted, Houston's mayor says." *FOX News*, September 26, 2018. www.foxnews.com/tech/robot-sex-brothel-slated-to-open-is-not-wanted-houstons-mayor-says

Burgess, Matt. "Digital Escapism: VR will allow us to live in the world we want to." *Factor*, October 14, 2014. www.factor-tech.com/connected-world/8747-digital-escapism-vr-will-allow-us-to-live-in-the-world-we-want-to/

Burns, Janet. "There's Now Evidence That Online Dating Causes Stronger, More Diverse Marriages." *Forbes*, October 25, 2017. www.forbes.com/sites/janetwburns/2017/10/25/theres-now-evidence-that-online-dating-causes-stronger-more-diverse-relationships/#760adde58bdf

Carroll, Tobias. "How Electric Dreams Compares to Philip K. Dick's Short Stories." *Vulture*, February 5, 2018. http://www.vulture.com/2018/02/electric-dreams-philip-k-dick-short-story-comparison.html

CBS Sports Staff. "Cowboys vs. Giants Odds: Sunday Night Football Picks, Predictions from Proven Model on 51–35 Run." *CBS Sports*, September 16, 2018. https://www.cbssports.com/nfl/news/cowboys-vs-giants-odds-sunday-night-football-picks-predictions-from-proven-model-on-51-35-run/

Chaney, Jen. "From Veep to Scandal, How TV Foreshadowed the Presidential Election." *Vulture*, November 3, 2016. www.vulture.com/2016/11/tv-foreshadowed-the-presidential-election.html

Clark, Travis. "All 19 Episodes of '*Black Mirror*' Ranked from Worst to Best." *Business Insider*, September 10, 2018. https://www.businessinsider.com/every-black-mirror-episode-on-netflix-ranked-from-worst-to-best-2018-5

"Clarke as ICT Promoter." Accessed April 9, 2018. www.arthurcclarke.org/site/sri-lanka/clarke-and-sri-lanka/communications/

Clifford, Catherine. "Elon Musk: 'Mark my words—A.I. is far more dangerous than nukes.'" *CNBC*, March 13, 2018. https://www.cnbc.com/2018/03/13/elon-musk-at-sxsw-a-i-is-more-dangerous-than-nuclear-weapons.html

Clifford, Catherine. "Facebook CEO Mark

Zuckerberg: Elon Musk's doomsday AI predictions are 'pretty irresponsible.'" *CNBC,* July 24, 2017. https://www.cnbc.com/2017/07/24/mark-zuckerberg-elon-musks-doomsday-ai-predictions-are-irresponsible.html

Clifford, Catherine. "Warren Buffett and Bill Gates think it's crazy to view job-stealing robots as bad." *CNBC,* February 3, 2017. https://www.cnbc.com/2017/02/03/warren-buffett-and-bill-gates-think-its-crazy-to-view-robots-as-bad.html

Cockburn, Harry. "China blacklists millions of people from booking flights as 'social credit' system introduced." *The Independent,* November 22, 2018. https://www.independent.co.uk/news/world/asia/china-social-credit-system-flight-booking-blacklisted-beijing-points-a8646316.html

Cohen, David. "How Much Time Will the Average Person Spend on Social Media During Their Life?" *Adweek,* March 22, 2017. http://www.adweek.com/digital/mediakix-time-spent-social-media-infographic/

Collin, Robbie. "Black Mirror Season 3, Shut Up and Dance review: 'soul-scorching, dark and riveting." *The Daily Telegraph,* October 2016. https://www.telegraph.co.uk/on-demand/0/black-mirror-season-3-shut-up-and-dance-review-soul-scorching-da/

Commons, Jess. "*Black Mirror's* Charlie Brooker: 'I Feel Sorry for Millennials. You get a Bad Rep!" *Grazia,* October 22, 2016. https://grazia daily.co.uk/life/tv-and-film/black-mirror-season-3-charlie-brooker-san-junipero/

Constine, Josh. "Facebook changes mission statement to 'bring the world closer together.'" *TechCrunch,* June 22, 2017. https://techcrunch.com/2017/06/22/bring-the-world-closer-together/

Crawford, Kate, and Vladan Joler. "Anatomy of an AI System, The Amazon Echo As An Anatomical Map of Human Labor, Data and Planetary Resources." *AI Now Institute and Share Lab,* September 7, 2018. https://anatomyof.ai.

Dailymail.com Reporter. "Bill Murray laments the rise of social media: 'People document their life rather than live it.'" *Daily Mail,* June 1, 2018. http://www.dailymail.co.uk/tvshowbiz/article-5795959/Bill-Murray-laments-rise-social-media-People-document-life-live-it.html

Damiani, Jesse. "*Black Mirror*: Bandersnatch Could Become Netflix's Secret Marketing Weapon." *The Verge,* January 2, 2019. https://www.theverge.com/2019/1/2/18165182/black-mirror-bandersnatch-netflix-interactive-strategy-marketing

Das, Reenita. "Virtual Reality: The Alternative to Marijuana and Opioids for Pain Management." *Forbes,* May 31, 2018. www.forbes.com/sites/reenitadas/2018/05/31/virtual-reality-the-alternative-to-marijuana-and-opioids-for-pain-management/#laf0f7d151d6

Dastin, Jeffrey. "'Kill your foster parents': Amazon's Alexa talks murder, sex in AI experiment." *Reuters,* December 21, 2018. www.reuters.com/article/us-amazon-com-alexa-insight/kill-your-foster-parents-amazons-alexa-talks-murder-sx-in-ai-experiment-idUSKCN1)K1AJ

Datsin, Jeffrey. "Amazon scraps secret AI recruiting tool that showed bias against women." *Reuters,* October 9, 2018. https://www.reuters.com/article/us-amazon-com-jobs-automation-insight/amazon-scraps-secret-ai-recruiting-tool-that-showed-bias-against-women-idUSKCN1MK08G

Dawsey, Josh. "In reversal, Giuliani now says Trump should do interview with Mueller team." *The Washington Post,* May 23, 2018. https://www.washingtonpost.com/politics/in-reversal-giuliani-now-says-trump-should-do-interview-with-mueller-team/2018/05/23/82f8fa24-5eb8-11e8-9ee3-49d6d4814c4c_story.html?utm_term=.6d43b59cb1a7

Dershowitz, Alan. "An op-ed by Professor Alan Dershowitz: warming up to torture?" *Harvard Law Today,* October 7, 2006. www.today.law.harvard.edu/an-op-ed-by-professor-alan-dershowitz-warming-up-to-torture/

Dershowitz, Alan. "Should we fight terror with torture?" *Independent,* July 3, 2006. www.independent.co.uk/news/world/americas/alan-dershowitz-should-we-fight-terror-with-torture-6096463.html

Dewey, Caitlin. "Everyone you know will be able to rate you on the terrifying 'Yelp for people'—whether you want them to or not." *The Washington Post,* September 30, 2015. https://www.washingtonpost.com/news/the-intersect/wp/2015/10/05/after-internet-backlash-peeple-co-founder-will-revise-her-app-to-make-it-positive/?utm_term=.385382e0c425

Dewey, Caitlin. "Peeple, the terrifying 'Yelp for people' is (sort of) launching on March 7." *The Washington Post,* March 4, 2016. https://www.washingtonpost.com/news/the-intersect/wp/2015/10/05/after-internet-backlash-peeple-co-founder-will-revise-her-app-to-make-it-positive/?utm_term=.3766b90cd652

Donnelly, Matt, and Tim Molloy. "All 13 Black Mirror Episodes Ranked, from Good to Mind-Blowing." *The Wrap,* August 12, 2007.

https://www.thewrap.com/all-19-black-mirror-episodes-ranked-from-good-to-mind-blowing-photos/

Dowd, Maureen. "Elon Musk's Billion-Dollar Crusade to Stop the A.I. Apocalypse." *Vanity Fair*, April 2017. https://www.vanityfair.com/news/2017/03/elon-musk-billion-dollar-crusade-to-stop-ai-space-x

Dunbar, R.I.M. "Do online social media cut through the constraints that limit the size of offline social networks?" *The Royal Society Publishing*, January 20, 2016. www.rsos.royalsocietypublishing.org/content/3/1/150292)

Ellis, Ryan. "The Scorpion and the Frog: A Tale of Modern Capitalism." *Forbes*, April 24, 2015. www.forbes.com/sites/ryanellis/2015/04/24/the-scorpion-and-the-frog-a-tale-of-modern-capitalism/#4da67cd76f7a

"Enter Search Term Here, Forever." *The New York Times*, August 21, 2006, A16.

Eugenios, Jillian. "Ray Kurzweil: Humans will be hybrids by 2030." *CNN Tech*, June 4, 2015. http://money.cnn.com/2015/06/03/technology/ray-kurzweil-predictions/index.html

Farrell, Henry. "Hackers used a fish tank to break into a Vegas casino. We're all in trouble." *The Washington Post*, September 4, 2018. https://www.washingtonpost.com/news/monkey-cage/wp/2018/09/04/hackers-used-a-fishtank-to-break-into-a-vegas-casino-were-all-in-trouble/?utm_term=.7dccf8071984

Feldman, Josh. "Alan Dershowitz and Richard Painter Get in Tense Clash: Mueller May Be a Good American But 'You're Not.'" *Mediaite*, May 5, 2018. https://www.mediaite.com/tv/alan-dershowitz-and-richard-painter-get-in-tense-clash-mueller-may-be-a-good-american-but-youre-not/

Friedersdorf, Coor. "Tucker Carlson Is Hurting America Again." *The Atlantic*, June 20, 2018. https://www.theatlantic.com/politics/archive/2018/06/tucker-carlson-is-hurting-america-again/563138/

Friend, Tad. "How Frightened Should We Be of A.I.?" *The New Yorker*, May 7, 2018. https://www.newyorker.com/magazine/2018/05/14/how-frightened-should-we-be-of-ai

Frier, Sarah. "America's Teens are Choosing YouTube over Facebook." *Bloomberg*, May 31, 2018. https://www.bloomberg.com/news/articles/2018-05-31/america-s-teens-are-choosing-youtube-over-facebook

Fuchs, Erin. "The tech execs who have called out Facebook's trust problem." *Yahoo Finance*, May 16, 2018. https://finance.yahoo.com/news/tech-execs-called-facebooks-trust-problem-152935213.html (quoting Marc Benioff, *CBS This Morning*, May 16, 2018, https://www.cbsnews.com/video/salesforce-ceo-marc-benioff-calls-for-national-privacy-law/)

Galeon, Dom, and Christianna Reedy. "Kurzweil Claims that the Singularity Will Happen by 2045." *Futurism*, October 5, 2017. https://futurism.com/kurzweil-claims-that-the-singularity-will-happen-by-2045/

Gaydos, Ryan. "Filmmaker David Lynch believes Trump could be one of the greatest presidents in history." *FOX News*, June 25, 2018. http://www.foxnews.com/entertainment/2018/06/25/filmmaker-david-lynch-believes-trump-could-be-one-greatest-presidents-in-history.html

Gibbs, Samuel. "Alpha Zero AI Beats Champion Chess Program after teaching itself in four hours." *The Guardian*, December 7, 2017. https://www.theguardian.com/technology/2017/dec/07/alphazero-google-deepmind-ai-beats-champion-program-teaching-itself-to-play-four-hours

Golgowski, Nina. "Washington teen jumps to death after being shamed in online video taken by dad." *NY Daily News*, June 5, 2015. www.nydailynews.com/news/national/teen-kills-public-shaming-allegedly-dad-article-1.2247168

"GOP Rep on Trump Jr.—Ocasio-Cortez Twitter Feud: 'Social Media Is Making Us All Stupid.'" FOX News Insider, December 10, 2018. http://insider.foxnews.com/2018/12/10/donald-trump-jr-and-alexandria-ocasio-cortez-spar-social-media-outnumbered-reacts

Gordon, Bryony. "Charlie Brooker on *Black Mirror*: 'It's not a technological problem we have, it's a human one.'" *The Telegraph*, December 16, 2014. https://www.telegraph.co.uk/culture/tvandradio/11260768/Charlie-Brooker-Its-not-a-technological-problem-we-have-its-a-human-one.html

Gottfried, Jeffrey, and Elisa Shearer. "News Use Across Social Media Platforms." *Pew Research Center*, May 26, 2016. www.journalism.org/2016/05/26/news-use-across-social-media-platforms-2016.

Grynbaum, Michael M. "The New Yorker Festival Boots Bannon, and Liberals are Torn." *The New York Times*, September 4, 2018. https://www.nytimes.com/2018/09/04/business/media/bannon-new-yorker-festival-liberals.html

"The Guardian view on Internet privacy: it's the psychology, stupid." *The Guardian*, February 8, 2018. www.theguardian.com/global/commentisfree/2018/feb/08/the-guardian-view-on-internet-privacy-its-the-psychology-stupid

Haas, Benjamin. "Chinese man 'marries' robot he built himself." *The Guardian*, April 4, 2017. https://www.theguardian.com/world/2017/apr/04/chinese-man-marries-robot-built-himself

Hall, Gina. "Amazon's latest drone prototypes can carry packages up to 5 pounds." *Silicon Valley Business Journal*, November 30, 2015. www.bizjournals.com/sanjose/news/2015/11/30/amazons-latest-drone-prototypes-can-carry-packages.html

Hamilton, Isobel Asher. "People kicking these food delivery robots is an early insight into how cruel humans could be to robots." *Business Insider*, June 9, 2018. https://www.businessinsider.com/people-are-kicking-starship-technologies-food-delivery-robots-2018-6

Handlen, Zack. "*Black Mirror* finds love (and a great episode) in a hopeful place." *The A.V. Club*, October 24, 2016. www.tv.avclub.com/black-mirror-finds-love-and-a-great-episode-in-a-hope-1798189275

Handlen, Zack. "No one's watching the watchmen on a so-so Black Mirror." *The A.V. Club*, October 23, 2016. https://tv.avclub.com/no-one-s-watching-the-watchmen-on-a-so-so-black-mirror-1798189235

Harmon, Elliot. "No, Section 230 Does Not Require Platforms to be 'Neutral.'" *Electronic Frontier Foundation*, April 12, 2018. https://www.eff.org/deeplinks/2018/04/no-section-230-does-not-require-platforms-be-neutral

Hawkes, Rebecca. "*Black Mirror*'s Charlie Brooker on predicting Trump, and the 'love' story that terrified him." *The Telegraph*, February 20, 2017. https://www.telegraph.co.uk/on-demand/0/black-mirrors-charlie-brooker-predicting-donald-trump-love-story/

Hawks, John Twelve. "New surveillance states have placed us in an invisible prison" *Salon*, September 15, 2014. www.salon.com/2014/09/14/john_twelve_hawks_new_surveillance_states_have_placed_us_in_an_invisible_prison/

Hayes, Dade, and Patrick Hipes. "Twilight Zone Series Reboot in Works at CBS All Access." *Deadline*, November 1, 2017. http://deadline.com/2017/11/twilight-zone-reboot-cbs-all-access-1202200631/

Hellard, Bobby. "How an episode of *Black Mirror* became a creepy reality." *i-D vice*, November 13, 2018. https://i-d.vice.com/en_uk/article/nepbdg/black-mirror-artificial-intelligence-roman-mazurenko

Hibberd, James. "Black Mirror postmortem: Showrunner talks Season 3 twists." *Entertainment Weekly*, October 21, 2016. http://ew.com/article/2016/10/23/black-mirror-postmortem-interview-season-3/

Hintze, Arend. "What an artificial intelligence researcher fears about AI." *Salon*, January 6, 2018. https://www.salon.com/2018/01/06/what-an-artificial-intelligence-researcher-fears-about-ai_partner/

Hogan, Michael. "*Black Mirror*: The National Anthem, Channel 4, review." *The Telegraph*, December 4, 2011. https://www.telegraph.co.uk/culture/tvandradio/8932095/Black-Mirror-The-National-Anthem-Channel-4-review.html

Holley, Peter. "Bill Gates on dangers of artificial intelligence: 'I don't understand why some people are not concerned." *The Washington Post*, January 29, 2015. https://www.washingtonpost.com/news/the-switch/wp/2015/01/28/bill-gates-on-dangers-of-artificial-intelligence-dont-understand-why-some-people-are-not-concerned/?utm_term=.037f1f650fe4&noredirect=on

Holub, Christian. "Black Mirror creator explains what a Trump episode would look like: Highlights from 5/21/17 Vulture Festival discussion with Andrew Sullivan." *Entertainment Weekly*, May 21, 2017. https://ew.com/tv/2017/05/21/black-mirror-vulture-fest-panel/

Howell, Elizabeth. "Parallel Universes: Theories and Evidence." Spacewww, May 9, 2018. www.space.com/32728-parallel-universes.html

Hvistendahl, Mara. "Inside China's Vast New Experiment In Social Ranking." *Wired*, December 14, 2017. www.wired.com/story/age-of-social-credit

"'Jeff, Do You Even Care?': Hannity Blasts CNN President for Anti-Trump Bias." *Fox News Insider*, June 26, 2017. www.insider.foxnews.com/2017/06/26/sean-hannity-cnn-fake-news-jeff-zucker-destroy-donald-trump-administration-scaramucci

Jeffery, Morgan. "'*Black Mirror*' series two 'The Waldo Moment' review." *Digital Spy*, February 25, 2013. http://www.digitalspy.com/tv/black-mirror/news/a461004/black-mirror-series-two-the-waldo-moment-review/

Jones, Daniel. "Alexa, will we divorce?" *The Sun*, November 29, 2018. www.thesun.co.uk/tech/7854556/virtual-assistants-amazon-alexa-relationship-break-up/

Joseph, Rebecca. "Frequent social media users nearly 3 times more likely to have depression: study." *Global News*, March 26, 2016. https://globalnews.ca/news/2601572/frequent-social-media-users-nearly-3-times-more-likely-to-have-depression-study/

"Joseph Goebbels on The Big Lie." *Jewish Virtual*

Library, http://www.jewishvirtuallibrary.org/joseph-goebbels-on-the-quot-big-lie-quot

JPost staff. "Top 5 Most Egregious Anti-Israel Headlines in the International Media." *Jerusalem Post*, August 17, 2016. https://www.jpost.com/Arab-Israeli-Conflict/Top-5-most-egregious-anti-Israel-headlines-in-the-international-media-464351

Kane, Suzanne. "Smartphone Use in America: Is it Contributing to Cognitive Decline?" *PsychCentral*, July 8, 2018. www.psychcentral.com/blog/smartphone-use-in-america-is-it-contributing-to-cognitive-decline/

Kelly, Laura. "Teen suicide rate suddenly rises with heavy use of smartphones, social media." *The Washington Times*, November 14, 2017. www.washingtontimes.com/news/2017/nov/14/teen-suicides-rise-with-smartphone-social-media-us/

Kharpal, Arjun. "Stephen Hawking says A.I. could be 'worst event in the history of our civilization.'" *CNBC*, November 6, 2017. https://www.cnbc.com/2017/11/06/stephen-hawking-ai-could-be-worst-event-in-civilization.html

Kim, Monica. "The Good and the Bad of Escaping to Virtual Reality." *The Atlantic*, February 8, 2015. www.theatlantic.com/health/archive/2015/02/the-good-and-the-bad-of-escaping-to-virtual-reality/385134

Knight, Will. "Biased Algorithms are Everywhere, and No One Seems to Care." *MIT Technology Review*, July 12, 2017. https://www.technologyreview.com/s/608248/biased-algorithms-are-everywhere-and-no-one-seems-to-care/

Koblin, John. "After Racist Tweet, Roseanne Barr's Show Is Canceled by ABC." *The New York Times*, May 29, 2018. https://www.nytimes.com/2018/05/29/business/media/roseanne-barr-offensive-tweets.html

Kosoff, Maya. "Apple Predicts *Black Mirror* Memory Implants Could Soon Be a Reality." *Vanity Fair*, April 25, 2017. https://www.vanityfair.com/news/2017/04/apple-exec-predicts-black-mirror-tech-could-soon-be-a-reality

Krishna, Swapna. "Russians used fake social accounts to gather Americans' personal data." *Engadget*, March 7, 2018. www.engadget.com/2018/03/07/russians-faken-social-media-accounts-steal-personal-data/

Kuss, Daria J., and Mark D. Griffiths. "Online Social Networking and Addiction—A Review of the Psychological Literature." *International Gaming Research Unit, Psychology Division, Nottingham Trent University*, August 29, 2011. www.mdpi.com/1660-4601/8/9/3528/htm?hc_location=ufi

LaFrance, Adrienne. "How *The Twilight Zone* Predicted Our Paranoid Present." *The Atlantic*, December 31, 2013. https://www.theatlantic.com/entertainment/archive/2013/12/how-em-the-twilight-zone-em-predicted-our-paranoid-present/282700/

Lardieri, Alexa. "Amazon Employees Protesting Sale of Facial Recognition Software." *U.S. News & World Report*, October 18, 2018. www.usnews.com/news/politics/articles/2018-10-18/amazon-employees-protesting-sale-of-facial-recognition-software

Lee, Benjamin. "*Black Mirror* Review—Charlie Brooker's splashy new series is still a sinister marvel." *The Guardian*, September 16, 2016. www.theguardian.com/tv-and-radio/2016/sep/16/black-mirror-first-look-review-charlie-brooker

Lee, Dave. "Pokemon Go: Hiding Pikachu may hold key to AR's future." *BBC News*, June 28, 2018. www.bbc.com/news/technology-44638604

Levey, Curt. "Supreme Court Ruling in cell phone case is a victory for our privacy rights." Foxnewswww, June 22, 2018. https://www.foxnews.com/opinion/supreme-court-ruling-in-cell-phone-case-is-a-victory-for-our-privacy-rights

Levy, Steven. "Bill Gates and President Bill Clinton on the NSA, Safe Sex, and American Exceptionalism." *Wired*, November 12, 2013. www.wired.com/2013/11/bill-gates-bill-clinton-wired/

Levy, Steven. "What Deep Blue Tells Us About AI in 2017." *Wired*, May 23, 2017. https://www.wired.com/2017/05/what-deep-blue-tells-us-about-ai-in-2017/

Li, Chris. "'Black Mirror' Isn't Just About Technology. It's About Us." *The Gospel Coalition*, December 29, 2017. https://www.thegospelcoalition.org/article/black-mirror-isnt-just-technology-us/

"The Lost Meaning of Objectivity." *The American Press Institute*. Accessed October 15, 2018. https://www.americanpressinstitute.org/journalism-essentials/bias-objectivity/lost-meaning-objectivity/

Maier, Lilly. "Mark Cuban Advises Trump to Invest $100 Billion in Robotics." *Forward*, December 19, 2016. https://forward.com/fast-forward/357571/mark-cuban-advises-trump-to-invest-100-billion-in-robotics/

Mandes, Evan. "What Happened to Alan Dershowitz: How a Liberal Harvard Professor Became Trump's Most Distinguished Defender on TV, Freaked Out His Friends and Got the Legal World Up in Arms." *Politico*, May 11,

2018. https://www.politico.com/magazine/story/2018/05/11/alan-dershowitz-donald-trump-what-happened-218359

Martin, George. "China 'launches an app that tells you if you are within 500 yards of someone in debt—and encourages you to report them if they seem capable of paying up.'" *Daily Mail*, January 22, 2019. https://www.dailymail.co.uk/news/article-6620879/China-launches-app-tells-500-yards-debt.html

Marvizon, Dr. Juan Carlos. "Not Just Intelligence: why humans deserve to be treated better than animals." December 6, 2016. https://speakingofresearch.com/2016/12/06/not-just-intelligence-why-humans-deserve-to-be-treated-better-than-animals/

Matthews, Hayley. "Online Dating Statistics: Dating Stats from 2017." *Zoosk*, December 3, 2017. www.zoosk.com/date-mix/online-dating-advice/online-dating-statistics-dating-stats-2017/

Matyszczyk, Chris. "The 1 Reason Why You Should Worry About Google Most of All (It Involves a Word that Might be New to You)." Incwww, May 6, 2018. https://www.inc.com/chris-matyszczyk/the-1-reason-why-you-should-fear-google-most-of-all-it-involves-a-word-that-might-be-new-to-you.html

McCluskey, Megan. "15 Times *The Simpsons* Accurately Predicted the Future." *Time Magazine*, updated February 26, 2018, originally published March 9, 2017. http://time.com/4667462/simpsons-predictions-donald-trump-lady-gaga/.

McGregor, Jena. "Some Swedish workers are getting microchips implanted in their hands," *The Washington Post*, April 4, 2017. www.washingtonpost.com/news/on-leadership/wp/2017/04/04/some-swedish-workers-are-getting-microchips-implanted-in-their-hands/?noredirect=on&utm_term=.7389c41ff39f

Mehta, Ivan. "Amazon's new patent will allow Alexa to detect a cough or a cold." *The Next Web*, October 15, 2018. https://thenextweb.com/artificial-intelligence/2018/10/15/amazons-new-patent-will-allow-alexa-to-detect-your-illness/

Meslow, Scott. "The Best TV Episodes of 2016." *GQ*, December 15, 2016. www.gq.com/story/best-tv-2016

Minor, Jordan. "*The Flintstones* Internet of Living Things." Geekwww, January 30, 2017. www.geek.com/tech/the-flintstones-internet-of-living-things-1686807/

Moniuszko, Sara M. "'Black Mirror' Season 4 includes a timely episode on power dynamics and sexual harassment." *USA Today*, December 29, 2017. www.usatoday.com/story/life/entertainthis/2017/12/29/black-mirrors-u-s-s-callister-freakishly-similar-highlights-societys-problem-power-today/974052001/

Moraes, Lisa de. "Sci-Fi Anthology *Black Mirror* Repeats TV Movie Win with Donald Trumpian 'USS Callister—Emmys." *Deadline Hollywood*, September 8, 2018. https://deadline.com/2018/09/uss-callister-black-mirror-wins-best-tv-movie-emmy-1202460277/

Mulane, Alex. "*Black Mirror* Season 3: 'Hated in the Nation' review: a blockbuster with a sting in its tail." *Digital Spy*, October 23, 2016. http://www.digitalspy.com/tv/black-mirror/news/a811894/black-mirror-season-3-hated-in-the-nation-review/

Naughton, John. "Steven Pinker: Fighting Talk from the Prophet of Peace." *The Guardian*, October 15, 2011. www.theguardian.com/science/2011/oct/15/steven-pinker-better-angels-violence-interview

Neuburger, Jeffrey. "FOSTA Signed into Law, Amends CDA Section 230 to Allow Enforcement against Online Providers for Knowingly Facilitating Sex Trafficking." *Proskauer Rose*, April 11, 2018. https://newmedialaw.proskauer.com/2018/04/11/fosta-signed-into-law-amends-cda-section-230-to-allow-enforcement-against-online-providers-for-knowingly-facilitating-sex-trafficking/

Neuburger, Jeffrey. "YouTube Protected by CDA Immunity Over Claims that it Provided Material Support to Terrorists." *Proskauer Rose*, November 14, 2017. www.newmedialaw.proskauer.com/2017/11/14/youtube-protected-by-cda-immunity-over-claims-that-it-provided-material-support-to-terrorists/

Noonan, Keith. "Why Is Everyone Talking About iQiyi stock?" *The Motley Fool*, June 25, 2018. https://www.fool.com/investing/2018/06/25/why-is-everyone-talking-about-iqiyi-stock.aspx

Nunez, Michael. "Former Facebook Workers: We Routinely Suppressed Conservative News." *Gizmodo*, May 9, 2016. www.gizmodo.com/former-facebook-workers-we-routinely-suppressed-conser-1775461006

Nussbaum, Emily. "Button-Pusher: The Seductive Dystopia of 'Black Mirror.'" *The New Yorker*, January 5, 2015. https://www.newyorker.com/magazine/2015/01/05/button-pusher

"Only 1 in 3 U.S. Marriage Proposals Are a Surprise; Engagement Ring Spend Rise, According to The Knot 2017 Jewelry and Engagement Study." *The Knot*, November 9, 2017. https://www.prnewswire.com/news-releases/only-1-in-3-us-marriage-proposals-are-a-surprise-engagement-ring-spend-rises-according-to-the-knot-2017-jewelry—engagement-study-300552669.html

Origgi, Gloria. "Say Goodbye to the Information Age: It's All About Reputation Now." *Fast Company,* April 28, 2018. https://www.fastcompany.com/40565050/say-goodbye-to-the-information-age-its-all-about-reputation-now

Ortiz, Aimee. "Terrifying Boston Dynamics robots, '*Black Mirror,*' and the end of the world." *Boston Globe,* January 5, 2018. https://www.bostonglobe.com/arts/2018/01/05/boston-dynamics-black-mirror-and-end-world/cL9RYkg6O6MqyPuhmgxVjP/story.html

"Parents sue game distributor over son's suicide." *China Daily,* May 12, 2006. www.chinadaily.com.cn/china/2006-05/12/content_588456.htm.

Parham, Jason. "Why Black Mirror's Most Controversial New Episode Is Its Most Important." *Wired,* January 6, 2018. https://www.wired.com/story/black-mirror-black-museum/

Pham, Sherrise. "You can now get kicked off Uber in Australia for being rude to drivers." *CNN Tech,* September 5, 2018. money.cnn.com/2018/09/05/technology/uber-australia-new-zealand-riders/index.html

Picchi, Aimee. "Amazon's Patent for Caging Workers was 'Bad' Idea, Exec Admits." *CBS News Money Watch,* September 11, 2018. https://www.cbsnews.com/news/amazons-patent-for-caging-workers-was-a-bad-idea-exec-admits/

Polonski, Vyacheslav. "How artificial intelligence conquered democracy." *The Conversation,* August 8, 2017. https://theconversation.com/how-artificial-intelligence-conquered-democracy-77675

Poniewozik, James. "Review: '*Black Mirror*' Finds Terror, and Soul, in the Machine." *The New York Times,* October 20, 2016. https://www.nytimes.com/2016/10/21/arts/television/review-blacfk-mirror-finds-terror-and-soul-in-the-machine.html

Ponti, Crystal. "Rise of the Robot Bees: Tiny Drones Turned into Artificial Pollinators." *NPR,* March 3, 2017. www.npr.org/sections/thesalt/2017/03/03/517785082/rise-of-the-robot-bees-tiny-drones-turned-into-artificial-pollinators

"Privacy and Technology," *ACLU.* Accessed November 4, 2018. www.aclu.org/issues/privacy-technology

Puchko, Kristy. "The New Yorker, Steve Bannon and Why We're Mad at Malcolm Gladwell." *Pajiba,* September 4, 2018. http://www.pajiba.com/politics/the-new-yorker-steve-bannon-and-why-were-mad-at-malcolm-gladwell.php

Rago, Joseph. "Status Reporter." *The Wall Street Journal,* March 11, 2006. https://www.wsj.com/articles/SB114204279173895576

Rawden, Jessica. "Bryce Dallas Howard Reveals Why She Gained 30 Pounds for Black Mirror." *Cinema Blend,* August 2018. https://www.cinemablend.com/television/2455424/bryce-dallas-howard-reveals-why-she-gained-30-pounds-for-black-mirror

Raysman, Richard. "Ethics in Social Media." *Practicing Law Institute,* March 15, 2018.

Regev, Amit. "Drone Deliveries are No Longer Pie in the Sky." *Forbes,* April 10, 2018. www.forbes.com/sites/startupnationcentral/2018/04/10/drone-deliveries-are-no-longer-pie-in-the-sky/#30ac02cc4188

Reicher, Stephen D., and S. Alexander Haslam. "Trump's Appeal: What Psychology Tells Us." *Scientific American,* March 1, 2017. https://www.scientificamerican.com/article/trump-rsquo-s-appeal-what-psychology-tells-us/

Rentoul, John. *The Top 10: Misattributed Quotations. The Independent,* August 25, 2017. https://www.independent.co.uk/voices/the-top-10-misattributed-quotations-a7910361.html

Riley, Charles. "YouTube, Apple and Facebook remove content from InfoWars and Alex Jones." *CNN,* August 6, 2018. https://money.cnn.com/2018/08/06/technology/facebook-infowars-alex-jones/index.html

Rogers, Katie, and Engel Bromwich. "The Hoaxes, Fake News and Misinformation We Saw On Election Day." *New York Times,* November 8, 2016. www.nytimes.com/2016/11/09/us/politics/debunk-fake-news-election-day.html.

Rosen, Rebecca J. "'I've Created a Monster': On the Regrets of Inventors." *The Atlantic,* November 23, 2011. https://www.theatlantic.com/technology/archive/2011/11/ive-created-a-monster-on-the-regrets-of-inventors/249044/

Rosenberg, Scott A. "The Sneeze and the fury of 'Snotgirl.'" *amNY,* May 30, 2018.

Rothman, Joshua. "Are We Already Living in Virtual Reality?" *The New Yorker,* April 2, 2018. www.newyorker.com/magazine/2018/04/02/are-we-already-living-in-virtual-reality

Ryan, Maureen et al. "Bandersnatch Has Many Paths But Do Any of Them Add Up to Anything?" *The New York Times,* January 4, 2019. https://www.nytimes.com/2019/01/04/arts/television/bandersnatch-black-mirror-netflix.html

Salam, Maya. "*The Simpsons* Has Predicted a

Lot/ Most of It Can Be Explained." *The New York Times*, February 2, 2018. https://www.nytimes.com/2018/02/02/arts/television/simpsons-prediction-future.html.

Scheff, Sue. "Was 2017 the Rise of Online Shaming?" *Huffpost*, December 2017. https://www.huffingtonpost.com/entry/was-2017-the-rise-of-online-shaming_us_5a43fa33e4b0d86c803c748f

Scibelli, Anthony. "Why *The Flintstones* Takes Place in a Post-Apocalyptic Future." *Cracked*, June 20, 2012. www.cracked.com/quick-fixes/why-flintstones-takes-place-in-post-apocalyptic-future/

Selk, Avi. "The Violent Rally Trump Can't Move Past." *The Washington Post*, April 3, 2017. https://www.washingtonpost.com/news/the-fix/wp/2017/04/03/the-violent-rally-trump-cant-move-past/?noredirect=on&utm_term=.fe10e1fc880e

Selyukh, Alina. "Section 230: A Key Legal Shield for Facebook, Google Is About to Change." *NPR*, March 21, 2018. https://www.npr.org/sections/alltechconsidered/2018/03/21/591622450/section-230-a-key-legal-shield-for-facebook-google-is-about-to-change

Semuels, Alana. "I Delivered Packages for Amazon and It Was a Nightmare." *The Atlantic*, June 25, 2018. https://www.theatlantic.com/business/archive/2018/06/amazon-flex-workers/563444/

Shih, Clara. "Hearsay Social CEO Clara Shih: 5 tech trends to watch in 2015." *Fortune*, January 28, 2015. www.fortune.com/2015/01/28/hearsay-social-ceo-clara-shih-5-tech-trends-to-watch-in-2015/

Siegel, Ethan. "Is There Another 'You' Out There in a Parallel Universe." *Forbes*, November 18, 2016. https://www.forbes.com/sites/startswithabang/2016/11/18/is-there-another-you-out-there-in-a-parallel-universe/#79f5b11a634f

Sims, David. "Black Mirror: 'White Bear.'" *AV/TV Club*, December 10, 2013. www.tv.avclub.com/black-mirror-white-bear-1798178958

Solomon, Shoshanna. "Late president Peres delivers hologram message at Israel Innovation Summit." *The Times of Israel*, October 25, 2018. www.timesofisrael.com/late-president-peres-delivers-hologram-message-at-israel-innovation-summit/

Solomon-Brady, Harvey. "Sex doll rental company will make a replica of your dead lover." *New York Post*, October 16, 2018. www.nypost.com/2018/10/16/sex-doll-rental-company-will-make-a-replica-of-your-dead-lover/

Solon, Olivia. "Amazon patents wristband that tracks warehouse workers' movements." *The Guardian*, January 31, 2018. www.theguardian.com/technology/2018/jan/31/amazon-warehouse-wristband-tracking

Speicher, Abby. "Drone Laws: The History of Drone Regulations and Laws." *Dart Drones*, November 9, 2016. www.dartdrones.com/blog/drone-laws/

Stanley, Jay. "New Technology Renews Old Fears of Manipulation and Control." *American Civil Liberties Union*, August 1, 2014. https://www.aclu.org/blog/national-security/new-technology-renews-old-fears-manipulation-and-control

Stern, Marlow. "Inside 'San Junipero': The Magical '*Black Mirror*' Episode That Will Help Take Your Mind Off Trump." *The Daily Beast*, November 27, 2016. www.thedailybeast.com/inside-san-junipero-the-magical-black-mirror-episode-that-will-help-take-your-mind-off-trump

Stewart, Dan. "Why David Cameron's 'Pig-Gate' Scandal Isn't Going Away." *Time Magazine*, September 21, 2015. http://time.com/4043311/david-cameron-pig-gate-scandal/

Stewart, Sara. "Locked up for 14 years, these brothers learned everything they know from 5,000 movies." *New York Post*, June 9, 2015. www.nypost.com/2015/06/09/how-6-brothers-learned-about-the-world-by-watching-5000-movies/

Stolworthy, Jacob. "Emmys 2017: *Black Mirror* Episode 'San Junipero' wins two awards." *The Independent*, September 18, 2017. https://www.independent.co.uk/arts-entertainment/tv/news/emmys-2017-winners-black-mirror-san-junipero-charlie-brooker-outstanding-writing-tv-movie-a7952266.html

Sulleyman, Aatif. "Elon Musk Slams Proposal to Create an Artificial Intelligence 'God' that People Will Worship." *The Independent*, October 24, 2017. https://www.independent.co.uk/life-style/gadgets-and-tech/news/ai-god-elon-musk-artificial-intelligence-religion-anthony-levandowski-way-of-the-future-a8017296.html

Surkes, Sue. "As influence of AI, big data grows, cyber experts discuss tech safety and trust." *The Times of Israel*, November 15, 2018. https://www.timesofisrael.com/as-influence-of-ai-big-data-grows-cyber-experts-discuss-tech-safety-and-trust/.

Svetlik, Joe. "First look at 'Better Call Saul season 2." *uSwitch*, February 8, 2016. https://www.uswitch.com/tv/news/2016/02/first_look_at_better_call_saul_season_two/

Sweet, William. "Jeremy Bentham (1748–1832).

Internet Encyclopedia of Philosophy. Accessed January 4, 2019. www.iep.utm.edu/bentham

Tallerico, Brian. "Every Major Easter Egg in Black Mirror Season Four." *Vulture*, January 4, 2018. http://www.vulture.com/2018/01/black-mirror-season-4-every-easter-egg.html

Telegraph Reporters. "Online dating ad banned after scientific claims were dismissed as 'fake news.'" *The Telegraph*, January 3, 2018. www.telegraph.co.uk/news/2018/01/03/online-dating-ad-banned-scientific-claims-dismissed-fake-news/

Thompson, Avery. "Google Accidentally Broke Japan's Internet." *Popular Mechanics*, August 28, 2017. https://www.popularmechanics.com/technology/news/a27971/google-accidentally-broke-japans-internet/

Tinline, Phil. "The Art of the Big Lie: the history of fake news." *New Statesman*, March 17, 2018. https://www.newstatesman.com/world/2018/03/art-big-lie-history-fake-news

Totenberg, Nina. "In Major Privacy Win, Supreme Court Rules Police Need Warrant to Track Your Cellphone." *NPR*, June 22, 2018. https://www.npr.org/2018/06/22/605007387/supreme-court-rules-police-need-warrant-to-get-location-information-from-cell-to

Vanian, Jonathan. "Everything to Know About President Donald Trump's New Drone Program." *Fortune*, October 25, 2017. www.fortune.com/2017/10/25/donald-trump-drone-program/

Vanian, Jonathan. "The Multi-Billion Dollar Robotics Market Is About to Boom." *Fortune*, February 24, 2016. http://fortune.com/2016/02/24/robotics-market-multi-billion-boom/

Vasquez, Zach. "The Truth About Killer Robots: the year's most terrifying documentary." *The Guardian*, November 26, 2018. https://www.theguardian.com/film/2018/nov/26/the-truth-about-killer-robots-the-years-most-terrifying-documentary

Vincent, James. "Automation Threatens 800 Million Jobs, but Technology Could Still Save Us, says report." *The Verge*, November 30, 2017. https://www.theverge.com/2017/11/30/16719092/automation-robots-jobs-global-800-million-forecast.

Vincent, James. "Tim Cook Warns of 'Data-Industrial Complex' in Call for Comprehensive U.S. privacy laws." *The Verge*, October 24, 2018. https://www.theverge.com/2018/10/24/18017842/tim-cook-data-privacy-laws-us-speech-brussels

"Virtual Reality vs. Augmented Reality." *Augment*, October 6, 2015, www.augment.com/blog/virtual-reality-vs-augmented-reality/

"Walt Disney's Carousel of Progress." November 23, 2017. www.travelwiththemagic.com/walt-disney's-carousel-progress/

Watson, Alice G. "6 Ways Social Media Affects Our Mental Health." *Forbes*, June 30, 2017. https://www.forbes.com/sites/alicegwalton/2017/06/30/a-run-down-of-social-medias-effects-on-our-mental-health/#188a61592e5a

The Week Staff. "China's Black Mirror moment." *The Week*, February 3, 2018. www.theweek.com/articles/752442/chinas-black-mirror-moment

Weller, Chris. "Bill Gates and Steve Jobs raised their kids tech-free—and it should have been a red flag." *Business Insider*, January 10, 2018. https://www.businessinsider.com/screen-time-limits-bill-gates-steve-jobs-red-flag-2017-10

Whiteman, Honors. "Loneliness a bigger killer than obesity, say researchers." *Medical News Today*, August 6, 2017. www.medicalnewstoday.com/articles/318723.php

Wiesel, Elie. "A God Who Remembers." *NPR*, April 7, 2008. www.npr.org/2008/04/07/89357808/a-god-who-remembers

Williams, Rhiannon. "Prisoners 'could serve 1,000 year sentence in eight hours.'" *The Telegraph*, March 14, 2014. www.telegraph.co.uk/technology/news/10697529/Prisoners-could-serve-1000-year-sentence-in-eight-hours.html

Wolchover, Natalie. "Concerns of an Artificial Intelligence Pioneer." *Quanta Magazine*, April 21, 2015. www.quantamagazine.org/artificial-intelligence-aligned-with-human-values-qa-with-stuart-russell-20150421/

Worrall, Simon. "Yes, Animals Think and Feel. Here's How We Know." *National Geographic*, July 15, 2015. www.news.nationalgeographic.com/2015/07/150714-animal-dog-thinking-feelings-brain-science/

Youn, Soo. "24 Amazon workers sent to hospital after robot accidentally unleashes bear spray." *ABC News*, December 6, 2018. https://abcnews.go.com/US/24-amazon-workers-hospital-bear-repellent-accident/story?id=59625712

Zetlin, Minda. "The 9 Most Weird and Hilarious Questions Congress Asked Mark Zuckerberg." Incwww, April 12, 2018. https://www.inc.com/minda-zetlin/mark-zuckerberg-congress-hearings-funny-stupid-questions.html

Zevallos, Dr. Zuleyka. "What Is Otherness." Accessed September 8, 2018. www.othersociologist.com/otherness-resources

Bibliography

Court Cases

Brandenburg v. Ohio, 395 U.S. 444 (1969).
Carpenter v. United States, 484 U.S. _ (2018).
Florida v. Jardines, 569 U.S. 1 (2013).
Furman v. Georgia, 408 U.S. 238 (1972).
Maryland v. King, 569 U.S. 435 (2013).
New Jersey v. T.L.O., 469 U.S. 325 (1985).
Rainbow Country Rentals and Retail, Inc. v. Ameritech Publishing, Inc., 205 Wis. 153 (2005).
Riley V. California, 573 U.S. _ (2014).
Terry v. Ohio, 392 U.S. 1 (1968).
United States v. Dionisio, 410 U.S. 1 (1973).
United States v. Jones, 565 U.S. 400 (2012).
United States v. Mara, 410 U.S. 19 (1973).
Veronia School District 47J v. Acton, 515 U.S. 646 (1995).

Music

Arlen, Harold and Yip Harburg. *If I Only Had a Heart*. Jack Haley. The Wizard of Oz, 1939.
Arlen, Harold and Yip Harburg. *Over the Rainbow*. Judy Garland. The Wizard of Oz, 1939.
Bacharach, Burt and Hal David. *(There's) Always Something There to Remind Me*. Lou Johnson, Reprise, 1964.
Carlisle, Belinda. *Heaven Is a Place on Earth*. Ocean Way Studios, 1987.
Crawford, Shep. *I'd Rather*. Luther Vandross. J Records, 2002.
Croce, Jim. *Time in A Bottle*. ABC, 1972.
Joel, Billy. *All You Want to Do Is Dance*. Columbia Records, 1976.
Joel, Billy. *Piano Man*. Columbia Records, 1973.
Joel, Billy. *Sometimes a Fantasy*. Columbia Records, 1980.
Joel, Billy. *Souvenir*. Columbia Records, 1974.
Joel, Billy. *This Is the Time*. Columbia Records, 1986.

Social Media Content

Clark, Dave. Twitter Post. September 7, 201.
Gladwell, Malcolm. Twitter Post. September 3, 2018.
Murray, Bill. Twitter Post.
Rogen, Seth. Twitter Post. September 16, 2018.
Serling, Anne. Twitter Post. March 7, 2018.

Dictionaries

American Heritage Dictionary, Fifth Edition, s.v. "populism," accessed May 1, 2018.

Google Dictionary, s.v. "categorical imperative," accessed December 1, 2018.

Other Website Content

"Actus Reus." *Legal Information Institute, Cornell University*. Accessed June 25, 2018. https://www.law.cornell.edu/wex/actus_reus
"AIEQ." Accessed November 8, 2018. http://www.equbotetf.com/about-aieq/
"Ball Memes." Accessed May 15, 2018. https://ballmemes.com/i/the-realest-people-dont-have-a-lot-of-friends-you-7bf1282f09f142ed96cae6c3b3908e95
"Black Mirror." *IMDb*. Accessed July 18, 2018. https://www.imdb.com/title/tt2085059/
"Black Mirror: Awards." *IMDb*. Accessed July 18, 2018. https://www.imdb.com/title/tt2085059/awards
Buffett, Warren. quoted in "Warren Buffett: The Inner Scorecard." *Farnam Street*. Accessed May 14, 2018. https://www.fs.blog/2016/08/the-inner-scorecard/
"But-for test." *Legal Information Institute, Cornell Law School*. Accessed April 7, 2018. www.law.cornell.edu/wex/but-for_test
"Carl Jung: 'Who looks outside dreams; who looks inside awakes.,' quoting from a letter addressed to Fanny Bowditch, October 22, 1916. See post on February 8, 2018, https://carljungdepthpsychologysite.blog/2018/02/08/carl-jung-i-am-afraid-that-the-mere-fact-of-my-presence-takes-you-away-from-yourself/#.W7ULiddKjHY
"Conspiracy." *Justia*. Accessed April 9, 2018. www.justia.com/criminal/offenses/inchoate-crimes/conspiracy/
"Daily time spent on social networking by internet users worldwide from 2012 to 2017 (in minutes)." *The Statistics Portal, Statista*. Accessed June 4, 2018. https://www.statista.com/statistics/433871/daily-social-media-usage-worldwide/
"Electric Dreams: Awards." *IMDb*. Accessed July 18, 2018. https://www.imdb.com/title/tt5711280/awards
"Facebook Community Standards Policy." Accessed November 14, 2018. https://www.facebook.com/communitystandards/
"First-Degree Murder." *Justia*. Accessed August 18, 2018. https://www.justia.com/criminal/offenses/homicide/first-degree-murder/
"47 U.S. Code Section 230—Protection for private blocking and screening of offensive material." Accessed July 16, 2018. https://www.law.cornell.edu/uscode/text/47/230

Bibliography

"Google Terms of Service—Privacy & Terms." Last modified October 25, 2017, https://policies.google.com/terms?hl=en.

Groupthink definition. Accessed October 17, 2018. https://www.google.com/search?q=groupthink&rlz=1C1GGRV_enUS752US752&oq=groupthink&aqs=chrome..69i57j0l5.1743j0j4&sourceid=chrome&ie=UTF-8

Hand, Learned. "The Spirit of Liberty" speech, 1944. Accessed September 17, 2018. https://www.btboces.org/Downloads/1_The%20Spirit%20of%20Liberty%20by%20Learned%20Hand.pdf

"Holy Hill Hermitage." Accessed September 25, 2018. www.holyhill.ie/hafiz-of-shiraz/

King, Martin Luther, Jr. *The King Center*. Accessed December 5, 2018. www.thekingcenter.org/blog/mlk-quote-week-sticking-love

King, Martin Luther, Jr. Address at the Fourth Annual Institute on Nonviolence and Social Change at Bethel Point Baptist Church, December 3, 1969, *The Martin Luther King, Jr. Research and Education Institute*. Accessed December 5, 2018. www.kings.institute.stanford.edu/king-papers/documents/address-fourth-annual-institute-nonviolence-and-social-change-bethel-baptist-0

"Meme." Accessed September 20, 2018. me.me/i/1998-don't-get-in-a-car-with-strangers-2008-don't-e17714799d0e4cb6a9823247ef06df90

"Mens Rea." *Legal Information Institute, Cornell University*. Accessed July 16, 2018. https://www.law.cornell.edu/wex/mens_rea

"The Mercury Theatre on the Air." Accessed October 8, 2018. www.mercurytheatre.info

"Number of monthly active Facebook users worldwide as of 4th quarter 2017." Accessed August 3, 2018. www.statista.com/statistics/264810/number-of-monthly-active-facebook-users-worldwide/

1970 interview conducted by James Gunn, *Literature in Science Fiction series*, with Rod Serling, at https://www.youtube.com/watch?v=0wfazePQzj8). Accessed July 3, 2018.

"Online Dating—Statistics & Facts." Accessed November 1, 2018. www.statistica.com/topics/2158/online-dating/

pinterest.com/pin/507006870540879597/?lp=true. Accessed August 1, 2018.

"Proximate cause." *Legal Information Institute, Cornell Law School*. Accessed May 9, 2018. www.law.cornell.edu/wex/proximate_cause

"Reflection of Light." *Science Learning Hub*. Accessed November 9, 2018. www.sciencelearn.org.nz/resources/48-reflection-of-light

"Second-Degree Murder." *Justia*. Accessed August 18, 2018. https://www.justia.com/criminal/offenses/homicide/second-degree-murder/

"A Selection of Supreme Court Cases Involving the Fourth Amendment & the Body." *American Bar Association*. Accessed August 19, 2018. www.americanbar.org/content/dam/aba/images-.../BodySearchCases_list.docx

"Standards of Care and the 'Reasonable Person.'" *FindLaw*. Accessed August 20, 2018. www.injury.findlaw.com/accident-injury-law/standards-of-care-and-the-reasonable-person.html

"12 Alarming Cyber Security Facts and Stats." *Cybint: Barbri Cyber Solutions*, March 16, 2018, https://www.cybintsolutions.com/cyber-security-facts-stats/

"The Ultimate Guide to Mixed Reality (MR) Technology." Accessed May 4, 2018. www.realitytechnologies.com/mixed-reality

"The Ultimate Quotation Repository." Accessed June 15, 2018. www.quodIbid.com/quotes/1400/max-frisch/technology-is-a-way-of-organizing-the-universe

"Why does Uncle Ben always tell Peter Parker 'With Great Power Comes Great Responsibility.'" *Quora*. Accessed October 1, 2018. www.quora.com/why-does-uncle-ben-always-tell-peter-parker-with-great-power-comes-great-responsibility

Wiesel, Elie. *The Elie Wiesel Foundation for Humanity*. Accessed November 30, 2018. www.eliewieselfoundation.org/about/

Wiesel, Elie. Nobel lecture, December 11, 1986. Accessed December 4, 2018. www.nobelprize.org/prizes/peace/1986/wiesel/lecture/

www.brainyquote.com/quotes/Aeschylus_383359. Accessed September 25, 2018.

www.brainyquote.com/quotes/anselm_kiefer_334618. Accessed May 4, 2018.

www.brainyquote.com/quotes/arthur_m_schlesinger_109503. Accessed May 1, 2018.

www.brainyquote.com/quotes/barbara_kingsolver_161793. Accessed May 15, 2018.

www.brainyquote.com/quotes/john_dewey_163896. Accessed May 29, 2018.

www.brainyquote.com/quotes/Michael_de_montaigne_138368. Accessed November 8, 2018.

www.brainyquote.com/quotes/soren_kierkegaard_105030. Accessed August 1, 2018.

www.brainyquote.com/quotes/susumu_tonegawa_731820. Accessed November 6, 2018.

www.brainyquote.com/quotes/tupac_shakur_100941. Accessed July 28, 2018.

www.criminal-law.freeadvice.com. Accessed October 5, 2018.

www.quoteinvestigator.com/2017/03/19/candle/. Accessed July 25, 2018.

Bibliography

www.quotes.net/quote/52460. Accessed June 14, 2018.

www.quotespictures.com/a-photographer-went-to-a-socialite-party-in-new-york-as-he-entered-the-front-door-the-host-said-i-love-your-pictures-clever-quotes/. Accessed August 9, 2018.

"Your Fourth Amendment Rights: Landmark Cases." *Judicial Learning Center*. Accessed August 19, 2018. www.judiciallearningcenter.org/your-4th-amendment-rights/

Index

ACLU 19, 49, 128–129
Actus reus 92, 94
AI 2, 177, 191–192, 194, 197–200, 202, 214–215
Alexa 1, 88, 100–101, 165, 191, 201, 215
All You Want to Do Is Dance 217
The Allegory of the Cave 139
Amazon 21–22, 30, 33–34, 37, 100, 115, 129, 191, 201–202, 211–212, 215, 218
Amusing Ourselves to Death 51
Apple 26, 65, 105
Arendt, Hannah 98
Arkangel 9, 20, 70, 100, 116, 119–122, 130, 137, 158, 167
Armstrong, Jesse 111
artificial intelligence 6–7, 10–11, 20–22, 25–27, 29–30, 33–34, 66, 88–89, 91, 101, 115, 155, 172, 177, 191–204, 213–214, 216; *see also* AI
augmented reality 9, 33, 138, 151, 153, 155, 159, 168, 198
Autofac 10, 23, 32, 34, 100, 122, 190, 196, 201, 202–204, 208–210, 212
automation 26, 28, 33–35, 108, 191, 203–204

Bailenson, Jeremy 77, 154, 157
Bandersnatch 69, 91, 146–148
Barrat, James 192, 195–196
Bauer, Jack 130, 134
Bauman, Zygmunt 178
Be Right Back 65, 101, 115–116, 125, 173–174, 185, 202, 208
Bentham, Jeremy 16
Bernays, Edward 41
Big Data 6, 81–82
The Big Lie 8, 51, 59–61
Black Museum 18, 20, 23–25, 29, 70, 119, 136–137, 162–163, 165–166, 187, 189, 204
Blascovich, Jim 77, 154, 157
blonde 73–74, 84
Bostrom, Nick 195, 197
Bowles, Nellie 14, 75
Brooks, David 73
brunette 73–74, 81, 84–86
Buffett, Warren 74

USS Callister 22, 70, 161–162, 166, 172, 200, 204, 217
Calo, M. Ryan 99, 101, 105, 116, 124, 131, 173–174, 186
Carlson, Tucker 54–55, 65
Carousel of Progress 10, 209, 212
Carpenter v. United States 124
categorical imperative 134
civil liberties 124, 129, 169
Clarke, Sir Arthur C. 220
Communications Decency Act of 1996 21, 66
The Commuter 159–160, 204
Cook, Tim 13, 65
Crazy Diamond 24, 185
The Creepy Line 58, 64, 192
Crocodile 9, 20, 23, 70, 101, 106, 112, 114, 118, 131, 133, 206, 208
Cuban, Mark 192
cultivation theory 10, 27, 197, 214

daughter universes 147
Dershowitz, Alan 133–134, 183–184
Dick, Philip K. 22
digital clones 138–139, 161–162, 183
digital cookie 165, 167–168
digital copies/digital copy 10, 146, 155, 161–166, 168–170, 176, 178, 184, 186, 187, 188
digital divide 14–15
disinformation 8, 15, 51–54, 62, 64–65, 180
Dolezal, Rachel 42–43
drones 32, 100, 122, 201–202, 211

eHarmony 89–90
Eighth Amendment 169
The Entire History of You 9, 25, 70, 101, 103, 106, 109, 118, 131, 160, 206, 208
Epstein, Dr. Robert 56
Etzioni, Amitai 130

Facebook 15, 57–58, 65–68, 76, 78–79, 83, 126, 129, 136, 173, 191, 195
The Father Thing 170, 172, 209
fatherland card 83, 100, 115, 132
Fifteen Million Merits 12, 24, 67, 70, 81, 98, 153
First Amendment 67, 124

Index

Force majeure 16
Fourth Amendment 123–125
Frankenstein (films) 198, 200
Frankenstein, Dr. Victor (fictional character) 17, 199
Friend, Tad 191, 196
Frisch, Max 150

Gates, Bill 14, 194
GDPR 127
Good, I.J. 192
Google 8, 29, 55–58, 64, 68, 127, 129, 136, 182, 192, 197, 214

Handlen, Zack 71–72
Hang the DJ 9, 23, 30, 65, 86–90, 100–101, 143, 145, 162–163
Hated in the Nation 9, 62, 70–71, 78, 91, 94–96, 119, 122, 127, 129, 131, 135–136, 162, 200
Heaven Is a Place on Earth 23
Hintze, Arend 17, 193, 195, 197
Hitchcock, Alfred 37
Hodge, Douglas M. 29
The Hood Maker 9, 70, 101, 103, 105, 117–118, 129, 131–132, 134, 179, 182
Human Is 170, 172, 205, 208
hybrid reality 151

Impossible Planet 153, 206
infinite universes theory 146

Jobs, Steve 14, 22
Joel, Billy 153, 154, 206, 217
Jones, Annabel 173, 180
Judaism 14

Kang 36
Kerr, Orin 123–124
Keslowitz, Justin 127
Kill All Others 9, 34, 43–44, 46, 50, 53–54, 61, 63, 70, 82, 100–101, 115–117, 119, 122, 128–129, 131, 179
King, Martin Luther, Jr. 44, 221
Kurzweil, Ray 29, 31, 145, 150, 176, 184, 189, 192, 197, 219

LaFrance, Adrienne 28
Laws of Robotics 201
Luddites 1, 14

The Matrix 141, 152, 196
Matthews, Hayley 89
McLuhan, Marshall 8, 41–43, 45–46, 52, 54, 62, 116
McWorld 30
Men Against Fire 9, 62–63, 70, 101, 104, 118, 138, 140, 180–181
Mens rea 92–93
Metalhead 10, 23, 190, 206, 212, 214
Mr. Whipple 34–35, 38
mixed reality 151, 177

multiverse theory 146
Musk, Elon 17, 31, 95, 143, 182, 184, 190, 194, 196–197, 219

The National Anthem 25, 62–63, 65, 69–70, 128
The New York Times 14, 75, 149
Nosedive 9, 23, 25, 70, 73–74, 76, 79–81, 83–84, 95, 100, 102, 115–116, 118, 120, 135, 179, 205, 211, 217
nostalgia 203–206, 208–212, 221

The Office 7, 13, 40, 79, 99, 116, 154, 156, 191, 211, 214
One Candidate 41, 43–44, 46, 50, 54, 63, 119
Orwell, George 85, 104, 129, 131; *see also* Orwellian
Orwellian 81, 129
The Other 178, 182

parallel universe theory 147
Peres, Shimon 29
Peterson, Jordan B. 38, 58
Piano Man 154
Plato 139, 141
Playtest 24, 106, 137, 155, 159, 198, 204
Postman, Neil 51
Pozdorovkin, Maxim 182, 191, 192

quantum mechanics 147

Rand, Ayn 98
Real Life 137, 155–157, 159, 204
replacement culture 10, 203–204, 208–209
Richtel, Matt 13, 29, 75
robots 2, 11, 27, 29, 33, 38, 40, 85, 101, 107, 115–116, 143, 171, 174, 176–177, 181–182, 187, 189–195, 198–199, 201–202, 209, 212–214, 216–217
Rossum's Universal Robots 199

Safe & Sound 8–9, 25, 41, 51, 53, 61, 63, 70, 82, 100, 115, 119–120, 122, 128–129, 131, 140, 179
San Junipero 10, 22–24, 144–145, 151, 162–163, 173, 176, 205–206
The Scorpion and the Frog 38
Semuels, Alana 33–34, 150
Serling, Rod 28–29, 36, 38, 61, 111, 181, 185, 197, 216, 221
Sesame Credit 80–81
Shih, Clara 101
Shut Up & Dance 15, 25, 61, 63, 69–71, 75, 82, 100, 116, 118, 122, 135–136, 162
Sideshow Bob 14, 30
Simpson, Bart 199
Simpson, Homer 39, 42, 60, 161
Simpson, Lisa 55, 57–58, 199
The Simpsons 2, 6–7, 11, 14, 30, 36, 42, 50, 53, 55, 57–58, 60, 99, 104, 142, 147, 161, 179, 199, 207, 213
singularity (concept) 192
Singularity (film) 196

singularity theorem 146
Socrates 36
Sometimes a Fantasy 153
Souvenir (song) 206
spectrum 10, 21, 165, 167, 175, 177–178, 182–184, 189
Swanson, Ron 97, 205, 216–217

(There's) Always Something There to Remind Me 23
Third Party Doctrine 124
This Is the Time 207
Time in a Bottle 218
The Truman Show 7, 142
Trump, Donald 8, 43–44, 47–51, 192
The Twilight Zone 5, 7, 8, 11–12, 25–29, 34, 38, 40, 61, 85, 103, 107, 115, 118, 128, 131, 140–143, 146, 153, 154, 170–171, 174, 179, 181, 183, 185, 187–188, 196, 204–207, 211–214, 216, 219
Twitter 2–3, 15, 44–46, 49, 51, 76, 83, 126

utilitarian 16, 134, 171, 208

virtual reality 7, 9, 33, 77, 116, 141, 144, 150–160

The Waldo Moment 8, 41, 44–45, 47–48, 63, 70, 128, 163
Walton, Alice G. 79
The War of the Worlds 41–42, 52
Westin, Alan 98, 121
White, Walter 221
White Bear 23–24, 59, 62, 70–72, 106, 140, 149
White Christmas 24–25, 62, 70, 100, 111, 122, 138, 158, 162, 164–167, 170, 186–189, 204
Wiesel, Elie 106, 219
The Wizard of Oz 7, 46, 183

YouTube 21, 48, 50, 58

Zuckerberg, Mark 126, 195

www.ingramcontent.com/pod-product-compliance
Ingram Content Group UK Ltd.
Pitfield, Milton Keynes, MK11 3LW, UK
UKHW041926140426
5217IPUK00014B/338